John Lee

DuPont

(3L) $100

Du Pont
The Making of an Admiral

ALSO BY JAMES M. MERRILL

The Rebel Shore
Quarter-Deck and Fo'c's'le
Uncommon Valor
Target Tokyo: The Halsey-Doolittle Raid
Spurs to Glory
Battle Flags South
William Tecumseh Sherman
The USA: A Short History of the American Republic
A Sailor's Admiral: A Biography of William F. Halsey

Du Pont

The Making of an Admiral

A Biography of
Samuel Francis Du Pont

James M. Merrill

Dodd, Mead & Company
New York

Part of Chapter I appeared in a different form in James
M. Merrill, "The First Cruise of a Delaware Midshipman: Samuel Francis Du Pont and the *Franklin*," *Delaware History* 20 (1983): 256–68.

Part of Chapter III appeared in a different form in
James M. Merrill, "Midshipman Du Pont and the
Cruise of *North Carolina*, 1825–1827," *The Ameri-
can Neptune* 60 (1980): 211–25.

Published by Dodd, Mead & Company, Inc.
79 Madison Avenue, New York, N.Y. 10016
Distributed in Canada by
McClelland and Stewart Limited, Toronto
Manufactured in the United States of America

Designed by Erich Hobbing

First Edition

Library of Congress Cataloging-in-Publication Data

Merrill, James M.
Du Pont, the making of an admiral.

Bibliography: p.
Includes index.
1. Du Pont, Samuel Francis, 1803–1865. 2. Admirals
—United States—Biography. 3. United States. Navy—
Biography. 4. United States—History, Naval—To 1900.
I. Title.
E182.D87M47 1986   359'.0092'4 [B]   86-9034
ISBN 0-396-08855-4

For Ann

Contents

Contents

Preface

Samuel Francis Du Pont was the first of this distinguished family to enter the armed forces. He left home at the age of fourteen as a midshipman. During his career he served on board the *Franklin,* the famed *Constitution,* the *Ohio,* and other ships in the Mediterranean. He lived through the greatest of all naval revolutions, the change from sail to steam, from wood to iron, from smoothbore to rifled cannon, and from paddle wheels to propellers.

Du Pont served with distinction during the Mexican War in command of the *Cyane* off the Californian and Mexican coasts. After the war, he helped establish the Naval Academy at Annapolis, and was superintendent of the lavish Crystal Palace Exhibition, New York's first world's fair. His pre–Civil War career was crowned when the Navy Department appointed him to command the steam frigate *Minnesota,* the pride of the Navy, which sailed for China in 1857 on a highly sensitive diplomatic mission. On the eve of the Civil War, Du Pont was the best known and most admired officer in the Navy.

When the Civil War started, Secretary of the Navy Gideon Welles assigned him to chair the Blockade Board, which mapped strategy for the entire naval effort against the Confederacy. Soon he commanded the South Atlantic Blockading Squadron, capturing Port Royal, South Carolina, one of the first Union victories of the war. In 1863 his monitors steamed into Charleston Harbor and into tragedy for Du Pont.

Admiral Du Pont's papers, preserved in the Hagley Museum and Library in Greenville, Delaware, are the single richest collection of private correspondence relating to the nineteenth-century United States Navy. Numbering almost 21,000 items, the papers cover a fifty-nine-year period. The most significant part of the collection is Du Pont's "journal letters," detailed accounts of his life while at sea. Instead of keeping a journal, as many officers did, he addressed these letters to his wife, Sophie, hoping that they would serve as a record of his naval career.

This biography is based almost exclusively on these papers.

In writing this book, my thanks go to President E. Arthur Trabant, Provost L. Leon Campbell, and Dean Helen Gouldner of the University of Delaware for granting me a year's sabbatical leave to work on this project, and to the Henry E. Huntington Library for awarding me a summer fellowship.

The Hagley Museum and Library is an excellent place to pursue research. Of the staff I would like to thank Richmond D. Williams, John Beverley Riggs, Betty-Bright Low, Daniel T. Muir, Marjorie G. McNinch, and Carol Hallman.

I am indebted to my editor, Cynthia Vartan, for her encouragement, and to my friend, Marie Perrone of the University of Delaware, for typing the manuscript. Last, my sincere thanks go to my wife, Ann, who undertook research, copyedited, made suggestions, and inserted or deleted a sentence or two.

I

"I hope some day to do honor to my country"

The sun shone brightly and the sea was smooth near Port Royal, South Carolina, on 7 November 1861, seven months after the Civil War had erupted. At 8 A.M. a Union flotilla of fourteen warships, commanded by Flag Officer Samuel Francis Du Pont, moved into Port Royal Sound. The main attack force, led by the frigate *Wabash,* "the destroying angel," with Du Pont on board, was followed by the frigate *Susquehanna.* To the starboard, a flanking unit of five gunboats sheered off from the main column, and headed into the northern section of Port Royal Sound to engage any enemy vessels lurking up the rivers.

Behind the parapets of the two Confederate forts, drums rolled as men cheered and hurried to their stations. As the Union steamers closed on the forts, the guns were brought to bear directly on the *Wabash.* When Du Pont's flagship was within full range, and nearly abreast of Fort Walker, the fort's cannon thundered. An officer on the *Wabash* shouted, "Cock your lock, blow your match, stand by, ready, [fire]!" Guns flashed.

The battle raged. The Union flotilla pounded the enemy works at a rate of twenty-four shells per minute. Within the forts, Confederates, fighting "like Tigers," felt alarm. Despite their salvos, the *Wabash* and *Susquehanna* passed and repassed their batteries.

By early afternoon, with their defenses ripped up and only a few guns still in working order, the Rebels streamed out of the forts and fled "like quicksilver" into the woods. At 2:30 P.M. the Stars and Stripes floated over the soil of South Carolina. With the capture of

1

Port Royal, the Union Navy gained the finest natural harbor on the southern coast, which would serve as a base for the South Atlantic Blockading Squadron.

That evening, as Union campfires on the beach and the red, white, and blue lanterns of the gunboats illuminated the harbor, sailors chorused:

> *All hail! the victory's won!*
> *The day's ours, the work is done;*
> *Columbia's ships and Union men*
> *Have conquered, as they will again.*

On board the *Wabash,* Du Pont rejoiced, "The magnitude of our operations is growing upon me and the blow is ringing all over this Southern country." Flag Officer Samuel Francis Du Pont, United States Navy, stood at the height of his profession.

Samuel Francis Du Pont* was born on 27 September 1803 at Bergen Point (now Bayonne), New Jersey, the fourth child and second surviving son of Victor Marie du Pont and his wife, Gabrielle Josephine de la Fite de Pelleport. His brother Charles and sister Amelia had also been born in the United States, at Charleston, South Carolina, where their father had represented France as consul until 1798. In that year Victor du Pont and his family had sailed back home to France. Frustrated by the political and financial upheaval created by the French Revolution, he confronted a cloudy future there.

Once in France again, Victor du Pont discovered his father immersed in grand designs. Philosopher, economist, author, and statesman, who had been ennobled by the King of France, Pierre Samuel Du Pont de Nemours was one of a generation of intellectuals, who had steered France on a new course. During the Revolution, his ardor for reform had failed to meet the standards set by more radical men, and his devotion to the Royal Family twice cost him his freedom.

In 1799 Du Pont de Nemours made the decision to migrate with his family to the United States, where he planned to found a com-

---

*Unlike other members of his immediate family, he chose to capitalize the particle of his name.

2

pany for land speculation and commercial development, utilizing the talents of his sons, Victor and Eleuthère Irénée, and his son-in-law.

In January 1800 Du Pont de Nemours and his family set up their household—called "Bon Séjour"—on Bergen Point across from Staten Island. Their knowledge of the United States was not recent. Du Pont de Nemours had maintained a long and lasting friendship with Benjamin Franklin, and his American contacts had widened to include a circle of acquaintances. A friend since his days as minister to the Court of France, Thomas Jefferson had appreciated Du Pont de Nemours's support for American independence during the negotiations that preceded the Treaty of Paris in 1783.

Warned by Jefferson of the risks involved in land speculation, Du Pont de Nemours abandoned thought of his more grandiose ventures. With barely enough capital, Irénée du Pont purchased land in Delaware in 1802 for a gunpowder manufactory employing techniques he had mastered earlier while a student in a French powder works.

Hoping to stabilize his business schemes, Du Pont de Nemours returned to France in 1802. His son Victor, who headed the importing firm Victor du Pont de Nemours & Co. in New York City, moved into "Bon Séjour" with his family.

Victor du Pont had adopted the ways of America and was the dominant influence over his children's early years. His wife, Gabrielle Josephine de la Fite de Pelleport, possessed charm and a fine intellect and was well educated. She had been reared at Versailles, the daughter of the Marquis de Pelleport, captain of the Swiss Guard in the home of the king's brother, the Comte d'Artois.

In 1804 the French government refused to honor Victor du Pont's drafts in payment for military supplies. Steps to halt increasing debts failed, and a year later the importing house went bankrupt. The Victor du Pont family left New Jersey and journeyed to an upstate New York settlement in Genesee County, where they held some land. Here Victor du Pont tried to start anew, but his venture failed and all his assets were sold to meet his creditors' demands. Finally the beleaguered family moved to Delaware to join Irénée along the banks of the Brandywine.

Victor du Pont shared a partnership, manufacturing cloth from the wool of his brother's flocks. He and his family moved to Louviers, into a two-story house that sat on the north bank of the Brandywine, across from the Eleutherian Mills, where Irénée's powder mills and residence were situated.

At Louviers the young du Ponts were exposed to a sophisticated and cultured society. Frequent visits by fashionable and fascinating people, stimulating conversation in both French and English, introduced them at an early age to the larger world beyond the Brandywine.

Since intellect was highly esteemed, almost revered in the du Pont household, the library was filled with good books, most of them in French. They included the works of Montaigne, Voltaire, the four-volume edition of Rousseau's *Confessions*. British authors were not neglected. The shelves were well stocked with English classics, such as John Milton's *Paradise Lost,* David Hume's *The History of England,* Henry Fielding's *The History of Tom Jones A Foundling,* and eight volumes of *The Spectator*. A few American works dotted the shelves, too.

In 1812, when he was nine years old, Samuel Francis Du Pont, known to his friends as Frank, entered a private boarding school in Germantown, Pennsylvania, Mr. Blondin Constant's Mount Airy College. Forty miles north of Wilmington, Delaware, surrounded by woods, Germantown had become a summer resort for the wealthy. Mount Airy College had gained a reputation for the quality of its students and the excellence of its instruction.

When the War of 1812 burst upon the nation, both du Pont industries along the Brandywine were challenged—the powder mills of Irénée du Pont were confronted by the expansion needed to fill increased government orders, and the woolen company was beset by financial woes. In straitened circumstances, Victor du Pont prepared to hand over the management of the woolen mill to his elder son, Charles. It was Frank's future and choice of a career that preoccupied Victor du Pont.* As his father considered suitable options, Frank's illustrious grandfather, Du Pont de Nemours, suddenly reappeared in the United States. Victor du Pont and his father traveled to Monticello, Virginia, to seek Thomas Jefferson's advice and help in obtaining an appointment for Frank as a midshipman

---

* The details concerning the du Pont family come from John D. Hayes, ed., *Samuel Francis Du Pont. A Selection from His Civil War Letters* (Ithaca, N.Y., 1969), I: xlviii–liii; H. A. du Pont, *Rear-Admiral Samuel Francis Du Pont, United States Navy* (New York, 1926), pp. 3–7; and Marshall W. Fishwick, *Launching an Admiral: The Boyhood of Samuel Francis Du Pont* (Wilmington, Del., 19—), pp. 7–9, 17.

in the Navy. They broke their journey with a stop in Washington, where they called on President James Madison to gain his support for the appointment. It is not surprising that with such influence, Frank Du Pont was accepted. To insure Frank's future, his elders also gained a place for him at the United States Military Academy at West Point. In correspondence with Du Pont de Nemours, Jefferson expressed his wish that the youngster would rise in rank from midshipman to become one of the "high Admirals" of the United States Navy.

Although he was to carve an eminent career in the Navy, young Du Pont had never expressed a wish for a life at sea. His father, experiencing severe financial problems and with little money to underwrite his son's education, believed that the Navy offered the boy an honorable profession. His future settled, Frank set out to live up to his family's expectations. Later, in 1839, when reflecting on his entrance into the naval service, while not casting any aspersions on his parents, he admitted, "but I cannot but wish that they had had means, to have given me a full collegiate education, with a design to civil pursuits. I am however resigned & happy. . . ."

On 19 December 1815 Frank Du Pont, studying at Mount Airy College, received his commission as midshipman in the United States Navy. He promptly answered Secretary of the Navy Benjamin Crowninshield, "I accept with joi and hope that . . . my future conduct will warrant your approbation. Enclosed is my oath."

During the early nineteenth century, in the United States Navy as in its British counterpart, political influence was important in securing an appointment as a midshipman. Thus candidates accepted for this rank varied in background and education. Unlike the Army, which trained its officer candidates at West Point, the Navy followed an apprentice system, which was individualistic and frequently haphazard.

John Paul Jones of Revolutionary War fame was an early advocate of a broad education for midshipmen. Ship handling and seamanship were necessary but not sufficient. Jones emphasized that these young men, who would eventually become America's ambassadors, should have an excellent command of English, written and oral; a knowledge of foreign languages; a grounding in international law; and sufficient mathematics to solve navigational problems. During this era of slow communication, Jones was conscious of the awesome responsibility a naval captain was sometimes forced to assume for decisions that affected foreign policy. Two captains of the early Navy, Charles Stewart and John Rodgers, endorsed the apprenticeship training and suggested that the best and cheapest school for midshipmen was the deck of a ship.

To become eligible for promotion to lieutenant, midshipmen could submit their names to the Secretary of the Navy for examination before a board of naval captains, which tested their competence in navigation and seamanship and evaluated their moral fitness. These boards were composed of three or more members, and frequently contained a commodore or chaplain in addition to the captains. The ordeal was oral. Each candidate was questioned individually, and was sometimes asked to demonstrate a piece of equipment or to solve a problem at a chalkboard.

Before a midshipman could apply for examination, he was required to have spent a prescribed number of years at sea and have reached a certain age. These requirements varied under different administrations from two to three years of sea duty and from eighteen to twenty-one years of age. The interval between examinations also varied.

After appearing before the board, a candidate knew immediately whether he had succeeded, but not his standing on the list of those who had passed. Midshipmen who qualified were registered as "passed for promotion" and were called passed midshipmen.

The year before Frank received his commission, 1814, the United States and Great Britain signed the Treaty of Ghent, ending the War of 1812, a war that fostered a surge of nationalism in America and a new appreciation of the Navy for its exploits on the high seas.

At the start of hostilities the United States Navy numbered sixteen seagoing vessels. The pride of the Navy was its three frigates, *Constitution, United States,* and *President,* which had been designed to outclass all others. They hurled a heavier broadside than the British frigates, and were heavily timbered and planked, yet with such fine, clean lines under water that they could outsail almost anything that floated.

The British commander had under him ninety-seven sail, including eleven ships of the line, and thirty-four frigates. The conquerors of the Nile and Trafalgar during the Napoleonic wars were confident of beating any vessel not more than twice its size.

The United States Navy's early victories at sea thrilled Americans. The *Constitution* knocked the ship of the line *Guerriere* helpless in two hours and a half, and reduced the frigate *Java* to a useless hulk. The sloop of war *Hornet,* after a close fight of fifteen minutes, sank the *Peacock.* The *United States* captured the frigate *Macedonian.* Although the strategic value of these victories was slight, the value to the American people's morale, after military reverses, was beyond calculation. Congress enthusiastically voted funds for six additional frigates and four ships of the line, none of which was completed in time to see action in the war.

On being commissioned, Frank did not ship out immediately. He continued his studies at Mount Airy College, preparing himself for the life of a midshipman. His courses included mathematics, languages, history, and geography. He preferred history as it proved more exciting, more interesting, and more instructive than his other studies.

Frank Du Pont was a handsome lad: tall with curly chestnut hair, dark blue eyes, and a firm mouth. He possessed a winning personality and made social contacts easily.

In May 1817, although only fourteen years old, Frank left his boyhood behind and traveled to the Philadelphia Navy Yard to join the much admired seventy-nine-gun *Franklin* for his first cruise. The youthful midshipman was motivated by a deep sense of family, honor, and love of country. "J'espère un jour de faire honneur à ma patrie," * he wrote his mother.

The *Franklin* was a ship of beauty. Her white decks, bright paint work, and orderly arrangement of tackle all attested to the skill and efficiency of the ordinary American seaman.

Frank was to sail in her under Commodore Charles Stewart, who had distinguished himself in the War of 1812. Stewart was to assume command of the Mediterranean Squadron. His junior, Captain Henry Ballard, was in actual command of the ship.

Going on board, Frank followed a ship's boy down the ladder into the lower gundeck and then into the twilight of the 'tween decks. Here a new midshipman could easily lose his sense of direction, not knowing whether he was walking forward or aft. After a few days, newcomers learned their way around the ship. Frank quickly mastered the routine, knew his stations, when the ship was at quarters, and when he was on watch.

The young men he met in the *Franklin* came from widely scat-

---

* "I hope some day to do honor to my country."

7

tered points throughout the nation, and from every imaginable background. A few were older, midshipmen who, through lack of patronage or failure to pass the necessary examinations, had never succeeded in earning promotion.

The "reefers," as midshipmen were then called, lived in the dampness of steerage, a section of the berth deck, below the main deck, where the principal cannon were placed. Below the ship's waterline, headroom measured only a few inches over five feet. Steerage lay abaft the crew's quarters, and forward of the wardroom, where the officers messed.

It had no lighting or ventilation except what came through the main deck when the hatches were open and from lanterns hanging from the beams. Reefers lacked privacy. Along the bulkheads the midshipmen arranged their personal lockers and, at night, they slung their hammocks from hooks projecting from the beams. Each midshipman was assigned a boy from the crew to stow the hammock in the morning. Shelves were laden with crockery and stores, and each reefer in the mess had a camp stool. Workmen had secured the mess table to the deck. Toilet facilities were two washstands and basins into which water was poured from a deck bucket.

Frank found his new uniform satisfactory—the blue cloth waistcoat, the standing collar with a diamond formed of gold lace on each side, the sleeves with three small buttons, and the white trousers. "My waistcoat fits me very snug and I live it very well." He also appreciated the mattress for his hammock, which his father had sent: "the only fault is . . . that it is a foot and a half too short, but I have fixed it so it will answer." To supplement his pay of $19 a month and one ration a day, the family sent him beets and cabbages, but he required shoes more than vegetables, and wrote, "I wish you would send me my shoes as soon as possible."

Victor du Pont visited his son on board the *Franklin* while she was still at the Philadelphia Navy Yard. He wrote his wife, "Nicholson, a midshipman of the frigate *Congress*, told me that Francis was very well, that officers from the *Franklin* had been often on board his ship and had all spoken in the highest terms of our dear son, that it was astonishing how fast he was learning, and that he was very active and well-behaved, concluding with the statement that there was not a *man* on board more beloved by his superiors and more respected by those under him."

Later, a naval surgeon and friend pointed out to Victor du Pont the one drawback to his son's popularity, "the other officers are so fond of him that they will spoil him. Even Morgan, who has never spoiled anybody, will be able to do it, so fond is he of him. He conducts himself with the greatest propriety, astonishingly so for a boy of his age."

On board the *Franklin*, officers kept the reefers busy, learning shipboard routine, assigning the crew to watches, and gathering stores on shore. Frank was duly impressed when with the pomp "of one of the greatest days that ever took place on board the U.S. Ship *Franklin*," high Army and Navy officers boarded the ship, including Commodore Alexander Murray, who was commanding officer at Philadelphia, General William Duncan, former superintendent of the United States Military Academy, and their aides. They attended a ceremony at which prominent Philadelphians presented Commodore Stewart with a gilt-edged sword, voted to him by the Commonwealth of Pennsylvania for his "glorious victory during the late war." "All the above mentioned," Frank wrote, "are at present very busy devouring a splendid Dinner in the Cabin. . . ."

In mid-October Frank stood in awe as he watched the *Franklin*'s crew surging up the shrouds and out along the yards. As the canvas thundered out from the yards, the ship's sails filled to the wind. She was underway. More canvas thundered and hardened from the yards. The *Franklin* maneuvered down the curving Delaware River, across Delaware Bay and, taking departure from Cape May, New Jersey, headed out to sea. Homesick, Frank wrote his brother, Charles, "I . . . bid you farewell. . . . I hope that I will have the . . . pleasure of being in all your arms . . . two years from thence after perhaps seeing the country [France] of my beloved farther [sic] and mother. Therefore I bid adieu to all my friends on Both Sides of the Brandywine."

Once clear of land's sheltering arm, the motion of the ship became violent. A gale struck. The *Franklin* rolled, heaved, and rolled repeatedly. Fortunately, Frank had good sea legs, and was proud of avoiding the seasickness that afflicted so many of the officers while underway in heavy seas. "They did not see daylight at all until we came to anchor, they were so seasick."

After a sojourn at Hampton Roads, Virginia, the *Franklin* anchored at Annapolis, Maryland. Once ashore, Frank collected sea shells for his cousin Eleuthera's collection. After he had roamed the town and inspected the State House, he concluded that Wilmington was a much better place to live. During this stopover, Richard Rush, the newly appointed minister to Great Britain, his wife, children, and one cow boarded the *Franklin* as passengers for the voyage to England.

Frank's homesickness was momentarily banished by thoughts of the forthcoming voyage to the Mediterranean. To his widowed cousin, Mrs. Victorine Bauduy, he wrote, "It is certainly the first time which I have been so far from my friends and perhaps the first time I have so strongly felt the happiness which we enjoy when we are home.

"However," he continued, "when I think of what beautiful countries I am going to visit and what curiosities I will see, and at the end of two years if I can give a good account of myself what a joyful heart will return in the arms of my dear friends. Certainly with such a joyful prospect as this who would not consent to undergo a few hardships, which may come in my way."

In late November 1817 the *Franklin* sailed out of Hampton Roads and took departure for Europe. Frequently, officers exercised the reefers in managing the sails and yards of the mizzenmast. Four of the oldest midshipmen kept watch in succession on the forecastle and had the forward sails under their charge. Divided into three watches, other middies took turns at deck duty. They saw to it that the officer of the deck's orders to the crew were executed, and mustered the men at night. They learned the ancient arts of splicing and sailmaking, shiphandling, and navigation. To navigate the ship, officers relied on the old time-sight method of finding longitude from altitudes, logarithms, and the chronometer.

The midshipmen were quickly apprised of the various responsibilities of the officers on board. Under the captain came the first lieutenant, the second in command. In the captain's absence, he had complete responsibility for the ship. Some captains left everything to their first lieutenants; others meddled with routine details.

The master and master's mate directed the course of the routine, under the captain or first lieutenant's supervision, and commanded all the seamen in sailing the ship. The purser was in charge of all the stores and kept accounts of everything that was received or delivered. The surgeon was responsible for the health of the ship. Larger ships and vessels making a voyage of two or three years had a chaplain on board to care for the spiritual welfare of the crew, and to act as a schoolteacher for the midshipmen.

Among the petty officers, the gunner's mate handled the ordnance, shot, powder, and small arms. The carpenter oversaw the caulking of the ship, stopped the leaks, and kept the vessel seaworthy. The boatswain was responsible for all the cordage, sails, and rigging, while the quartermaster cared for the hold, keeping it in order and preparing it for stowing. The coxswain had charge of the ship's skiff, directing its comings and goings.

While the middies acquired hands-on proficiency in their shipboard duties on the *Franklin,* the chaplain taught them English composition, international law, and instructed them in French and Italian. Much of a reefer's education depended on his own initiative. With a passion for self-improvement, Frank devoured books in history and philosophy borrowed from Captain Ballard's personal library. "I assure you," he wrote his cousin Victorine Bauduy, "that all my leisure hours are occupied by reading & studying. Captain Ballard has given me permission to use whatever books I please out of the Cabin and I assure you I take advantage of his kind offer."

Although the midshipmen worked hard under constant pressure, they found time for horseplay. They chased one another over the rigging, boxed and wrestled, and entertained themselves with sea ballads.

The officers and men of the *Franklin* spotted foreign land for the first time at the Isle of Wight, and soon the ship lay anchored in the port of Cowes, discharging Rush and his family. Since American warships were infrequent visitors in British waters at this time, the *Franklin* lured curious townspeople to the wharves.

After several days at Cowes, the *Franklin* upped anchor and stood southeastward to round Cape St. Vincent, headed for Gibraltar and the Mediterranean. That harbor was crammed with shipping, for the naval power of England in the Mediterranean was based there. Once the *Franklin* anchored, Commodore Stewart's gig drew alongside. The gig then skimmed across the harbor to carry Stewart to the port admiral. Failing to find the Mediterranean Squadron at Gibraltar—"the best fortified place I ever saw"—the *Franklin* got underway and maneuvered out to sea.

Like other squadrons that patrolled the Pacific, the Caribbean off the coast of Brazil, and the East Indian waters, the Mediterranean Squadron's major mission was to protect American lives, property, and a growing commerce; to increase the opportunities of commercial intercourse; and to boost the efficiency of the Navy by affording active service to officers and crews. On their cruises in foreign waters, captains were ordered to collect information relating to the social, political, and economic conditions of the countries they visited.

Steering eastward from Gibraltar, the *Franklin* freely sailed across the Mediterranean toward Syracuse, Sicily. Day by day the wind held fair. The watches changed, drills were executed. The Mediterranean was the finest school for an officer. The constant activity and experience in shiphandling in proximity to the shore, entering and leaving all kinds of ports, and the contact with the best ships of England and France gave the United States Squadron a standard for comparison, a standard to equal or excel. Meeting with the naval officers of these European nations and with the people of highly civilized backgrounds all helped to stimulate interests and cultivate manners, which no other station could supply.

When the *Franklin* reached Syracuse, the ship's company were united with the rest of the squadron: the seventy-four-gun *Washington,* the frigate *United States,* the sloop of war *Erie,* and the brig *Shark*. Once on liberty, the gleeful midshipmen toured "the curiosities of this once celebrated place." In their dress coats and cocked hats, they excitedly explored the streets of Syracuse, the ruins of the ancient Greek theater and the Latin Colosseum, and the stone quarries, where they discovered "a cave called Dionysius ear," carved out by early Greek prisoners of war. "If you stand at the bottom of it and whisper," Frank described, "you can hear it reecho as if you had spoken very loud. . . . They fired a little gun about the length of my finger and it roared louder than our thirty-two pounders when we fire them." The reefers returned that night, exhausted, to pace the quarter-deck for four dreary hours.

Soon the *Franklin, Washington,* and *United States* got underway and reached Messina, Sicily, the next day. Thirty-five years before, an earthquake had jolted the city, leaving few remains of antiquity. Although disappointed at the lack of "curiosities," Frank and his shipmates were determined to see Messina anyway, despite the street beggars who overwhelmed them. They "are all around you," Frank explained, ". . . and if you give a farthing to one you will have in less than five minutes a thousand around chasing you all over."

Throughout the spring of 1818 the squadron continued to cruise the Mediterranean to "show the flag." "I can say now," Frank boasted, "that I have seen three quarters of the Globe which is more than many persons can say."

Tunis's relics disappointed Frank. He wrote his father, "I must say that since I have been in this Sea I have not seen anything that I think worthwhile of sending home to you, but there is time enough before I go home."

He concluded, "It has only been six months since I left you although it has appeared more and it would still appear longer if it was not that I always have something to do and it is much more pleasant in the company of a number of vessels [*Washington* and *Erie*] than to sail alone. Your eyes are always turned towards the other ships to see who beats sailing which I say with pleasure is the Franklin. With half the quantity of sail we set, we run the rest of the Squadron out of sight in twelve hours time."

Later, he bragged, "The Franklin, she is certainly one of the greatest ships that ever floated . . . [and] I venture to say the neatest ship."

The middies worked hard. Regulations required that each of them keep a journal. They recorded the courses steered, the wind directions, shipboard occurrences, descriptions of ports, and general remarks. These journals were intended to give middies practice in spelling, writing, and composition. Each month Captain Ballard reviewed their contents and, while underway, every midshipman's "day's work"—his sun and star sights, or in cloudy weather his dead-reckoning estimates of the ship's position—had to be handed in daily.

By late April the Mediterranean Squadron lay anchored off Leghorn. Built along the western slope of Italy, Leghorn is within twelve miles of Pisa. The reefers lost little time in riding out to see "the wonderful leaning tower . . . one of the seven wonders of the world." "I could not ascertain how many feet high it was," Frank informed his father, "but it is very high indeed. I walked to the top and I assure [you] I was very tired when I got up there."

At Naples the crew witnessed the arrival on board of the Emperor of Austria and the King of Naples along with an assortment of princes, princesses, dukes, and counts. The emperor, Frank wrote, was "as ugly as any old fellow I ever wish to see . . . he had on an old cocked hat, put me in mind of a haystack as anything else." The king was handsomer, but Frank commented on his "decayed teeth, I suppose on account of eating so much *macarony*."

In early June the *Franklin* arrived at Gibraltar. Frank's life had been so occupied with shipboard routine and duties that regret over leaving the Brandywine and home had been crowded aside. "I am happy to say," he wrote his father, "the Mediterranean agrees with me very well and [I] like it better and better every day. I have not been on the Doctor's list. . . ."

That summer the *Franklin* sailed eastward across the Mediterranean to Palermo, which faced the Tyrrhenian Sea on the northern coast of Sicily. The reefers went sightseeing. With its thousands of years of history under the domination of many cultures, Palermo was filled with massive cathedrals, Norman churches with Gothic towers, and chapels gilded with mosaics. The Arabs had contributed palm, orange, lemon, and olive trees, and with their sharp eye for beauty had left a heritage of lovely gardens centered with graceful fountains.

Commodore Stewart received permission for his midshipmen to tour the Royal Palace, sometimes called the Palace of the Normans. "This [garden] is really elegant," Frank wrote. "It is altogether in the Chinese style. The garden is full of Pheasants and rabbits and nobody is allowed to shoot them but for the king himself. The garden is spacious and handsome. . . ."

The midshipmen also visited another palace in a town not far from Palermo. Frank was struck by the yard surrounding the palace with its "great number of animals with men's heads on them, & human bodies with heads of wild animals on them." He was disappointed with the palace itself because "it did not appear comfortable, & the hideous figures outside are very disgusting and I do not think the man is happy to whom it belongs." While in Palermo Frank attended the opera, but was "very little entertained" as there was no dancing and "very bad singing." Visitors daily thronged on board the *Franklin,* keeping her officers alert as they showed the ship.

In November Captain Ballard, whom Frank admired, asked the youngster to accompany him when he took command of the sloop of war *Erie.* Frank was not only impressed that Ballard had requested him but he also wished to sail on a smaller ship. He enjoyed the officers on board the *Erie* better than those on board the *Franklin,* and especially liked First Lieutenant Robert F. Stockton, "a smart and correct officer as well as obliging."

On the *Erie,* Frank was "better satisfied than I have been since I left home." The *Erie* "works smarter, looks better than any ship in the Squadron," he boasted. Small ships had advantages. Commodore Stewart sent the *Erie* "knocking about" the Mediterranean, anchoring at ports not frequented by the larger warships, and her midshipmen had many more privileges than their counterparts on the *Franklin*. "You will find it strange," he announced, "that I should prefer a small ship like this than a large fine ship like the one I left. . . . I don't think that if you were to pick the whole Navy you would not find a set more happy than we are. We have a captain who does everything to make us happy and a [first] lieutenant who seconds the notion."

At home in Delaware, Victor du Pont, the recipient of these enthusiastic accounts, worried that Frank had made a mistake shipping on the *Erie*, believing her not as seaworthy as the *Franklin*. "I give you my word," Frank reassured his brother Charles, "that I would rather go around the world in her than the Franklin." The *Franklin* rolled and pitched in rough seas, while the *Erie* "would be riding like a little duck in the water. I have been in a pretty heavy blow on both of them, and I am able to judge."

In February 1819, the *Erie* arrived at Messina for repairs at its navy yard. The pre-Lenten carnival ashore was in full swing with its "rejoicings," masquerade balls, and parties for the officers and midshipmen. But Du Pont and the other reefers soon learned it was exceedingly difficult to line up dates for these affairs as all the "proper young ladies" had been spoken for weeks ahead of time.

During the *Erie*'s sojourn at Messina, the new regulations regarding promotion to passed midshipman were published. They were strict and required reefers to know geometry, trigonometry, navigation, and astronomy. Frank, who strongly supported proficiency in these subjects, quipped, "it will keep them from promoting some that do not know the stem from the stern. . . ."

Since a plague raged in Gibraltar in mid-June, the *Erie* stayed clear and dropped anchor in Algeciras Bay, Spain, nine miles from "The Rock." Algeciras was a "miserable place," "really tiresome." Its only attraction was its bullfights.

With little to interest him ashore, bored with shipboard routine, Frank craved the drama of a shooting war with Spain, sailing gallantly into battle or "something or other to put us in motion." The Spanish king had not yet agreed to a treaty ceding Florida to the United States. "I presume, however," Frank admitted, "it is of very little importance. We can take the Floridas as easy without his name on it." His eagerness for action against the Spanish fleet was balanced by his wish to return home to his family and friends. He was "anxious to press my foot once more on the soil of freedom."

In mid-August 1819, the *Erie* combed the Atlantic Ocean around the Azores for a pirate ship that had plundered a heavily laden American brig. When the *Erie* finally reached Gibraltar empty-handed—the plague had waned—orders for home awaited her. Frank felt no regret to be leaving the Mediterranean as his thoughts were focused on Louviers.

After side ventures chasing marauders and slavers on her return voyage to the United States, the *Erie* finally sighted Sandy Hook on 20 January 1820 and entered New York Harbor, where she moored. For Frank, returning to his native soil after an absence of several years was an experience fraught with excitement and anticipation. When Lieutenant Stockton, now commanding the sloop, refused to grant leaves to its officers, Frank complained, "I assure you it is really distressing to me to be so near from home and not able to get there, however these little privations will take place and must be put up with. . . . I am very lonesome and would much rather be jumping about in a NW [northwest] gale than lashed alongside of a wharf in New York."

He managed to get home to Delaware by February. During his cruise, he had seen exotic coasts, explored strange lands, gained a knowledge of the ways of the sea, and matured into a fine seaman loyal to the Navy. His tour of duty had Americanized him. No longer were most of his letters written in French.

Frank's immediate future seemed uncertain. On leave midshipmen received half pay. Eventually Frank resolved to master mathematics at home under the tutelage of his cousin, Victorine Bauduy. He hoped for an assignment to a ship bound for Cape Horn after a period of study. He preferred this course to returning to the *Erie* in New York Harbor.

To his friend Lieutenant Garrett Pendergrast on the *Erie*, he confided, "I will have nothing to disturb me [at home] as I would have if I was to stay by the ship. I am pretty certain that I can get into active service when I want to, that is if there is a ship going out."

II

"I found the Constitution...
a very superior ship"

The Navy Department cut short Frank's time at home, assigning him to the Philadelphia Navy Yard for temporary duty. Soon, with permission of his commodore, Frank reentered Mount Airy College. In addition to courses in geography, English, and French, the college emphasized mathematics, "hammering away at Geometry [and] Arithmetic." Frank admired his mathematics teacher, who paid attention to "scholars, and particularly me." Blondin Constant, himself, taught geography, and a retired sea captain tutored the students in English. Between classes, Frank and the captain met occasionally to "talk a little *rope.*" He told Garrett Pendergrast, "I am applying myself to the different branches necessary in our profession." Although fascinated with his studies, Frank found campus life "dreary," especially after the exhilaration of his cruise on the *Franklin.* He yearned for home. To his cousin Eleuthera, he wrote, "I can find nothing around me worth speaking of. This old college is always the same, and I assure [you] it is not the least handsome in the world, and had I not made it a duty when I came here to keep myself pretty close to my studies, I am afraid that I should find it a difficult matter to kill time. I must however confess that studying and reading will not at all times keep me from getting [a] little *home sick.* It will certainly appear strange to you, after a separation of two years one of a few months would produce this effect, it is nevertheless true."

Students at Mount Airy College arose at 4:30 A.M. to study for an hour before breakfast. They then went to classes from 8 until

17

12. After a two-hour lunch break, they again filed into the classrooms until 5. The small boys went to bed at 8, while Frank and the upperclassmen retired at 10. Letters from home made Frank more homesick. "The Brandywine," he wrote Eleuthera, "it appears is nothing but gaiety. I regret much at not being at all your little festivals. You made my mouth water (as the saying is) when I read about the fine cherries and strawberries."

"To receive the love and esteem of my relations and friends is the height of my ambition," he told Victorine, "and I will ever endeavor to prove them that it is not misplaced. . . . It appears that you have nothing but *tea parties,* visitings, &c. on the Brandywine."

Vacation commenced in September. Frank requested service on the *Constitution,* "Old Ironsides," but to his disgust the Navy Department assigned him to the schooner *Alligator.* He immediately urged his father to use his influence in Washington to have the orders changed. They were. In March 1821, Frank exulted to Pendergrast, "Well, I have succeeded . . . in getting clear of the Alligator." He still hoped for the *Constitution,* anxious to sail again to evade the boring routine of life at Mount Airy College.

To his delight, orders for the *Constitution* arrived, and he set out for Boston, where the frigate lay moored. He was waylaid in New York by his old shipmates. They hosted a dinner on board the *Franklin* at the Brooklyn Navy Yard. "After we had dinner . . ." he wrote Charles, "we got the Band down in the steerage and danced till nine or ten o'clock."

Leaving New York City, he arrived in Boston on 14 April 1821. Smartly turned out in regulation white pants, white vest, and navy-blue pea jacket resplendent with brass buttons and midshipman's insignia, a visored cap on his head, Frank boarded the *Constitution.* He received a cordial welcome from his new shipmates. "I found the Constitution," he wrote Alfred du Pont, "what I had always heard of her, a very superior ship. She is the handsomest I have ever seen and as perfectly sound as when she was first built." Although the lieutenants on board were "a very great set," he found "the captain was not stylish enough for her," and he thought the steerage was much too small.

The *Constitution* had been constructed at Boston and was launched in 1797. Hundreds of midshipmen had received their training on her decks. Through each of the fifteen ports on either side of her main battery, guns were placed close to her waterline. Three masts towered well over 150 feet from her deck. Her overall length was 200 feet and her extreme width, 40 feet 6 inches.

Her spar or top deck, which rose fourteen feet above her waterline, swept from stem to stern without a break. Immediately before her mizzenmast was the wheel, and in front of it opened three companionways, the captain's, wardroom, and steerage. Amidships, before the mainmast, was the pinnace with a capacity of seventy men; at either end the crew's companionways opened. On this deck were twenty thirty-two-pounder carronades. Aft, on her port and starboard sides, were davits from which hung the whaleboats. The gig was suspended from her stern. Extending in every direction above the deck was a huge web of rigging. To learn the names of the ropes was indeed an accomplishment for new midshipmen.

Below the spar deck was the gun deck. The after part of the gun deck was partitioned to form the skipper's quarters, which consisted of two cabins, one behind the other. On either side of the after cabin was a tiny stateroom; that on the starboard side was occupied by the commodore when the ship carried one, and that on the port side by the captain. The galley was forward. In the bow lay the anchor gear. Along the gun deck on either side was the *Constitution*'s main battery of twenty-four pounders.

Below the gun deck lay the berth deck. In the bow was the sick bay. Directly back of the sick bay lay the brig. Aft, on the starboard side, was the purser's office and, behind it, the carpenter's cabin. On the port side were the sailmaker's cabin and the warrant officers' mess. The center section was the steerage, which was separated from the berth deck by a wooden partition. Behind the steerage was the wardroom from which the officers' staterooms opened on the starboard and port sides.

On the orlop deck, the next deck below, and in the hold, the crew stored provisions and reserve materials. The spirit room, the grocer's vaults, the sail room, the water tanks, the paint room, the smithy, and the yeoman's storeroom were located here.*

In May 1821 the *Constitution* got underway, and after an uneventful cruise of twenty-one days, anchored at Gibraltar. The ship could have made the passage in seventeen days "with all ease" as

---

* Material concerning the *Constitution* is in Henry L. Burr, *Education in the Early Navy* (Philadelphia, 1939), pp. 68–69.

she had a fair wind, but she carried little sail. "The Constitution," he told Victorine, "is a first rate sailer."

Returning from liberty, Frank denounced the port to his brother, "Gibraltar has not changed the least. I met the same persons, the same jackasses parading the streets as when I was here before."

In July the *Constitution* visited Florence. "I must say," Frank wrote his sister Amelia, "that I never enjoyed myself away from home, so much in my life." The midshipmen toured Florence in a carriage.

The *Constitution* returned to Gibraltar in mid-August. From there the frigate sailed to the Spanish town of Port Mahon on the island of Minorca, the winter rendezvous of American vessels on duty in the Mediterranean. The town's harbor was one of the finest in the Mediterranean, well protected from gales, and of easy access. Minorca had been conquered successively by Carthaginians, Romans, Moors, Spaniards, the Corsairs under Barbarossa, the British, and the French. It had been retaken by the British, and finally had been acquired by the Spanish in 1802.

The captain restricted the midshipmen's liberty to one day in three. Enlisted men swarmed ashore only to get drunk on the *vino negro,* or to dance the fandango with the native women. They usually returned to the ship inebriated and exhausted, many of them battered from fistfights.

When the midshipmen went on liberty, they rented donkeys and rode throughout the island. They explored the back roads and farm pastures in quest of archaeological sites and discovered the remains of many pagan altars. They bought figs and almonds from the natives for their starved palates.

On 9 October the *Constitution* was again underway, sailing to Genoa, Leghorn, Tripoli, and Algiers before ending her cruise at Gibraltar on 23 November, "making a very handsome cruise of 44 days without anchoring." Frank wrote Pendergrast, "we merely showed ourselves off the above mentioned ports. Everything on board goes pretty well. This is the easiest going . . . that you ever heard of. . . . The Commodore is no disciplinarian . . . but he is one of the most generous and good natured old souls I ever had anything to do with. He stands by the reefers on occasions and [helps] them out in all their difficulties."

Throughout the cruise Frank studied for the examination for lieutenant. He thanked Pendergrast for an eight-page letter with its "useful and beneficial advice." "Time shall not be lost," he wrote.

"I promise you faithfully that every moment shall be put to the very best advantage with information that you . . . have given me. . . . I am in hopes [that I] . . . will show you that your good opinion has not been wholly unfounded. . . . I have studied spherics before but have forgotten them. I shall resume the study immediately."

To Charles, Frank wrote, "I am determined to see what application hard study will bring forth. I have payed the very greatest attention to the seamanship part of my profession since I have been out, and in the future mathematics will have its share of my time, tho' I assure you it is much more difficult to become a thorough-bred seaman than a mathematician."

During January, February, and early March 1822, the *Constitution* lay at Port Mahon. During the annual festival, "Mahon was a gay place, masquerade Balls every evening, opera, &c.," Frank told Charles, "in fact so much that I did not devote as much time to study as I fully expected."

In mid-March the *Constitution* sailed for Gibraltar, and the midshipmen were "heartily glad." For two weeks in April the frigate visited Cadiz, where Frank told Amelia, "women are generally good looking and dressed mostly in Black without hats but veils."

This second cruise to the Mediterranean began to pall. He complained to Victorine, "The Mediterranean has still but few attractions for me; visiting the same ports every day and not even all those, that I saw when up here before. If I had not visited Florence, this cruise in the Mediterranean would have tired me to death." To Alfred du Pont he noted, "everything is dull enough in this quarter. My stock of news is always at a very low ebb."

In the summer of 1822 Frank left the *Constitution* in Gibraltar to return home expecting to sit for the examinations for promotion. When he arrived, he learned that no midshipmen of his date of commission would be permitted to take it that year. As usual when confronted by serious impediment, he looked for family or friends in high places to exert pressure. This time he urged his father to intervene. Victor du Pont wrote his friend Captain David Porter to see if he could "possibly do anything." Frank visited Commodore William Bainbridge in Philadelphia, hoping that he would use his influence to sway the Navy Department. The commodore tactfully suggested that Frank write the Secretary of the Navy about his "situation." Unfortunately, Frank discovered that the secretary was not in Washington at the time.

Realizing that string pulling by his friends and family could accomplish nothing, Frank decided to go to sea again, and take the examination in the fall of 1823. In late September he wrote the secretary, who had returned to the capital, "Sir: Having left the Frigate Constitution in the Mediterranean for the purpose of offering myself for examination this year and finding on my arrival that my date has not been included that there is no possibility of my being admitted I am desirous of going to sea and would be thankful for orders to the Congress." To make sure he received such orders, he wrote Captain Porter for help.

Frank soon received the coveted assignment and sailed on the *Congress,* Captain James Biddle commanding. The frigate arrived in the West Indies in early December 1822 to hunt down freebooters lurking in the Caribbean.

The pirates frequently used Cuba and Puerto Rico as bases, as the Spanish authorities of those islands, resentful of the help given by the United States to their revolted South American colonies, winked at piratical activity. Freebooters sailed out of Cuban and Puerto Rican harbors, some flying the Jolly Roger, but most showing a plain blood-red ensign. They preyed on American merchantmen, which led the Navy Department in 1822 to establish the West Indies Squadron.

The *Congress* cruised the Caribbean. After three days at St. Barthélémy, the *Congress* ran over to St. Thomas, then sailed to Puerto Rico. Leaving Puerto Rico on 13 December, the *Congress* arrived at La Guaira, Venezuela, six days later. Together with a Mr. Myers, the captain of an American brig, and Captain Biddle, Du Pont crossed the mountains on horseback in threatening weather and rode into Caracas, fifteen miles away. Almost immediately they received word from La Guaira that a gale had struck the port. Every vessel except the *Congress* had been driven ashore. In a torrential downpour they set off for the coast, hiring three men to slash a way through the blown-down trees across the road.

Myers, Biddle, and Du Pont struggled into La Guaira in the evening. Twenty-one vessels lay grounded on shore, some destroyed, including Myers's brig. Forty seamen had already lost their lives. The *Congress* "was riding by her last cable, having parted two. The sea was rolling so high that there was no possibility of getting on board." Frank and Biddle sat up the whole night watching the frigate, expecting at any moment that she too would helplessly go aground. "No one person on board had the most distant idea of being saved," Frank later told Charles. The storm abated the next morning and by diving through surf Frank and Biddle finally reached the ship. With a favoring wind, the frigate made sail and stood out to sea, "glad to leave so detestable an harbour."

The *Congress* lay off La Guaira for two days, attempting to aid the stricken vessels, then, taking departure, arrived at Curaçao. The townspeople pleased the officers of the *Congress* by hosting two fancy dress balls—"the society is very good and the ladies all speak English."

"The cruise," Frank wrote Victorine, ". . . altogether has not been unpleasant so far, but still not pleasant enough to keep me from regretting [leaving] the Mediterranean." To Pendergrast he wrote: "I like Capt. B[iddle] very much. He has his eccentricities, as all men have, and is a little austere, but on the whole, is a friend to his officers if they deserve his friendship."

After patrolling the Caribbean for several months, the *Congress* returned to Norfolk for overhaul on 9 April 1823. The cruise around the Caribbean had taken 150 days, of which 112 were at sea. But the frigate, much to Frank's disgust, had not captured any pirate ships.

While she was being outfitted, the Navy Department assigned the *Congress* to the Mediterranean Squadron, with orders to take Hugh Nelson, minister to Spain, to Cadiz, and Caesar Augustus Rodney, minister to Argentina, to Buenos Aires. Since the ship was destined for New Castle, Delaware, to take on board Rodney and his family, Du Pont gained permission to go home and pick up the ship when she arrived in the Delaware River.

While in Delaware, Du Pont learned that no examinations for promotion would be given in 1823. The Secretary of the Navy had informed Biddle in Norfolk that he had been "so much pestered" by passed midshipmen about promoting them to lieutenant that he was determined not to give any more examinations until these passed midshipmen were raised in rank. "So you see," Frank told Pendergrast, "my bright prospects are fast fading away, however I am young and determined to buffet it out and keep at sea, and I think I have pretty well done so already, and I can tell you that I conceive myself no inconsiderable seaman." Later he complained, "This shameful conduct [of the Secretary of the Navy] has put me *far far* behind. . . . I am still an unpassed midshipman because they will not examine me."

Frank boarded the *Congress* at New Castle in late June 1823.

The ministers, their families, and baggage jammed the ship. Rodney found it necessary to take with him a huge number of personal items, 527 in all. Included were eleven bedsteads, two butter churns, an old washing machine, and three saddles, together with a menagerie of four dogs and three cats. All his articles were enough to fill a large merchantman. To make room for this luggage in the hold, the crew hoisted up 100 barrels of provisions and stowed them on the berth deck, where carpenters erected three storerooms. Excess items littered the deck and encroached on the space allotted to the enlisted men. "In consequence," wrote Biddle, ". . . of all this furniture being on board, my pride has been severely mortified at the unsightly appearance of every part of the ship." *

The *Congress* finally got underway. When she reached the Virginia capes, a gale struck. Surrounded by huge wave crests, the ship rolled and pitched as water surged over the decks. After two hectic days, the wind and sea abated and six young ladies appeared on deck for the first time. Officers helped them "spend their time as agreeably as possible." On the passage, "fine regular courtships [are] going on, notwithstanding there is considerable competition," Frank wrote Victorine, "but I believe that each of both parties, have chosen their favorites, and if we had a Chaplain on board, I would not be surprised to see several matches, as for my part, I have neither been remarkable for my indifference, nor for my particular attention, to the ladies, but have done everything in my power to oblige and serve Mr. Rodney in any way—not only because he is in bad health, but as the friend of my uncle."

The *Congress* arrived in Gibraltar in mid-July 1823. After depositing Nelson and his family at Cadiz, the frigate headed for South America. The ship reached Rio de Janeiro in late September. "I wish I could speak . . . well of the city," Frank wrote Victorine, "but it has nothing to recommend it. The streets are narrow and filthy, the Inhabitants are very uncouth and half civilized, and are at least one hundred & fifty years behind us."

The ladies on board the *Congress* had withstood the voyage well. "They have helped in great measure to while away the dull hours at sea," Frank gossiped to Victorine, "but alas! we are going to lose them. . . . I suspect the separation will be hard on some. I think

---

* See Nicholas B. Wainwright, "Voyage of the Frigate *Congress*, 1823," *Pennsylvania Magazine of History and Biography* (1951): LXXV, 170–78.

they have made three of four conquests. . . . Some of our gentlemen are certainly much smitten, this is certainly the most astonishing circumstance I can relate to you. The impressions, however, I am in hopes are not so deep, but that, the almost sovereign remedy—salt water and a little absence will be able to do away with them. . . . I see my pen is leading me on to little scandal so I think I had better stop it or change the subject."

Frank's thoughts turned to the Brandywine. "I anticipate much pleasure at home this winter. I hope we will have plenty of snow when I get with you again. . . . I think I shall stop longer than I did last time, for I begin to find that there is not much gained by keeping so constantly at sea."

After leaving Rodney and his family at Rio de Janeiro, where they boarded a merchant ship for Buenos Aries, the *Congress* sailed for Norfolk, arriving in mid-December.

After a sojourn with his family, Frank, accompanied by his uncle Irénée, who had political clout in the capital, traveled to Washington to see Secretary of the Navy Samuel Lee Stoddard about taking the passed midshipman's examination for promotion.

To reach the Navy Department, they passed close to the White House. The mansion had been rebuilt and repainted after severe damage to it by the British in the War of 1812. To the west of the chief executive's house stood the Navy Department building. It was not large, and its plain classical façade was identical in appearance to its neighbor, used by the Army, and to the buildings of the State Department and Treasury to the east of the White House.

Once inside the Navy Department Frank and his uncle bypassed the auditor's office on the first floor and continued upstairs, where they skirted office Number 8, which housed the three powerful Navy commissioners.* Next door to the commissioners, men worked designing future vessels for the service. On entering room Number 1, the office of the Secretary of the Navy, they learned to their regret that Stoddard was out of town.

Frank and his uncle then visited Captain David Porter and Captain Charles Morris, before returning to the Navy Department to

---

* The establishment of a board of Navy Commissioners dated from 1815. The board consisted of three captains appointed by the President and confirmed by the Senate. The duty of these commissioners was to attend to all matters connected with the Navy under the supervision of the Secretary of the Navy. The board remained in existence until 1842. Since that date, however, several secretaries appointed boards to formulate naval policies.

see the chief clerk. No one had information about the examination but they were told that the secretary would soon return to Washington. "I hope . . . he may," an arrogant Frank wrote his father, "as I would much rather deal with him than an upstart clerk, in fact it is beneath my dignity of an officer to have any transactions with them, and if they were made to feel it they would not assume so many airs, but Mr. Hay [chief clerk] is so much courted by Lieuts. and Captains that it has turned his head."

Typically, that June the heat in the city was "excessive." "In fact," Frank told his father, "my coat has not been dry since I have been here and I am heartily sick and tired of Washington."

"If there were no examination," he continued, "the best thing I can do is to get orders to the North Carolina or Constitution."

Irénée du Pont met with Commodore John Rodgers and told him of Frank's desire to go to sea again. Rodgers replied that he would be happy to have young Du Pont with him on his cruise to the Mediterranean in the *North Carolina*.

III

"God knows . . . I have worked hard enough"

In October 1824 the handsome yet balding, neatly attired midshipman boarded the *North Carolina,* the pride of the nation, which lay moored at the navy yard in Norfolk. She was destined to become the flagship of the Mediterranean Squadron. Designed by William Doughty, launched in 1820 at the Philadelphia Navy Yard and with a bust of Sir Walter Raleigh as the figurehead, the stately square-rigged line-of-battle ship measured 380 feet in extreme length and 280 feet in extreme height, from the top of her mainmast to the bottom of the keel.

When Frank, who was then twenty-one years old, came on board the *North Carolina* his messmates welcomed him and teased him about his being the oldest midshipman in the Mediterranean Squadron, "senior of my grade." Undoubtedly the middies and the entire ship's company were excited when on 25 October, amid naval pomp and ceremony, General Lafayette, the American Revolutionary War hero, and his entourage, who were on a triumphal tour of the United States, came on board to inspect the ship.

In addition to his regular duties on board ship, Du Pont was studying for the examination for lieutenant and had already decided "to devote every moment of my time, not only to the practical but to the scientific part of my profession, and will do all in my power to obtain the name of a skillful seaman, and scientific officer."

"I am well aware, as you say," he wrote his father, "that everything depends on this cruise, and rely upon it, I shall govern myself accordingly."

Although not as beautifully proportioned as the frigates of the *Constitution* class, and not as fast, the *North Carolina* was "the *Show Ship*" of the Navy. Pierced for 102 guns, she actually mounted only 94, a ship capable of throwing a greater weight of metal than any man-of-war afloat at that time.

By 1824 the *North Carolina* was sadly in need of a complete overhaul. Officers and crew worked hard repairing the ship and readying her for sea. When Du Pont stepped on board, she was "pretty advanced" with the repair work, "considering what has been done to her. She has been literally pulled to pieces. She was in an astonishing unsound state, & has been entirely, or nearly planked over from the water."

"I thought that once on board this ship we should be a little settled," Frank wrote, "and have some time to ourselves, but my troubles on busy days have only commenced."

Frank was promoted to master's mate and quickly learned that First Lieutenant Matthew C. Perry was a competent and progressive officer, but a tough taskmaster. "I have charge of one of the decks as a master's mate," he explained to his father, "which keeps me employed from daylight until 8 ock without the least interruption. I can scarcely get my meals, and, indeed, I am never seated at the table more than two minutes, without hearing myself repeatedly called by the first lieutenant with some new order to execute."

Perry liked his oldest midshipman. "Indirectly," Frank continued to his father, "I have been informed that I have a warm friend in him. He certainly appears friendly. I hope he may continue so for what ever opinion we may have of a person, there is nothing gained by making an enemy of him, and there is sometimes a great deal lost, and I have always found it a good rule to make as many friends as possible, when you can do so without sacrificing principle or feeling."

The *North Carolina* was supposed to carry a crew of 960, but in December the "ship was entirely too crowded, with both officers and men," Frank wrote. "We have now on board one thousand and twenty souls."

One evening he described the scene below decks: "If you could see me at this moment you would laugh if you did not pity me. . . . everyone is in his hammock, my head takes [bumps] against one [hammock], my elbow [against] another, my legs crammed between two trunks, and old stump of a pen without knife to mend it, a solitary candle in an old lanthorn, the table . . . is loaded with small trunks, clothes, books, and shoes and [a] thousand other articles, not forgetting a large piece of canvas, intended to represent a table cloth. . . ."

Commodore John Rodgers, the designated commander of the Mediterranean Squadron, clambered on board the *North Carolina* on 18 December 1824, as sailors manned the yards, fired off a salute, and hoisted his broad pendant—thirteen stars on a blue field—and everything was done with "considerable form." "The old Commodore himself was dressed off in his full uniform," commented Du Pont, "and did really look and no doubt felt good." Then the senior naval officer on active duty, Rodgers was a disciplinarian and put the fear of God into those who served under him.

As soon as repairs were finished, the *North Carolina* was to sail for the Mediterranean to join the squadron. In 1824 the State and Navy departments had multiple reasons for bolstering the squadron by adding the *North Carolina* and the frigate *Constitution*.

The Greek struggle for independence against Turkey and the quasi-war between Algiers and Great Britain disturbed the peace of the area and endangered America's trade. Pirates plagued the sea, menacing unarmed merchant vessels. A ship like the *North Carolina* and an enlarged squadron would help guard merchantmen, scatter pirates, and impress the fleets of European nations. In Rodgers's opinion the American Squadron was the superior of any ever seen in Asia Minor.

Rodgers also had orders to undertake a strategic and, indeed, delicate diplomatic mission. The Department of State wished him to prepare the way for negotiations leading to a commercial treaty with the Ottoman Empire, a treaty to protect the trading rights of Americans and to insure free access of Yankee ships to the Black Sea, opening up trade with Russia.

President James Monroe's emissary to the sultan had discovered that complicated intrigues pervaded the Turkish court, making it almost impossible for an American to confer privately in Constantinople with the minister of foreign affairs, Reis Effendi. Ambassadors of European powers skillfully exerted their influence to prevent the sultan from negotiating with the United States, fearing that such a treaty might infringe on their own privileged trading rights.

The American emissary had learned, however, that if Commodore Rodgers conferred with Capudan Pasha Khosew, Lord High

Admiral of the Turkish Navy, the third most powerful official in the Ottoman Empire and a warm friend of the United States, about the possibility of a commercial agreement, an opening wedge might be gained and negotiations could take place at a later date. The State Department advised Rodgers that he was merely to "sound out" the Capudan Pasha, "not treat with him."

At this meeting between the two officers, Rodgers was to submit American proposals and ascertain the Ottoman Empire's terms for such a treaty. In return, the Capudan Pasha would confer directly with the sultan.

Another motive led the Navy Department to order Rodgers to the Mediterranean. In the mid-1820s the squadron required the reinstatement of stern discipline. Naval officers had tarnished the reputation of the Navy by their drunkenness, their fights ashore, their gambling, and their duels. The Secretary of the Navy was sure that nothing but the firm hand of Commodore Rodgers could cure their habits and curb their vices. The *North Carolina* was to be the model of discipline, and her arrival in the Mediterranean was to restore the standing that the squadron had previously enjoyed under the commands of Stephen Decatur, William Bainbridge, Isaac Chauncey, and Charles Stewart.

From the moment Rodgers stepped on board, Frank Du Pont noticed a marked change in discipline. He reported, "everything is yet hurly burly hard work from morning to night together with the severest discipline.

"Our commodore," he continued, "says that there has been an unjustifiable relaxation of discipline in the Navy and he is determined to revive it & to do [so] he intends punishing every offender to the fullest extent of the laws.

"The fact is that half the officers . . . are half frightened to death. As for my part, I take every thing very easy. I have been 9 years in the service without suspension or arrest and I think I can go through this cruise without it. I know my duty, can do it, and am willing to do it, if more is required, I cannot help it, however I see my way clear, and do not anticipate any trouble, as many do.

"At all events," he added, "we will see discipline, order, & style carried to its highest pitch."

As work progressed on the *North Carolina*—the men "are rubbing up, and [she is] beginning to look like a man of war"—Rodgers promoted Du Pont again, this time to sailing master, to serve directly under First Lieutenant Perry. "I am as you may suppose in high spirits about it," Frank wrote his father, "for more reasons than one, not only for the satisfaction of having at last emerged from the laborious, disagreeable & often unthankful office of mids[hipma]n, but also for the great pleasure it will be to . . . all my friends."

To his sister Amelia he wrote, "the great prospects opened for me [on] this cruise buoy me up and I feel life and vigour sufficient to go through anything, the fact is I feel more like a man than I ever did, the chance of my speedy promotion to some sort of responsibility, makes me feel my importance and I hope to return to you, with an excellent knowledge of my profession, and a considerable standing among my superiors. . . ."

In January 1825 the *North Carolina* sailed for a shakedown cruise in the Chesapeake. Leaving the ship at Ragged Point, Maryland, not far from the mouth of the Potomac, Rodgers journeyed up to Washington to bid farewell to his family and his friends at the Navy Department. He returned to the ship on the steamboat *Washington,* accompanied by President James Monroe, Secretary of the Navy Samuel L. Southard and, said Frank, "about 40 more great fish from Washington." They inspected the *North Carolina* and congratulated Rodgers on the ship's neatness and order and her library containing eleven hundred volumes. Once the notables departed, the *North Carolina* moved down to Hampton Roads. On 27 March she upped anchor and made sail with a moderate breeze. At 6 P.M. she passed Cape Henry, discharged the pilot, and set a course for Europe.

After a "boisterous passage" of thirty-three days, the *North Carolina* arrived at Gibraltar. Frank's friend, Lieutenant Alexander Slidell Mackenzie, United States Navy, was on furlough and had been traveling in Spain. He described the arrival of the *North Carolina:* "After much weary expectation, the ship was at length signaled from the tower, and, climbing to the top of the Rock, I saw her coming down before a gentle levanto, with skysails and studdingsails—a perfect cloud of snow-white canvas. By and by the lighter sails were drawn in and disposed of. Europe was doubled and left behind, and the gallant ship stood boldly into the harbor, with yards a little braced, sails all filled and asleep, and hull just careening enough to improve the beauty of the broadside. . . . nothing could exceed the beauty of the spectacle."

When the *North Carolina* arrived on station at Gibraltar, the Mediterranean Squadron was then anchored in Messina. It consisted of the frigate *Constitution,* corvette *Cyane,* sloops of war *Erie* and *Ontario,* and the schooner *Nonesuch.*

While awaiting the squadron's return to Gibraltar, the *North Carolina* entertained visitors. "She is really worth looking at," Frank said. "The English are delighted with her and with us."

Rodgers provisioned the ship and then got her underway and showed the flag at Málaga, Algeciras, and Tangier.

Once the *Constitution, Ontario, Cyane,* and *Erie* reached Gibraltar, the squadron sailed for the Aegean Sea. They first called at the island of Póros to replenish their water supply and to give the officers an opportunity to go tour the "relicks of antiquity." While *North Carolina* lay anchored, a Greek slave trader came alongside with two white and one black Turkish women and offered them to Rodgers at $40 a head. After much hassling and many threats with the slave trader, Rodgers dispatched Perry in the gig to the Greek boat and, after bargaining, purchased the three women for a total of $50. Rodgers's object was to free them, but this was impossible to do at Póros. The women pleaded with Rodgers to take them to the United States, but he was unable to extend shipboard hospitality. The commodore took the "poor unfortunate creatures" to the first safe place, Smyrna, the next port of call. After they were decently clothed, they went ashore to shift for themselves.

In a street in Smyrna, an executioner decapitated two men, a Greek and an Armenian who had been convicted of coining counterfeit money. Such actions and "the horrid exhibition afterwards" shocked Frank and his shipmates. "It is astonishing what indifference such scenes are regarded by the natives," noted Rodgers in his journal. "Indeed so far from evincing the least commiseration, the first impulse of the Turk is to spit upon, & spurn them as they pass."

After leaving Smyrna, the squadron crossed the Aegean to Nauplia in the Gulf of Argolis. There the Greek revolutionary government struggled against the army of Ibrahim Pasha, which had overrun the Peloponnesus. The Greeks hoped the appearance of the Yankee ships meant American intervention in their favor; but the United States Navy kept to its policy of strict neutrality. "The Greeks are yet struggling," reported Frank, "but I believe loosing gradually what ever advantage they have ever possessed." While at Nauplia Frank witnessed with interest the reception on board of the celebrated English author and adventurer Edward John Trelawney "in a splendid Albanian suit, with black and curling mustachios, looking altogether like the most dashing buccaneer."

Unable to gain information of the whereabouts of the Turkish fleet and the Capudan Pasha and, as the season was advanced, the commodore decided to postpone negotiations until the following year. Leaving the *Ontario* to protect American commerce in the Aegean Sea, the squadron sailed for Gibraltar.

The responsibilities of sailing master gained for Frank invaluable experience and imbued him with renewed confidence. "I have proven to my superiors that I can perform it [my duty] without being watched," he wrote his father, "and they no longer keep that strict eye over me, that they formerly did, but leave everything to my own discretion a confidence to some that might be injurious, but to me it has been the greatest incentive."

Frank added, "my time is much pleasanter than it was formerly, everything goes on more easily and comfortable, the path that was so thorny, and so full of stubbles at first, has by constant friction and bustling over it, become comparatively smooth & even, the experience I have gained enable me to perform my duty better with more ease to myself. . . ."

Early in November the frigate *Brandywine* joined the American forces at Gibraltar. Before the end of November the squadron arrived at Port Mahon to spend the winter months. Rodgers wrote Secretary of State Henry Clay, "Indeed, in every port in the Archipelago, where the squadron has been, whether among the Greeks or the Turks, we have experienced nothing but respect, kindness, and hospitality." Officers and crew began overhauling and repairing the *North Carolina*. After several months of "heavy work" the ship "was the most splendid piece of machinery that ever set in the water, her looks and fine order are beyond description."

"I have had a hand in getting her so," Frank wrote Victorine Bauduy, "but God knows . . . that I have to work hard enough, and I am kept moving from sunrise until sunset, with scarcely time to get my meals. . . ."

Despite the work Frank continued studying for his examination and, at every opportunity, read books from the ship's library, volumes that ranged from Herodotus to the writings of modern travelers to the Near East.

In December Frank and three other midshipmen—"three very smart young men"—passed the "fiery ordeal" of their examination for lieutenant. "The examination was long, strict, and tedious, beyond measure," Du Pont wrote his father. "The struggle was long but glorious, and I do say without any hesitation that I acquited myself handsomely and better than my most sanguine anticipations led me to expect. I was in, seven hours on seamanship, and you may rely on it I had more shoals, Rocks, and gales of wind, to encounter than I ever had or ever expect to see. . . ."

The examining board presented the four passed midshipmen with a certificate. On receiving his, Du Pont made "a gracious reply and retired from the Cabin one of the happiest fellows in the world."

Known throughout the Navy as a stern disciplinarian, Rodgers continued to mete out punishments. Courts-martial and floggings were frequent. Five midshipmen were convicted of engaging "in gaming at . . . tables kept by a certain notorious gambler . . . in the town of Mahon." "The discipline," Du Pont explained, is ". . . as severe as was foretold, I am perfectly willing if it is extended alike to all, which it will no doubt."

Rodgers forbade officers to frequent gambling halls ashore as it led to "ultimate ruin and disgrace." He issued "some pretty severe general orders" to his officers, prohibiting dueling, defaming superiors, or wearing civilian dress ashore. Midshipmen could not lend money to one another or become indebted to "foreign tradesmen," and their visits ashore were curtailed. Rodgers, stressed Du Pont, was the only commodore who "has taken any steps, and highly necessary ones they were, of guarding the morals of officers, by checking this as much as possible by setting a good example himself."

The harsh discipline turned the *North Carolina* into a "hard ship," but Frank got along "astonishingly well" with the commodore. To his father, he wrote that Rodgers "flies in a tremendous passion now & then, but tis' soon over and bears no malice after, but with the other one [the captain] it is one continual roar & bustle, his haughty overbearing disposition never relents, and with one who is vested with so much power and influence as he is, it makes it still more horrible. We have many heavy squalls together, but I am too much the Lawyer for him, and take good care never to commit myself.

"I have now," he continued, "become a man, feel myself one and am determined to conduct myself like one."

On 10 April 1826 the squadron sailed from Port Mahon. After touching at Gibraltar, Rodgers attempted to contact the Turkish fleet and the Capudan Pasha. The ships called at Algiers, Tunis, Mílos, Póros, Delos, and arrived at the roadstead of Vourla, twenty miles from Smyrna, on 19 June.

Ten days later the squadron left Smyrna still searching for the Turkish ships, and anchored off Tenedos three days later. The governor of Tenedos boarded the *North Carolina* but, after an exchange of pleasantries, became evasive about the whereabouts of the Capudan Pasha. Midshipmen, of course, were in ignorance of the complexities of Rodgers's mission but, Frank wrote, the commodore has "some little business (God only know[s] what) with the Porte and we . . . [are] waiting for an opportunity to transact it with the Captain Pasha who . . . [is] expected out soon with his fleet. . . ."

On 4 July 1826 at 10 A.M. the *North Carolina*'s crew sighted Turkish ships "pouring forth" from the Dardanelles. As the fleet—twenty-three sail (battleships, frigates, and corvettes) commanded by the Capudan Bey, next in rank to the pasha—passed the *North Carolina,* a frigate stuck fast on a rock, losing her rudder. Desiring to inspect the damage to his grounded ship himself, the Capudan Pasha arrived at Tenedos. This gave Rodgers the chance for the long-awaited interview. The Turkish admiral sent his flag lieutenant and dragoman to inform the commodore of his arrival, and of his wish to see him on shore the next day.

Rodgers expressed his regrets about the grounded frigate. The dragoman intimated that the Capudan Pasha planned to behead the captain if Rodgers failed to intercede. Rodgers agreed to make the request, if by so doing "I could save the life of a fellow creature."

On 6 July the commodore left the *North Carolina* with David W. Offley, the American consul at Smyrna, George B. English, the interpreter, and several officers.

The meeting was cordial. Rodgers said he hoped the two nations would negotiate a treaty of friendship and commerce on the principle that citizens of the United States and Turkey and the Ottoman subjects in the United States should each enjoy all the privileges of the most favored nation; and that these were the only terms that could be accepted by the United States.

The pasha answered that he would make all this known to the sultan, assuring Rodgers that he had no doubt that through his influence everything would lead to conclusions satisfactory to both countries.

Before heading back to his flagship, Rodgers interceded and won a reprieve for the captain of the grounded frigate.

On this cruise the commodore afforded his officers an opportunity to tour the Plains of Troy, and the reputed tombs of Ajax and Achilles. Frank cut his name on the remaining columns of the Temple of Minerva.

On 11 July the squadron anchored at Mytilene Roads in Lesbos. Three days later the pasha's fleet appeared and, after it anchored, the *North Carolina* fired a salute of twenty-one guns, which was immediately returned.

At 2:30 P.M. on 15 July the pasha came on board, arriving in a "splendid barge" of twenty oars. The Yankees fired a salute and manned the yards. The pasha inspected the crew at quarters. Watching proudly, Frank wrote later, "he was amazed beyond description, and well he might have been. I have never seen in my life so beautiful a display, nine hundred men, all dressed alike, with their clothes as white as driven snow, a blue belt, ornamented with stars, around each waist, and a handsome black hat with the ships name in Gilt letters, together with the officers in full dress, at their quarters ready for action, made it a sight grand beyond description."

The pasha expressed his astonishment with the *North Carolina* and told the officers that he had been in both England and France, but "had never seen anything to compare to it." Frank added, "(whether he really thought so I cannot say), but I am sure he never did for I do not believe there ever was a ship in the same order."

Rodgers conducted the pasha over the entire ship, "which he scrutinized with peculiar attention and evident satisfaction." After remaining on board for two hours, the pasha took leave in a "very cordial manner," expressing friendship and respect for the United States.

On the next day, Rodgers, accompanied by several officers, returned the pasha's visit, and the Turks treated the Yankees "with great cordiality and distinction."

The Capudan Pasha reported that he had written the sultan, informing him of the wishes of the President of the United States, and assured Rodgers that he should have no fear concerning the outcome in which they were mutually interested.

When Rodgers left the Turkish flagship, the Capudan Pasha's flag, then flying at the main, was struck, and another, the imperial flag, was hoisted as if the sultan himself were on board. That had never been done for an officer of any European nation. The pasha explained that this "extraordinary honor" was the mark of respect for America.

Commodore Rodgers wrote to Henry Clay, ". . . judging from the distinguished manner in which he received me, and the unrestrained scope he gave to his expressions of respect and good will towards our government and country, as ought to leave no doubt on my mind, but that the meeting will have the desired effect, and that it will hereafter prove to have been an important step towards the opening of negotiation that shall secure to the United States many important commercial advantages. . . ."

Rodgers was well pleased with the conferences, which ultimately led to the first treaty between the United States and Turkey.

On the afternoon of 18 July 1826 the American Squadron got underway and, after making a tack to windward, each ship bore up in succession and ran through the Turkish fleet. On coming abreast of the flag of the Capudan Pasha, the *North Carolina* crew gave three cheers while the band played "Hail Columbia." The commodore had never seen such a sight before and suspected it would "without doubt, leave a lasting impression on the mind not only of the Capudan, but on that of every other Turk who happened to witness the scene."

Although Frank had been officially promoted to lieutenant in April, he received "the first tidings" in September, when his father wrote him the news. By November Frank still had not officially received his commission and was "still continuing the arduous and drudge duty of [sailing] master." He told Lieutenant Perry that he would "attend to the [sailing master's] duty with pleasure," but declined wearing the lieutenant's uniform until he should be "regularly installed as a lieut."

"It was altogether discordant to my feelings," Frank wrote, "to commence my career as a lieut. by attending the duties of a subordinate grade."

Slowly the relations between Du Pont and the commodore deteriorated. Rodgers offered Du Pont the privileges and the uniform, but not the duties of a lieutenant because he had no one to replace him as sailing master.

37

To learn that his service could not be spared was "a very fine compliment," Frank wrote, ". . . but it is a poor way to repay them by keeping me in a subordinate situation.

"I . . . am determined not [to] show any degree of impatience as I had been advanced by him [Rodgers] to a very responsible situation tho' the obligation is certainly repaid by my having borne my duty . . . and done it *thoroughly*."

His frustration eventually led to "some little dispute" with Rodgers. Frank, considering himself "under no obligations to Commodore Rodgers," could no longer continue as sailing master while entitled to the position of lieutenant. Rodgers refused to relieve him of his duties. Frank contended that the commodore "fully intended that I continue as master until the end of the cruise, this I thought was too hard. I had been a slave for two years, had worked night & day, and as a recompense for it was made to continue on, perhaps a year longer . . . and be denied in every sense of the word the dignity, time &c [to] which I was fully entitled was more than I had patience enough to endure."

Frank applied for duty on board the schooner *Porpoise,* and on 15 December 1826 Rodgers angrily complied with his wishes.

"I have perhaps lost his [Rodgers's] friendship but not his respect," Frank advised his father. "At all events I am ready, willing and able to perform my duty at all times. The rupture was not of my seeking. I wanted to obtain my rank on board of his ship. I could not succeed, sought it elsewhere and found it. This is my crime and no more."

Life was freer on board the *Porpoise.* As first lieutenant he "breathed a different atmosphere. I am no longer in constant dread of being found fault with or being arrested. Thank god I have escaped the latter so far and I do not now see the slightest reason to apprehend it."

The pleasures of the cruise failed to last. In April 1827 Du Pont received "the killing tidings" of his father's death and desperately wished to start home immediately. Aware that the *Porpoise* might remain in the Mediterranean for another year, while the *North Carolina* was scheduled to return to the United States, he rejoined his old ship as a "Supernumerary L[ieutenan]t." The commodore was "not inhuman enough" to deny Du Pont his change of duty. "Altho," Frank wrote his brother, "I can never feel any regard or esteem for him [Rodgers], I give him full credit for his conduct on this occasion.

"My footing on board," said Du Pont, "is all that I could wish, I am on duty, the hatchet is buried, and all is quiet."

The *North Carolina* sailed to the United States via Cape Haitien, Port-au-Prince, Havana, and Key West, arriving at Hampton Roads on 29 July 1827, ending a twenty-eight-month cruise.

IV

"During the crisis . . . all of you flashed across my mind"

After his return to Louviers, amid family and friends, Frank, then twenty-four years old, questioned his choice of a naval career. He would never completely adjust to the death of his father, "one of those losses which nothing can repair." He cherished his Sundays along the Brandywine, "everything around me is calm and quiet, the stillness not being even diluted by the usual exhilarating sound of our Water Wheels. . . ."

He envied his close friend and former messmate, Dr. John Wily, who had settled down in Brooklyn and was enjoying "the society of a fond wife, the caresses of darling children, & all the comforts of a domestic life, with full leisure to follow . . . literary pursuits & means to receive friends in a simple but cordial manner."

Frank wrote Wily in April 1828: "Depend upon it this is the right way, there is no other course to compare to it, and I only wish to God that it was already in my power to speak from experience, but I trust that such happiness is still in reserve for me. At all events I look forward to it with the fondest and most cheering anticipation. You must not suppose from all this nonsense I am *caught*, it is perhaps the want of being so entirely, that makes me misera-ble. . . .

"I find I cannot live without being in love," Frank continued, "and for the want of *l'argent content* have never been able to follow

it up, but had to commence at once to struggle against it, & no
sooner do I succeed than I find myself in the same situation with
the next woman I meet (for I am not taken in by pretty faces). I am
getting old fast, the warmth of my temperament shows itself constantly. . . . My hair is nearly all gone, & when you see me expect
to meet an old young man. . . . I begin to despise the service and
will remain on shore as long as I possibly can."

Although Frank enjoyed country life—the walks and horseback
rides, "the picturesque views, shady bowers and running brooks"—
he was discontented and uncertain. "So you see," he wrote Wily,
"everyone but me has a particular object of attraction & Occupation & I lead a kind of general life of devotion to all them, & tho'
I am well aware of the . . . powerful attachment they all have for
me, induced perhaps by my frequent absences, I still feel a void &
want *something more.*"

To Garrett Pendergrast he described his situation: "It is true I am
a marrying man, but like many others who go a great deal into
society & talk much about it, we are always the longest in getting
fixed. I have seen several women that in my opinion possess every
quality that constitutes a good wife, but . . . they are always poor.

"I have never yet been struck by a woman who had a fortune,"
he continued, "and as I never would marry one had she the mines
of Golconda that was deficient in other matters, I am not in a situation myself to take a poor one. . . . As long as I remain single, I
am perfectly independent, but my loaf will not bear dividing. God
knows I wish it were double the size you may rely on it I should
not be selfish with it. I have also an aristocratic feeling ridiculous
enough it is true, but which I cannot shake off, this tends also to
diminish the chance for I will confess to you that I attend to
caste. . . ."

Discouraged in his search for the perfect wife, Frank questioned
whether a naval officer should ever marry and have children since
he would be at sea much of the time. To Pendergrast he conceded
that children were a source of great joy, "but when you consider
the long moments of care and anxiety constantly attendant on a
growing family, the possibility and in our profession the probability
of being cut off from it when your parental Guardianship is most
wanted, and the still more terrible chance of having children grow
up unworthy of you, really I think one ought to bear up readily
against what is generally but what I think improperly considered a

41

misfortune, laying aside the laudable wish to meet the views of our Creator and the natural vanity of handing down your name, and perhaps seeing it exalted by your flesh and blood.

"I think a navy officer is perhaps better off without a family whatever may be his circumstances," he continued. "Your wife is then your sole idol and I think when engaged in a distant and hazardous service your anxiety for her will be as much as you will overcome without surrounding her with a numerous progeny to assist in tearing your heart strings to pieces."

In the fall months of 1828 at Louviers, Frank began taking a strong interest in politics, especially the presidential race between Andrew Jackson and John Quincy Adams. This concern would stay with him for the rest of his life. He had fully intended to travel to Washington to see the inauguration, the "coronation of King Andrew Jackson," but family circumstances prevented him. Frank was anti-Jackson and heartily disagreed with the new President's appointment of a "miserable cabinet." "I could start up a thousand objections" to the cabinet appointments, he told Pendergrast, "and give you whole sheets on the subject. . . . who the Devil is Mr. Ingham [Samuel D., Secretary of the Treasury], a miserable political agitator . . . who never administered the affairs of anything larger than a little [news] paper."

Like most naval officers, Frank's constant concern was the appointment of the Secretary of the Navy. He asked Pendergrast, who was in Washington at the time, to write him about John Branch. "I am . . . afraid he is an old Fogy."

Several months later, after intense reading of the newspapers, Frank wrote Pendergrast that "Old Jackson is a mere tool, his energy is gone, he cannot possibly live more than a year, and we shall then have the arch hypocrite [John C.] Calhoun [Vice President], which will mend the matter but little, as in duty bound I support Old Hickory but I believe him surrounded by a more corrupt faction than has existed in this country before."

During the early months of his leave, Frank had enjoyed relaxing at home renewing his close relationship with his mother and sisters, and visiting cousins and friends. "After a wandering apprenticeship of ten years," he explained to Pendergrast, "deprived except at short intervals of the counsels and example of your relations, exposed at an early age to all the vicissitudes and vices strewed in a sailor's path, it is delightful to find one's self at length restored to the bosom of his family, with the cheering consciousness that the worst had been encountered and overcome. . . ."

As his leave lengthened into months, Frank grew restless and wished for orders to the West Indies "or anywhere else." Daily he looked for word from the Navy Department. "I have everything down to a shirt button," he told Pendergrast. "I shall have no objection to go to sea, but if I am going to be pen[ne]d up in some Dock Yard it will be very hard, for anything like employment I am always ready and willing."

During his stay at Louviers, Frank lost weight. "I . . . grow thinner every year," he wrote Pendergrast. "I shall soon make a good representation of an Egyptian mummy; if I do not dry up entirely." He measured six feet one inch tall "with shoes," and weighed only 150 pounds. To compensate for his "almost bald head," he grew "a pair of whiskers that would do honour to a French Grenadier."

In the spring of 1829 Frank fancied himself deeply in love with Caroline Morris, daughter of Mr. and Mrs. Anthony Morris, a well-to-do family of Philadelphia. The couple became engaged. Because Mr. Morris was extremely ill, Frank was unable to "speak to her [mother] on the subject," and was uncertain of her approval of and consent to her daughter's marriage to a man of his profession. Frank received the blessings of his own mother, who "saw my feelings were too deeply involved to have combatted them strenuously, even if her own had not gone with mine."

To Victorine, Frank expressed his admiration of Caroline. "You have seen the person of my choice, with the mildest of dispositions she possesses solidity of character, & with a spirit naturally gay and lively. She is industrious and domestic in habits. Her family is respected and had been so for generations back, & her education has been and is still well attended to.

"I think there are many congenial points between us and my anticipations are of the most cheering kind," he continued. "As to worldly matters I do not know how I stand, sailor like, I have not thought much about them. I have understood however that she has expectations, if so well and good, for I am free to confess that I am not one of those, who consider money an objection. I can make as good use of it as any man tho' I am at the same time well satisfied, that the sum of human happiness does not depend upon the sum of anything of that kind."

Orders arrived for Frank early in the summer of 1829 to join the

Ontario, Captain Alexander Wadsworth commanding, for a three-year cruise to the Mediterranean. Although eager for a sea assignment, he regretted leaving Caroline and was concerned for his beloved mother, who was advancing in age and who had "hopes of keeping me with her for a long time."

He boarded the *Ontario* in Philadelphia on her way to New York. At the Brooklyn Navy Yard, Frank wrote his mother that the *Ontario* was a "good sailer."

The wardroom, "as our apartment is called," proved comfortable and "neatly fitted up." Furniture included a bed, bureau, and chair, "the whole neatly curtained off." The officers enlisted a first-rate steward and fine servants "so that we are as well fixed in these things as possible. Indeed we have taken some pains & paid considerable attention to these little comforts & amenities, for they tend greatly to blunt the bitter pill of separation from home and friends," he wrote Victorine.

"I can safely say," he confided to his sister Amelia, "that I have never been in a mess since my entrance into the service that I was so much pleased with. We have all thus far shown a unity of feeling & purpose, that promises a most agreeable & harmonious cruise. Our ship is already in beautiful order & the admiration of all those who have seen her."

In mid-August the *Ontario* got underway from her mooring at the Brooklyn Navy Yard and moved out into the river. Major Henry Lee and his family came on board destined for Algiers where he was to become the new consul. On 17 August Commodore Isaac Chauncey boarded the ship to say good-bye. The *Ontario* met him with a salute, and the crew, aloft, gave him three cheers. Commodore Chauncey was "highly pleased" with the *Ontario* and paid compliments to the officers, who wore full dress uniforms in honor of his visit.

On 21 August the ship got underway from New York at 10 A.M., but owing to a head wind she made little progress, and was compelled to anchor off Sandy Hook. On the following day she upped anchor and was out into the Atlantic. The crossing proved "perilous." The *Ontario* encountered "A Gale wind such as I never before witnessed." In the afternoon of 8 September the ship's company realized foul weather was ahead, and the crew hauled in the sails as the wind increased.

Frank graphically described the situation to Charles: "By 4 p.m.

we were under *very* little canvas. . . . The sea was however rising so high and so rapidly that it was determined to 'Lay the ship to' that is bring her head nearer the direction of the wind & sea. . . . While performing this evolution and while laying in a most exposed situation with all one side to wind & sea, we were struck with the hardest squall I ever felt, and were completely thrown over until every Gun on that side was completely buried in the water, the ship laid almost motionless, the force of the wind kept her over, & the immense body of water laying on the Deck kept her from rising over the waves; at this critical moment when more than one stout heart gave up all for lost, though none showed its inward throbbings, the only alternative left, which was to get the ship before the wind was immediately resorted to, & executed with skill & intrepidity. In a few moments we had the satisfaction to see her yield to the first efforts of the helm & well distributed sail, everything was done to ease the ship by a proper distribution of the weight in her, & we were soon scudding gallantly before the gale at the rate of 10 . . . miles per hour. We were obliged to keep the stern of the vessel directly to meet the coming waves that were so terrific indeed, the least deviation bringing one or the other side exposed to them they would then break over us & we had about two feet water washing from side to side. . . . I believe but few ships were ever extricated from a similar situation.

"During the crisis, Home, Ma, all of you flashed across my mind, but it was only a flash, the next moment I was . . . up to my waist in water getting the Fore sheet aft, upon which all really depended. Many of the men were alarmed & all looked to their officers, as sailors always will in trying occasions, for support, and I am proud to say, they received all the comfort that coolness, energy, and decision could give them. I believe if any one among us had felt like flinching he had only to turn to his neighbour. The stern determined look he would have there encountered would have banished all thoughts of alarm.

"It certainly was a trying situation, and as little as I might care about being in a similar one, I am far from sorry that it happened, independent of the experience gained, it is a feeling of some satisfaction, whatever confidence one may have in himself, to know that his nerve and his head have been fairly tested & not found wanting, and one of the first internal reflections I made after all was over was how I am sure of myself in any situation I care not what it is.

"I have been in many gales & in the winter of '27 in the Gulf Lyons we had one Com[modore] R[odgers] put down as the hardest he had ever witnessed, but never could see the slightest danger before, and I am therefore certain that this was by far more severe than any others I had been in."

On 17 September 1829 the crew with relief heard the cry "Land Ho!" from the masthead. The ship's company clamored on deck and her officers with spyglasses marked "every object as it rose in view." An hour's sail brought the *Ontario* within full view of Cape St. Vincent. The ship passed Cape Trafalgar on the morning of the 18th and entered the Straits of Gibraltar. She anchored in the harbor of Gibraltar the same day, having made the passage from New York in twenty-seven days. Frank went ashore to see old friends, and dined with Mr. Henry, the American consul. "Gibraltar," he wrote Victorine, "is certainly a highly interesting place to a stranger, not merely as a splendid specimen of military engineering & being one of the most impregnable Fortresses in the world, but you find congregated within its Walls persons from all quarters of the Globe. . . ."

Leaving Gibraltar, the *Ontario* dropped anchor at Algiers on 2 October after "a long and disagreeable passage" of nine days, encountering a "continual succession of gales," accompanied by "terrific thunder and lightning." Frank speculated that the *Ontario* had so little fair weather since leaving New York that "some spell is upon us. I believe, however, that Jonah was among the passengers since we have landed them all, the beautiful sky, gentle breezes and pure air of the Mediterranean are again bringing us cheerfulness and comfort."

In Delaware at Eleutherian Mills the nineteen-year-old Sophie Madeleine du Pont, one of Frank's cousins, the youngest daughter of Irénée du Pont, sat writing with hero worship in her heart.

> *Star of Hope! gleam on the pillow*
> *Bless the Soul that sighs on thee*
> *Bless the sailors lonely pillow*
> *Far at Sea!*

. . . .

Star of God! yet safely guide him
To the shore he lov'd for me!
Long tempestuous waves have tried him
Far at Sea! *

Sophie, having read all of Frank's letters to her sisters, composed these lines for her cousin, whom all the younger du Ponts admired.

Left motherless at an early age, Sophie had been reared at Eleutherian Mills by her oldest sister, Victorine Bauduy who, widowed after a brief ten weeks of married life, managed the house for her father. As Sophie matured into a young lady, she assisted her sister in running the household and corresponded frequently with her brother, Henry, a cadet at West Point. She was ambitious for Henry and did not hesitate to chide him on his academic performance when she felt he was neglecting his studies.

Sophie never traveled from Eleutherian Mills except to attend boarding school or to visit friends in Philadelphia. An avid reader, she expanded her understanding of the world through books and periodicals, especially those relating to her special interests of history and travel. Fluent and literate in English and French, she was now learning Spanish. A devout Christian, she taught Sunday school and sought to perfect herself by prayer and examining her conscience.

Despite the rural setting of the gunpowder mills and the family residence—a Georgian-style mansion overlooking the powder yards along Brandywine Creek—Eleutherian Mills was a hospitable household frequently entertaining extended family and guests. As Frank suggested, the du Ponts welcomed his betrothed, Caroline Morris, on her frequent visits to Delaware, and made her feel at home.

When in Philadelphia, Frank's cousins often saw Caroline and went to parties as her guest. Of one soiree, Sophie wrote her sister, "there were very few ladies, & a *great many* gentlemen, but almost every one were perfect strangers to me. . . . You ask me what conquests I made. Candidly, they are all briefly summed up in that little word, None. . . . I saw Caroline often—she was sometimes affectionate to me. . . ."

---

* This quote and some of the details in this chapter about Sophie du Pont and Frank come from Betty-Bright Low and Jacqueline Hinsley, "A Family Party: Daily Life on the Brandywine 1823–1833, Caricatured by Sophie Madeleine Du Pont" (Wilmington, Del., 19—).

"Caroline Morris is [a] lively pleasant girl enough—not pretty, nor homely, but betwixt & between. I rather like her than otherwise," Sophie wrote Henry at West Point.

Sophie professed to be happy for Frank and Caroline. She herself had just broken off her engagement to a young man, and confided to her diary, "I thought a great deal about the importance of marriage vows—When I declined entering on that state, it was chiefly because I disliked the person proposed as my companion in it. I think if I had been so unhappy as to have formed an attachment, I should have forgotten everything else. My desire is, that my sister Eleu[thera] should marry & I remain single, to live with Pa & sister and to be their comfort & take care of them when they grow old. But God who orderth all aright, may order differently for me, yet should I ever marry, I desire it may only be one who loves & serves God—who is a sincere Christian—& I wish to think always of this, & to keep a watch over my heart, that I may not suffer its affections to be won, ever by anyone who does not afford that character. My own thoughts are, I shall not easily *love now*. I thank God for making me escape an unhappy union, & for the possession of a happy home & friends who are pleased to retain me in it."

Since there were few eligible men in Sophie's life, she relied on the companionship of women. Sophie's youthful relationships with members of her own sex exhibited an unusual intensity and she found herself emotionally attracted to casual acquaintances. While her behavior toward new friends was circumspect, she sustained close relationships with long-time friends. She wrote in her diary, "During this visit, I saw Elizabeth Smith 7 times, which was more than I ever saw of her before. I took a great fancy to her. I think I am very apt to take fancies to people I know very little, particularly if they are pretty, & give them credit for every virtue under Heaven, I love them ere I know them well. I think 'tis what is called in French *engonement*. Elizabeth's beautiful black eyes haunt me even now. Their glance seemed to bewitch one when I was with her, I could not weary of looking on her lovely face. . . . I think I shall not soon forget her parting kiss. . . . I felt as if I *loved* her then. . . ."

In early November 1829 Sophie wrote Henry at West Point, "last night there came a letter from cousin Frank from Gibraltar, the first we have received since his arrival in Europe. He gives an account of a dreadful storm they had on the 8th of September. . . . they were very near being lost. A squall struck the ship and threw it on the side, and for some minutes they had given up all hopes. . . . Poor Cousin! To think that he is exposed every hour to similar accidents, is indeed dreadful! My poor Aunt must feel this terribly. How trying it is to know those we love [are] exposed continually to the recurrence of imminent peril! Yet it is gratifying to know they bear it with such noble courage as Frank does, particularly when we consider that the navy was never his *choice*, nor does he like it now."

This last sentence is revealing; Frank must have confessed his distaste for the Navy in conversation with his cousins. He would have preferred to pursue a civil career, and entered the Navy only to avoid becoming a burden to his family. Throughout his career Frank every so often wrote that he abhorred the Navy, and regretted not electing another profession, preferably farming.

By mid-October 1829 the *Ontario* lay anchored in Port Mahon. Frank carped about the condition of the Mediterranean Squadron. As was to become his habit, he was critical of his superiors, and complained of the squadron commodore, Captain William Montgomery Crane, who kept his ships moored permanently in the "miserable hole" of Port Mahon, instead of patrolling the sea. He accused Crane of being unenergetic and of depriving the squadron officers of nautical experience. In a searing opinion, he noted to Charles that all the midshipmen applied to remain in the squadron when the *Delaware* sailed for the States as they had seen "neither duty nor the Mediterranean" and "have been idling their time & are all disgracefully in debt. . . ."

When Crane was relieved by Captain James Biddle, a friend from *Congress* days, Frank applauded. "We shall . . . have better discipline at last," he wrote. This admiration, though, soon was transformed into outright dislike of the new commodore. On this cruise to the Mediterranean a defiant Frank was constantly irritated by senior officers. Although he professed a high regard for authority, he abhorred incompetence, felt himself qualified to judge men who outranked him, and did not hesitate to embroil himself in controversy.

Frank wanted the deadwood that clogged the higher echelon of the Navy eliminated. He and other young officers felt stymied by the system that denied them promotion. He continued to debase and criticize his superiors throughout the decades ahead. While some of his comments were biased, there can be no doubt that there were inefficient, superannuated officers commanding ships at sea. Frank was not alone in his evaluation of his superiors; in recognition of the situation, Congress in 1855 established an Efficiency Board to weed out incompetents.

It was not until his promotion to captain and his assignment to an important mission in the Far East, that Frank altered his stance and refrained from censuring those in power. After he accrued seniority and achieved his goal, his perspective altered.

After serving as counsel for a fellow officer at a court-martial, a cocksure Frank confided to Wily, "I believe . . . I am looked upon as [one of] the leaders of the rebels. . . . I stood by the weak against the strong. I asserted my rights & those of others, by talking long & loud—right & left . . . & I intend to do so wherever I may go."

The *Ontario* visited Barcelona and Gibraltar, then got underway for Algiers in threatening weather. After reaching Málaga, the ship ran into a severe gale. Torrents of rain poured down and the wind increased. The *Ontario* alternately plunged heavily, and rose again, laboring. Under shortened sail she rode more easily, but as the wind on her beam grew stronger, she was bowing down to it as she ricocheted through the waves. For six days the *Ontario* withstood the onslaughts of the Mediterranean gale and when the wind at last subsided, her officers discovered that they had drifted to within twelve miles of Gibraltar. Consequently, the *Ontario* "bore up" and anchored in the harbor. The officers and crew were "pretty well fagged out . . . hoarse from hollering and with our stock of dry clothes expended."

Frank's acquaintances on shore greeted him with disbelief. They thought the *Ontario* had been among twenty vessels wrecked between Gibraltar and Málaga. The storm had been "most terrible & nothing like it having been known for sixteen years." After his Atlantic crossing and Mediterranean adventure Frank concluded that the *Ontario* was "certainly the finest and safest [ship] I have ever been in."

Critical of Captain Wadsworth for having left Gibraltar when weather threatened, Frank wrote Charles, "Unfortunately our Captain, besides being fidgety, is *nobody* in any capacity. He may have been a very good subordinate, but this thing responsibility crushes him down, & if I thought a command was ever to make me as miserable, yea one hundredth part as much so, I should waist but very few more days in the Navy. He is a fool in spite of experience, though I believe a very good hearted man. I hope for his sake he will leave in a year, for if we were to have six months more such weather as we have lately encountered he would die of anxiety."

Despite his sour assessment, Frank passed the time in Gibraltar "pleasantly." "Our mess," he wrote Charles, "is a pattern of harmony, my room comfortable & books attractive. I have added much to my nautical knowledge & experience."

Christmas 1829 found the *Ontario* anchored at Port Mahon, waiting to go into the navy yard for overhaul. To overcome the tedium of winter, Frank hired a Spanish instructor and a fencing master. "This with my books and the duty of the ship will help me through it," he confided to Victorine.

In late February 1830 the *Ontario* took departure for Marseilles. Once again a gale struck the ship—"yards & mast were all down, & nothing but the lower storm sails could be shown," he wrote Amelia. But on 2 March the sky cleared and the weather turned mild. "Such is the variable climate of the Mediterranean & the vicissitudes of a sailor's life, but this variety keeps up the excitement and infuses energy in all your actions," he continued. "I have added much to my stock of experience and would not shrink tomorrow from command of a ship in the most trying situation."

By 5 March the *Ontario* was "snugly anchored" in the inner harbor of Marseilles. After a pleasant interlude, the ship got underway to cruise the Mediterranean.

On this voyage Frank soon catalogued his dissatisfaction with the *Ontario*'s new skipper, Captain William L. Gordon. "Let me spit some venom upon a reptile which I have let off lightly," he wrote Wily. "A man who is in strange company when he finds himself among gentlemen—who, one day is a vain, conceited, arrogant bully—the next, a pliant, submissive sycophant. A man who is to such an extent, that some have been charitable enough to ascribe it to a constitutional infirmity.

"To be honorable and independent is to insure his anathema—to be a cringing hypocrite, is to be certain of his embrace—a sort of military *martinet,* who sends forth bullying bulletins—as insulting in their tone as they are execrable in their English—a man who fortuitous circumstances have placed over his betters—who came among us . . . [and] found a little paradise upon the waters, but . . . converted it in[to] a floating Hell. . . ."

Despite this assessment of the captain, Frank was enjoying this

51

cruise, which "adds much to my professional knowledge," he wrote Wily. He admired the first lieutenant, George N. Hollins, "one of the most amiable men . . . that I have ever known, is industrious, indefatigable, and a fine seaman." Frank was pleased with the ship and his messmates. "There is a jolly set sitting about the mess table," he wrote a friend, "singing, laughing, talking, playing the Guitar, flute & god knows what so that I am in a perfect bedlam."

During this period Frank received letters from Caroline Morris, who often spoke of the du Ponts' kindness while she was visiting Delaware. He also had letters from Victorine that expressed "a prepossession in favour of my fair friend." "This induces me to believe," Frank wrote back, "that she has not suffered in your estimation by a longer acquaintance. If this should be the case, it will be the source of no ordinary satisfaction, for no one has a higher opinion of your discernment than myself. I have studied her character closely, a thousand times more than I ever did any other woman's and am fully convinced my most sanguine expectations will be realised, that she is deeply attached to me I am fully convinced."

Separation was giving Frank the opportunity to review his relationship with Caroline, and Victorine's charitable assessment of her may have eased his increasing doubts about his engagement.

After visiting Gibraltar in the fall of 1830, the *Ontario* again anchored at Port Mahon. "The Squadron is in beautiful order," he wrote, "and any American would be proud of it." He noted that Commodore James Biddle was at Port Mahon for the winter, renting a house on shore, "where he intends to hold *soirees*." "Though I am not one of his [Biddle's] admirers and have not called upon him since he has been on station, I think he does much to sustain the dignity of the flag."

Instead of having all ships anchored at Port Mahon for the winter, Biddle ordered the *Ontario* to Smyrna, "which if possible is more stupid & even more out of the world." Here Frank and Lieutenant William Ogden gained permission to tour Constantinople for three weeks.

During his stay there, Frank claimed that he saw "everybody & everything." After twelve days sightseeing, he wrote Amelia, "I never found myself flagging not even for a moment . . . and have come to the conclusion that if I had but one city to see, that city should be Constantinople. I had formed no idea of its extent and still less of the peculiar character of the scenery."

After more sightseeing and personal interviews with the sultan and other Turkish dignitaries, Frank and Ogden departed for Smyrna in early January 1831. "Time passes off here much more agreeably than at Mahon," Frank wrote Amelia. "There is a ball every Thursday at the casino, where you meet agreeable society and good music."

However, by the spring of 1831, Frank declared "This long respite from sea service has been to most of us tedious and irksome." No letters, no newspapers, no books from home. "I have never felt so cut off from them [friends on the Brandywine] before," he complained to Charles. "I feel it . . . while writing this letter, as if we had no longer any subjects in common."

Supply ships failed to arrive. The officers and men on board the *Ontario* managed to make their provisions hold out. The "paltry sum" of $2,000 given to the ship by Biddle had long since evaporated, and the crew was dependent on the generosity of the merchants on shore.

To Charles he fumed, "There is no one who will submit with more cheerfulness than myself to the necessary restraints & privations of the service, but to smart under the selfish whims, of a nervous & splenetic old bachelor is rather more than I can endure with patience. . . ."

A bored and disgruntled Frank "killed six days of time" by touring the interior on horseback with five friends, penetrating as far as Alaşehir. After skirting several long caravans, the party finally reached the spot where Sardis once stood. Here Frank and his friends dismounted and commenced the exhausting ascent to the acropolis. By a narrow and dangerous path, they struggled to the pinnacle. Frank was enchanted to recall that the plain before him had "once reverberated with Xerxes' countless hosts," Lydians, Medes, and Persians. "But my thoughts," he told Eleuthera, "strayed to the Brandywine." There among the ruins Frank carved the name "Sophie" on an overturned stone column of the church. On his return from his voyage in the *North Carolina* in 1827, he had discovered that his cousin Sophie du Pont had grown into a modest and intelligent young lady. A natural friendship had developed between the young neighbors, uncomplicated by conscious physical attraction. Saltwater and absence were altering his feelings toward Caroline, and he felt trapped by his engagement to her. He was of a generation that felt it necessary to find an honorable way to terminate a solemn commitment. In emotional turmoil, his thoughts strayed to home.

By June the *Ontario* was again in Port Mahon, along with the *Constellation, Brandywine, Concord,* and *Boston.* Lieutenant Dale then left the *Ontario* to return to the States. "This leaves me 2d Lieut." Frank's commission date was 19 December 1815. His appraisal of his new duties changed when he received the list of promotions. Although the number of lieutenants promoted was respectable, "still what prospects are left for us at the other end, those of 1814 just promoted."

"What a failure the Navy has been to me," he confided to Wily. "Eight & twenty years of age, & the second Lt. of a sloop of war! Whenever I think of it which begins to [be] always, I am disgusted, heartily so."

During the winter of 1831–32 the *Ontario* was at Port Mahon. In April, with orders from home, the ship upped anchor and sailed westward, touching at Cape Verde off the coast of Africa, picking up the trade winds. Heading toward home at last, Frank was moved to write:

> *Tis sweet to hear the watch Dog's honest bark*
> *By deep mouth'd welcome as we draw near home*
> *Tis sweet to know there is an eye will mark*
> *Our coming, & look brither when we come*
> *Tis sweet to be awakened by the Lark,*
> *Or lulled by the fall waters, sweet the hum*
> *Of Bees, the voice of Girls, the Song of Birds,*
> *The lisp of Children & their earliest words.*

"If you go to sea," Frank wrote Charles Henry Davis later, "the Mediterranean has many inducements over the other stations—the number of vessels, the possibility of changing ships if you are not suited, & the greater ease of getting home, & many other reasons make it the most desirable cruise."

On 4 May 1832 the *Ontario* picked up the Norfolk pilot. Frank groused that the ship was anchoring at Norfolk rather than New York. "My usual infernal luck," he complained to Wily in Brooklyn. "I never but once returned to any other port. It has taken away half the pleasure of getting in. I had promised myself so much satisfaction with you & my other friends in Henry Street."

V

"In a few words she is an angel"

In Delaware the entire du Pont family anticipated Frank's return from Virginia. Although Sophie Madeline kept up a brave front while entertaining Caroline Morris, she had never approved of the engagement. She had deep feelings herself for Frank. "Frank has arrived!" she revealed in her diary, "he is safe, he is once more in his native land, in a few weeks, perhaps in *one,* we shall see him! . . . But yet I cannot feel that joy I felt the last time he came. When I think of seeing him again amongst us, all seems delightful, but immediately I think of his marriage. Oh *that thought* is still too painful! In a month perhaps, Frank, dear Frank, whom I love next to my brothers, & as a brother, whom all looked up to as to one superior, on whom our brightest hopes are set. He will have formed that tie, which I fear will seal his destiny, to be an unhappy one! I cannot bear the thought of that event, I never could. I always looked on it with regret & grief. . . ."

On Thursday, 18 May Frank returned home.

"Till he came," Sophie divulged in her diary, "I was so agitated I could scarce do anything—was this right? I know it was *not,* for it was not with joyful feelings, & I thought more on the painful results his return *might have,* than on the great blessing & joy we should feel his safe return to be. I was calm when he was here, & *cold* too, I fear. But as soon as he was gone, the tears *would* come. I sat down & let them flow for some moments, I scarce knew why.

"I felt I ought to say something about Caroline. I introduced the subject by asking if he was going to Phila—his answer was hurried, & I thought embarrassed—my courage failed me & I said nothing.

This was yielding weakly to the sinful timidity of my nature. What, not even to say to him I wished his happiness in the most important event of his life! & how *can* he love or care for me!"

That spring, Frank, his feelings for Caroline altered, searched for an honorable way of breaking his engagement to her. He journeyed to Philadelphia, hoping for a pretext that would allow him to withdraw his proposal. To his relief, he discovered that his misgivings were shared by Caroline. Their parting appeared amiable.

"My affair is off, all off," Frank wrote Pendergrast. "In a moment of illusion, and hastened by being on the eve of separation, I entered into a most hasty, ill suited, uncongenial engagement."

For nearly three years, he continued, "I was prey to contending emotions. On the one hand my honor recoiling with horror, at inflicting a wound which might be more or less lasting—on the other, crushed at the thought of an ill assorted union. . . . I thus passed my time in misery, guilt & deceit—for I was constantly exerting myself to sustain that natural, gay laughing buo[y]ancy of my character, which alas independent of all such matters is fast leaving me. Since my return however, my star began to glimmer again, an unexpected opening offered itself, this with an increase of fortune already great, enabled me to make a retreat without sacrificing my honor, or the happiness of another."

To Charles Henry Davis, Frank confided: "The thing was brought about by *myself* or rather I availed myself of an opening to do it— and I trust I stand sufficiently high in your estimation, for you to believe me when I tell you that I did it without compromising my honor, and what was equally sacred, the happiness of the Lady."

Sophie divulged in her diary: "I could never, no never, realise that engagement—I did *not expect* its dissolution, yet it has not surprised me, & I only find it hard to believe that there ever *was* an engagement. Ever since his return, I saw he did not love her. The very first day he came, when I spoke of Phila, & he turned his head away & spoke of hedges, I *knew* he did not love her. Yet I scarce dared admit the idea to myself, much less tell another. . . . I do *know* in fact, he is *right*, he has acted as principle required, as his duty to God & man required."

Three days later, somewhat hypocritically, she wrote, "Cousin F[rank] dined here—exerted himself to be cheerful & animated. The more I see of him the more my heart bleeds for C[aroline]. What will *earth* give her to replace this treasure? I pray the *Lord* may be her comforter."

Again she noted in her diary: "It is evident that C[aroline] and her family expected [the wedding]. . . . Poor soul—could I believe that she was at all able to appreciate or understand Frank's merit, & that she loved him, as he deserves to be loved, I should indeed deem her miserable!"

During the summer of 1832 Frank enjoyed the company of his family and the "calm pleasure of country life." He wrote Pendergrast, "I have a fine horse, which I make frequent use of." He made a point of seeing Sophie almost daily, taking her on long walks in the country, escorting her to horse races in Chester, Pennsylvania, and sharing rides with her in his new gig.

"My cousin," Sophie confided to her diary, "has not been here today. He so seldom misses coming for a day that it seems *unnatural* not to have seen him. When he first came home this summer, I remember what happiness I thought 'twould be, after so long a separation, to see him every day. And this is a happiness to which habit has not yet in the least rendered me accustomed or indifferent. Each time I look again on that dear face, I feel anew the pleasure of his return."

Again she wrote, "I do not know why I felt *awkward* at meeting my cousin, & receiving the little tokens he brought me—otherwise than it is *my nature* to be awkward & embarrassed."

In September, Irénée du Pont hosted a dinner party for the governor of Delaware, David Hazzard. As Irénée had to survey a farm and did not expect to return until 1 o'clock, and since most of the du Pont children had other plans, Frank and Sophie received the notables and "promenaded" them through the mills. "Our cousin," Sophie wrote to Henry, "was here by twelve & we sat in *laughing* expectation of our *distinguished* till *one o'clock*." Irénée finally arrived with the governor and, after a dinner of lamb with mint, the guests departed. "Our governor is very gracious & serene in manner," Sophie told Henry. "He called cousin nothing but *Col*[onel] Du Pont to Frank's great amusement."

In another letter to him, Sophie described a gift: "You ought to see what a pretty little piece of lava Cousin Frank brought me, as a weight to hold down my paper! It is a little treasure tome, for it conjures up visions of Etna & Vesuvius, of Italy & history & poetry & Romance, & dearer than all, of the one to whose kindness I owe the possession of the talisman."

As fall blended into winter, Frank wrote Davis, "I will pass the winter with my friends here, both my inclination and duty prompt me, as they are lonesome & it is the best time to enjoy those domestic comforts & endearments, which our long cruises are but too apt to make us think slightingly of, but give us most erratic habits. I am beset with invitations from all quarters."

Suffering severely from intestinal problems, Frank visited a doctor whose examinations proved "more disagreeable than painful." The doctor prescribed stale bread and milk, morning and evening, meat once a day with rice and potatoes. "I have not tasted wine for a month," he groused. In mid-December 1832 Frank went to New York to see John Wily. While in the city he attended "all the Balls" and met with former messmates. In his long midnight talks with Wily, he confessed his love for Sophie.

After his return from New York, Frank journeyed to Philadelphia where the famed actress, Fanny Kemble, was giving her farewell appearance in *The Hunchback*. When he arrived at the theater he was denied entrance by a crowd swarming about the lobby. Later, he was "compensated" by meeting Miss Kemble at Nicholas Biddle's home at a huge party given in her honor. Senator Henry Clay of Kentucky was there. Frank described the festivities as a "handsome Tea Party & I enjoyed myself very much. Miss Fanny sang twice, and the last time an amazing little ditty from her own composition, which delighted the company." Frank managed to talk to her, "but it was heavy dragging," and her enunciation "was exceedingly ponderous."

Frank was called to New York again on Navy business and did not return to Delaware for Christmas. "Cousin Frank has never come home for Christmas Day," an aggrieved Sophie wrote Henry. "Every day, every *hour*, we expected him—neither he nor a letter appeared. . . . it has been a very great disappointment to his mother and all here, that he should be away at this season of festivity. . . ."

Frank arrived back in Delaware on 31 December, in time to join the family on New Year's Day in "that delightful exchange of warm & cordial feelings in our home circle, which the New Year so agreeable revives. . . . most of us dined at my uncle's, where we exchanged little presents, the compliments of the season, the joy of the children, & the friendly communion of all, made us perhaps as happy a little community as could be found anywhere," he wrote Pendergrast.

A happy Sophie informed Henry: "Our dear cousin returned home yesterday, just in good time for the Day. . . . You may think what a pleasure it was to have him in our circle once more. . . . We had the usual interchange of presents . . . & Cousin Frank gave me the most beautiful book I ever saw, Rogers Italy. This embellished with the finest engravings, at almost every page. . . . Its greatest value . . . is the kindness which remembered me, & wished to give me pleasure. Indeed this is the great charm of this annual interchange of tokens, not that we have so many pretty things, but that we have so many things to tell our hearts each hour of the day, of the affection & interest of our nearest & dearest. . . ."

During January 1833 Frank stayed "in my winter quarters without interruption." The month "glided swiftly on, with the assistance of books, periodicals, & papers, an occasional ride or drive to Wilmington, which has recently been enlivened by two or three canvas back suppers, when after the delicious bird itself, champagne, & cards were the idols most worshiped."

Frank often went up to Philadelphia that winter for the opera and parties. One ball "exceeded any thing of the kind in this country, not excepting the renowned city of the Gotham," he bragged to Wily. The host opened ten rooms, "the walls of which were hung in crimson & gold drapery." Frank and his friends danced until four o'clock in the morning.

Frank and Sophie became engaged in March 1833. "It was not until our ride home" from New Castle, Sophie wrote Henry, "that I had the least idea that our cousin's regard for me was *more* than that of a cousin."

"I have . . . his assurance," she noted in her diary, "that he respects, that he will endeavour to share, my religious principles & feelings. The wildest hope or wish my heart ever imagined could never have reached the rapture of this thought. He will not only be my friend for time, but for eternity!"

The engagement had the complete approval of both du Pont families. "My uncle said he had long wished it," a jubilant Frank wrote Wily. "All my friends shed tears of joy, all said it was as it should be."

Frank had known his cousin "long & well," and he concluded that his "morbid instability of character has alone prevented our coming together long ere this." He was delighted that "her education has been very much attended to, and she has profited by it.

"She is pious," he praised, "but that piety, which inspires the greatest respect, which is the very reverse of fanaticism & bigotry, which adds to her cheerfulness, instead of producing affected melancholy & gravity. . . . In a few words she is an angel of purity & sensibility—her mind is well staid & every way calculated to improve my own.

"To say something of her style of beauty . . . I have not the descriptive talent. . . . She is middle size . . . face long but cheek full & dimpled, small mouth & beautiful teeth—eyes blue & hair light in great profusion, complexion clear with color—when silent expression pensive—when talking or laughing, cheerful & very animated. . . . She is pretty, good, & sensible & looks about eighteen."

Shortly after the engagement was announced, Frank was off to Baltimore to act as a groomsman at George Hollins's wedding. He wrote Sophie often. "The wedding was gay & pleasant. . . ." The bride looked "pretty & interesting," but in Frank's estimation was not the woman "to have united my friend George. . . . He now has an amiable wife, who loves him but who will never make him what he is susceptible of being made."

Throughout his stay in Baltimore, Frank's friends entertained with festive parties, balls, and dinners. From his discussions with Navy colleagues, Frank concluded "that the Navy is in the decline, & not a favorite with the Gov't. If I could make a thousand dollars at anything else, with a certainty of not getting below it, I would willingly embrace the chance—& cry quits with Uncle Sam."

When Frank returned from Maryland, he and Sophie fixed the date for a June wedding. "We shall settle down in the midst of friends long tried," he wrote Pendergrast, "and scenes long familiar. . . . I look forward with inexpressable joy to our union."

Sophie arranged her trousseau and made visits to acquaintances in Wilmington and Philadephia. In April she went off to Alexandria, Virginia, to see friends. "How lost I feel without you! . . ." Frank wrote her. "I find that great is the difference between *you going* & *my remaining* & when the reverse is the case.

"How I count the days & hours when you will be mine . . . ," he continued. "I have heard it said that as a man draws near thirty, the warm feelings of his heart get tempered down, that instead of being quick & enthusiastic, he is cold & calculating—but surely this is not my case—almost the very reverse. I can look back and analyze past sentiments & how different were they from the present ones. I feel now a vigorous elasticity of mind that inspires a confidence in the future, which I never experienced before. . . ."

On the following day, Frank wrote, "How I think of June, do not say you think it coming too soon. . . . When I have you with me I feel so happy & contented. . . . But the moment I leave you, I wish to return & then begin to count the days & hours until you will be mine."

Sophie did not share his anticipation. A poignant entry in her diary reveals her qualms: "When I come to my own sweet little room, my paradise as I have jokingly called it, & remember the blessed sabbath hours; the pure thoughts & feelings awakened & cherished in them here. I think, will it ever be so again? I shrink extremely from my marriage. When with Frank if he speaks to me, he can charm & make me believe almost anything. When I am here alone in the presence of my God, I am oftentimes overwhelmed with grief and terror. Everything I look upon here troubles my heart with sadness, & I don't know how I can ever support this next week, but thro' His aid whose strength is sufficient for us."

As the wedding neared, Frank wrote Wily: "I don't know whether the wedding will be large or confined to the family & the immediate attendants. As I told you my uncle is queer about some things, & it will all depend upon his wishes, which are law and gospel to his daughters."

The couple was married in the parlor of Eleutherian Mills on 27 June 1833. Charlotte Cazenove, Sophie's intimate, and her cousin Ella joined Eleuthera as bridesmaids. Frank had Henry du Pont and naval officers John Wily and William Ogden as groomsmen.* "We had a very pleasant wedding," Frank told Pendergrast, "and the kindness of our country neighbors & Wilmington friends have kept us quite gay—the weather favouring us greatly it being both clear & cool."

On their honeymoon, Frank and Sophie went first to New York City, where they met his old messmates on board the *Delaware*. They spent ten days at West Point, "one of the most agreeable spots in the country—the very best hotel in the U.S.—a delightful situation." They enjoyed the "exercise of cadets . . . such as artillery &

---

* Some of the details of Frank and Sophie's relationship come from Betty-Bright Low and Jacqueline Hinsley, "A Family Party: Daily Life on the Brandywine 1823–1833, Caricatured by Sophie Madeleine Du Pont" (Wilmington, Del., 19—).

shell firing, [and] infantry tactics. . . . I never spent a pleasanter week in my life," Frank wrote.

They then journeyed upriver to Albany, visited Trenton Falls near Utica ("More curious than Niagara"), crossed over to Lebanon and, from there, to the "lovely & incomparable town of Northampton." They rode through the beautiful Connecticut Valley, and returned to New York City from Hartford.

In September 1833 Frank learned that his friend Charles Henry Davis was about to sail on board the *Vincennes*. Frank wrote that he did not want Davis to leave "without the assurance that I shall always cherish the acquaintance we have formed, and will do all in my power to foster an intimacy, which has afforded me already so many moments of unalloyed satisfaction & pleasure." He assured Davis that although he was now married, he had "no thoughts of resigning. . . ."

Frank and Sophie moved from Eleutherian Mills across the creek to Louviers, the Victor du Pont home, where his mother, sisters Amelia and Julia, Julia's three young children, and Ella resided. Sophie agonized at leaving Eleutherian Mills and dreaded making her home with her in-laws.

At Louviers, Frank hoped to spend the winter, "quietly & advantageously, spending my mornings, in *earnest study*, and the evenings in social converse & polite literature."

During the fall Frank spent a few days in Philadelphia, staying at the U.S. Hotel. He went to the navy yard and transacted business, but "a knot of officers in high ferment" detained him until a late hour. They were carping about a bill presented to Congress by the Secretary of the Navy, Levi Woodbury, which would reduce the shore pay of officers. "The atrocity of the plan . . . consists of robbing all junior officers, from Lieutenants down, in order to increase the pay of Captains," Frank explained to Sophie.

Frank returned to the navy yard, where again the discussion turned to Secretary Woodbury and the bad feeling created by his proposal.

The Navy Bill was actually intended to "give every grade the compensation of its corresponding rank in the Army," and Woodbury was "finally brought to think that the higher ranks ought to be better paid, but would not have it said, that the aggregate expense of the Navy was increased under his reign, so Yankee like, he resorts to a Yankee trick—and robs the poor Middies & others to the amount of about twenty eight thousand a year, & puts it in the pockets of others."

As Du Pont was convinced that the Navy Bill could not pass the Congress, he let the matter drop.

He was not anxious to sail until summer. "I should have no objection then, as I wish to take another cruise," he wrote, "& will then settle down if I can more permanently & solidly than I can at present with orders hanging over me."

During this time Frank and other officers helped create a lyceum, a center for the education of naval officers. "I believe," Frank had written Pendergrast in December 1832, "that the present improved moral condition of the Navy and its growing intelligence will authorize an attempt to establish a society, which will be as creditable to its founders and supporters, as it will be permanently beneficial to the . . . class which it is intended to protect." He hoped that the center would endow a fund, the interest of which would be sufficient to provide an ample annual pension for Navy widows. "I can see," Frank concluded, "in my mind's eye a brilliant association, conducted by men of honor & delicacy."

The lyceum system, then expanding across the northern part of the United States, was a comprehensive American scheme of adult education, catering to a popular desire for self-improvement and scientific knowledge. A group of people would raise funds to finance a lyceum, which would attract lecturers on literary and cultural subjects. Scientists would exhibit specimens or set up apparatus and perform experiments before the members.*

The United States Naval Lyceum established at the Brooklyn Navy Yard in 1833 provided officers stationed in the New York area with a high form of recreation. The constitution of the Naval Lyceum declared that it was created "in order to promote the diffusion of useful knowledge, to foster a spirit of harmony and a community of interest in the service, and to cement the links which unite us as professional brethren." Matthew C. Perry urged the Navy Department to add an extra story to the office structure then being built in the yard, and there the Lyceum had its lecture hall, cabinet, library, and reading room, open daily from 9 A.M. to sunset. Every Tuesday evening a session was held for papers and discussion. This "is the leading event in Navy affairs," a jubilant Frank wrote Pendergrast. The annual dues were set at one dollar, "sufficient to keep them supplied with leading newspapers and periodicals, & new

---

* Some of the information concerning the Naval Lyceum comes from Samuel Eliot Morison, *"Old Bruin," Commodore Matthew C. Perry* (Boston, 1967), pp. 133–34.

Books." The Lyceum received extensive donations for engravings, maps, statues, and busts from many wealthy New Yorkers. Contributions of books supplied by officers after their cruises filled the cabinets.

"The Lyceum," Frank wrote Davis, "is under excellent management, and well organized."

That autumn Sophie suffered a miscarriage and her health deteriorated so that Frank delayed active duty at sea. He carried her to the sofa bed in her room each morning to let her hear the birds and see the garden from the window. Never robust since her fall at a ferryboat eight years previously, she had severe pains in her knee and also was plagued by intermittent lower back problems and bursitis. Physicians treated her with morphine and for a while she was addicted.

Frank had planned to spend time in Washington listening to the Senate debates while Sophie visited friends in Alexandria. His eagerness to attend the congressional debates, "which have never been so brilliant as this Session," was tempered by his concern for Sophie's delayed recovery, which caused him "uneasiness and required medical attendance." He wrote Pendergrast: ". . . she's been an invalid, more or less, all fall and recovers her strength very slowly."

That winter, in spite of worry over Sophie's health, Frank wrote Davis: "its been a most happy time for me. I have seen in bolder relief the inestimable qualities & virtues of my better half—her patience, contentment, perfect cheerfulness & Happiness though suffering at times considerably, taking an interest in my studies, readings, in all matters naval or political. . . . She has a delightful knowledge of Botany & Natural History and an exquisite taste & talent for Poetry."

"I am happy to my heart's content," he wrote Pendergrast, "with the society of my lovely wife . . . [and] good books. I never care about leaving the fireside." He devoted several hours a day to a course in astronomy, "which I consider more a pleasure than a study—in fact the days are not long enough for me & I retire every night, firmly resolved to get up by dawn, but alas there I stick and have not yet crawled out before eight."

"I have not found the days long enough," he reiterated to Davis, ". . . it has been the happiest period of my whole life—most certainly that which has been the best employed."

Naval matters, however, continued to occupy his thoughts. The

Secretary of the Navy's annual report for 1833 was "filled as usual with suggestions that are never attended to, and repeated from year to year until the heart is made sick—it is also filled with arithmetical calculations of different expenses, showing the man [secretary] . . . [is] daily haunted by Dollars & cents, & not able to get beyond them."

A board of five Navy captains had begun a revision of *The Rules and Regulations for the Naval Service.* "Well," Frank exploded to Davis, "I could not believe my own eyes—a greater abortion you cannot conceive. . . . There is not an article which if good does not already exist either in the printed Laws or internal Rules—and all that is new is decidedly bad. . . . to sum up the whole matter, those gentlemen were only occupied about themselves—to increase their power . . . [and] to reserve all the good berths to themselves. . . ." Young officers under the captains' revised regulations could not expect to receive command of a squadron or a station for fifteen or twenty years. "In fact the discontent is so great that I think there is no possible chance of its getting through."

While primarily focused on naval affairs, Frank's frustration also included the entire Jackson administration. "The distress in the country," he complained, "has spread far and wide, all business is nearly at an end, failures have followed failures in all the large cities, produce is down to nothing—all this has aroused the whole country—& a degree of excitement exists never known before. Meetings upon meetings have been called—delegation upon delegation have been sent to Washington. . . . The President received them courteously at first, but would immediately break out in a towering passion.

"The last elections . . . [have] brought from the West a lower set of men than were ever before known in Congress—men who never expected to get there, who never would but for the Jackson fever, which will leave more bitter traces in this country than the cholera."

Congress adjourned on 30 June 1834, "and as usual the Navy was left among the 'unfinished business.'" Frank had kept up with the debates in newspapers, which "threw a spice of variety to my other occupations." He evaluated the leading congressmen who had played a conspicuous part in the session. "I must admit," he wrote Davis, "that tho' my personal predilection inclines for another [Henry Clay] I must award the palm for gigantic mind . . . powers of argument, and for grasping every subject with the strength of a giant, making bones crack as he goes along, with no equal in the science of analysis, for all this & indeed everything else in the qualifications of an orator & statesman, your fellow statesman [Daniel] Webster has left behind his great & brilliant rivals, and all impartial judges at Washington admit it."

In early July 1834 Frank left Louviers for Philadelphia to hear Daniel Webster give the Fourth of July oration. The hall was jammed with congressional notables and "a sprinkling of ladies." Frank's seat was near the speaker's platform and he "saw and heard . . . to great advantage" as Webster "thundered forth for three quarters of an hour in [a] manner really sublime & beautiful."

To Davis he wrote, "the department appears to have forgotten me, which I am the more glad of as my wife is still an invalid, not having left her bed since January—her general health is excellent, but [she is] suffering from some of those complaints peculiar to women." Frank had taken Sophie to Philadelphia to receive "the best advice. Her recovery will be certain and permanent, but will require some months."

Frank realized, however, that the Navy Department would certainly assign him next to sea duty. "After that," he wrote, "I can settle down as I intended. My hobby is still to kill my own mutton & raise my own turnips on a snug farm with a snug house, & a Spare Room in it for a valued friend, like yourself for instance."

In mid-July orders came to report to the sloop of war *Erie*. As Frank knew that the new Secretary of the Navy, Mahlon Dickerson, was in Philadelphia, he went to the navy yard immediately to see if his orders could be canceled. His principal reason for this request, he explained to Dickerson, was Sophie's illness. The secretary replied that something surely could be done, and suggested that Du Pont contact the chief clerk of the Navy, John Boyle, in Washington. Frank wrote: "I trust there will be no objection [about revoking the orders]. And that our sense of public duty will permit you to grant . . . [this] request." By return mail Frank learned that the orders had been canceled.

Sophie's health was not the only reason for Frank's unwillingness to serve on the *Erie*. He admitted to Davis that with his length of service he had been ordered "at the *eleventh* hour to fill up some vacancy on board a sloop of war, whose officers had all been duly notified & had six weeks to prepare." He also confided that if he went on a sloop of war it would be as first lieutenant. "The fact is my dander was up . . . & it is well enough that these fellows should know that you are not so dependent upon them, as to put up with any trampling upon."

The new secretary "is a plain man, extremely polite & unostentatious, a bachelor with a large income, but as thoroughly ignorant of all matters connected with the Dept. over which he has been called [on] to preside, as you can well conceive." In a later evaluation he suggested that "Dickerson appears affable & Politic—lazy as the Devil and profoundly ignorant of all naval matters."

During the summer of 1834 Frank was "hard at work farming." "My mind is fully made up," he wrote Pendergrast, "to settle down in that vocation as soon as I have added another three years to my service."

In November Frank's father-in-law, Irénée du Pont, passed away, "an awful bereavement." "I loved him as a full son," he told Davis.

On a trip to Washington in December Frank paid his respects to Secretary Dickerson, who received him "cordially." Frank reemphasized that he was not desirous of shipping out until his wife had "fully recovered." Dickerson was unwilling to give him any assurances. Frank continued on to John Boyle, "who is in reality the Secretary," he told Sophie. Frank again stressed his desire to remain ashore. "Old Boyle was or rather appeared delighted to see me," and "promised me faithfully" that no orders would be issued until he knew they "would be agreeable."

Frank was beginning to yearn for the companionship of close friends like Davis and Pendergrast. In a moment of nostalgia, he wrote Davis: "I have always looked upon my cruise in the Ontario as the brightest period of my professional life—it was performed after the ardour & thoughtlessness of youth had fortunately yielded to the stability of manhood, & when I could look upon scenes & men around me with calmer discernment than had been my wont. The harmony of our mess has often been contrasted in my mind, with the unsociable, distrustful, quarrelsome, indeed every trait in the scale of misery, which has marked that of almost every ship which has since been commissioned. I wish, therefore, those days to live in my memory, and how can that more happily [be] accomplished than by receiving occasionally the vivifying impulse of your delightful pen.

"When I speak of going to sea," Frank complained, "it is only in case of being compelled. I partake of that deep & widely pervading disgust for the Navy, which is increasing it appears to me in all classes of that corps. What is it owing to? It would appear that the seniors have lost confidence in their juniors. No one gives a tone to the *morale*—esprit de corps is dying away—the Department, it matters not under whose direction, is always wretchedly administered—first by a man, whose whole energy is devoted to saving six pences [Woodbury], who talks to officers of their high *'wages'* &c then another [Dickerson] who . . . has the old Bug bear responsibility staring him in the face & is in daily apprehension of being shot by his own shadow."

Summer 1835 arrived. At Louviers Frank was enjoying the life of a gentleman farmer. "You are aware," he wrote Davis, "that one of my own Castles in Utopia has been a Farmer's life. . . . Well, this summer I determined to see if bright theoretical visions would not vanish before a little hard experience, and I consequently entered body & soul into the direction of the extensive Farm around us belonging to the concern, and which the absence of one of the family [E. I. du Pont] left to my guidance. I have been at it therefore, not as a looker on . . . but took hold in good earnest. What was a preference has grown in a passion, and my mind for the future is fully made up. I never have been so hale, so strong, so happy in my life. But before I can follow up present views, a bitter pill must be swallowed, the . . . confinement of a cruise must be endured, and I have determined to go soon, that I may be back soon."

After receiving the news that Davis had brought his bark safely around Cape Horn, "one of the dreaded promontories . . . always a feather in any man's cap," he continued, "We are all seamen & navigators . . . but we have not all been tried.

"I am tired of the Mediterr^n and as an officer would desire to double the cape, having been to Brazil and the W. Indies. . . . The first lieutenancy of a ship in time of war I might covet, now, I can only say I do not shrink from the task—entire success at it depends upon many contingencies beyond a man's control & independent of his fitness, that it afford no positive evidence of a man's merit, and none whatever of competency to fill a higher grade."

During a trip to Philadelphia in October Frank wrote Sophie, "I have a good piece of news, that will delight you. . . . It is that no vessels are to be sent to sea *until* the Spring. The appropriations have given out. I hope it is the case—it is about too good to be true."

On his return to Delaware, he learned that the United States Naval Lyceum was planning to publish a journal. "Through its medium," he wrote a friend, "much good I think may be effected. . . . There is one subject which I think may be discussed to the evident advantage of the Navy. I mean its discipline. . . . We have reached an important era in the Navy & it deserves to be chronicled. It is a favorable moment to hold up, expose, and arrest the scenes & events which have stigmatised our name for many years, & the last three or four in particular.

"It strikes me," Frank continued, "that a set of . . . essays, covering the whole ground, commencing with a general view, & then going into details—written with clearness, firmness & spirit, but without abuse, might do much to restore a proper moral tone in the Navy, and that harmony which at this moment has entirely abandoned its ranks."

During early November Frank traveled to New York to see Wily. To Sophie, he wrote: ". . . on our approach to New York, a feeling of homesickness came over me, so new & unusual for *me*—that I could not but think with deep feeling, how much greater than I myself had anticipated would be the trail in store for us. I said if I feel this way on leaving home for a few days on a visit of pleasure what will it bid when I approach this same city, having bid adieu to Sophie for years."

When Frank returned to the Brandywine, orders awaited him.

VI

"Everything has favored me so far"

"Judge my astonishment," Frank wrote Pendergrast, at receiving orders to report to the sloop of war *Warren* as first lieutenant. Fitting out at the Philadelphia Navy Yard, the *Warren,* Captain William V. Taylor commanding, was bound for the West Indies. Frank preferred a cruise to the West Indies to one in the Pacific or Mediterranean. "If my wife should not mend during the winter, I could soon get home from Pensacola." "It is awful to go with Taylor," he suggested. "Taylor is one of those men that are crushed down by responsibility—the command of the Rec[eiving] ship at Boston nearly upset him."

"You know . . . the unhappy individual who is to be my Captain," Frank confided to Davis. "Write me all you know about his good points and weak ones so that I may know how to shape my course."

Leaving Sophie "will be a hard trial," he continued, "my poor wife has to exert her fortitude but her health is so much improved that she had made up her mind like a woman of sense."

Frank left Louviers on 22 November 1835 for Philadelphia and the *Warren.* At the navy yard he met with Pendergrast and, together, they visited the sloop. "I went over . . . every hole & corner," he wrote Sophie, "and was not a little disgusted . . . she is rough & untidy—but I still think she can be made comfortable and I hope all will go well." * Frank called on the captain at his lodgings

* From this chapter onward, unless otherwise indicated, all quotes in this book are from Frank's letters to Sophie.

in the city only to discover him absent. "I fear from what I hear he is a great simpleton."

On 1 December seventy seamen from New York arrived for duty on the *Warren.* "They are represented as good men generally—with some first rate Seamen among them."

The only officers to have arrived on board the *Warren* were Frank and Lieutenant Ebenezer Farrand, "who appears to be a sensible young man with stability of character." Frank's morale plummeted when a new batch of seamen came on board, half of them drunk. In his small cabin he described himself as "gloomy, thoughtful & melancholy"; the *Warren* as "cold, cheerless, & comfortless."

Finally on 13 December, after all the officers and crew had assembled, the *Warren* got underway for New Castle, Delaware. On the run, the ship encountered ice, which "I thought at one time would have cut us in two," Frank wrote Pendergrast. "I protected the ship all I could. . . . The men worked like men, & I found the midshipmen smart & attentive." Frank had been happy to leave Philadelphia because, despite his vigilance, the men could easily find liquor there—"now we shall have them all sober, & in order."

After loading gunpowder at New Castle, the *Warren* sailed down the Delaware River. "Dearest Sophie, precious Sophie, the wind is fair this morning, & it is 'all hands up anchor.' God bless you. Say Farewell to all."

Maneuvering down the river and bay, many of the *Warren*'s seamen became disabled, most of them "frosted" from casting the lead line. Although Frank relieved them every fifteen minutes, three out of five came below with their "hands in the most pitiable situation, some of them as transparent as glass." With close attention to detail, Frank stationed a sentry in the galley, where the fire was located, since seamen coming off duty "would instinctively rush towards the fire." Most of the men recovered, although their hands remained "extremely tender, more delicate poor fellows than any lady's." A few developed "immense blisters & large sores."

On 18 December the sloop entered Hampton Roads and anchored near Norfolk. While underway, Frank's spirits had risen. "I like the Captain better as I see more of him, not that I have discovered he knows more, but he is kindhearted & very well disposed & if I do not require him to assume any responsibility, I do not doubt I shall get all I wish out of him." Frank found the crew the "most willing, obedient set I ever saw. I have not punished a single one."

71

"I am well pleased with my messmates," and "I think we shall all get on very harmoniously together."

At Norfolk the *Warren* took on supplies, and a fresh draft of men arrived. On Christmas Eve, Frank's attention was focused on Sophie: "How often I have thought of you today—though constantly busy my thoughts have constantly wandered to you. . . . I never was in better trim to go to sea. My mind is not quite so much at ease for I cannot prevent myself from feeling occasional anxiety for you."

In a letter to Davis, Frank indicated that he enjoyed the responsibility he carried as first lieutenant. "From the material I have to work upon, if the Capt. will permit me, I think I can make a ship that will not dishonor his pendant." Frank continued to admire his second lieutenant, Farrand, who was "a fine, sensible, energetic, little man, an old cruiser in the West Indies . . . an excellent officer & agreeable companion."

In fine, clear weather the *Warren* sailed from Norfolk on 28 December. The first day out Frank stationed the men at the guns and exercised them. "The men are still awkward & the green hands so seasick that it was necessary to be on the lookout." The wind picked up. It squalled. It thundered. The *Warren* "rolled very deep and was extremely wet, the water on the upper deck washing from one side to the other all the time." The captain habitually failed to appear on deck at night, "which keeps me more up. . . . But I wish to study the qualities of the ship under all circumstances so that I may know how to manage her in bad weather. She has performed very well so far and much better than I anticipated."

On the voyage southward, the men "do as well as I could expect." He found it necessary to punish only three seamen. "It is the most painful part of my duty, & I feel more repugnance than ever to whipping. I feel, however, the responsibility, which is great, of not permitting the slightest shadow of insubordination and I am convinced that strict . . . justice, tempered with mercy, where it can possibly be applied, is the best way of insuring the least degree of corporal punishment. Things as yet promise fair & if I did not want to see you so much Sophie, more than I can tell you, I should be very happy on board. Sometimes Sophie I think I will never leave you again."

On the first Sunday out of Norfolk, Frank, strongly influenced by his wife's piety, distributed Bibles and religious tracts to the men.

"Many are reading them between the guns. On New Years Day 100 stopped their ration of liquor and are now receiving the amount in money in lieu. . . . This circumstance will add much to the good order of the ship, & their health will [be] materially benefitted, for strong drink in the tropical region is particularly injurious. I think many more will follow the example. I hope, by spring, only a few of the old Tars who are used to it in all climates will drink any Grog."

In January 1836 the *Warren* made landfall, passing between the islands of Caicos and Mayaguana. Frank stood on deck the whole night "to relieve the Capt. from excessive anxiety he feels at approaching land, from want of confidence in himself, more than incapacity; he is perfectly miserable when going through any passages."

The *Warren* sailed through the Windward Passage. Frank used his position to make "great improvements in the Ship & if I can only have a month at Pensacola & the Captain will give up some of his old school notions, I will make his ship the crack one of the fleet."

Along the south side of Cuba, the *Warren* became becalmed for several days. Frank took advantage of this interval to write Sophie a long letter, telling her of the routine the ship observed on Sundays. Before breakfast, the men cleared the ship "in every part." Afterward they bathed and turned out in white suits. Officers inspected the "mess things" on the berth deck.

As the ship's bell rang 11 A.M. the officers and men went aft. The clerk read the assemblage four prayers from *The Book of Common Prayer*. Next, Captain Taylor read *The Articles of War*. Then the crew mustered and passed inspection before eating. After dinner some of the men lounged between the guns, several perusing their Bibles and tracts. "Of course many do not, but they have sufficient respect not to interfere or even jest with those who do."

On that particular Sunday, after his morning duties were finished, Frank cultivated Sophie's approval by reading a chapter from "the little book" she had given him for Sunday mornings, and the fifth chapter of Matthew, which she liked.

"Everyone on board is cheerful & contented. I have yet had no trouble whatever with the men or officers, a few of the former have been punished, but very few indeed. I could not have been more fortunate than I have been in this respect. Some of the midship[n] came on board with bad characters—here they have been respectful and have performed their duties with cheerfulness & alacrity—they are a very fine set altogether. I like my mess mates better every day—good officers on deck, & obliging friends *below*. I have seen nothing yet to change my opinion, that mildness & consistency with no system of Favoritism will discipline a crew in less time than coercion & cruelty. It is surprising ever to myself how smart they work the ship already."

During the 1820s Americans had begun to settle in Texas, occupying huge tracts of land. To stop this flood of aliens, Mexico prohibited further immigration in 1830, although the law proved impossible to enforce. As soon as the Mexican government enacted this restriction, the Texans began to seek independence. When their demands for what amounted to local autonomy were rebuffed they resorted to force. In 1835 a series of armed skirmishes quickly escalated into a full-scale rebellion, the Texans receiving much military and financial aid from American "volunteers."

By 21 January 1836 the *Warren* was within sixty miles of the Texas coast. Frank was not slow to express himself on Captain Taylor's shortcomings. "The Captain is a well disposed man, unfortunately [he] makes himself miserable by anticipating ills of all description instead of being thankful for present blessings. . . . he is at the time of life when a command is irksome and harrassing—he feels no pride in it, & only thinks of getting through it without accident—this station is the worst in the world for him, as he dreads the land & is always harping of the effects of the currents. . . . he is not a man either that you can comfort or relieve, for he is very sensitive if you say anything that leads him to suppose that you consider him more timid than others.

"His orders leave much to his discretion, which is unfortunate— for he is much too old to command at sea."

The *Warren* patrolled off the coast and showed the flag off Galveston, headquarters of "the American Renegades." The *Warren*'s mission was to prevent any "undue severity" on the part of the Mexicans against American citizens or property, "which however they have a full right to exercise."

To Pendergrast, Frank summed up the situation: "We have a mixed crew, that is, we have some men equal to any I ever saw, & some as utterly worthless—I mean as to capacity—there has not been a man reported for insolence yet—they are very orderly, but very green. They however work the guns very decently & Reef very handsomely.

"The ship is a fine one, & lays to better than any vessel I ever saw—but is a perfect tub as to sailing. . . .

"I am getting very tired out here & want badly to get to Pensacola—to get some letters from my wife. I have run out of work, that is of all that can be done at sea."

In early February the *Warren* was still patrolling off Galveston. Frank had become bored with the duty and isolation. He complained of the steady diet of corned beef, ham, and tongue. The sloop failed to sight any other ships and "might as well have been in the South Pacific."

In a few days the *Warren* sailed for Pensacola, and on 11 February she was off the Mississippi River. "All is pleasant and quiet. I get along very easily & quietly in the execution of my duty. All on board appear to be happy & contented & altogether things have surpassed my most sanguine anticipation and I can say without arrogance that I am satisfied with my own exertions & those around me.

"So far we have been fortunate with regard to casualities. No one has fallen from aloft or overboard. No one has been injured in any way. I always feel some apprehension in heavy blows about men getting overboard—for we have no means of saving the poor fellows—the boats would be overwhelmed by the waves carrying down a dozen with them attempting to save one."

The ship sailed into Pensacola. "This is a beautiful harbor," he wrote Amelia, "and of great extent formed by a deep bay of many miles shut off from the sea by a long low island."

Once anchored, overhaul began, refitting the rigging, and caulking and painting the ship. "The Capt. has been very kind and has assented to my views, some of them too are contrary to what he has heretofore been accustomed to. . . . He appears however much pleased with me."

War was raging in Florida. In 1835, Seminole Indians, led by Chief Osceola and supported by runaway slaves, had risen in rebellion against the American government. Thus began a costly war that was to drag on into the 1840s.

Prior to arrival in Pensacola, the *Warren*'s officers had learned from a pilot boat off Mobile that American troops had been massacred by Seminoles at Tampa Bay. The *Vandalia* had sailed immediately from Pensacola to reinforce the town. Several days after the *Warren* had anchored a steamboat arrived from Tampa Bay with the news that the marines and army troops, garrisoned at the fort, had marched in pursuit of "the poor ill fated indians." Frank believed that it would require 10,000 men to put down the Indians. "We wish to drive them beyond the Mississippi & they desire to cling to the land of their Fathers. Goaded in this way, & maddened by indulging in a vice we learnt them. . . . they rise & seek redress, we then ring the knell of destruction. So it is, so it has been, it appears ever to be, & the Fate of the aborigenes of the Western World, it would seem had been ordained for some inscrutable purpose. . . . it is an inglorious warfare.

"I was struck & touched at the eloquent & feeling, & true manner you spoke of their [Indians] terrible fate . . . which in all probability awaits them. . . ."

Work on the *Warren* continued. "A good seaman attends to all his duties, but the landsmen* are generally hard subjects and the quickest way is to whip them to the mark. But I found by speaking to them, listening to their excuses, & shaming them, & giving them the choice of coming the next morning with their things clean, or to be punished, that I have not to whip a single man for his bright work—as it is called among them. It is very usual to have a great deal of Iron work about a ship kept bright."

The Captain was from "the old school," where discipline was of "a severe killing kind, which I myself had seen produces nothing but heart burnings & bickerings ending in arrests and courts martial.

"Brought up in such a school, he cannot comprehend how things can go on smoothly without whipping [and] scolding. . . . He said the other day, 'You give me nothing to do or to say about the ship—everything appears to go on with so little trouble & all on board appear cheerful. I never saw men look so happy. . . .' "

Accustomed to harsher discipline, Taylor continued, " 'I have not yet heard you reprimand one of them [midshipmen]. I never saw such little whipping either, which I am rejoiced at, for I have seen

---

* A landsman is an inexperienced sailor, rated below an ordinary seaman.

so much of it & done so much of it—that I had determined against it for the future, and feared that you might be one of the flogging men, & we might disagree. . . .' "

Taylor then added, " 'but you have a way of speaking to the men that I never heard before—it appears to have more effect upon them, than I ever thought mere talking could have on sailors.' "

As the days progressed, the *Warren* moved closer to the navy yard for refitting. The officers and crew "literally tore the poor *Warren* to pieces," as Frank took the opportunity to have the ship arranged "to my taste, which will I think render her more efficient & secure & at the same time as neat as a ship can be." At the navy yard, carpenters, blacksmiths, and sailmakers repaired "everything in their different departments."

Frank habitually rose at 6 A.M. and never sat down "but at meals." "I am so interested that I never feel fatigued even at night." The *Constitution* and *St. Louis* "are doing the same work pretty much, so that the navy yard is quite a scene of activity, filled with mechanics, sailors, Lieutenants, and Midshipmen."

The crew's work, discipline and self-restraint were heartening. "Tho' we've had so many of them on shore, or in boats going up to Pensacola," he had not seen one of his seamen drunk, while each night a half-dozen men belonging to the *Constitution* and *St. Louis* "went off in that condition."

Unfortunately, one incident forced Frank to take stern measures. The boat sent to town returned one evening with three drunken sailors who had behaved insolently to the officers in charge. "They had been excellent men, and were good seamen. Still it was important to check instantaneously such conduct to show the crew that although mild means & the mildest treatment indeed had been pursued, still it arose from no weakness or want of firmness. I therefore went to the capt. the next morning & told him that he must make an example of the men, that I was sorry to give him such a task, but the men deserved more than I had a right to give them. He did so, the effect was of the best kind." After their flogging, the sailors apologized to the officers of the boat and declared that they "richly merited" what they had received.

Commodore Alexander J. Dallas, commanding the naval forces in the West Indies and Mexican Gulf, felt compelled to hasten the repairs on the *Warren* as he anticipated receiving orders to dispatch her to some trouble spot. "He lands every day in the Yard, & pokes his nose everywhere, asking every mechanic what he is doing." Boarding the sloop frequently, Dallas was "fidgety & hurrying us very much." "All this however has not dampened my energies in making *a ship of the old craft.*"

"I think it," Frank wrote Pendergrast, "more elegantly fitted than anything I ever saw. . . . we are comfortably fixed, have the finest wardroom & have the most harmonious mess in the Squadron."

Frank relaxed by strolling along the wide expanse of beach. On one occasion Taylor asked to accompany him. "I agreed without hesitation for it is a source of constant worrying to me to see him so lost . . . so totally divested of all resources. He makes no friends or not even acquaintances." They walked along the beach from the navy yard to the lighthouse, then returned to the *Warren* before sundown.

"I feel great concern . . . about our Captain," he told Pendergrast. "I have told you already of his great nervousness & anxiety about his command & the responsibilities attached to it." The captain "is now two days in bed with a violent nervous attack at the idea of going to sea. . . . he appears to have little or no command over his feelings. . . . His mind . . . has been impaired by his nervous temperament & advancing years, & render him entirely unfit for command."

Prodded by Dallas and concerned about Taylor, Frank welcomed an afternoon diversion of "a little Tea Party" ashore. The affair attracted naval officers from the *Warren* and other ships in the yard, with a sprinkling of wives.

In early March the *Warren* received orders to complete its preparations for sea and get underway for Havana, before proceeding to Key West, Florida. "We have done a tremendous week's work and I hope we have seen the worst & hardest of our labour. . . . I am glad we are going. . . . Our ship has been greatly improved & [is] I think *twice* the vessel we found her." Foul weather prevented the *Warren*'s immediate departure.

The weather turned fair and the *Warren* sailed for Havana. The captain became confined to his bed. Frank, as first lieutenant, took charge of the ship, and brought her into Havana Harbor on 23 March after a seventy-two-hour trip. The channel was "the narrowest I have ever seen & circuitous." The *Warren* grazed the walls of the town first one side, then the other. High banks intercepted the wind, "requiring the greatest vigilance & activity to keep the ship clear." The harbor itself was jammed with shipping, and on several occasions the *Warren* almost rammed small craft. "nothing but a miracle saved us. It was a most spirit stirring scene & highly exciting."

Gazing out his porthole, the captain "was in fear & trembling. . . . I never pitied a man so much in my life."

The *Warren* anchored in "fine style, a splendid termination of a fine voyage." The officers and men appeared "highly delighted," and Frank received many compliments and congratulations on "my first essay as Captain & I confess to *you* Sophie I was not a little *proud.*" In excusing the brevity of his letter, he wrote: "I am too much fatigued . . . my eyes trouble me very much, from straining in *looking* out & from want of sleep—otherwise I am in most excellent health & in the finest spirits."

In the almost unbearable heat, Frank lost a great deal of weight, "so that I am a good deal *a la* Greyhound again, & burnt like a black mulatto." Ashore he purchased a broad-brimmed straw hat, "which is great protection to me & comfort."

On 1 April the *Warren* sailed for Key West. The captain, again in command, almost ran the ship aground. After this harrowing experience, he called for Frank to resume command, and he took to his bed again. "I was glad we left Havana when we did—though I was perfectly well while there, the heat and closeness of the harbor and some exposure to the sun had generated in me a great deal of bile, and the morning we came out, the sea being high I was with almost every one on board sea sick, something quite unusual with me."

The *Warren* came to anchor off Key West on Easter Sunday after an uneventful voyage. "I have read the 24th Chapter of Luke & have thought of you and your devotions all day."

Some of the inhabitants of Key West "are what are called 'wreckers.' " Every year hundreds of vessels were grounded on the Florida reefs. The wreckers' boats would cruise offshore, watching the movements of "some poor fellow" approaching the reefs. The moment the ship ran afoul, the wreckers would bear down, hoist out the cargo, and bring it into Key West, where they had it adjudicated by the resident judge, who generally apportioned two-thirds of the property to the wreckers, the other third to the insurers. The wreckers then shipped the salvaged merchandise from Key West, growing rich on the proceeds. "There are now men living on this barren Key worth hundreds of thousands of dollars." Shippers accused the wreckers of putting up lights at night on the Key, which, being mistaken for the regular lighthouses, led "many vessels astray. . . ." The population here "though apparently gentlemen are lawless & reckless. . . . I am told there are a few excellent people here. . . . They have established a Sunday school on the Key."

While in Key West Frank busied himself "giving a *finishing touch* to the ship. . . . I think I have made great improvements & they all say that the officers of the Squadron will not know the ship on our return to Pensacola. I paint inside tomorrow & after that is done we shall have nothing to do but keep the ship clean & protect ourselves from the sun. I have worked the crew very hard since we sailed, & am desirous to give them rest, time to make their clothes, & straw hats &c. They are well behaved men & first class Seamen. . . ."

On 11 April the *Warren* had an unexpected visitor. Frank was summoned to the deck in haste to receive a revenue cutter. "A fine looking man" in full uniform stepped on board. At first Frank mistook him for a French admiral and was about to address him in that language, when the visitor introduced himself as General Alexander Macomb, commander of the American troops in Florida. After greeting the general, Frank changed into his white dress uniform. General Macomb inspected the ship and "appeared much gratified." Frank apologized for not firing the customary salute, "but we had a seaman quite sick & [the] concussion might injure him." The general confided to Frank that the Seminole hostilities were "far from being terminated. If this is the case the Army will suffer terribly during the coming months. . . . the mosquitoes alone are a formidable enemy—& the marshes & morasses very unhealthy."

After Macomb reboarded the revenue cutter, Frank sent the crew aloft to give him three cheers. "He appeared to have been highly delighted, stood up in the boat & waved his hat."

The seriously ill seaman who had contracted "a bilious fever" died just before the *Warren* sailed. The night he succumbed Frank canceled plans to attend a ball in Key West, as "I could not bring myself to leave the scene of death."

The *Warren* sailed on 16 April and reanchored in Havana Harbor the following day. "You can scarcely imagine the perfect Forest of Shipping around us. The American ensign predominates but there are Spanish, English, Bremen, Sardinian, French [and] Russian" ships.

If the *Warren* did not soon sail for home, Frank considered asking to leave the ship to return to Delaware for he sorely missed Sophie, "but this would be wrong & against the interest of both. For it would make me lose the advantages of this arduous cruise however short it may be. . . . I have some *magnificent* & *curious* . . . plants for you from Key West. Oh if you could see them I think you would be much astonished."

By the 19th the *Warren* was underway again, and after six days at sea she arrived at Pensacola. Immediately after the sloop anchored, Frank received orders to report to the frigate *Constellation* as first lieutenant. Commodore Dallas had passed over two senior officers in selecting him for the assignment. When Dallas informed Captain Taylor of his decision, Taylor behaved "very kindly" and commented that it was a deserved promotion. To Taylor, the commodore explained the basis of his choice: he needed " 'just such an officer as you have described Mr. D[u Pont] to be in your last report. . . . I have no Captain—and I want an officer that will relieve me of all trouble & anxiety.' "

Frank's feelings about this advancement were ambivalent. Professionally the orders came under the "most flattering circumstances, & I think will be attended with very material advantages to both of us—but they throw a gloom on the prospect of an early return. . . . Though I know so well that you would be resigned to anything that would contribute to my personal gratification & professional advancement, still my heart yearns so to see you again.

"I have been entirely passive in the affair . . . it has sought me— it is considered a great comp[limen]t paid to me & the situation thought a very desirable one, as I perform the duties of Captain under Com. Dallas. . . ."

To a friend, Frank characterized his new situation: "In a professional point of view & for my personal benefit hereafter, it may be considered a fortunate event. . . . [It is] the very best thing that could have happened to me [as] it throws me at once out of the sloops and out of the frigates except as first lieutenant. . . . I am now the youngest lieut. holding this place in the service."

Frank had arrived on the *Warren* as a young, ambitious officer eager to advance in a career that he had not freely chosen, a career that he felt had been forced on him by economic realities. On the whole, he evaluated his experience as a positive one. "I had found her . . . unsafe, uncomfortable, unsightly. I worked upon her until

I thought her *handsome*—until she sailed not so 'damn badly'—until she worked like a Pilot boat. . . . I feel really pleased & indeed consider myself fortunate in having taken the cruise in the *Warren*—thrown entirely upon my own resources, occasionally in trying situations, and on one or two occasions taking the ship from Port to Port—the Captain all the while a steady occupant of his cot, have added much to my professional experience and has given me a degree of confidence which I trust never to lose—the last time we went to the Havana I carried her over from anchorage to anchorage in 72 hours from this place [Pensacola] . . . and found the excitement delightful."

In another vein Frank wrote: "I . . . feel as if at my present age I might command a ship & enjoy it—but in twenty years hence, should I live that long, I shall be a dam' old fogy, afraid of my shadow—cold perspiration starting at every pore at the sight of a little coloured water & as for a reef . . . it would throw me into histrionics or convulsive throbs & gestures. . . . Surely a system which produces such results cannot be the proper one for a great & growing maritime power.

"You well know that this is not an individual picture—it applies strictly to nine out of ten of our commanders afloat, & to those who have been so for the last ten or fifteen years. We have doubtless some Captains who have great professional knowledge, but even those have lost the true Sailor feeling—from the infrequency of command they are more alive to the possibility of misfortune during its continuance—they prefer Port to Sea—their minds are ever employed in foreseeing danger, & forming plans to arrest its consequences. Such mental occupation shackles present action, and instead of the bold & even reckless seaman rising with the emergencies of the moment—fruitful in resources—confident & cheerful in their application—with unblanched cheek, and well directed energies . . . we have men overpowered by anxiety & responsibility, men converted by the present system, from naturally dauntless characters, into drivelling old imbeciles, exciting in their inferiors feelings of pity, scorn & contempt—instead of admiration, attachment & respect."

Frank hoped to go to sea immediately in the *Constellation*—"it is there from all I have learned that I could be of most service to the Com[modore]—he . . . [is] always desirous that his 1st Lt. should be on deck in bad weather, play captain as it is called—as I have pretty good experience at this, it would come quite natural."

To a midshipman who was returning north, Frank entrusted a small box for delivery to Sophie. It contained a few of the "little things, which I have gathered for you—for it has been my happiest occupation to collect whatever I think would interest you." There were shells from the Florida reefs and Key West, and loose musk-mellon seeds from Havana, Frank having been "struck with the immense size of them."

He conveyed his admiration of the *Constellation* to Sophie. "This is a noble Frigate . . . in beautiful order, a crew of three hundred and fifty men that would do your eyes good to look at. The mess is [a] very agreeable one & the Commodore [is] a very mild easy man to deal with."

After attending a church service in Pensacola, where he listened to "a most Christian-like charitable sermon," he wrote Sophie, "I have never contemplated religion or knew what it really was I may say, until I saw it in you. It has lent a charm to your natural vitures. I feared you would be too serious, and instead I found you cheerful, happy, [and] contented."

Frank was relieved to learn from Sophie's letters that her health continued to improve and, "I am more & more satisfied at what has passed, it is decidedly for the best. . . . It throws me very, very far ahead. I am delightfully situated on board."

The *Vandalia* returned to Pensacola from Tampa and her officers reported on the Seminole War. "The Indian war has ceased for the present—the whites have been baffled, outwitted, outmanaged in every instance; I am told Gen[1] [Winfield] Scott is greatly mortified—too much was expected of him—the *total* ignorance of the face of the country—the impossibility to procure guides—the impenetrable nature of the thickets for anything like masses or columns of men—with the perfect shelter they afford to the Indians, . . . more than counterbalances all the numbers that can be brought against them."

Men at the Pensacola Navy Yard armed steamboats to ply the Chattahoochee River transporting troops and provisions. Frank implored the commodore for command of the expedition, but he declined, "saying he would be compelled to leave in a few weeks perhaps himself to go down in one of the corvettes to the coast of Mexico and that I could not be spared as he had no captain to his ship. I made the offer sincerely and willingly. . . . I must confess I feel a great yearning to get clear of the monotony of our life here."

The days spent in Pensacola were tedious. "We unbent our sails and sent them to the navy yard to keep them out of the dews & rains. I regret this as I wanted to go out in the ship. You must sail in a vessel to become thoroughly identified with it—but I also regret on the Commodore's account because I think he ought to go out for the benefit of the Junior Officers, if for nothing else."

Frank suspected that the reason the *Constellation* did not sail was that she was "tied by silken cords," as a "desperate courtship" existed between Dallas and "a certain fair lady." "I do not admire her and I think the Commodore might do much better for himself." He characterized her as "not pretty—a little deaf and I think a good deal of a nonentity." Her sorties on board, frequently with other ladies, provided "food" for the officers, who growled in undertones about a "Petty Coat government."

Good news arrived from Texas in mid-May 1836. The Texans had captured Mexican General Santa Anna, "which will soon terminate the war." "It has been a most unprecedented stroke of good fortune. It is now probable that Texas will be annexed to the U.S. Santa Anna is a cruel man, & has carried on the war, with that blood thirsty feeling which has characterized all the revolutions of the South American States and those of Mexico."

Monotony continued at Pensacola. "There is no society," Frank wrote Davis, "that can afford me any interest, & my only amusement is to take the seine occasionally & sweep the Lagoons or sail about the Bayous in a beautiful boat the Commodore gave me the other day."

"The monotony," he admitted to Sophie, "is so very great that it makes the task no easy one. I have no acquaintances on shore that I care a fig for, or that can interest me—so that I have landed but three or four times since I joined this ship—they all tell me I ought to go out more."

When in early June Commodore Dallas traveled to Tallahassee on business for a week, Frank had command of the *Constellation*. Torrents of rain fell on Pensacola. "Sailors are like young ducks, fond of being in the rain & you have actually to drive them below to get them out of it—in many respects they are like children. You cannot get them half the time to put on dry clothes, & hardy as they are, it is a fruitful source of sickness in this climate."

Using his authority, Frank oversaw the complete overhaul of the rigging. "The ship was in good order when I joined her, but I want her to be in better [shape] before all the ships come in."

In mid-June Frank received orders to join the schooner *Grampus* as her captain—his first command. He was taking over for a sick captain "in no way qualified to continue in command, as he never ought to have left his home." "I have to go off immediately to Tampico but will be back by 1 August. The schooner is a fine vessel, an excellent 'Sea Boat' as it is termed." Although the *Grampus* may have been an excellent sailer, Frank discovered her to be "in horrid order." He threw himself in the work and "with the cordial assistance of all on board got things decent & comfortable."

"I can scarcely expect to retain the command of the *Grampus,* as she is the command of a much older officer. Should I be relieved on my return I shall thus get clear out of the Squadron. Besides I can now come home whenever I may wish to apply."

The command of the *Grampus* "is considered here as a great piece of good luck. I hope it may prove so. I shall do my duty as I have ever done and I hope all, dear Sophie, will go equally well with me. . . . What a flurry I am in Dear Sophie. What excitement. . . ."

On board the schooner, Frank described his cabin "as snug a little place as you can well imagine. It is small, very small, but still I have every comfort around me, though it will take me some time to accustom myself to *being alone.*

"This vessel is an excellent one, and far safer than the *Warren.* I have sailed in one [schooner] before & feel at home in the management of them." The *Grampus* carried twelve guns, three lieutenants, "an excellent Physician," the regular complement of officers of other grades, and a crew of seventy men.

Frank was ordered to fall in with Captain Taylor in the *Warren* off the Mexican coast, and to pass him orders to communicate with American consuls at Tampico and Vera Cruz. If the *Grampus* failed to rendezvous with the *Warren,* Frank was to communicate with the consuls himself, and offer passage to any American citizens who might wish to come on board, should they be permitted to leave Mexico, "which is doubtful."

Dallas informed Frank that the Mexican government had laid an embargo on all foreign vessels. The military command had promised that the persons and property of all foreign countries would be respected, but Frank feared that the government might not be able to effect this "against the popular excitement of the lower classes, which, since the capture of Santa Anna has been known to them, is very great.

"Our vessels of war not being able to enter any of their ports & being obliged to lay off some miles, can be of no further use except what may arise from their mere presence." The Mexicans had raised 17,000 men for the Army to carry on the war in Texas.

"Everything has favored me so far. I have successfully advanced into responsible stations since I left you—through the mercy of a kind Providence, I have so far succeeded in them & with a continued trust in it, I have hope still to prosper. I am going on a service which may result in great benefit to some of my countrymen, perhaps to the safety of their lives. I am therefore in good spirits—ready & willing to do my duty wherever it may lie."

While Frank prepared the *Grampus* for sea, the *Warren* hove into sight on 21 June. Immediately, Dallas transferred Frank to the *Warren* as her captain. Taylor had become sick on board the *Warren*, which returned a month ahead of schedule. Dallas ordered Du Pont to sail for the Mexican coast in company with the *Grampus*. Frank was optimistic for "The health of all on board is excellent. I am *delighted* for I am almost sure now to see you in October. . . .

"All are delighted at my getting the command. Everything promises well dear Sophie."

Captain Taylor left the ship on 23 June, suffering from "Mental and nervous attacks," and "now I am in possession of the Cabin where I have spent many an hour as a guest."

On 25 June the *Warren* and *Grampus* got underway from Pensacola. By 6 July they were 100 miles from Tampico and, two days later, they proceeded to Vera Cruz. As they neared the harbor, Frank watched a pilot boat come toward the ships. This proved that American relations with Mexico were "undisturbed."

Frank promptly dispatched a lieutenant on shore to communicate with the American consul, Dr. Burrough. From the lieutenant Frank learned that American commerce had suffered "no aggression or interruption and that no apprehension was entered by the Americans residing there either for themselves or their property. This was very satisfactory news for it necessarily curtailed my visit."

On 9 July Frank went ashore, and with the consul he called on the governor general. "The visit passed off very well, was long & sociable & I retired after making arrangements with him for an exchange of customary salute."

On 10 July the *Warren* and *Grampus* got underway from Vera Cruz for Tampico. "It was a great relief to me to find myself away from Vera Cruz, for I could no[t] but feel some apprehension about the health of the crew." Before arriving at Vera Cruz, several of the seamen had been "attacked seriously with scurvy & the whole crew were more or less affected with it." For that reason the *Warren* had remained two days at Vera Cruz taking on fresh provisions. The crew laid in large quantities of vegetables, principally pumpkins and onions, "both by the bye [are] the sweetest & finest in the world." "The crew is still living on them & this with the limes & lime juice have completely arrested the . . . symptoms."

Dangerous reefs and small islands between Vera Cruz and Tampico required "vigilance and caution, for I found there was no dependence to be placed in the books of directions, nor in the recent experience of others, for the currents baffle . . . all individual experience. . . . I found them directly the reverse of what Capt. Taylor found them."

The ships anchored at Tampico on 13 July. Immediately an American came on board the *Warren*. The Republic of Mexico, he said, was still "in a very settled state." The feeling in favor of General Santa Anna at Tampico was not strong, "although all parties are united against Texas. They are making great efforts to raise another army to march there. . . . But the treasury is exhausted & . . . the Mexican government cannot raise a dollar. . . ."

"I have had great satisfaction in my command of this ship, nothing of an unpleasant nature has occurred. The officers all do their duty, the men are cheerful and contented. The first lieutenant . . . is an entirely reformed man. Captain Taylor did not treat him properly, but since I have been here, he has taken the greatest interest in his duty & we have together got the old ship back to her good looks. . . . She is a perfect menagerie. . . . She is full of parrots, macaws &c, all of them learning to talk. We have also a pair of armadillos, funny little things. . . .

"I am impatient to get to Pensacola for your letters and to see what disposition will be made of me. . . . I have determined to decline the command of . . . [a] schooner, if offered me. . . . My ambition has been satisfied by getting this ship however short may be the period. . . ."

In late July 1836 the *Warren* and *Grampus* upped anchor in Tampico and got underway for Pensacola. As soon as the ships reached port, Frank filed his official report: "I have . . . the satisfaction to state that our commerce with the Republic of Mexico has of late suffered no aggression, and that no apprehension is at present entertained by citizens of the United States residing in that country, either for their persons or property."

He went ashore to see the commodore. Dallas had married in Frank's absence, and was "as happy as a man can be." Questioned about a leave, the commodore replied that "he would do all he could for me, [but] that he really thought he could not spare me."

The commodore's marriage had enlivened the social life of Pensacola. "We shall have for some time to come considerable gaiety." Almost every night someone hosted a party, banquet, or dinner. One ball held on board the *St. Louis* was "really beautiful. The hangings and draperies were composed of flags with wreaths and garlands intertwined with evergreens and flowers, and brilliant chandeliers made entirely of the ship's arms, bayonets and pistols." The crew shot off fireworks from atop the masts, "all so professional, but all very beautiful. . . . The whole affair went off very well . . . if one may judge from the lateness of the hour. . . ."

At another ball, "which was by far the most agreeable," Frank danced every dance. "Indeed I do not know what came over me, but I felt on that occasion more of that lightheartedness of yore than I have experienced in years.

"A combination of circumstances made me feel like this—the good accounts of your health, the prospect of seeing you soon, and my present agreeable situation, just returned from my first cruise as capt. an agreeable relief from the drudgery of first lieutenant."

Reports reached Pensacola from the steamboat expedition up the Chattahoochee River. Naval personnel were "in good spirits, but have found no service in which to gain Laurels, being employed to transport militia and provisions." Frank was among the naval officers who were apprehensive about the introduction of steam as a source of power. Learning of serious accidents on board the steamboats, he wrote, "As we predicted some of the sailors would get caught in the Engines." On board one of the boats while still at Pensacola, "one of our best seaman was drawn in by the Fly Wheel—they were a half hour extracting him, his limb had been taken off."

Out of boredom, Frank had volunteered to lead this expedition. Now he wrote Pendergrast that he was glad "I did not press the matter, and I escaped the most onerous, disgusting service, that ever poor devils went upon—though they all went off with visions of

Indian glory, [and] promotion . . . floating before them—instead of which the transportation of corn & militia men with bilious fever bring them to the Jaws of death, where many of the poor sailors did enter, while others deserted."

From Sophie's letters, Frank learned that she had been reading books on Mexico. "You do know what additional interest I took in Mexico from the knowledge that you were reading its history and that you knew so much of it. This is one of many feelings of contact if I may use the phrase which has made my union with you, one of such perfect happiness. You take an interest in everything, small & great. . . . I travel, you read—it is well for me that I do, for you would soon leave me far behind."

The government's policy toward the situation in Texas provoked Frank's criticism. "We have all in the Squadron been perfectly disgusted—perhaps the more so, from being behind the scenes a little & knowing the utterly worthless class which have populated & are now governing that province [Texas]—most of their leading men in the Govt. are fugitives from justice, but the Conduct of Congress is too reprehensible, passing resolutions by acclamation in favor of receiving Texas in[to] the Union, or rather acknowledging her independence—that very Congress would *not have dared* taken such a step, if one of Canada's [provinces] had been in question. The manner in which Mexico has been treated throughout this affair, is most unworthy of a great nation. . . . I have no patience on this subject—for I can no more bear bullying in nations, than in individuals."

The calm on board the *Warren* ended one evening in early August. When her officers returned to the ship from shore, they witnessed "scenes of riot & drunkenness with faces bloody & scarred—altogether the conduct worthy of brutes in the most abject state, & all the result of excess drink." Frank and fellow officers quickly restored order.

The following day, Frank mustered the crew, who by then were "clean & sober." Five were missing, "having gone off doubtless in a drunken frolic." "Everything is quiet & orderly on board, but I have had a great deal of punishment to inflict, more than during the whole cruise previous, & it has wrung my heart—it was however absolutely requisite, & I have not ordered a lash that I was not perfectly satisfied of its justice & propriety & absolutely necessary. It . . . [is] all the effect of Liquor, which they had succeeded in smuggling on board in spite of every vigilance, the consequence was that the ship was full of drunken men . . . making them insubordinate & insolent to the officers. By redoubling the vigilance I detected the channel through which the poison was brought—this & the inflicting of the full extent of the Law has made them all recover their senses, & usual good conduct."

In late August Captain Webb of the *Vandalia* relieved Frank on board the *Warren*. Du Pont left Pensacola on a steam packet. In evaluation Frank wrote Pendergrast: "This ended my West Indian cruise, a cruise more filled with professional satisfaction to myself than any I have yet made. I had no trouble or difficulty personal or professional—enjoyed my health, & trust made some new & sincere friends—and instead of abusing I shall bless the old *Warren* the longest day I live."

VII

"I have taken a wise step"

On his return home after nearly a year's absence, Frank found Sophie's health much better. They spent three weeks together in Philadelphia, where she consulted a new physician. She was now able to walk short distances and, if as he hoped, she continued to gain strength through the winter months, Frank convinced himself that a little sea bathing the following summer either at Cape May or Newport, Rhode Island, would insure "a permanent & thorough recovery."

Frank remained on the Brandywine and did not return to the West Indian Squadron as Sophie's health, "though greatly improved is just in that state as to require all my time & attention, in order to insure a perfect restoration which I trust we now have within our grasp." He was looking forward to a quiet winter, he wrote Davis, "in the domestic intercourse of those we love, with the accessories of books & periodical literature, and other plentiful enjoyments which daily present themselves in the country."

During that winter of 1836–37 Frank mulled over his experiences in the West Indies and set down his theories on naval discipline and the internal organization of a warship, which he had tested on the *Warren* as first lieutenant and captain. He did this in a long letter of advice to his friend Alexander Slidell* who was about to sail as a first lieutenant on the *Independence*. "The Discipline of the service has undergone & is still under a process of change—in some things for the better—in others less so. The men are infinitely more subordinate than formerly—the officers less so. You will find it I

---

* Slidell added Mackenzie to his name, from that of a maternal uncle, around 1838, and was thereafter known as Alexander Slidell Mackenzie.

think an easy matter to establish most thorough good conduct among the former, with one twentieth the whipping heretofore used—consistency—no favoritism—great firmness & severity at times—enough to convince them you can use the lash & that most soundly, but would infinitely prefer not being compelled to resort to it will readily effect all you may wish—half the punishments I have seen inflicted in the Navy, were done in such a manner and under such circumstances that the men were led to believe the officers took personal satisfaction in the matter. . . .

"For minor offenses the plan of 'stopping the Grog' is a good one—though the present system of giving the men money in lieu deprives you materially of this check—great vigilance is necessary after the issue of this money, or you will be almost driven to regret the introduction of temperance among the sailors, for the proceeds nearly all go for liquor, and with the present negligent race of midship[n] it is almost impossible to arrest the smuggling."

Frank continued, "Inspect the crew at quarters every morning—be very rigid at first. . . . exact from the Lieutenants strict attention on deck & to their Divisions, discourage intimacies with the Midship[n], the prevailing sin of the day. As to the latter, if any one can get along with them it will be yourself, who unites firmness of character with mildness of manner. Make no difference as to the Pass[d] Midship[n] except by giving them the higher duties belonging to the grade. . . . For the Ships boys a great deal may be done & we may bring up in a few years a fine class for Petty Officers. . . ."

The national political scene, especially in regard to naval affairs, continued to hold Frank's interest. He voiced his concern to Davis: ". . . if the country in general is out of joint [under President Van Buren] what shall I say of the Navy in particular—Driveling imbecility—sullen obstinacy—*penny saving,* still hold the helm of our doomed Department. . . . The only ray of comfort I can give you, is that the darkest hour of the night is just before dawn, so have we been brought so low, if we move at all we must rise." He was particularly critical of Secretary of the Navy Mahlon Dickerson, who in the interest of economy did not spend all the money allotted to the Navy, but returned a portion of it to the Treasury. "Public attention has at length been awakened to the utter incompetency of the Head of the Dept.—he has consequently been attacked, exposed, vilified, torn into shreds, right and left on the floor of the Congress—and would you believe it, not a voice was raised in his defense. . . . The continued stay in office [is] because of some wretched political or party consideration."

In June 1837, Frank conducted Sophie and Victorine to Warm Springs, Virginia. Sophie's Philadelphia physician had stressed that the waters would "most likely . . . insure very decided and permanent relief." Every day Sophie was carried to the baths in a sedan chair. The water in the main bath, noted for the treatment of painful and irregular menstruation, was kept at a temperature of 96 degrees.

The visit to Warm Springs was curtailed by the illness of Frank's mother, who died in early December 1837. "The absence of a mother's love & watchful interest in our lives is generally felt. . . ." Frank wrote of her to Pendergrast, "To a grace & charm indescribable in the performance of her domestic duties, my sainted mother possessed that delightful trait, which illicits unreserved confidence—for years she had been the depository of my inmost thoughts—an intellectual counsellor—a never failing & judicious friend."

During that winter Frank expressed concern to Davis about the conduct of the war in Florida, "which . . . continues at this moment at the rate of $73,000 per diem and though we have *turned* the Indians, disregarding flags of truce, and are using treacherous means to entrap their chiefs, we are still whipped, and that soundly at every encounter." Compared to the plight of the Indians, "Slavery seems to me merciful. . . ."

In late February 1838, Frank traveled to Washington and spent his time listening to the debates in Congress, dining with friends, and visiting the navy yard. He delayed putting in an appearance at the Navy Department as "Dickerson still holds on—he is sufficiently in his dotage to cling to office." When he finally reported he discovered that he "had barely escaped orders to the *Erie*. . . . this . . . closes all danger for the present" for sea duty. The *Pennsylvania* or *Ohio* were scheduled for the Mediterranean in the summer, but "made no application."

Learning from a friend that Lieutenant Cornelius K. Stribling had been paid a commander's wage while captaining the *Peacock*—"a case not half so strong as mine"—Frank seesawed between the auditor's office and "old Dickerson's" a half-dozen times until "I finally succeeded in getting Mr. Dickerson to put hands on paper & say that the appropriate commander of a sloop of war was a *commander,* which settles all future cases, to the no small joy of the auditor, who thanked me for the good I had done—saying he had been for fourteen months trying to get the same."

In glee over his victory at the Navy Department he exulted to Pendergrast, "I got my claim . . . for pay as a Commander while in command of the *Warren,* as hard a fight however as ever a man had—the imbecility of that office is beyond credence."

While in Washington, Frank, dubious about the practical application of steam propulsion in war, became fascinated with the new experimental steam frigate, *Fulton II,* which had been constructed under the supervision of his friend, Matthew C. Perry, now known in Navy circles as "the father of the steam Navy." Frank told Pendergrast, ". . . if she is a failure I would give much to have the details, & particularly, the delays, doubts, mismanagement, changes of draft, & model &c &c—which I believe were continued & repeated during her construction—[Joshua] Humphreys [the builder] . . . a little frightened about it . . . pretended to express the greatest surprise, at her being sent to sea by the Dept.—said it was never contemplated to have her anything but harbor defence—now when Perry left Washington with orders in his pocket he appealed to me to go with him, & spoke of cruising on the coast with more interested service afterwards &c."

"The Steam Frigate," he speculated to Davis, "is a failure I believe in toto. . . ."

Later, learning more about *Fulton II* from Pendergrast, Frank wrote, "The whole business was even worse than I believed. . . . I was amused at the whole conduct of my friend Perry—evidently impressed with the failure of the Fulton, but fearing to say so like a man. . . ."

Analyzing steam propulsion for use on warships, Frank wrote a lengthy treatise critical of the *Fulton II.* "It would seem that an experiment involving a very material if not total change in the Science of naval warfare prosecuted and completed at enormous expense has signally failed. . . ."

Du Pont expressed concern that although the *Fulton II* had been "exhibited under a considerable flourish of trumpets," no official report or authorized account of the ship's performance or capabilities had been furnished to the public, "but all had been silence and reserve and in the absence of other testimony, we have been apt to form a judgment from the facts presented in the Public papers— which facts it must be admitted go far to bear out the verdict of 'Total Failure.' . . .

"The Frigate [under the command of Perry] sailed or steamed out of New York . . . and the next thing we hear, is that [she] has taken shelter from an ordinary blow under the Delaware Breakwater," a blow "which a Charleston Steam Packet, built for carrying passengers and not for the purposes of war, would have scorned to run from. . . . The Chief Naval Constructor . . . [was] heard to express great surprise that the dept. should think of sending the Fulton to sea—she having been built solely for Port defence, which must have meant of course N. Y. Harb^r and Sound."

During the summer of 1838 Frank and Sophie went to Cape May to vacation, he hoping that she would be "much benefited by the Sea bathing."

Later that summer Frank learned that James K. Paulding had succeeded Dickerson as Secretary of the Navy. "I have some hopes for Paulding," he commented to Pendergrast, ". . . he is a gentleman and thus far, so superior to some of the Party hacks from the Senate or House, which we were threatened with."

Feeling optimistic about Sophie's health, Frank decided to apply for a ship. Leaving his wife at Cape May he traveled to Washington to meet with Secretary Paulding. After discussing naval matters, Paulding asked Frank if he could do anything for him. Frank replied that he had already made application to go to sea on the *Ohio*. When the secretary asked whether he had been to the Mediterranean, Frank answered, "frequently." The interview ended without Paulding committing himself.

Later Frank learned from a friend that his application had reached the Navy Department and that Commodore Isaac Hull, recently appointed to command the Mediterranean Squadron, had requested him. Commodore Hull was a hero of the War of 1812. He had commanded the *Constitution* in her historic victory over the *Guerriere,* making optimum use of his ship's superiority and his well-trained crew. To Sophie, Frank wrote: "My impression is that I *will be* ordered [to the *Ohio*], and all I have seen & heard here, has fully confirmed me that I have taken a wise step, & for our future & mutual good—Dearest Sophie take heart it is all for the best."

After a restful summer at Cape May, Frank and Sophie returned to Louviers in late August 1838 to await his orders. "I feel insecure at present," he admitted to Pendergrast, "and thus debarred from entering into plans for the future. My wife is well enough for me to leave her and with one cruise more I may settle down . . . and go to farming in good earnest. Should we get together in the *Ohio* it would do much to reconcile me to the cruise or rather seperation."

Orders came in early fall and Frank left Sophie for Boston and the line-of-battle ship *Ohio*, Commodore Hull's flagship. Frank's good friend Pendergrast was on board.

VIII

"I have never been so exasperated"

When Frank arrived in Boston and boarded the *Ohio*, Captain Joseph Smith commanding, he confronted a situation that left him dumbfounded and angry. Naval regulations strictly forbade women from being quartered on naval vessels without a special permit from the Secretary of the Navy. However, Mrs. Hull and Miss Hart, the wife and sister-in-law of the commodore, had obtained the necessary permission to cross the Atlantic in the *Ohio* with the distinct understanding that while the vessel was in European waters they were to reside on shore. To make room for the ladies, Hull ordered the lieutenants to leave their accommodations on the berth deck, to which they were entitled by naval regulations, and to take up quarters on the orlop deck, the lowermost deck. Located below the waterline, the orlop deck was used to store provisions and reserve materials. The spirit room, grocer's vaults, and sail room were there. This region also contained the bread room, water tanks, and paint room, along with the smithy's and yeoman's storerooms.

In cool climates, this change in berthing would have proven of little consequence, but in the hot weather of the Mediterranean it would entail hardship to those concerned as the orlop deck was without light and received scanty ventilation.

The undesirable character of the lieutenants' quarters was tested during the passage of the *Ohio* from Boston to New York. Frank and his messmates resisted these living arrangements when the ship anchored. Du Pont, all other lieutenants, the surgeon, and the purser angrily petitioned Secretary Paulding.

"U.S. Ship *Ohio,* New York, October 20, 1838. Sir: We the . . . officers of the *Ohio,* beg leave to lay before you a statement of the facts in relation to the quarters which have been allotted to us on board this ship.

"In so doing we are impelled by no other than proper motives—motives which spring from what we conceive to be due to our rank, to the discipline of the service, the efficiency of the ship, and our natural physical wants.

"In the first place, rooms on the orlop deck have been assigned to us, where neither light nor air can penetrate, and in none of which under the most favorable circumstances can candle light be dispensed with. The closeness of these apartments is such, that our experienced Fleet surgeon gives it most unhesitatingly as his opinion that serious ill health must ensue to the occupants during a three years' cruise. This opinion is confirmed by that of every medical officer who has seen this new system of accommodations introduced in our line of battle ships. . . .

"In the ordinary duties of the ship, requiring the presence of all hands, in going to quarters, in case of fire, squalls, or any other sudden emergency, the sea officers instead of heading or leading the crew, must inevitably be the last to reach their respective stations. In case of mutiny, a dozen men could with perfect ease, and in a moment of time, completely cut off all communication between the commander and the few officers of the watch, and all other officers of every grade.

"The arrangement of which we complain had its origin in the French navy, but was soon abandoned on the score of health. . . . The *North Carolina* was so fitted when she last sailed from the United States. Her officers were as strenuously opposed to the orlop as ourselves, but became in a measure reconciled in consequence of having an airy apartment where reading and writing could be done by daylight, and which, during the summer heats, could be used as a temporary sleeping place. The *Ohio* was also fitted in the same manner by Commodore [Charles D.] Ridgeley at this yard, and subsequently approved on inspection by the Commissioners; but at Boston we were deprived of that part of the main gun-deck destined for our messroom, and the . . . officers [were] sent to mess in the lower gun deck, displacing in their turn, the larger messes of Passed Midshipmen and Midshipmen, who have now to live altogether in the orlop.

"We delayed making this communication, being desirous of giving the new arrangement a fair trial. Our passage from Boston afforded this, and after mature deliberation, we feel it a duty we owe to ourselves, to our brother officers who may follow us in this class of ships, and to the service generally, to request of you to investigate the matter, confident that your decision will be based upon strict justice and whatever may be due to the true interest of the navy. . . ."*

While the *Ohio* was in New York, Sophie took up residence at Mrs. Ellery's boarding house in Brooklyn. Frank was fortunate to be able to slip away for short visits with her, and when he could not leave the vessel, he jotted her notes. In one, he disclosed "the ship is more cold, damp and gloomy than ever. . . ." After Sophie returned home in late November, Frank was without a confidante.

"Nothing has *officially* transpired with regard to our apartments," Frank wrote shortly after her departure. "But the Commodore has received a communication which I am told has made him pretty savage. He has kept the contents. Part of it however informs him that Capt. [Robert F.] Stockton is to go in the ship [as first lieutenant], & [is] to have the main gundeck cabin, unless he & Capt. Smith can agree to live together, if not the latter I presume must go in the Poop. . . . but all is silence with regard to what concerns us. . . ."

Officers and crew readied the *Ohio* for sea. For one whole day Frank took charge of the men stowing powder on board ship. That same evening he went to see Hull and "bearded the old Commodore in his den—spent an hour. Mrs. Hull & Miss Hart were very polite & cordial—the old gentleman in good humour."

After the close of this visit, Hull handed Frank a note for Captain Smith, a reply to the lieutenants' letter to the Secretary of the Navy. Paulding had referred the entire matter of the orlop deck controversy to the Navy commissioners, whose lengthy reply, Frank felt, was based "on false premises throughout." "They even go so far as to say they are not aware of having approved the apartments as fitted at New York, and as I predicted they say the charge of want of air is removed by pipes which had been put into our rooms,

---

* This letter and other official correspondence relating to the orlop question comes from H. A. du Pont, *Rear-Admiral Samuel Francis Du Pont, United States Navy* (New York, 1926), pp. 19–42.

which are stopping up to prevent the foul air from coming to us from the decks where the men sleep. I will frankly tell you that I have never been so exasperated or felt so strongly in my life on any subject. . . . What further course we are to pursue is not yet determined upon. I promise you to be prudent . . . [and to control] my feelings of great indignation, indignation that could only spring from a just cause and firm basis. As for Mr. Paulding, I give up. . . . He has started off with infinitely more pretensions than Mr. Dickerson, but I believe candidly will fall even behind him."

Captain Smith, Frank wrote, "has behaved like a man of uprightness & rectitude in the matter, and repeated today that he did not hesitate to say that but for Com. Hull taking his family they [he and Hull] would have lived together. . . . I left the ship . . . at 1 ock under feelings of despondency & disgust, but rallied a little after landing."

On returning to the *Ohio* after spending his afternoon in the city on mess business, Frank tried to write Sophie again, but on opening his desk drawer he spilled his inkstand, "deluging everything—things are in such confusion about me that I cannot write with any comfort."

He was so disgusted over the officers' accommodations that he sent anonymously "a long commentary" to the editor of the New York *Courier*, detailing conditions on the *Ohio*. "I have no assistance mental or otherwise but sound advice from prudent men such as Pendergrast. I feel nothing. . . ."

Frank's mood was not improved when his attempt to raise a fund for the ship's library met with indifference. "I presume we shall go without. I can't do everything, for it really seems to me no one cares about what does not immediately interest himself. I wanted to have got a few books myself."

Friday, 28 November, was "a gala day" on the *Ohio*. The commodore entertained the mayor of New York City on board. Everything "went off well. I was extra polite to Mrs. Hull, who is very grateful & cordial. The only thing that kills me is to see the old man [Hull] so cut down by these matters [the berthing complaints], but was our only hope or chance of ever having this vile system changed."

To Sophie in Delaware, Frank sent the issue of the *Courier* that contained his commentary. "Today [1 December] a paper is to be mailed to you containing the whole story of our quarters. I like

100

myself in print better than in manuscript. . . . The editor of the Courier had a letter from Paulding yesterday touching on the subject. . . . I told him [the editor] to lay great stress on the point of our perfect harmony on board, regard for the Com^e & Capt., & for the Secret[ary] himself. I think the Navy Board [of Commissioners] will *shake* for once—& the whole fire being directed on them leaves but the slightest personal risk. The papers here are unanimous against them. . . . Altogether I am perfectly delighted there was no faux pas in the printing.

"The sensation [caused] . . . by our publication is immense. . . . the whole edition of the paper, including the weekly paper was sold out before 10 ock. The editor . . . was stopped frequently to find out who the author of the comments were." Captain Smith suspected Frank and let him know that he felt "it was in bad state." Later Frank wrote Sophie, "Everything I have heard goes to confirm that I have not made a single mistake as to any matter asserted as facts. . . . The truth is the Commissioners did not imagine there would be nerve enough to publish the correspondence."

The protest letter from the lieutenants to Paulding and Frank's commentary created a public relations problem for the authorities in Washington and cast Commodore Hull in an unfavorable light. The special privilege accorded his family, although not without precedent, was repugnant to American public opinion since for the benefit of two members of his immediate family, his subordinate officers were deprived of reasonable comfort.

That the orlop controversy gave rise to widespread criticism is evidenced by Paulding's letter to Hull, dated 30 November, which contained the following: "I feel assured that, in order to quiet the *clamors of dissatisfaction expressed in every quarter,* as well as for the benefit of the service generally, you will willingly sacrifice [the ladies' passage in the *Ohio*] to my wishes, and those of the President."

Hull quickly answered that as permission had been freely granted and that as great expense had been incurred and as no other arrangements had been made for the ladies ashore, they would be "in absolutely an unprotected condition."

The commodore hurried preparations to sail before Paulding could reply. The *Ohio,* with Hull's family on board, got underway for Europe on 6 December 1838, with the lieutenants still quartered on the orlop deck.

Immediately after sailing from New York, Frank assured Sophie, "I am satisfied with what I have done & go with a perfectly light conscience. . . . I would have given much to have had you with me, but I have had so much happiness while you were with me, that I shall not complain. No words can convey to you the thought and intensity of my feelings toward you Sophie. . . . the weather is fine and the wind is fair. . . . Pray for me as I shall for you."

As the uncomfortable voyage continued, he wrote, "I never have felt so deeply our separation. I have discovered you were more necessary to my existence than I was aware of. Now that I cannot at any moment go to you I feel how much I am losing, how desolate I really am. You must therefore expect to see me return in a year, if such a thing can be brought about & this is always practicable if properly managed."

By 22 December the *Ohio* was 800 miles from Gibraltar. The wind was fair. But, Frank told Sophie, "the ship sails like a witch. . . . she is uncomfortable to a degree that I have never seen— the three decks above the orlop have not been dry since we sailed, a good many of the crew are sick & the officers suffering . . . many of them from sore throats.

"Our mess room [is] the most wet, close black hole that you can possibly picture to yourself. . . . the lamp & two candles, literally only making darkness visible."

While at sea, probably as a result of the wardroom officers' petition and the public furor over their quarters, Hull directed Captain Smith to conduct a special investigation on the alleged disadvantages of the orlop deck for berthing the officers. At the end of December Smith submitted the following report to the Secretary of the Navy.

"The officers generally are intelligent and competent and evince a disposition to exert themselves to make the ship what it is desirable she should be. The ship accommodates her officers and crew as well as ships of her class can, as far as I am able to judge. I have . . . made inquiry of the officers occupying rooms on the orlop deck, as to their convenience and comfort, and they stated that their apartments had been quite comfortable, and much more so than they had expected to find them.

"Thus far the deck has proved extremely comfortable to all whose berths are there, and much more so, in my opinion, than any other deck could have been made for all its occupants. The orlop deck can be and has been kept clean and dry and well ventilated by windsails, and I have perceived no ill effects, and as far as I have learned, no instance of ill health is attributable to, or exists in consequence of, sleeping or messing on that deck."

Frank was dismayed. The captain's evaluation came during December when the *Ohio* sailed in the Atlantic, a time when the difficulties relating to ventilation could be much more readily surmounted than during the hot summer months.

"That Capt. Smith has a perfect right, to give his opinion of the orlop deck no one can deny, but to leave it to be clearly & distinctly inferred that those officers who objected to being berthed there, and respectfully set forth their objections to the Secretary of the Navy—have found this berthing quite comfortable, better than what they expected—is what is wholly deplorable—Capt. Smith had not a vestige of authority for this assumption. . . . Quite comfortable! this is sheer . . . mockery. . . . Smith's letter . . . has filled us with indignation. Not the slightest change has undergone in the mind of every one of us who signed the letter in relation to the orlop—and not a man of us was consulted by Capt. S[mith]."

Casualties mounted during the crossing. Dr. Van Wyck suffered an apoplectic fit that left him insensible for days. Lieutenant J. S. Missroon stumbled and fell on a coil of rope, breaking a leg. Lieutenant R. L. Browing sprained an ankle severely. A seaman fell while reefing from the end of the "Fore topsail yard," but fortunately went overboard instead of hitting the deck. The boatswain ran aft and tossed over a rope, which the man caught and hauled him up without injury. Another seaman, not so fortunate, fell from the main topsail yard onto the deck, and was instantly killed. "I was just ascending the ladder to go on deck, the noise he made in striking was terrible & not to be mistaken. He was a handsome young man—had not been to sea before—was stationed aloft from choice, was fearless & ambitious, but had not yet attained the grasp & inconceivable tenacity which enable sailors to cling aloft like squirrels. . . .

"Our chaplain who is a simple hearted, amiable man—of negative character however . . . gave us a good prayer and in a few remarks alluded to the recent melancholy death—but without effect, & not in the language which could reach a seaman's better nature."

Sophie's evangelizing and deep concern for Frank's spiritual well-being were bearing fruit. He began a regular course of Bible study, "which I long wished to do, to become better acquainted with its history—to do that which would please you my own precious heart." He came to enjoy reading the Bible. "I like it better & better, what was rather a task or done as a duty, I do now from inclination." On night watches he discussed religion with Pendergrast. "I told him that unfortunately I could not explain to him all I felt, or answer knotty questions—but that the most perfect conviction had come over my mind . . . that my ideas of religion as applicable to things of this world had changed—and after describing all the excellence, happiness, truth, cheerfulness, which I had seen make part & parcel of it—he said, 'I presume, in such a character, you have described your wife.' "

Every evening before Frank went on watch, he read a daily verse from his little book and, on closing it, he kissed it where his wife had written, "a keepsake from Sophia." Coming off watch, he would kneel beside his bed and with "whole heart & soul" pray to "Him to bless you, in every way you could wish. . . ."

His interest in salvation kindled, he supported Lieutenant Guert Gansevoort's request to the chaplain for Sunday school instruction for the seventy boys on board. Frank regarded the youngsters as "very promising, if properly attended to, though I am sorry to say there seems to be some old school notions prevailing among the higher officers, who probably think that hard knocks & cuffs is the readiest way of making sailors."

Gansevoort located an excellent teacher on board, who "will command sufficient respect and is found of the boys. . . . I can see in this apprenticeship system if properly managed, the means of manning our Navy with a set of seamen such as the world never saw, raising immeasurably the standard of their class, & giving a new tone & character to this calling. . . ."

Disagreement over the officers' berthing arrangements did not alter Frank's continued admiration of Captain Smith: "He has a few kinks, but these we must get used to & recollect that we all have our faults & peculiarities—he is affable, accessible, & kind—I believe he wishes for nothing more than that we may be happy & comfortable—he is a superior seaman, immensely cool, & gives us full authority in our watches."

As the *Ohio* approached Europe, Frank was aware of a camaraderie in the officers' mess that was getting "better and better every day." "There is a degree of kind feeling & amiability in the department of each & every one to the other, that must be rare in so large a mess. As yet not an unkind word has passed—and I cannot convey to you better the state which I wish to describe them by quoting the words of [the] Captain . . . [of the Marines] who said to me . . . 'Why Sir, I look upon it as *an extraordinary* mess. . . .' "

On 30 December the weather was clear and the sea calm, when the lookout spotted snowcapped mountains. Everyone on board was disappointed when Hull decided not to put in at Gibraltar. "This is the first of those little inconveniences, which though trifling . . . , are not so to me, & which we must expect to meet with during the cruise, arising from the Com^e having his family on board."

It was 4 January 1839 before the *Ohio* joined the *Cyane* at anchor at Port Mahon. Here, Captain Stockton left the ship and Pendergrast assumed the duties as first lieutenant "to the great joy of all on board."

That Frank found separation from Sophie difficult is suggested by the endearments with which he ended his letters to her. He closed one, "Farewell once more my own beloved wife—object of my dearest affection & happiness on earth. I want to hear . . . how everything goes with you—oh Sophie how much you are to me—how I love you—how my heart yearns for you—how it seems to cling to you daily & hourly."

On an evening ashore Frank called on an old friend, the Dutch consul, and his family. At their home he met Lieutenant Charles Heywood of the United States Navy and his wife, and Mrs. Adams, an old acquaintance, who was married to another lieutenant. The ladies came on board the *Ohio* the next day to call on Mrs. Hull and Miss Hart. "It seemed curious to see . . . American officers' wives dressed in Spanish style without bonnets, etc. they are . . . very pretty women."

Shipboard routine continued in Port Mahon. "The ship is improving fast in her appearance & if Smith & the Commodore had the good sense not to interfere too much with the first lieutenant, they would be much better pleased in the end than with their own exertions."

The ladies still lived on board and "must die of ennui, they land occasionally for a short walk, but I think we see less of them than ever." Frank escorted them one afternoon on a visit to Mrs. Heywood and Mrs. Adams and generously took the occasion to invite

Miss Hart to accompany him on "any . . . excursion she wished." She postponed "the matter *indefinitely*, though having just expressed such a desire. . . ." "They . . . say nothing offensive . . . but do not certainly meet you half way, in bringing about anything like a cordial intercourse—and as Pendergrast says, [they] are the hardest people to talk to he ever had anything to do with. They want to get the old man ashore, who would die out of the ship, & they cannot well leave him."

Frank depicted them as socially inept. "They are unobtrusive and so far harmless—but instead of providing a little life & spirit in a social way in the ship, they are the most destitute of any *savoir faire* in this line of any persons I have ever met." Mrs. Hull and Miss Hart finally went ashore to live in Port Mahon until the *Ohio* was ready to sail again.

Du Pont lost himself in his work on board. "I am interested & believe efficient in the duties of the ship—for I find it one of the most agreeable pastimes here, to be on deck during the day & have as much duty as Pender[st] can push upon me. . . . On the other hand the night watches, where there is nothing . . . to occupy you, come very tough. I get through them partly by . . . my thoughts of home & my own Sophie."

His respect for the men increased. "I am much better pleased with our crew than I expected, they only require a little training to bring them back to what they should be—they are remarkable in one respect—I have never seen under the circumstances so little drunkenness. . . . Six hundred out of the eight hundred & fifty stop their ration of whiskey & take money in lieu. . . ."

Conditions on the orlop deck continued to frustrate all the lieutenants. "I have given up all hopes of redress, which I believe is the case with every member of the mess. . . . Though I find inconveniences increasing daily with the Orlop, I have settled down into great composure under it. The deck outside is kept clean by rubbing with stones and sand, and the dust covers everything in our rooms—it is impossible to keep a garment out of your drawer."

One day the captain and commander of a British warship came on board. Since Smith and Hull were ashore, Pendergrast and Du Pont escorted them through the ship. When they came to the orlop deck, "we had a full discussion of the subject. As you may suppose I was well pleased to find every assertion in the comments fully sustained and more." The orlop experiment had been tried on the

Thunderer and another British ship of the line, but had been given up "on the score of health & the manifest impropriety of confining all the officers to one part of the ship."

The lieutenants on the *Ohio* converted an area on the lower gun deck into a lounge. "We have a fine Sofa across the stern, with good cushions. My red curtains from the *Warren* having come to good purpose & through the skill of an upholsterer on board, make quite an appearance. The orlop I think, however, is getting more disagreeable. . . . for I occasionally get a headache when I remain too long. I regret this much, for I do not read as much as I wish or ever have leisure for, of late, but as soon as the painting is done in the mess room this will be a very good place."

Since sailing from New York, Hull and his wife had been extremely fearful of Secretary Paulding's reaction to the ladies making the cruise, after he had expressly asked Hull to put them ashore in the United States. It was not until April that a letter arrived from him. Paulding asked Hull not to think of a successor—his services could not be spared—and assured him that he could keep his family with him. "This," Frank told Sophie, "is the end of the *grand battle* a result which causes me neither surprise or mortification. . . . The odds were all against us in those quarters from whence any action could come. . . . Besides the consciousness of having claimed with manliness our rights, and of having submitted to a proper & I may add cheerful acquiescence & favorable tone to the decree against us, we have another subject of consolation of having exposed the rottenness of the navy board, bringing down upon them the ire and indignation of the whole country. . . . I rejoice in this because it will give a new impulse to the navy & not from any personal triumph."

Mrs. Hull and Miss Hart visited the ship in mid-April. "They were in high spirits & I must do them justice, today, polite, cordial & pleasant—they were so much relieved that joy & satisfaction evidently preponderated over any air of triumph—I hope they may continue in this good vein. . . ." The ladies were to remain in Port Mahon when the *Ohio* sailed for Gibraltar.

The crew prepared the *Ohio* to get underway, hauling up our "onerous anchors, buried well, after three months of uninterrupted imbedding." On an evening in mid-April the ship set a course for Gibraltar, "everyone feeling pleased and invigorated by the fine sea breeze."

On the following day the sentences of courts-martial of four men were carried out. One seaman received sixty lashes—"he is a stout irishman and stood it well." The other sentences were "very mild," but one seaman fainted after he received twenty-five of the thirty-nine lashes that he was to receive. Crew members took him down. Most men who received lashes put a piece of lead in their mouths, bit down, and clenched their jaws, which created saliva, relieving the thirst that immediately ensued. This seaman, however, had swallowed his lead, nearly choking when the lashes commenced. After recovering, crew members brought him up again, but Pendergrast suggested to Captain Smith that he dispense with the rest of the punishment, which he did. "I trust and believe that salutary consequences will result from this, during the cruise. It is very harrowing to see a fellow creature thus degraded, but I am so firmly convinced that disorder, inefficiency & mutiny are so unavoidably the result of doing away with corporal punishment that I can witness such scenes, & execute them, as I would any other disagreeable duty arising from stern necessity."

One sailor who had deserted "showed a good deal of character" after he had received his lashes. He asked Captain Smith for permission to speak. He declared, " 'I have been punished, sir, but I hope that what has passed will not be put down against me in [the] future. I hope I shall not be looked upon as a black sheep in the ship—I intend to do my duty like a man, for I am both able & willing to do it!'

"I was delighted with this manly, but perfectly respectful bearing. There is no undue severity in the ship. None of the lieutenants are severe men, if we have a fault [it is] . . . in being too lenient. . . ."

The orlop deck "degradation" still rankled Frank and his messmates. On entering his room one evening, Frank heard the midshipmen talking loudly in their hammocks outside. One of them, abreast of the surgeon's and chaplain's door, indulged in a "strain of conversation," which would have insured an enlisted man a dozen lashes. Frank reported the incident to Pendergrast, who severely reprimanded the reefer. Captain Smith asked Frank about the trouble. He replied sarcastically that "this was part of the beautiful arrangement" of the orlop deck. "He turned off the conversation quick enough."

"The evil continued with great additional impropriety & outrage the following night." Pendergrast reported it to Smith "in such terms

& with such emphasis as roused him from his apathy." He told Pendergrast he would like to have a written report. Quickly, Frank wrote up all the midshipmen's remarks, presenting "a disgusting dialogue" of the language, which Pendergrast sent to the captain. Smith called up all the middies and "things have gone better since.

"Smith's indifference about the objections of the orlop, while he is suspected of lending himself to its being perpetuated in the service by his reports to the navy board has drawn off from him much of the kind feeling which was generally felt for him by the officers.

"These things have me load another *thirty-two pounder* [cannon] against the Navy Board, and I have filled it to the muzzle. I have not yet sent it, wishing to ponder over it well, & not desiring to do anything that can injure me in any way."

On the evening of 15 April lookouts on the *Ohio* sighted the southern coast of Spain. "Though some thirty miles off, the old man was up the whole night. I found him on deck at 4 ock this AM, in a dead calm, having complained to [the lieutenant] on the mid watch that the sea was not wide enough for a ship of this class. He is gradually usurping Smith's command from him. . . ." Stricken with rheumatism in Port Mahon, Smith had changed "as he was much bolder on the cruise across the Atlantic." "If I had ever permitted them [Hull and Smith] to trouble me while in charge of the deck, I should doubtless be more annoyed, but as I have perfect control of the ship & crew in my watch, I execute their orders, cheerfully & implicitly, but in the way I think things should be done—and never let them confuse me. . . . But they seem to me, when . . . some of the younger ones are in charge, to take particular pains & pleasure in adding to any little difficulty which may occur."

On Sunday, 21 April, the *Ohio* entered Gibraltar harbor. When anchoring, Frank stationed himself on the main gun deck among the anchor cables. The crew let go the anchors. Chain cables rumbled. Immense pieces of oak timber cased in heavy iron, around which the cables were twisted to moderate their velocity, presented "a stream of living fire. . . . the noise of the chain & the trembling of the whole ship made up a pandemonium awful to behold. . . ."

When the crew let go the anchors, one chain "in one of its wildest contortions" struck Frank's right instep. "The pain was severe but not enough to unnerve me in the slightest degree. I immediately felt my ankle joint, and finding all was right there I sent [a man] for a slipper, pulled off my boot and attended to duty on one leg until all was secure."

With the anchors out, Frank went below, pulled off his stocking to see the extent of the damage—"all the top of the foot was black, but no bones hurt, the ankle safe, and I was truly grateful & relieved. The Dr. gave me a solution which in ten minutes drew out every particle of discoloration. I will be on duty tomorrow. . . . My escape of a broken limb was most providential, for the chain must have passed very near me before it struck me, for on looking, my pantaloons were much torn above the foot."

While at Gibraltar the crew mended the broken anchor chain and "had endless work with anchors" for five successive days, "which wore out officers & men, rendered doubly annoying, by the peevish interference & nervous anxiety of the *old man.*"

After just a week at Gibraltar, the *Ohio* was underway, headed out into the Atlantic off the western coast of Spain "without an object in view, [and] no plan laid."

"I will not enlarge on this but must quote the words of . . . [a] messmate, who said in the gravest manner, 'the truth is, its the *vacancy of mind* that troubles the old gentlemen.' . . . nothing could describe better the true state of the case." As Captain Smith's rheumatism worsened, Hull was daily "more restive & usurping more & more the former's duty, making him pretty sick of his business. Some here growl a good deal, & it must be confessed there is cause, but for my part, it has struck me so *en ridicule,* that it is a course of *merriment,* & not dissatisfaction. I have long since given up the idea of having an interesting cruise. . . ."

IX

"I . . . accept no half measure, no compromise"

On 3 May the *Ohio* was "still knocking about on the wide ocean." The weather was fine, the winds moderate. "I enjoy good health and am contented in mind; I think I have disciplined myself a good deal, and do not give way as I did to fits of impatience. . . . [Although] the old man [is] without mind, without resources, & without curiosity . . . I keep from . . . [grumbling], first because I think it would be agreeable to you, and secondly, the character of a fault finder is unamiable, and very apt to grow upon us."

While the *Ohio* was at sea, everyone's diet for seventeen days consisted of ham, salt beef, salt pork, tongue, and codfish along with pea or bean soup and potatoes. Frank joked, "We shall be fairly pickled. . . . I miss vegetables, & always grow thin on salt provisions."

On 16 May the *Ohio* maneuvered outside the Lisbon harbor. Rumors scurried about the ship that the captain would refuse to go in and anchor. "I could not have conceived & you could not imagine such childish, whimsical, wavering, peevish conduct as had been exhibited by *le vieux* [Hull] on this passage—complaining and whining about winds & weather, but afraid to avail himself of either when fine or fair. . . ."

While off Lisbon, the captain sent a circular to the lieutenants calling on them to state their opinion in writing as to the qualities of the *Ohio*. Frank told Sophie, ". . . of course I did not lose the opportunity of giving the orlop *a shot.*"

In his official letter, Frank replied, ". . . as a Man of War . . .

111

I consider her the finest line of battleship I have seen or sailed in—except the Franklin in some points of view."

But, he continued, "As a man of war, in the usual and more comprehensive sense of the term, I think her efficiency sensibly impaired by the highly improper berthing of her sea lieutenants. . . . In the sudden exigency of night quarters the lieutenant, instead of being the first man in his division to aid and cheer on his men to extra exertion by his immediate presence and example, he will be the last person to make his appearance. . . . I consider the discipline of the ship to have been seriously affected. . . ."

In late May, after visiting Lisbon, the *Ohio* got underway and, on 11 June, anchored in Port Mahon. Immediately Mrs. Hull and Miss Hart rejoined the ship, which then sailed for Marseilles. Here Frank received a packet of letters from Sophie, "letters which mitigate so materially the pangs of absence, letters which I can read with pleasure and profit over and over again, and which during our summer's cruise will be my constant intellectual companions."

After reading and rereading all the letters, Frank settled himself in his room and wrote, "I have done my duty on board of this ship with zeal & cheerfulness, such as never animated me before, and strange to say, I have never been brought in slightest collision with either Captain or Commodore—everyone nearly of the others have been to the one or the other for something unpleasant—on duty I have never received from either a petulant word or look, nor have I had occasion. I trust I should not except under some extraordinary circumstance ever show anything approaching such feelings to them.

"I am a thorough man of wars man, in all such matters, I go for implied obedience . . . & cheerful obedience to duty. . . . I heard the other day a compliment paid me. . . . Capt. S[mith] in speaking of officers generally told [Lt. Sylvanus W.] Godon . . . that he considered me the best officer he had sailed with . . . he liked my manner of carrying on my duty better than any officer's on board, and so with the old man. . . . he consider[s] me ahead & front of all the officers . . . he said 'I like him very much, he is a capital officer, I like to see him handle the ship &c,' but for all this neither of them can understand me—they cannot understand that an officer can contend for what he conceives his rights, and contend, too, strongly & boldly, and at the same time forget all such things, when he closes the door of his messroom behind him. . . ."

Through Captain Smith, Hull sent to the officers extracts of a letter he had received from the Secretary of the Navy. Paulding wrote, "The Department regrets the circumstances which have brought you to this conclusion [asking for reassignment] so adverse to the interests of the service; yet I cannot but hope that . . . a better feeling will prevail among the officers of the wardroom of the *Ohio*. But whether this anticipation is realized or whether it is not, the Dept. expects . . . you will retain your command . . . until by a firm and steady assertion of authority, in which you may rely upon it for support, you have suppressed that spirit of discontent which if permitted to triumph, will it is feared be fatal to the future character and discipline of the service.

"To revise that discipline was the design of the Dept. in fitting out one of the finest ships in the Navy and placing her under . . . [your] command. The selection of the junior officers was also made with a view to that object, and was intended by the Dept. as a compliment to each and all of them, in the confident expectation that having the eyes of their countrymen upon them, at home, and those of Europe abroad, they would be excited to an honorable ambition to sustain that reputation which had been acquired by a series of glorious victories.

"It is with deepest respect that the Dept. is forced to confess that so far its anticipations have not been realized. From the first, the spirit of discontent approaching insubordination, has prevailed among a portion of the officers, which manifested itself in disrespect to their commander, in appeals to the public as void of foundation as they were destitute of all manly consideration. . . ."

After reading Paulding's evaluation of their behavior, all the lieutenants "boiled over with indignation" and signed a letter, composed by Frank, which they delivered to Smith. In part, they wrote, "In answer to the very serious charges of 'discontent approaching insubordination.' . . . we have endeavored from the first moment of joining the ship at Boston, to sustain the high reputation of the service . . . and trust it will be found that our demeanor has been uniformly respectful to our superiors, and that we have exerted ourselves to the utmost faithfully and cheerfully to discharge all the duties assigned to us. . . .

"As regards our accommodations, we take occasion to state that our opinions on that head have not in the slightest degree changed since we had the honor to address the Dept. on that subject. Whatever we have urged against the messing and sleeping apartments of the ship, has been the offspring of feelings very different from discontent, insubordination or disrespect; we were actuated by a sense we conceived to be due to our ranks, as well as a desire to call attention to a system of accommodations, without precedent we believe in any other naval service."

To Sophie, a seething Frank wrote, "Mr. Paulding [thinks] this ship is a disgrace to the flag she bears, & he [is] held in utter contempt by all his officers for keeping her in such a condition. . . . [This is] why I am ready to despair."

The *Ohio* got underway from Marseilles with the *Cyane,* and by 26 June the ships reached Leghorn, "having given Toulon & Genoa the *go by.* . . . Our prospects of a pleasant cruise is at an end, it will be a hurried race around the coast, delays just sufficient to tantalize everyone, & all this without any earthly object. . . ."

Frank's opinion of the cruise changed when the captain gave permission for him and six other officers to visit Rome, although "the old Commodore grumbled" at Smith's releasing so many. The skipper of the *Cyane* decided to sail to Civitavecchia and land any officers who were desirous of going to Rome. Du Pont, Pendergrast, lieutenants W. L. Howard and Guert Gansevoort, ship's surgeon Dr. B. Ticknor, and Passed Midshipman William R. Rodgers boarded the *Cyane* on Thursday, 4 July, and on the next morning they arrived at Civitavecchia where they hired carriages to transport the party from both ships.

The group entered the Eternal City—"The most interesting of all cities"—before sunset. "The view of the Dome [of St. Peter's] had already come up to my highest expectation." Frank, who had been designated as tour leader, bargained for an hour, trying to locate proper lodgings—". . . this is the country of extortion *par excellence.* You are charged for everything you have except the air you breathe. . . .

"It seems to me my time is always taken up for other people, but that I do not mind, for I would suffer all the inconveniences which could be devised, & live on bread & water, to see what I have [already] seen."

On Friday the American delegation, seventeen in all, in dress uniforms, headed by the consul, were presented to Pope Gregory XVI. They were ushered into a private audience room. The officers and consul formed a semicircle around the pope, who was dressed in "a kind of cloak with a cap . . . a fine looking man of seventy-two."

114

During the audience, which lasted for a half-hour, the pope spoke of the American ships and declared he would visit them "with great pleasure," if they came to the mouth of the Tiber the following year. He complimented the Americans on their appearance, inquired about their visit to Rome, and asked questions about the American Navy.

For several days the party continued touring the city and its environs, visiting historic sites. On Tuesday, 16 July, at 4 A.M. the officers of the *Ohio* and *Cyane* clambered into carriages, which returned them to Naples and their ships.

On boarding the *Ohio*, the officers were quickly apprised of drastic change. Before leaving the ship, they had neglected to say goodbye to Commodore Hull who, as their boat pulled away for *Cyane*, "bounced out in a new character, swore like a trooper, pulled down his cap, said he had been treated with scandalous disrespect as a man & as an officer."

He protested bitterly that too many officers had been granted leave, complained that the "wrong set" had gone, and suggested that they be recalled. In his rage he refused liberty in Naples to the remaining officers and confined them to the ship until the leave party returned.

The morning after the travelers arrived back, Hull welcomed all officers except First Lieutenant Pendergrast, who was the target he selected "to concentrate his impotent threats upon."

When he encountered Frank, who touched hat respectfully and bowed, Hull snapped, " 'I hope you had a pleasant visit Sir!' "

" 'Very well indeed, Sir, I hope you have been well, Sir,' " Frank responded.

"My manner was that of perfect unconsciousness of having done wrong or of appearing to know that anybody had thought so. . . . My manner of late has been neither hot nor cold—distant but respectful. . . . This is all very unpleasant. . . . I find all my enjoyments have been at the expense of my messmates—that five lieuts. are retained on board, . . . & this done with the hope that the disappointment produced, will alienate the feelings of those who are confined to the ship, from those who are gone. . . ."

The *Ohio* was soon at sea, off the west coast of Sicily. To minimize the tensions on board, Frank buried himself in books. He commenced reading a French work on Italy, giving special attention to the chapters relating to Rome, "so that I might impress all the objects of interest & beauty on my mind. . . . I find that on a fair calculation we saw about one tenth of what is really curious & worth contemplating. Still we did well & considering the heat of the weather, accomplished as much as ever was done in that way before, for the same number of days." Studying the New Testament, Frank found "the works of art which I have seen illustrating it, have made me read it with great interest."

The officers' dissatisfaction with their living accommodations was unabated. Dr. Ticknor documented the air quality on the deck and in his room, and appended it to the daily sick report.

At the start of summer, the officers abandoned their rooms entirely during the daytime. Their quarters became "almost untenable at night . . . the suffering & consequent debility was quite severe." One lieutenant finally "got his dose" and became "the most violent denunciator" of conditions on the orlop deck. He urged Du Pont to draw up a letter to Smith requesting other quarters, but Frank refused. Finally under Du Pont's prodding, the lieutenant composed a letter to Captain Smith, which all the officers signed. Du Pont stated, "I would rather not have signed [it] . . . but the captain having invited communication, upon being spoken to on the subject, and knowing that if we permitted the summer to pass without complaint, it would be seized upon—I put my name to it, but stating distinctly that I would accept no half measure, no compromise. . . ."

The lieutenant sent the letter to the captain, "We beg leave to inform you, officially, which we do with great reluctance, that the suffocating closeness and extreme impurity of the atmosphere in our orlop rooms have rendered them no longer tenable, and would most respectfully request that other accommodations be assigned to us."

Captain Smith responded immediately: "I received your communication last evening. I regret extremely that you find your orlop rooms untenable from the suffocating closeness and extreme impurity of the atmosphere there. I have transmitted a copy of your communication to the Commander-in-chief, and requested instructions respecting it. The Commodore says, in reply, 'I do not feel myself at liberty to authorize any alterations in the ship under your command in relation to the accommodations of the officers; but I repeat, that your suggestion in relation to a part of the officers berthed on the orlop removing their cots and hammocks to the wardroom and main deck during the continuance of the warm weather meets my approbation.' Therefore no permanent alterations can be made until the pleasure of the government is known and instructions received upon the subject; but I will direct the first lieutenant to have temporary rooms made for your accommodation during the continuance of the warm weather."

Frank was stubbornly opposed to halfway measures. "As soon as I saw this," he wrote Sophie, "I determined to have nothing to do with the matter, and decided to remain where I was, and that my motives & position should be understood."

In his own letter to the captain, he set forth his position. "Sir. As it is my intention to decline occupying one of the places which you directed the first lieutenant to dispose of, for temporary sleeping accommodation to those officers who have complained of the suffocating state of the atmosphere in their rooms on the orlop—and as I should greatly regret if my so doing were attributed to an improper spirit I beg leave to say a few words in reply to your communication of yesterday. . . . I will speak freely but with feelings of the highest respect for my superiors.

"I am one of those Sir who believe, that Lieutenant is as much entitled by regulation, by usage, & by military propriety to a permanent and fixed apartment suitable to his rank . . . as the captain of a ship is to his cabin—and that a ship of this class is capable of affording such at least, as he would occupy in a frigate or sloop of war. I signed the letter of the 27th inst. representing the present state of the orlop rooms, under the impression that if the complaints contained in it were found to be well grounded, other permanent & usual accommodations would be given me—particularly as it had been generally understood, if not officially stated, that the present arrangement of berthing nearly all of the officers of the ship on the orlop was merely an experiment. But Commodore Hull having decided that he is not authorized to make any permanent change, of which he is of course the sole & proper judge, I prefer remaining where the Department has placed me as long as my health will endure it, rather than occupy quarters which I consider unfit for an officer holding the third rank known in our navy, and from which he may be ejected at any moment."

Frank regarded the issue as a matter of principle and was convinced that his course was the correct one. At the risk of jeopardizing his advancement, he rejected any compromise. His contention that his quarters on the orlop deck endangered his well-being were not borne out, although he was uncomfortable as the *Ohio* continued routine patrolling of the Mediterranean.

He assured Sophie of his excellent health. "I have not yet taken a grain of medicine since I saw you last, which I believe none of the mess but myself can say. . . . I never write or read now in my room, indeed it is impossible, this is a great privation." Later, he wrote, "Things on board are . . . bad, they are repugnant to my natural feelings of cordiality & kindness—but my conscience is clear, thoroughly so. . . ."

The *Ohio* sailed through the Aegean Sea. "This . . . is a favorite section . . . for me—studded with beautiful islands, included with deep & well sheltered harbours—no sunken dangers without, & the bluest sea that you can imagine, its navigation is exciting . . . & altogether interesting beyond description."

At the start of August the ship dropped anchor at Piraeus, the seaport of Athens. Frank and Lieutenants Missroon and Browning went ashore, and hired a carriage to drive into the city, four miles away. Although it was nearly sundown when they arrived in Athens, they lost no time walking out to see "a few of the antiquities." The next day, without Missroon, whose leg was bothering him, Frank and Browning toured Athens and its environs.

In the morning the three officers toured the Acropolis before returning to their hotel rooms. The next day the sightseers trekked back to the *Ohio*.

A few days later the officers and crew readied the ship for a visit from the King and Queen of Greece. In blistering heat—"the hottest day you ever knew"—the ship's company waited two hours for their appearance. Finally, at dusk, they came on board. Frank was not impressed with the King, whom he described as "deficient, showing no general intelligence." The Queen "was another affair, with a most amiable expression & manner, she speaks quick and to the point, and seems well educated and informed." The royal couple strolled about inspecting the lighted ship for two hours before going ashore.

Early the next morning the *Ohio* set sail. During the two-day cruise from Greece to the harbor of Vourla in the Gulf of Smyrna, drunkenness became a problem. The enlisted men had bought cologne water from Greek peddlers without the knowledge of the officers.

Captain Smith, Frank wrote, exhibited inconsistency in his handling of the sailors, "one day sermonizing & accepting promises, another, abuse mixed with low sailor slang, sometimes perfectly disgusting & always with a total absence of all dignity or manly exercise of authority."

Punishments were meted out unfairly. Smith ordered ten lashes each for three seamen, while a fourth, who was drunk with the others, and was "in addition exceedingly insolent & mutinous to the officers," received six lashes—"his previous character also being worse than that of the others."

"A sailor," Frank wrote Sophie, "is made up of the grossest vices, with a sprinkle of the highest virtues which adorn human nature—in other words his character is an anomaly, a perfect antithesis. He is immoral, profane, obscene, & nearly always intemperate & has no sense of obligation, or the binding effects of his word or oath. . . . Kindness and indulgence, if not tempered by very firm and efficient restraint, is totally thrown away upon him. . . .

"On the other hand, he is brave to recklessness, and humane in a very striking degree. No woman's heart is more alive to suffering humanity or ready to administer to its wants—his kindness and attention to a sick messmate are very notable, no personal risk ever checks him in the slightest degree in these duties—his purse is ever open to all charitable objects, and this is done with a cordial, off-handed manner, which adds much to the act itself. But while he will do all this, he will cheat, rob, & lie in all his dealings. . . .

"I have mentioned all these particulars because I wish to note them down, and thought they would add to your knowledge of a man of war life. . . ."

The town of Smyrna lay eight miles from the *Ohio*'s mooring at Vourla. "Our future movements are wrapped in mystery. They [Hull and Smith] seem quite contented here, and have not yet named a day for sailing. . . . It is a positive shame for so noble a ship to be in the hands of such men as the Com^e and Captain." During their sojourn in the Gulf of Smyrna, the ship's company found plentiful fresh water, and the surrounding islands offered suitable sites to land the men, which even the disgruntled Du Pont admitted was "conducive to their health, cleanliness and proper recreation."

At daylight on 20 August, the *Ohio* upped anchor and headed out. "Guess to where?" Frank rhetorically asked Sophie. "Mahon. We do not go to the interesting countries of Syria & Egypt where we have consuls and commerce."

A day's sail from Vourla, the *Ohio* encountered nineteen French and English warships lying at anchor at Tenedos. Frank described these vessels as "the last efforts in naval architecture, naval equipment & discipline of these great powers. . . . They have many new fixtures, which we have nothing of." Du Pont was displeased that Commodore Hull did not utilize the information on the political situation in the Near East offered him by the French and English admirals. "They are always frank & communicative to Americans, and if he [Hull] were capable of embodying it, could have made an interesting report to his own Government. But the old man is dead to everything but getting along without accident—the women have even lost all influence over his movements, they were exceedingly anxious it appears to visit Jerusalem."

He acknowledged his growing irritation and frustration. "My desire to see you & be with you, of course, increases . . . with my rising disgust & repugnance to my present life & I am sure that my navy feelings & character are fast leaving me. I see so much around me to sour me, & so little in prospect ahead."

By early September the *Ohio* lay anchored at Port Mahon and her female passengers had debarked to take up residence ashore. No sooner had the crew secured the ship than Frank informed Commodore Hull that "for reasons of a domestic nature" he wished permission to return to the United States. "It is with reluctance that I ask to be relieved from active duty; though the circumstances which lead me to do so touch me very nearly, I should not perhaps have yielded to them, had I not already seen a fair portion of active service, and if Capt. Smith had not officially informed the officers in June last, that he had one more lieutenant in the ship than he required."

Hull responded, "Under the circumstances I cannot grant your request at this time, but I will forward your application to the Navy Department, and in the meantime arrangements can be made to transfer any excess of officers which Capt. Smith may desire to be relieved of."

Frank, "much out of temper," wrote Hull again, stressing that "it is a source of deep regret that my request could not be granted. In justice to myself, I can only say that no stronger reasons in my mind could exist than those upon which my application was based, and Capt. Smith having declared that he had a surplus of sea lieutenants. I considered the moment particularly propitious to make it. . . . I beg leave . . . to state, with reasons to the arrangements which you inform me are to be made for transfering any excess of officers from the ship that any orders to that effect will be cheerfully received."

Frank had also written to Secretary of the Navy Paulding: "Reasons which touch me in my closest social relations, attended with circumstances which render them more than usually urgent, induce me to apply to the Navy Department for a leave of absence. I have been aided in overcoming the natural repugnance which an officer must feel in asking to be relieved from duty, by the recollection that I have seen a fair share of active service, having been some fourteen years out of some twenty-three on board a seagoing ship. . . . I trust it will be agreeable to the Department to grant me this request."

Frank was vexed by Hull's denial of his request. To Sophie, he confided, "I was . . . sore, disappointed, & chased about all this. Before I went to bed I read the 37 Psalm which you recommended in your letters. I could not but be struck with its . . . perfect adaptation to the state of my feelings, but I was still too much perturbed to profit by it as much as I should have done."

His deteriorating attitude toward his superiors affected his conduct toward them. He confessed that on morning watch, "I cut the old man without seeming to do so very effectually whenever he came out. . . ."

As was usual when he was thwarted, he urged his family to circumvent official channels and to intervene. He asked his brother Charles to exert pressure in Washington, "This old man having refused me permission I wish you therefore to give me your kind and best assistance in getting me clear. I fear, however, from Paulding's great ill humor against the whole navy in general & this ship in particular it will not be very easy. Besides I am not sure that this old commodore has not put in a word against me in forwarding my application. . . . if you should have any business in Baltimore, & it were not too much inconvenience . . . to go . . . [to Washington] . . . you would readily effect the matter. Should you [go] . . . be very guarded. P[aulding] is one of the bitterest men possible & I may be suspected of having more to do about the [orlop] quarters in this ship than my share."

To Sophie, he wrote, "Charles must get me a leave . . . at whatever cost. I would not remain in this ship for any consideration . . . everything is getting worse, annoyances increase which chafe me to death. . . ." In Washington Charles failed to obtain a leave, and Frank remained on board.

While the *Ohio* remained at Port Mahon, an explosive situation erupted on board. "A few bad men" became drunk and demanded that the whole crew leave the ship. Their behavior was "insolently mutinous, & highly disrespectful" to Smith. "It was one of those cases where a quick energetic course was required & everything would have been settled in a few minutes. The men should have been punished on the spot, & with extreme severity."

Captain Smith "temporised" and, with promises and apologies, persuaded the troublemakers to disband. The throng surrounding them cheered as they dispersed. That night several of the men jumped overboard in an attempt to swim to shore. Officers in boats pursued the deserters, overtook several in the water, and brought them back to the ship. Others gained the shore, but were captured and confined in "the calaboose (Jail)."

Drums beat to quarters. Hull appeared from his cabin and ordered the officers to divide themselves into two watches and to maintain a guard by rowing around the ship all night. The crew lighted all the lanterns on the decks, "indeed everything was done to stamp the event into importance which it no wise merited."

Hull "threw the onus on the Captain" for his lenience and for partiality in permitting some dozen men, known on board "as the married men," to visit their homes in Port Mahon every night.

The next day was Sunday. At muster, Pendergrast read Hull's general order and "here *le vieux* showed himself in no better light than his Captain. The order had neither point nor candor, nor nerve. The English of it was 'My lads you shall not go ashore, not because you have behaved like mutinous rascals, but because there is sickness, in Mahon & I am afraid you will catch it. . . .' "

After Pendergrast read the order, Hull stepped forward and delivered a speech "as deficient in force as the order." Following this, the master-at-arms punished the runaways at the gangway—"all done by the old man to Smith's disgust & mortification, who found himself thus stripped of his command." The captain went below in "an agony of disgust and if he had been a man would have thrown up his command at once."

Pendergrast insisted that the men be confined and court-martialed, and he told Smith that if he did wish to try the men, he would bring charges himself. This brought the captain to his senses and the men "were ironed."

"I had a low opinion of these men before, but when I saw the flag of my country permitted to be thus disgraced & the fame of a noble ship tarnished I could scarcely contain myself. Six men . . . allowed to throw a whole ship in convulsion, and measures taken which in spite of all that may be said . . . will stamp the proceeding as a serious mutiny. It was sufficiently disgraceful to the ship, but it need not have been. . . ."

"The coup de grace was an attempt by a word here, or an inuendo there, on the part of the drivelling & vindictive imbecility of *le vieux* to connect the feeling of the officers on the orlop question with the movement of the crew."

Meanwhile Lieutenant Browning reported two men for insolence. His insistence that they be disciplined displeased Commodore Hull, as the men were his favorites. In lieu of punishing the two culprits, Hull issued an order refusing liberty to all officers and enlisted men. "In fact, the most silly, ridiculous measures were persevered in—as I verily believed to punish the officers."

In early October the *Ohio* sailed out of Port Mahon in weather "stormy, gloomy, & disagreeable." Frank's mood matched the weather. He missed Sophie terribly and entertained thoughts of starting a family. "You have no family & . . . I do not agree with you that we are not likely to have any, for I believe God will bless you in that way yet, [although] not having had the care of one so far, has given you means of intellectual improvement which you could not have had." Several days later, he continued, "I think . . . sometimes, how I should doat on a daughter of yours that would be like you in every respect—but have I not you, dear, and, as long as you are spared me, I feel blessed, happy & content."

By mid-October the *Ohio* was sailing off the southern coast of Spain. It was a year since Frank had joined the ship in Boston harbor. To Sophie, he wrote, ". . . it has been to me a year of excitement, the extent of which, could I have foretold, would have deterred me from the thought of entering upon such a one. Still, I do not regret it, and I am disposed to think that it has by no means been thrown away. The details & knowledge of my profession have been firmly fixed within me, which cannot but . . . [further] my success hereafter in the responsibilities of command. My knowledge of naval administration & naval character, opinions, [and] prejudices . . . has vastly increased & has afforded me material for occasional deep thinking."

The orlop situation worsened. "A new evil has increased upon me in the shape of *bilge water,* the fetid odour from which is *killing,* though not dangerous; my room being near the pumps is filled with it, so much so as to turn the paint black. . . . The bilge water is decomposed seawater, which remains in the bottom of the ship, & cannot be drawn out, the pumps not being able to reach it & when the ship gets to pitching & rocking, it becomes stirred up & emits . . . [a] gas you can imagine."

The *Ohio* maneuvered off Málaga, where many American merchantmen lay anchored, waiting to load cargoes of fruit. Hull refused to run in and show the flag. "This poor old man does not understand at all the objects of his mission, or has not the nerve to execute it. I think he is the most miserable old goose to occupy such a station that I ever have seen. . . . I believe him to be a selfish bad man & a bad *old* man is terrible."

Frank went ashore when the *Ohio* made a short stop at Gibraltar and learned from the "utterly disgusted" American consul that many of the American cargo ships at Málaga had crews that were in a state of mutiny. The consul had procured assistance from the English sloop of war *Wasp* to quell the uprisings. "As for our men of war," Frank wrote Sophie, "it was useless to ask for them. I have become so disgusted with this ship that any change would be agreeable. . . ."

After departing from Gibraltar, the *Ohio* stopped briefly at Tenerife in the Canary Islands and put in at Madeira. She returned to The Rock before heading back to Port Mahon. Not far from Gibraltar a gale hit the ship. Rain "overpowered" the wind and "we had torrents of the former. For the first six hours, I think it blew as strong as I ever saw it. . . . The weather has been disagreeable. Rain, heavy squalls, and sea rough. But the ship has proved herself an admirable one—nothing is strained, & she rides over the highest waves with an ease which I have never before seen. . . . Generally these large ships strain & groan under their heavy armament, like some huge leviathan contending with the elements. . . . the old man is fretting & impatient, & frightened."

The weather moderated. When not on deck, Frank was absorbed in James Fenimore Cooper's *History of the Navy of the United States of America.* "I am exceedingly please[d] with it. . . . The facts have been collected with care, are related in a plain & sensible historical style, and with a degree of liberal impartiality that I admire prodigiously—his naval ideas are military & sound, and altogether I con-

sider the work creditable to the Navy, to the Country, & Mostly so
to the author, who in my humble estimation deserves the thanks of
the whole corps. . . . I wish Mr. Paulding would read it attentively
& ponder it well."

On 28 November the *Ohio* sailed into Port Mahon. The *Brandywine* joined her at anchor the same day. That Frank still nursed
a negative opinion of his superiors is illustrated by his comment, "It
is refreshing to meet one ship at least, commanded with dignity &
manly bearing."

At Port Mahon Frank was elated to receive letters from Sophie.
"The little keepsake & those sweet verses melted me, and I cried
like a child in the quietude of my orlop cell."

Since Mrs. Hull and Miss Hart were still in residence in Port
Mahon, Frank hoped that the commodore would live ashore during
the winter months, which would be "a great relief to all of us, for
he is an eye sore."

Pendergrast divided the officers into eight watches, which gave
them five days off in succession while in port. Frank considered
taking a room on shore where he could store his clothes, books,
writing materials and "other comforts." "It will be of service to me
after a year of sweat in the orlop, without any intermission."

The *Brandywine* upped anchor and got underway for France as
the *Ohio* went alongside the navy yard for overhaul. Hull joined
his family ashore and Captain Smith was "sufficiently sick as to be
literally off duty." With the first lieutenant in charge "things go on
systematically and smoothly."

Frank rented a room that had excellent light and a fireplace. He
rearranged everything from the mat on the floor to the sofa, tables,
and chairs. One door opened out onto a terrace—"altogether it's
about as comfortable *a fix* as you could wish." He admitted feeling
"a good deal of wear & tear on this last cruise, which was a severe
one," and enjoyed taking walks through the countryside.

On Christmas day 1839, he wrote Sophie ". . . this is Christmas,
and I have been thinking much, very much of you all morning. I
thought how quiet, peaceful & happy I would be by your side reading to you in your bible, and perhaps some sermon & discourse
suitable to the occasion, as we used to do of yore."

The *Brandywine* returned from France with the *Ohio*'s new chaplain, Reverend J. B. B. Wilmer, a replacement for Reverend John
W. Greer. Frank hoped that Wilmer would take the apprentice boys

in hand as "I never knew such a fine set of lads & young men in my life. . . ."

Members of the *Ohio*'s mess prodded Frank "to get up some little . . . amusement for them" on shore. At first he declined, then yielded and "soon got into the spirit." He arranged for the officers to host soirees once a week during the carnival season. The first affair took place in a five-room house in late December. "It was most brilliant & successful, being [graced] with the elite of Mahon," headed by the governor and Commodore and Mrs. Hull. The party commenced at seven and ended at midnight. Serenades provided the entertainment. Waiters passed cakes and sugarplums to the ladies and cups of chocolate and wine to the gentlemen.

During the *Ohio*'s previous layover in Port Mahon, her officers had lost considerable sums at the gambling tables. Under Frank's supervision, the Friday night parties brought a measure of refinement to Port Mahon's society. The *Brandywine*'s band supplied the musical entertainment. With the introduction of the soirees, gambling almost vanished, "a circumstance never known before in Mahon. I do not attribute this improvement alone to the soirees, but in bringing about an acquaintance with the society here, evening visiting has been introduced & learning to dance & studying Spanish, etc. here with the sad experience of last season certainly changed the course of many."

In January, "We had a most delightful soiree. . . . It was the fiesta of St. Antonio, the ladies were more numerous, more dressed, more delighted. I never saw in the same number so many pretty women. Everything as usual went off well. I never have enjoyed myself more out of America. I felt younger than I have done for many years, and danced every time until 2 in the morning. . . . the ladies here all make their own dresses, & dress their own hair, & you would be surprised to see the neatness & beauty of both."

Reverend Wilmer took a room next to Frank's on shore. Frank sized him up as "a perfectly guileless man, unacquainted with the world, pleasant & interesting in conversation, well educated, pious, zealous in his desire to do good."

On the following Sunday, Reverend Wilmer, on board the *Ohio* held "the best service I have yet seen in a man of war." Frank was so impressed with the sermon that he devoted an entire paragraph to it in a letter to Sophie.

Ashore, Frank and Wilmer discussed at length Commodore Hull.

Wilmer believed that the commodore was not responsible for the orlop deck berthing of officers and promised that at the end of the cruise he would write "a general remonstrance to the Department against it." The chaplain praised Frank to his face as "a brilliant officer, a good fellow, and a perfect gentleman," and advised him to "bury the hatchet, [out] of forbearance due to [Hull's] age and declining faculties."

After hearing him out, Frank replied that the question of accommodations had been buried by the officers, but "a system of the most grievous & ill natured procedures had marked the old man's command & exercise of authority—that he never had done anything for their [the officers'] pleasure—that his remarks were ill natured . . . and on some occasions false & outrageous—that all these were kept within the sphere of his power & prerogative, and that we had but to submit as inferiors. . . ."

Sophie had kindled Frank's interest in religion; Reverend Wilmer fanned the flame. After one of his sermons, Frank wrote Sophie, "He seemed to reach every man's bosom, & there were but few officers who had not a tear glistening in his eye. I was myself deeply affected, though I fully commanded my nerves. . . . altogether it was the most powerful & thrilling effect I ever heard. The silence of death reigned among the crew, and all seemed not only deeply absorbed, but stunned into motionless suspense, surprise, & awe."

The following evening, Frank visited Wilmer in his room to discuss religion. Frank spoke of his upbringing—"The sound moral precepts & high sense of honor which had been implanted in me by my parents." Frank had received comparatively little religious education. He recalled, "I was launched in the world at 13 . . . a *navy* world & all its corrupting tendencies . . . in short my life had been a blank to Religion until I was married, that a general change had come over me since then wrought by the indescribable character of my wife." The two men conversed far into the night.

On returning to his room, Frank was moved to write a few lines of poetry praising Sophie,

> *Blessed is she whose faithful heart receiveth*
> *Oer the wide seas such words of truth I love!*
> *The love that cannot fail, that ne'er deceiveth,*
> *That brings on earth the dawn of heaven above!*

Mail arrived at Port Mahon. A letter from Charles, who had met with Paulding in Washington, made it clear to Frank that he had no chance of obtaining leave. "I shall make no further effort & be resigned," Frank wrote Sophie.

From Charles's letter he also learned that Captain Smith had forwarded Frank's commentary concerning the orlop deck to the Navy Department.

Storming into the captain's cabin, Frank upbraided Smith angrily, " 'Understand me, Sir, you must not suppose that I would take back one iota of that letter, so far from it, if there is any one act of mine, more than another that I am pleased with while on board of this ship, it is the ground I therein assumed—But Sir the point was between me & my commander, its nature & import required no appeal to the Dept. & it could only have been sent there to *individualize me a little* in this Orlop controversy—but Sir you do not know me—I go for doing that which is right, that which my conscience approves & the best judgment I can bring to bear upon a question—after that, I am very regardless of consequences, & though it may seem strange to you Sir, I care not a fig what Mr. P[aulding] or anybody else may think. If I know & feel myself right, or what any Port Captain in the Navy may think—if I do wrong there are the laws, let each or all come forward, accuse, try & condemn if you can—let us have no secret underhanded business however. I will earn my bread by the labour of my hands & the sweat of my brow, if necessary, rather than submit to injustice. . . .' "

"I have lost all feelings of respect for nineteen twentieths of the Captains in the Navy," he told Sophie. "I look upon them as an inflated, ignorant, & stupid set of men selfish & grasping, & wholly unfit for the stations they occupy. . . . I doubt very much if there is a single ship goes to sea now, on board of which there is not one or more Lieuts. in every way more fit to command her than the Captain. . . ."

X

"The service is fast losing its hold on me"

In mid-March 1840 the leading townspeople of Port Mahon held a public masquerade ball in the town's theater. They invited the American consul and the officers on board the American ships and their families. Hull, his wife, and Miss Hart, as well as the family of the consul, attended, but left at an early hour. Many of the younger officers remained. Not long after the Hulls' departure, a riot occurred on the ballroom floor. Just as Frank descended the stairs from his box seat, he saw to his surprise many townsfolk milling around Passed Midshipman J. W. Read and Midshipman Somerville Nicholson of the *Brandywine.* Running over to the two Americans, Frank discovered them and a citizen of Port Mahon pushing one another. Neither midshipman seemed excited and, when asked what was the matter, Read informed Frank that he had been jostled by a Mahonese, "who was otherwise very offensive in his conduct."

Frank urged Read and Nicholson to avoid "being drawn into a 'row.'" They agreed and turned to follow Frank out of the crowd. Suddenly the Mahonese struck Nicholson a staggering blow, then pounced on Read and Du Pont. This signaled an attack by the Mahonese on the eleven American officers still at the ball. They were assailed from every direction. "We were compelled to defend ourselves, unless we preferred being beaten down and killed like dogs.

"I fell into the work like an unchained lion, and I am astonished myself . . . at the strength & activity which seemed to possess me." Some ladies in the boxes fainted, others shrieked.

Military guards, gripping muskets with fixed bayonets, rushed into the mêlée. Instead of driving the mass before them, they joined the assailants. The eleven officers defended themselves against some hundred individuals. The guards fell to work in the rear, clubbing several Americans to the floor. Read received nasty bruises on his thighs. Guards beat Midshipman George Chapman severely over his hips and back. Midshipman Alexander Dallas, gaining his feet after being knocked down, took a heavy blow in the back from the butt end of a musket. A musket struck Midshipman John Abbott in the jaw.

Finally Frank and the other officers dispersed the crowd momentarily. As Frank walked to another part of the ballroom, a soldier bashed him in the back, while a second charged with a bayonet. He narrowly avoided the thrust.

The Mahonese drove the officers out of the ballroom into the arcades beneath the boxes. The riot was finally quelled. "Through the mercy of God," Frank told Sophie, "no one was dangerously injured, although many were very seriously so & came within an inch of their lives." Du Pont gathered all the party together and they left the theater.

On returning to the *Ohio*, the officers reported the riot to Pendergrast, who had been at the theater but had not participated in the fighting, as he was Senior Officer Present. He sent his report to Commodore Hull, who sent a letter and Pendergrast's report to the governor. The governor sustained the conduct of the guards and offered no reparation. Hull refused to take further steps. "The fact is he [has] no spirit left. But I looked upon this in too serious a light, to be over in this way."

Angered by Hull's lack of support for his officers, Frank wrote his own report to the commodore: ". . . the Governor having justified the brutal and unheard of attack of the Soldiers, and your own communication showing that the information you have received has induced you to accept the Governor's explanations, I am compelled by what is due to my own honor, and in justice to the younger officers engaged on that occasion, to submit in some detail the circumstances of that painful occurrence."

Frank detailed a description of the affair and closed his report by declaring, ". . . I trust that you will not think it strange, still less disrespectful, that the officers who were thus outraged, and myself as well, should be wholly disappointed with the letter of the governor." He believed that the persons responsible should be stripped of authority and imprisoned.

"I find, sir, my situation a very embarrassing one. I am earnestly desirous of doing nothing that could bear the semblance of the slightest disrespect to yourself, or of . . . anything that might seem an improper spirit in not being satisfied with your decision in this case; still, the extent of the outrage, of which I have drawn but a faint picture, is so great, attended with circumstances so calculated to rouse my indignation as an officer and a citizen of the United States, that I think I owe it to myself; to the junior officers who were assaulted with me and to the defenceless and unoffending youths whose blood was shed on the occasion, to ask for redress through all the appeals which official propriety authorizes me to make." *

Frank asked Hull to be allowed to send a copy of this statement to the Delaware members of Congress. This would give them an opportunity to seek "through our minister at Madrid, or any other channel which may be deemed best, that reparation which I humbly submit, the case loudly calls for.

"I pushed the Commodore to insist upon some redress from the governor or I would refer the matter to the Govt."

Du Pont's remonstrance caused Hull to make "a complete surrender of his first position and [he] has come down hard upon the Gov. like a man, to prevent a recurrence. I had to use a little blustering in close of the letter, about going to Congress which I dislike to do, knowing so well that Congress would have done nothing. But it was the only way to rouse the old man."

Meanwhile Hull wrote the Navy Department, detailing his version of the incident. He took the opportunity to report that Pendergrast, Missroon, Godon, and Du Pont had previously failed to pay him proper respect.

Receiving the commodore's report, Secretary Paulding severely reprimanded the four lieutenants, a reprimand based on Hull's references to matters occurring prior to the ball. Paulding ordered it to be read before all the officers on board the *Ohio*.

At 11 A.M., 23 March 1840, the commodore and his aide boarded the ship and ordered all the senior officers on deck. Hull declared, "Gentlemen, I have sent for you to read a communication from the Secretary of the Navy. Some of you I understand talk of him as a Navy Agent, but I'll have you understand this comes from the President of the U.S. . . . You have treated me with contempt & dis-

---

* See H. A. du Pont, *Rear-Admiral Samuel Francis Du Pont, United States Navy* (New York, 1926), pp. 30–38.

respect. Some of you have not spoken to me for four months, there is a bad feeling all around, & it has been carried to another ship. . . ."

When he finished, the aide unrolled "the precious document. . . . This letter of Paulding's is beyond description," Frank wrote Sophie later, ". . . Filled with invective, foul innuendoes & bitter sarcasm. . . . *I* must be selected as a special victim. My letter to Cap^n Smith about not coming out of the orlop is alluded to as couched in disrespectful language. That my application to return had been disregarded, because I was not entitled to the indulgence. . . ."

After Hull read Paulding's reprimand, the officers turned and left. The junior officers then came on deck and were read Paulding's letter. Hull assured them that it was not meant for them, called them "his boys," warned them against making the department angry, and advised them to keep themselves "straight."

"This is," Frank advised Sophie, "one of the blackest pages of Naval History."

In response to this reprimand the four lieutenants wrote letters of conciliation to the commodore and the Secretary of the Navy.

Emboldened by the secretary's attitude, Hull ordered the four lieutenants to leave the squadron immediately and return to the United States in the store ship *Dormo,* which had been chartered to take home naval invalids from the Mediterranean. The lieutenants were to report by letter to the Secretary of the Navy on their arrival. Captain Smith, with a "sick ticket," and Dr. Ticknor, who had been relieved, were also returning on the *Dormo.*

The four officers moved ashore to await the store ship's arrival. The crew donated $500 to present Pendergrast and Du Pont with swords, but they themselves put a stop to it. Frank feared that "they will attack me [in Washington] on my orlop letter or to the one to Hull about the 'row' in Mahon. . . . We are sent home because we did not visit the Com's family—[the] . . . charge against us will dissolve into thin air, if we are allowed a hearing—depend upon this." Frank urged Sophie to contact his friends to "do anything to keep things cool at Washington about us before our arrival . . . for the pressure against us is heavy—& the issues they are endeavoring to make [are] false & foul. . . .

"The service is fast losing its hold on me as I have before told you. I wish I had never been placed in it, & been permitted to join the rest of the family in the more ordinary pursuits of life. I think men who feel strongly, of quick excitable temperament, are not fit for it—to be kept all one's life in a subordinate station, for the highest rank to be obtained alike by the intelligent & honorable, with the stupid . . . & immoral is a wrong state of things in my mind. One does not like to cast away . . . the labours of years, but in my present mood I think I could lay them down without a murmur. However a little sunshine drives away the mists of discontent and the mood I am in now will pass."

The *Dormo* sailed from Port Mahon on 14 April and, after a brief stay at Gibraltar, set a course for Boston. During the voyage Frank wrote down his thoughts about his relationship with Sophie. "I will have been married seven years this month, and the union has [been] to me one of . . . happiness and immeasurable profit. My precious Sophie has been an invalid most of this time, having been visited with constant physical suffering, and consequent trials still more severe to her refined feminine sensibilities. But I never knew her to commit an act that I would have had undone, or to utter a word that I would have had unsaid. She has been to me a judicious counsellor, a cheerful companion, a true friend, a loving wife. Her society has opened new sources of interest, new taste, [and] new delights.

"To the most angelic patience & resignation under trials and ailments, gentle, kind, and charitable, never so happy as when administering to the comfort & happiness of others, and always preferring the latter to herself, she adds qualities of the mind equally remarkable and attractive. Highly intellectual, highly educated and well informed, with refined literary tastes & poetic imagination . . . she unites the stronger traits of quick perception and sound judgment, and is with all so modest & diffident. . . . For over these qualities of the head & heart, a pure and holy Religion presides . . . guiding every movement—throwing in short its corrective & benign influence over every thought word, & deed. . . ."

After the *Dormo* arrived in Boston, Frank immediately departed for Delaware. In the quiet of home, he drafted a letter to Secretary Paulding, detailing the events of the past months. In part, it read, "Agreeable to an order from Commodore Hull of 31ˢᵗ March, I have the honor to report my arrival in the U.S. Though intending with as little delay as possible to solicit a personal interview, I will not lose a moment in removing if I can, the impressions which the course of the Comᵉ must create against me.

"Upwards of twenty four years in the service, a large portion of them actively employed in all classes of ships, and under commanders reputed for the severity of their discipline, I have passed through that period of time without reproach, as the records of the Department will testify. But I now find myself under no arrest or suspension, without charges, specifications, or explanation, and wholly unconscious of having done wrong, dismissed from the ship and squadron . . . in a manner and under circumstances calculated to reflect most injuriously upon my honor and reputation as an officer. A procedure which if emanating from the sentence of a Court Martial, would be considered among the most severe punishments which such a tribunal could inflict, short of positive dismissal from the service.

"On 23^d of March last with all the Ward Room officers of the *Ohio* and some others, I was sent for by Com^e Hull to listen to the reading of a communication from the Navy Department. That communication shows Sir, what unfavorable reports have reached you, reports concerning which I have been kept wholly in the dark, wholly ignorant while moving on with unabated zeal in the discharge of my duties. . . . The terrible censure applied to the officers generally was specially directed against me. . . . Commodore Hull . . . not satisfied with reading your communication to all the commissioned officers of the *Ohio* . . . sent for the Junior officers without exception . . . making remarks which reflected upon the character of his Lieutenants . . . [he] had . . . [your] communication also read to them, including that part concerning myself. I thus have been rebuked and punished in the most public manner, held up to the contempt of my juniors over whom I was in the daily exercise of authority, and all this without a hearing. . . . I have been deeply wounded Sir, by the severity of your censure, wholly undeserved. . . .

"It has been currently reported in the Navy Sir, that you have invited the officers to communicate with you unreservedly, if they have grieves to state them respectfully and your earnest desire to promote their welfare. Under this invitation I approach you Sir as an injured man; I appeal to you for Justice. . . ."

A week later Frank traveled to Washington. On his way he saw Louis McLane, statesman, diplomat, and family friend, who spoke a good deal of Paulding "in the most contemptuous terms. His unpopularity is excessive & conduces much to our strength."

Frank checked into Gadsby's, where he met Dr. Ticknor. They

decided to go to the Navy Department together and see Paulding and, "putting on our *harness,* about which his majesty the Secy is very particular, off we went."

At their arrival in audience room of the Navy Department, Frank asked a messenger to announce them to the secretary. " 'He is engaged just now with some of the members of Congress, but will soon be alone.' " Soon the congressional delegation came out of the office followed by Paulding. Seeing Frank and the doctor in full dress uniforms, he welcomed them. They bowed. Paulding hesitated "as if trying to recollect who it was." Suddenly, he said, " 'Mr. Du Pont I believe.' " He handed out his hand to Frank. "I had mine as straight as a Poker, but immediately accepted his." Frank introduced Ticknor. Then Paulding remarked, " 'I am sorry gentlemen I have to go over to the President's, it is Cabinet day. I shall be pleased to see you tomorrow morning.' " While returning to his office, he turned, and said, " 'I hope you have been well, Mr. Du Pont.' "

Frank replied, " 'Very well Sir, I hope you have enjoyed your health Sir.' " Paulding's manner exhibited "constrained, awkward graciousness, and I saw in a twinkling the reaction he had commenced."

On their way back to Gadsby's Frank told Ticknor, " 'it's all right, you'll find he is on the back track.' "

At the Washington Navy Yard, Frank related to his friend Captain Thomas H. Stevens the whole story, hoping that he would influence the secretary. "He stands very high with Paulding, & is one of the few favorites of the Dept." Pendergrast and Missroon arrived that day in Washington and reported that many Navy captains "are strong with us."

The next morning Frank had his interview with Paulding, who was "gracious, affable, & even kind." He spoke "as fair as a man could" and promised "to do everything that is right, urging me to let the matter rest in his hands, and not to carry it out of the Department, saying, 'I hope you will also have some patience, it is a delicate matter & I wish to read with attention and without interruption all the letters & reports—You shall have every line that Com^e H. has written about you, common justice demands that.' "

Paulding took the position that since verbal intercourse might be incorrectly recalled or interpreted, he wished "all to pass in writing on this subject, so that it may be filed & recorded." Frank agreed, but added, " 'I wish reparation for the injury done me by Com.

Hull in reading your communication to the juniors.' "

The secretary stopped him and said, " 'I must say this surprised me very much, & was not in accordance with my wishes or instructions—is such a thing ever done?' "

" 'No Sir,' " Frank replied, " 'it is one of the most extraordinary procedures I ever knew, & where an individual too was named as I was, it leaves me . . . without a shadow of defence, it is for such acts as these [that] I came here for your protection.' "

Seemingly "glad to be let off . . . more easy than he expected," Paulding said, " 'I trust the officers do not suppose that I have any personal feeling against you . . . [or the] others.' "

The secretary promised to reply to the officers' letters and added, " 'I presume you must all want to see your families, & this business can be as well transacted from a distance as by remaining here.' "

Du Pont finished by saying, " 'I find, Sir, I have after all spoken more, after y[ou]r request that all should be done in writing, than perhaps has been agreeable.' "

Paulding replied, " 'Not at all. I am very much pleased with this conversation.' "

The secretary followed Du Pont to the door and bade him good-bye. "I am sure," Frank wrote Sophie, "the thing that troubles him most, is the severity of his censure which has been much noticed in all our letters—We are now going to convey to him by intermediaries all that we could not say ourselves. . . . On the whole I am much pleased with our proceedings."

Before leaving Washington, he learned that Mrs. Hull and Miss Hart had reboarded the *Ohio* in Port Mahon, "bag & baggage," and that the ship was waiting for a wind to sail. "This was told to P[auldin]g . . . which seemed to stagger him." The Department "was so indignant that the ladies were continuing to cruise in the Ohio, that Paulding was going to send an order out to prevent them from returning home in the Ohio," Frank informed his friend Alexander Slidell Mackenzie.

Frank intervened to prevent such an order being sent. He told Mackenzie "that we had come for justice, had received it, but desired no retribution. It was true Mrs. Hull had turned me out of the ship, but I had no wish to turn her out. I am [a] pretty savage fellow in a chase, but it is foreign to my nature to triumph. To be involved in such affairs at all, is wholly repugnant to my feelings; I may pass with some of my friends as being Radically inclined, but they do me great injustice. If to be a Radical however consist[s] in a manly & unflinching assertion of rights secured by law & proper usage, a firm & legal resistance of wrong, a zealous discharge of duty & sincere devotion to the service, then I am perfectly willing to be considered."

Before returning home, Frank wrote Charles Davis, saying that he hoped he had acquainted him "with the nature of our return & dismissal from the Med^n Squadron, whose emblem of command should be a petticoat instead of a broad Pendant." After a lengthy condemnation of Hull, he added, "I am happy to say that our reception here has been most satisfactory." He confided that the "whole tone & feeling here is with us including the highest officers of the Government, even old Woodbury, the Atty-General, a personal friend of mine—and among the . . . Captains, we have met with every sympathy."

Frank urged Davis, who was living in Cambridge, Massachusetts, to go to the navy yard in Boston "in the most accidental way," and inform anyone of influence "casually how the land lies here [in Washington] with us. We want to wind up smoothly here."

After Frank's return to Louviers, he received a communication from Paulding, inviting him to visit the Department again and giving him the option of going to sea or staying on land. "He is also to write a letter," Frank told Pendergrast, "taking back his censure on the officers. He is convinced they have been wronged. The Com^e's last dispatches brought him to this conclusion."

Frank went to Washington to see the secretary. "The conduct of the Department," he wrote Davis, "has been admirable throughout, it has administered justice, & that with magnanimity. It has taken the whole onus of the business on its own shoulders, tracing our dismissal to P[auldin]g's letter . . . which severely censured us, & which was read to all the officers old & young. By this whole process, the justice which is awarded to us, falls with the least possible harshness on Hull."

At their meeting, Paulding read to Frank "the most full & magnanimous atonement to the officers of the Ohio that ever fell from an official functionary, & this is to be read to all persons who heard his letter of 16 Dec." Frank was convinced that since the officers had made no appeals to the public or Congress, "it had much to do with the result."

In part the secretary's letter to Hull read, ". . . In . . . promptly endeavoring to repair the injuries which may have been inflicted on the interests and feelings of these officials by an act which, though believed to be just and expedient at the time, is now, from subsequent explanations, admitted to have been otherwise, it is confidently expected that this example will have a salutary influence, and produce the restoration of that mutual harmony, respect, and confidence among the officers of the squadron in the Mediterranean, which is equally essential to the efficiency and reputation of the Navy and to the welfare of the country. . . ."

When Frank returned to Delaware, he took Sophie to Cape May for a short vacation. She reveled in their walks along the New Jersey shore. At the end of this pleasant interlude, having received a just resolution of his grievance and in response to gentle proddings of Paulding, Frank decided to rejoin the *Ohio* in the Mediterranean.

In early October 1840, he boarded the steamer *Britannia* at Boston for Europe. He had never before been on a transatlantic steamer, although his inspection of *Fulton II* at Washington had interested him in steam technology and its naval applications. He wrote Mackenzie from Boston setting forth his ideas on the probable effects the introduction of steam propulsion would have on warships.

"The Navy," he advised, "should consist of [one] hundred gun ships & steamers. The latter can never replace the former thank God, but I believe they will drive out everything below them. I hope Capt. Perry will turn out something handsome & efficient. I was much flattered two years ago by his offering me a situation with him. If I could have left home at the moment, I should have been tempted to join him & overcome my antipathy & prejudice against the sad change in our profession which we are threatened with, for the chivalry & mystic character of the sailor will vanish before it. We shall become mechanicians. . . . Besides I have no talents that way, so I stick to the ropes & sails & let others gather laurels amidst smoke & vapour as much as they please. . . .

"I would not have command of the Fulton or one of the new Frigates tomorrow. That steam is a necessary & powerful auxiliary to the Navy, must however be admitted, but in our day at least cannot in main replace or *lead* the large ships in action."

On board the *Britannia,* Frank eagerly learned all he could about steam. He talked at length with the engineer about the machinery, "and have been to see it as much as the intense heat will allow me. He is a Scot with such an accent I can hardly follow him. He is very fond . . . of his engines."

One evening the *Britannia* passed close to an English sailing ship and, although the wind was fair and she had all her sails set, "he seemed to be at anchor, so rapidly did we leave her—what a conquest is this steam over the elements—a journey of three thousand miles & be calculating within *hours* of the time of arrival is most extraordinary. With regard to these Atlantic steamers it is not so much in their swiftness that such brilliant results are attained as the ceaselessness of the *process*. Our engine has not been stopped one instant since we left Halifax, & the least we have gone has been nine miles [per hour], but mostly ten, & now eleven & twelve. . . . ."

The *Britannia* passed another English vessel moving in the same direction, "and it was a striking exhibition of steam over sails. We were going directly toward our port & in the eye of the wind at a rate of nine miles an hour, while she was standing off on a diagonal, some 60° from her course & at a rate of 5 the hour. The head wind & contrary sea have only impressed me more with the power steam."

On 15 October the *Britannia* arrived in Liverpool, having made the run from Boston in thirteen days and twelve hours—"this is good, but the same vessel has done better."

In England, Frank visited Birmingham, Warwick, Stratford-upon-Avon, Oxford, and London. The British railroads impressed him as "vastly superior to those in the U.S."

It was to be regretted that Americans were "so ignorant on Naval matters," he wrote. "In England it is quite different. . . . there is not a man or woman who does not know much of the British Navy, where noblemen go yachting for pleasure in the channel in Dec.—these naval matters are in the taste of the people, but with us, politics is the grand subject of all others."

Frank took a steamer to Antwerp, and while in Belgium he toured Brussels and tramped the battlefield at Waterloo.

Frank arrived in Paris in early November, realizing a lifelong dream. Sophie's nephew, James Bidermann—"a first rate fellow"—offered to be his guide. From Paris he wrote, "everything far exceeded my most sanguine expectations." Frank and his nephew visited museums, churches, gardens, "and points of interest such as the place de la Bastille." They attended the theater and opera. Frank described Versailles as "one of the wonders of the world. After all I had seen, I did not think I could be amazed further, but I was astounded. All other palaces seem to sink into secondary stations."

They toured the French countryside. "I have been delighted, instructed, & I hope informed by my journey. I have been cheerful & happy, but from some cause or other, I am more thoroughly American than I ever was in my life before. I have seen the land of my parents, the places where they once dwelt & moved, & there, with whom they conversed & were intimate in days past, all this I have done with feelings of deep sympathy, but I thank my God, that his providence led them to the other side of the waters & that my lot was there cast."

At the end of November Frank passed through Marseilles on his way to Toulon, where he missed making connections with the *Cyane*. He boarded a French steamer for Port Mahon and arrived there on 2 December 1840. He was reunited with Pendergrast, Missroon, and Godon when he rejoined the *Ohio*. After receiving a warm welcome from all the wardroom officers, he resumed his quarters in "the close air of the orlop."

The day after his arrival, he presented himself to the office. There he was introduced to the new commander, Captain E. A. F. La Vallette, a favorite of Hull's, and to Dr. Wilkinson, Ticknor's replacement. After Hull floundered "a little . . . like a struck Dolphin," Frank saluted "frankly & cordially," and handed Hull his orders. The conversation then became "unconstrained & Natural."

"True to my promise that I would return to pour oil on the waters," Frank wrote Sophie, "I find that spirit still within me and I trust nothing of an unpleasant kind will again occur. . . . In this ship all is quiet & harmony."

Several days later, he added, "I doubt if a man of war, with the same number on board was ever in a higher state of contentment & discipline. Our return has had the happiest effect, and I am now more than ever convinced that the Navy will be permanently benefitted by it."

Frank was overjoyed when he heard the news that General William Henry Harrison, "Old Tippecanoe," had been elected President over Martin Van Buren. "I wish to see if the Navy is to share the same neglect as from other Administrations—the leading men of the rising party are more essentially naval than any of the others. I know of more officers who have connecting links with the General than the whole Navy possessed before with those dirty fellows now in office."

As time passed, Frank came to regard Captain La Vallette as incompetent. "The Captain is no better than Smith . . . nor do I think half so good—for he stands in awe of the old man, more than the youngest midship[n] in the ship, whom he has disgusted in every way."

Ashore Frank found Port Mahon "dull" and socially drab. Although he attended Christmas services at the cathedral, he seldom ventured ashore, and for intellectual stimulation had "fallen back upon my books." As an antidote for boredom, he reinstated the Friday soirees, which he acknowledged were more successful than before. He was aware that the failure of Hull and the ladies to attend these parties was a snub and he was sensitive to the slight.

In 1837 an insurrection in the eastern provinces of Canada strained relations between the United States and England. Many Americans along the border, hopeful that the conflict might ultimately lead to the annexation of Canada by the United States, aided the rebels. After the initial uprising was suppressed, its defeated leaders found sanctuary and continued hostile raids into Canada from bases in the United States. In response Canadian officials crossed into the United States at night, and attacked and burned the American steamer, *Caroline,* which was supplying the dissidents. In the action an American was killed.

Amid mounting tension, Parliament ignored the American demand for reparations. When in 1840 Alexander McLeod, a Canadian suspected of participating in the action against the *Caroline,* was arrested in New York and brought to trial for murder and arson, the British government vigorously protested. It assumed responsibility and warned that McLeod's conviction would result in serious consequences. To the relief of the State Department, McLeod established an alibi and his trial resulted in his acquittal.

The furor over the McLeod case led to talk of hostilities. Frank believed that there was not "the slightest chance" of war—"commerce . . . which now rule[s] the world will . . . interfere again in this case to avert catastrophy. . . . The truth is nothing but an enemy's fleet, upon our coast, threatening the very existence of New York, will ever move our people. . . .

"You know how I feel as a citizen & Patriot, in this capacity I must wish to my country the blessings of an honorable peace—as any navy officer, the professional spark of ambition is within my breast & I am ready to lay down my life for my country & the

honor of my corps with zeal & alacrity—but the corps has been
. . . neglected. We shall be required and expected to do the work
of giants, while we are armed & prepared for an encounter with
pigmies.

"The English legislators know that in a war, the subjugation of
the U.S. is out of the question, however disastrous the war may
be—& they know that war will make the U.S. a great naval power,
& a great manufacturing nation—from these two sources the decline of England may begin."

His assessment caused him to scoff at the "old man," who Frank
wrote was "in positive terror of being blockaded next week by the
British fleet."

He roundly criticized the wardroom strategists: ". . . I wish . . .
my countrymen could have a little more national pride, in lieu of
vain boasting & silly vapouring, which seems to destroy all true
perception of our own vulnerable points, & the capabilities of England. We have much in our favor if a contest should come, very
much indeed to overcome the numerical superiority of the English. . . . The personel of the Navy . . . the country will have
reason to be proud of; but the work of giants is expected of them,
while the most inferior means are given them to accomplish it. . . .
Our good people [at home] now look upon the American Frigate as
a match for . . . [the] English . . . [ships]. Forgetting or never
knowing, that the latter have been gaining daily experience—are
fitted with all the improvements of the age—manned by a higher
order of seamen than ever before have been found in them—while
we have stood still—All these things we will feel, but only at the
commencement, after dearly bought experience, of both blood &
treasure we shall end and I believe gloriously, but we might so have
commenced."

The *Preble*'s arrival at Port Mahon brought news of a "threatening nature." The ship's company of the *Ohio* hastened preparations for sea. Crew members hauled up guns from the hold and
mounted them. They loaded extra provisions. A hurriedly called
council composed of officers from the *Ohio, Brandywine,* and *Preble,* after a meeting on board the *Brandywine,* advised Commodore
Hull to order the squadron back to the United States and place it
at the disposal of the Navy Department. They strongly believed that
the squadron was too inefficient to render effective service in the
Mediterranean. Hull disregarded their advice and refused to leave

the station unless he received orders from Secretary Paulding.

When the *Ohio* got underway from Port Mahon on 15 March 1841, the ladies remained ashore. "Everything is on a war footing." Frank urged Hull's staff to press him to go home "as the logical thing to do," but the commodore remained adamant.

In the Mediterranean off the coast of Spain, Frank wrote Sophie, ". . . every resource in the ship has been put to the test, to increase her efficiency & capability of resistance. The crew show an excellent spirit. . . . I think the ship will give a good account of herself and when the old man knows that *he is* in to fight, I have no doubt he will carry the ship into action with skill."

Officers realized that a shooting war, while not probable, was a possibility. "My life," Frank wrote Sophie, "belongs to my country, to serve her with zeal, with energy, with skill & devotion are the uppermost thoughts in my mind. I am seeking daily also to render my acts & conduct & thoughts more acceptable to God, which I feel will nerve me thrice over should the contest come. . . . I have great faith in your prayers, such prayers I am sure avail above. . . . I wish our country were better prepared."

Frank well remembered reading about the War of 1812, when a few English frigates with their boats had plundered American inland seas and burnt the nation's capital. Frank believed that confrontation of the English fleets of warships, flanked by "war steamers" would be "great and awful" at the first onset. Yet he stated he had "no fears of the results, not the slightest, for God has smiled upon our country through all her history, & will do so yet. . . ."

The *Ohio* rendezvoused with the *Preble*, who had just departed from Málaga harbor. Her officers relayed information that the tensions between Washington and London has eased. Frank appraised Hull's reaction. "You never saw a poor old man more elated—the pressures of a thousand pounds seem to have been lifted off him."

Throughout April and May the *Ohio* continued to patrol the Mediterranean. Finally, Hull received orders to return home. After the *Ohio* put in at Port Mahon to pick up the ladies, she stopped briefly at Málaga and Gibraltar before moving out into the Atlantic headed for Boston.

While at sea, Frank vented his feelings to Sophie. "Our mess still hangs together, but the cement is of scarcely sufficient tenacity to accomplish this—selfishness, selfishness, seems to be the pervading sin. I fear there is more of it in the Navy than elsewhere.

143

"Pendergrast said the other day, 'I never should have forgiven you, if you had not returned [to the *Ohio*], we should all have *gone to pieces* here if you had not come.' I told him I had done so because I considered it my duty to myself, to my rank, & to the Navy, but I doubted much, if any other man in it, situated as I had been, with so much to detain me, & so little to get, by coming, would have done it—that I looked upon all patriotism, esprit de corps, sense of right, manly & moral independence of spirit as gone in the Navy if it ever existed. Another thing that has strengthened my disgust for the Navy—is to survey & see what perfect absurdity, of what utterly baseless material its reputation is composed of.

"Take this present cruise—a more worthless execution of the objects intended to be accomplished cannot be selected—a man more wholly incapable, could not be selected—a man more unfit & unworthy to be placed over honorable men or in a high command. No man of any character can be associated with him & not form a contemptible opinion of him. Yet this cruise will be looked upon as successful. . . ."

On 14 July the *Ohio* eased into Boston Harbor. When Hull was relieved, Frank hurried home to Delaware and immediately took Sophie to Cape May for a well-earned vacation.

XI

"I feel in good spirits about the future"

During the War of 1812 and, indeed, for centuries preceding it, fighting ships had depended on sails for mobility, and on smooth-bore, muzzle-loading cannon for offensive operations. But in the period between 1815 and 1865, the navies of the world underwent momentous and revolutionary change. They adopted steam propulsion, propellers replaced paddle wheels, wooden sides and decks were strengthened by armor plate, iron hulls replaced wooden, smoothbores were outmoded by rifled cannon, and solid shot gave way to percussion-fused shells.

Of these various changes, the introduction of the steam warship was the most far reaching in its strategic and tactical consequences. No other invention so significantly influenced naval warfare and the basic elements contributing to sea power. The obvious advantage of steam over sail was to render ships independent of the wind. At first captains used engines primarily as auxiliaries to sails.

In 1814 Robert Fulton constructed the first steam paddle-wheel warship, the *Demologos,* sometimes called *Fulton I,* for the defense of New York Harbor. The *Demologos* stimulated little interest among American naval authorities. Except for the *Sea Gull,* which the Navy purchased to pursue pirates in the Caribbean, the *Demologos* remained the only steam warship in the United States Navy until she was destroyed by an explosion in 1829.

In 1835 Lieutenant Matthew C. Perry induced the Board of Navy Commissioners to commence construction of a steam warship, *Fulton II,* a wooden, side-wheel, harbor defense steamer. The satisfactory performance of *Fulton II* led Congress to authorize two additional steam warships, the wooden side-wheelers *Mississippi* and *Missouri*.

In 1842, Congress decided to build a gunboat for service on the Great Lakes. The Navy took a momentous step when it authorized an iron hull for this gunboat. As the only rolling mills capable of handling the ship's plates were in Pittsburgh, the *Michigan* was fabricated there, and assembled and launched at Erie, Pennsylvania.

By the 1840s, the advantages of steam propulsion were obvious, but so were its disadvantages. Paddle wheelers had serious drawbacks. A side-wheeler suffered from unequal stresses when rolling and tossing in heavy seas. Engines, boilers, and paddle wheels were all vulnerable to damage by enemy gunfire.

The reluctance of Americans to adopt steam was overcome by the development of the screw propeller. Through political influence, Captain Robert F. Stockton pressured the Navy in 1843 to authorize the building of the screw sloop of war *Princeton* to the specifications of the Swedish shipbuilder John Ericsson.

During the 1850s, the United States Navy launched the Merrimack class of fast, screw-propelled, steam wooden frigates. *Merrimack, Minnesota,* and *Roanoke* were generally regarded as the finest of their type in the world. By the outbreak of the Civil War in 1861, the navies of the United States, Great Britain, and France regarded fighting ships lacking steam propulsion as obsolete.

The adoption of the steam man-of-war drastically altered naval strategy and tactics. Warships could now move across oceans at a constant speed in direct lines, instead of traveling devious routes caused by the fluctuation of the prevailing winds. Although steam propulsion increased maneuverability, the logistics of supplying squadrons with fuel acted as a brake on full acceptance.

At approximately the same time as the United States was launching the *Demologos,* Henri-Joseph Paixhans of the French Army was inventing a gun that could fire explosive shells horizontally. This innovation was soon introduced into the French Navy and, later, into other navies of the world. Until Paixhans's shell gun, the thirty-two pounder had been the standard heavy broadside weapon of western navies. The effects of shell fire on unarmored, wooden ships was devastating.

In 1856, the United States Navy introduced a gun developed by Commander John Dahlgren, a gun that predominated in the naval engagements of the Civil War. These smoothbores were of nine-, ten-, and eleven-inch caliber, originally designed to fire shells, but later modified to use solid shot against the ironclads.

After the introduction of the smoothbore cannon, a new factor emerged, which influenced the trend of ordnance design. This was the introduction of the rifled gun. These began superseding the smoothbores, and with them came the elongated, pointed projectiles that displaced spherical shot and shell. The rifling in barrels gave spin to the steamlined projectiles, increasing range and accuracy. Although conservative Americans experimented with rifled cannon, the United States Navy long resisted the trend toward rifles and, throughout the Civil War and for years afterward, the smoothbore Dahlgren remained standard armament.

After the invention of the shell gun, forward-looking men perceived the necessity of introducing armor on warships. In 1859, France launched the first seagoing ironclad steamer, the *Gloire*. Two years later the British commissioned the *Warrior* and, during the Civil War, the United States sent to sea many iron-hulled monitors.

During the years between the War of 1812 and the Civil War, the primary function of the United States Navy was the promotion and protection of American trade. "A commerce such as ours," remarked the Secretary of the Navy in 1842, "*demands* protection of an adequate naval force. Our people . . . have a right to require the presence of our flag, to give assurance to all nations that their country has both the will and the power to protect them."

While the Navy maintained its frigates and sloops of war on distant stations, it sent others out on exploring and surveying expeditions. Certainly no voyage of the first half of the nineteenth century stimulated more interest than the United States Exploring Expedition (1838–42), commanded by Lieutenant Charles Wilkes, and none returned with as much information relating to the Pacific Ocean area. With a corps of scientists on board, the squadron discovered a broad sector of the Antarctic continent and many Pacific islands and reefs, surveyed numerous previously unknown waters, and explored what is now the northwest coast of the United States.

Unsuccessful attempts to open diplomatic relations with Japan led President Millard Fillmore to decide that a show of force was necessary. In command of the East India Squadron, Commodore Matthew C. Perry was asked to deliver a personal letter from the chief executive addressed to the Japanese emperor and was empow-

147

ered to negotiate a treaty guaranteeing protection for American lives and property in Japan and free access by United States' ships to ports for supplies and trade.

The paddle-wheel frigates *Mississippi* and *Susquehanna* and the sailing sloops of war *Plymouth* and *Saratoga* got underway for Japan from Hong Kong and dropped anchor in Edo Bay on 8 July 1853. This visit, followed by another in February 1854, resulted in Perry's negotiated treaty, which opened two Japanese ports to American shipping.

Official and unofficial reports of these ventures were published in the United States. Charles Wilkes's *The Narrative of the United States Exploring Expedition* became an immediate best-seller and earned much favorable publicity for the Navy. The first volume of Commodore Perry's *Narrative of the Expedition of an American Squadron to the China Seas and Japan* ranks among the classics of exploration and adventure.

After Frank and Sophie returned from their summer sojourn at Cape May, Frank's appraisal of his experience on the *Ohio* had changed. To Mackenzie, he wrote, "My cruise I look upon as the most important service of my life, and I would not on any account have exchanged my station on board for anything short of the command of a sloop of war." He remained deeply concerned with the efficiency of the Navy, and predicted, "If some means are not adopted to secure the commands of our ships & squadrons to men capable of filling those important stations, the Navy will lose all hold on the country."

Du Pont was heartened to learn that Abel P. Upshur had succeeded Paulding as Secretary of the Navy. "He is," Frank wrote Davis, "a noble & just man and I have the highest hopes of his administration. . . . he is going to push for getting all our ships in commiss[io]n & the building of twenty new sloops. . . . He is quite shocked at the chaotic state of the Dept.—says the Navy is governed without law."

In December, Frank set off for Washington to meet with Upshur and to ask for promotion to commander. The secretary told Frank to submit his request in writing and promised to lay Du Pont's case before the President.

Frank ran around Washington rallying support. He talked to Delaware senators Thomas Clayton and Richard H. Bayard. In particular he wanted the backing of Bayard, who sat on the Naval Affairs Committee. He also wrote the chairman of the Senate Naval Affairs Committee about his appointment, and asked Pendergrast, who had already been promoted, to say a word about him to the new naval secretary. "This would have more effect than all that has yet been done."

In March 1842, Frank returned to Washington to press Secretary Upshur about his promotion, to urge Senator Bayard to use his influence, and to prod his naval colleagues to appear before the Naval Affairs Committee on his behalf. "I do not think I can do anything more with proper self respect," he wrote Pendergrast.

In June the vessels of the Wilkes exploring expedition to the Pacific returned to New York Harbor. When the expedition had been sent out in 1838, it was poorly organized, badly equipped, and charged with an almost impossible task. Wilkes had kept things together in adversity and carried out his mission remarkably well. To achieve success, he had resorted to drastic measures. When he arrived in New York Harbor, Wilkes faced charges of cruelty, disobedience to orders, ordering illegal punishments, illegally detaching enlisted men from the Navy, and conduct unbecoming an officer. The Navy Department ordered a court-martial.

Frank was in Delaware when he learned of his appointment as a member of the court-martial to be held on board the *North Carolina*, the Navy's receiving ship, at the Brooklyn Navy Yard, beginning on 25 July.

When he arrived in New York to stay with his bachelor friend, Dr. Wily, in Brooklyn, he discovered that Wilkes was spoken of with extreme bitterness by everyone. He was pleased, as he wrote to Sophie, that Commodore Matthew C. Perry, commandant of the navy yard, considered the "placing of me on the Court Martial was the highest compliment that could have been paid me, & brought me before the Public at the close of my career as a Lieutenant, in the most honorable position."

In addition to Du Pont, members of the court included Commodore Charles Stewart, president, eight captains, two commanders, and one other lieutenant. Noting that there were only three members with whom he was acquainted, Wilkes argued that it was a "picked court" and believed most of the members were indisposed to do him justice. At Wilkes's request the court agreed to take up his case after those of his subordinate officers, Passed Midshipman

William May, lieutenants Robert E. Johnson and Robert F. Pinkney, and Assistant Surgeon C. F. B. Guillou.

The judge advocate was Charles H. Winder of Baltimore, whom Wilkes described as "a young man without any knowledge of law, and destitute of character, and devoid of truth, who was a pet of the Secretary, and ready to do his bidding." Philip Hamilton represented Wilkes, his friend.

The court was organized, and Frank thought "a good mood & general cordiality" marked its opening session. He had a young man's reaction to serving with so many high-ranking officers who, he believed, blocked his chances of promotion as long as they remained on active duty. To Pendergrast, he confided, "It is melancholy to see . . . the high physical condition of these old cocks, they look better & fresher than I remember any of them ten years ago."

The court first tried Passed Midshipman May on charges of "insubordination and mutinous conduct," and of "disrespect of his superior in the execution of his office." *

"One of the witnesses examined today," Frank explained to Sophie, "showed by his manner & tone, as well as the force of his words, that bitter & heartburning hostility which pervades the officers of the Exploring Exp. against their commander. The court is crowded with them, hanging on every word that is said with an intensity of interest & feeling that I have never seen equalled. I have seen frequently excitement on shipboard, & in squadrons, but the indignation which seems to pervade these young men, must have sprung from some cause not usual in the service. . . .

"On the other hand, Wilkes seems perfectly selfposs[ess]ed. He was examined today as a witness . . . he looks broken & very old, however."

Frank became convinced that all the charges lodged against the young officers were trivial and, he wrote, "those against Wilkes himself are not much more serious—he was a disagreeable, overbearing & disgusting commander, but I doubt if he has transcended his authority, & the whole matter could easily have been arranged by the Secret[ar]y."

After May's short trial, the court decided that he had been disrespectful, and sentenced him to be publicly reprimanded.

* For details of the Wilkes court-martial, see David B. Tyler, *The Wilkes Expedition* (Philadelphia, 1968), pp. 375–85.

When May's case ended, Frank wrote Sophie, "things occurred which astounded me, and I now do not regret my orders [to the court-martial], for I have done *good* & *can do more*. . . . I am useful here to the cause of justice & propriety."

Lieutenant Johnson's trial followed. Accused of giving away public property and of refusing to obey orders, Johnson was acquitted of both charges.

Assistant Surgeon Guillou's trial lasted three days. Of the six charges against him, the court decided he was guilty of four, including disobedience, neglect of duty, disrespect, and disobedience to orders. The court sentenced him to dismissal from the Navy.

Lieutenant Pinkney's trial—"long and tedious"—was complicated and lasted from 6 to 13 August. The court found him guilty on two of six charges, namely, "treating a superior with contempt" and "disobedience of orders." The court sentenced him to a public reprimand by the Secretary of the Navy and to six months' suspension from duty.

Wilkes's trial dragged on until 7 September. The "excited tone" of the judge advocate, whenever he mentioned Wilkes, caused uneasiness in the court. Frank earnestly believed such "impertinance" toward Wilkes was unjustified and asked several senior members of the court to intervene, but they refused. On 20 August "it went beyond endurance," and Frank himself interrupted and "arrested it."

"I am," he told Sophie, "determined to do justice to all, as far as it is in my power, & is proper with my age here—but I will not countenance arrogance towards Wilkes than I would sustain the latter in such a course towards others. . . .

"I find this the most wearisome duty that I have yet performed in the Navy. . . . On the other hand it is considered the most important duty that I could be ordered upon, & it would in no manner have done to have got excused. I am therefore patient under the vexation."

Later, during the proceedings, Frank confided to Sophie, "The trials have evinced nothing creditable to Wilkes' capacity as an officer, showing how unfit he was in many respects for his command. . . . On the other hand he seems to have laboured beyond precedent, & required others to do the same—his forte is a skillful use of instruments—but the young men under him say he is a great quack in real science."

After a long and tedious trial, the court exonerated Wilkes of all charges except those relating to illegal punishment, for which he received a Navy Department reprimand. Secretary Upshur's letter to Wilkes "is looked upon as the severest & most withering reprimand ever penned."

While the court was not in session Frank sought out friends. He dined with Missroon at the Astor, spent an evening at Commodore Perry's quarters, heard a sermon by Reverend Wilmer at the Navy Yard chapel, and called on Commodore Shubrick, who introduced him to James Fenimore Cooper, with whom he struck up "quite an acquaintance—I was struck more with his intelligence, than with his manner—he is very naval, fond of naval anecdotes, [and] tells [a] good many 'Joe Millers.' " He asked Sophie if she needed anything from New York. "I told you that orange has succeeded blue. Shawls are much worn. Velvet & embroidered velvet scarfs & mantellas are yet worn."

After sitting on other courts-martial at the Navy Yard, Frank returned home in mid-October. "I am heartily wearied with my judicial labours," he wrote Davis, "though not regretting on the whole my orders, however much they have broken up my social existence this last summer. The intimate knowledge which I have gained of the present condition of the Navy in general; the still greater insight into the characters of those who govern it—the meeting of many more acquaintances . . . have been valuable sources of consolation."

On 28 October 1842, Frank was promoted to commander, and in November he, Pendergrast, and two other officers were summoned to Washington by Secretary Upshur to help revise the *Rules and Regulations* of the Navy. Although he regarded the duty as "onerous & thankless," Frank could not refuse "such a compliment" from Upshur. He checked into Fuller's City Hotel and went to the navy yard to begin work.

In early December, the brig *Somers*, Alexander Slidell Mackenzie commanding, sailed into New York Harbor. Mackenzie was the brother-in-law of Commodore Perry. Other personnel of the *Somers* included First Lieutenant Guert Gansevoort; Lieutenant Matthew C. Perry Jr., who at twenty-one had eight years' naval service; Oliver H. Perry II, the commodore's seventeen-year-old son, who was captain's clerk; and Henry Rodgers, younger son of the old commodore.

Among those who had originally sailed in the *Somers* were Samuel Cromwell, a bearded, bewhiskered boatswain's mate and senior petty officer, and Elisa Small, captain of the main top. Both had served in slave ships before enlisting in the service, and Cromwell, if not a former pirate, had gained knowledge of piratical procedure. Also on board was nineteen-year-old midshipman Philip Spencer. This young man, recommended by Commodore Perry, belonged to one of the first families of New York. His father, John Canfield Spencer, a noted attorney of the Albany bar, was the current Secretary of War.

On her outward voyage the *Somers* was a happy ship. Along the west coast of Africa the brig patrolled and searched for slavers. But on her return passage to New York, the atmosphere on board the ship changed drastically. The crew grumbled and obeyed orders grudgingly. The *Somers* became the scene of near mutiny. In an apparent plot to seize the ship and convert her to piracy, Spencer had enlisted a score or more men.

Overestimating the seriousness of the affair, and aware of the risk of holding dangerous prisoners in irons, Mackenzie consulted his officers and on his own authority hanged Spencer, Cromwell, and Small from the yardarm. No courts-martial were held. When the brig arrived in New York, the incident aroused nationwide controversy.

Frank was in Washington when he read about the *Somers* affair in the *Intelligencer*. Immediately, on 19 December, he wrote Mackenzie. "The *Intelligencer* has just dropped from my hand and left me with awe & admiration; you have immortalized yourself, and should be placed in no emergency that you would not meet like a man. . . . What an awful alternative, but how nobly you have met it! No battle could have gained you so enviable a position. I have seen but few persons since the news has arrived, among those there is but one opinion.

"The benefit to result to the service from this is incalculable. I presume it will be a death blow to reinstatements of worthless officers through political influence. . . ."

The Navy Department convened a court of inquiry, which met on 28 December on board the *North Carolina*. The court was composed of three commodores, all veterans of the War of 1812. Charles Stewart was its president. Ogden Hoffman, federal attorney general for New York, served as judge advocate. Commodore Perry's son-in-law, John Hone, was Mackenzie's secretary. Perry received word from a congressman in Washington that Secretary of War

Spencer was urging that Mackenzie be tried for murder by a civilian court.

From Washington Frank wrote Mackenzie again. "I wish to assure you . . . of my entire devotion & my anxiety to serve you in some way or other." He said that he would come to New York to assist Mackenzie in the trial. "Your friends have no anxiety about the result but that every human being in the country should view in its fullest extent the heroism & self devotion of your conduct. . . . but to the class who are averse to [the] shedding of blood under any circumstances—to those who have no idea of the elements & consequences of mutinies on the high seas, or the responsibility which rest on those who have lives & property under their charge—there will be required a clear exhibition of the impending danger. . . .

"You must be prepared to find a bitter, unscrupulous, & very able & dexterous enemy in the Secretary of War—his machinations & his malignity go hand in hand—he will endeavor to set forth the transaction as an act of personal panic, instead of high moral courage. . . ."

In January 1843, Frank wrote Perry, "Public opinion is still divided, though I have reason to believe that a majority in both houses is with Mackenzie—other are savage in their opposition."

On board the *North Carolina* the court questioned every officer of the *Somers,* twenty-two enlisted men, and sixty-eight of the seventy-four apprentices.* The court sat until 19 January and the next day Commodore Stewart pronounced its findings—"The immediate execution of the prisoners was demanded by duty and justified by necessity." The conduct of Mackenzie and his officers "was prudent, calm and firm, and he and they honestly performed their duty to the service of their country."

But before the court of inquiry had adjourned, Secretary Upshur, at Mackenzie's request, ordered him tried by a court-martial. Mackenzie believed that only by a court-martial could he be properly vindicated of all charges. He feared that without such a proceeding Secretary Spencer might engineer his indictment on a murder charge in a civil court.

In Washington Frank worked to rig the court with members

---

*Background information on the court of inquiry and subsequent court-martial comes from Samuel Eliot Morison, *"Old Bruin," Commodore Matthew C. Perry* (Boston, 1967), pp. 144–62.

friendly to Mackenzie's cause. He contacted several eligible captains to see how they stood and interviewed Secretary Upshur at his home about the makeup of the court. "We have at last arranged a court which I think will please you," he wrote Commodore Perry on 23 January. Unfortunately for Mackenzie, Upshur changed his mind and withdrew four names that Frank had suggested. "I had my doubts about the court," Frank wrote Davis later. "I never liked the change which had been made in its composition at Washington."

The court-martial, composed of eleven captains and two commanders, with Captain John Downes as president, convened on board the *North Carolina* on 2 February and, shortly afterward, adjourned to the chapel in the navy yard. The judge advocate, William H. Norris Esq., was a relative of Spencer's. Counsel for the defense was Ebenezer Griffen Esq., "a lawyer of great reputation on criminal cases."

On the first day of the proceedings, Frank sat in attendance and afterward went to Commmodore Perry's quarters to meet with Mackenzie. His friend's supporters seemed profoundly grateful for Frank's services in Washington and thanked him for his help in forming the court. "Things look very well just now," Frank informed Sophie, "the court are all that could be wished." However, Frank was concerned that the judge advocate was "very raw," unacquainted as he was with his duties in a naval court, and "some think he is a tool of Mr. Spencer."

As the sessions continued Mackenzie appeared "calm, placid, & shows to great advantage—he is still sought out like a wild beast & people come in to Court and enquire first for him always. . . . McK^e is still deeply affected when the testimony touches the execution & its attendant scenes."

The "Court are doing & will do what is right. I think myself it is uncommonly sound in its sense of what is just & proper."

He spent many evenings with Perry and Mackenzie in the commodore's quarters. On one occasion, Du Pont, at his friend's request, accompanied Mackenzie to Griffen's quarters to hear the defense read. Already Frank regretted the choice of Griffen. As they heard the argument Du Pont offered many suggestions. "I may do more good in this way, than I have yet done, by keeping out any incongruous matter. I must tell you from all I have heard of Mr. G[riffen] it has not been a fortunate selection. He is an old lawyer, overwhelmed with the magnitude of his undertaking, says he is

writing for the *civilized* world, knows nothing of naval matters, &
is enormously high in charges [fees]—why he was selected I cannot
tell."

"The tone & spirit are unexceptionable," Frank wrote Davis,
"some parts excellent & eloquent, but so inferior to what . . . [oth-
ers] would have done that I was disappointed, though it was better
than I had been led to expect."

At Frank's suggestion, Mackenzie retained the services of Theodore Sedgwick Esq., a famed New York lawyer and publicist. He
was worried about Mackenzie. ". . . the tediousness of the trial has
nearly brought him to the end of his patience, & there are things
constantly occur[ring] which fret him dreadfully. For example . . .
Gansevoort's evidence was the worst & most perplexed I ever heard,
doing neither justice to himself nor to the cause, & in several in-
stances grating to McK beyond endurance—for example, making
himself appear very flourishing & heroic & McK occup[y]ing a secondary part, intentionally of course, yet importunate—but the principal point . . . escaped all the inimical reporters."

On the following day Frank arrived early at the navy yard and
counseled Gansevoort before he resumed his testimony hoping to
"do him service." His advice helped matters, for the lieutenant became a stalwart witness for the defense, withstood a vigorous cross-
examination, and flatly stated his belief that the *Somers* could never
have been brought into port but for the executions.

As the sessions dragged on, Frank returned home. On 21 February he wrote Pendergrast, "It was with difficulty that I could get
away from Brooklyn. Had I not been so long without a single quiet
day at home, I should have remained with McK, who . . . is left
without any intimate naval friend but Perry. I think I was of service
to him in a good many ways, but principally in a social way &
keeping his mind cheerful. He has had an awful road to travel, annoyances of every description were daily springing up, & the tediousness of the present trial. . . . The Judge Adv. is a scoundrel
. . . [and] very malicious. . . ."

A month later, learning that Mackenzie was ill, Frank interrupted
his visit home and went back to New York. He found Mackenzie
much better after "terrific treatment." After attending the trial, Frank
wrote Sophie, "I confess the infamy of the Jud. Adv. threw me off
balance for a little while & I never felt so much like trying to pick
a quarrel with a man & giving him a whipping, for ten years past."

Du Pont reported that a majority of the court were "savage against the Judge Adv.," and considered he was "a spy on their actions." Writing about Mackenzie's ordeal, Frank said, ". . . there never was a man so . . . infamously tortured in this country—on the other hand the public mind never was so much with him. . . . All the newspapers . . . have come to the rescue with a fierceness that has roused the whole community."

On 29 March as Mackenzie was in better health, Frank returned to Delaware where he received orders to report to the Ordnance Bureau, which sent him to New York for duty.

On 1 April the court-martial issued its verdict. It dropped two charges against Mackenzie. On every other charge the verdict was "not proved." During the nearly four months of the inquiry and trial, the *Somers* affair had been discussed nationwide. No case of the century, prior to the assassination of President Lincoln, aroused as much passion. Opinion varied. Captain Robert F. Stockton, who refused service on the court on the ground that he had already made up his mind, would have voted to hang Mackenzie. Several hundred New York and Boston merchants signed memorials to Mackenzie, praising his conduct. Support also came from a series of letters to the press by Richard Henry Dana, author of *Two Years Before the Mast,* who knew life at sea from the common sailor's point of view.

A strong anonymous attack on Mackenzie was made in the pamphlet *Cruise of the Somers: Illustration of the Despotism and the Unmanly Conduct of Commander Mackenzie.* A far more cutting review came from the pen of James Fenimore Cooper. In his *Review of the Proceedings of the Naval Court Martial,* he used every argument to prove Mackenzie to be an incompetent commander.

At the Brooklyn Navy Yard Frank was delighted to find Missroon assigned to the same duty with the Ordnance Bureau. "There are an immense number of old guns, unfit for use, which must be marked as such, shot also." Captain Alexander Wadsworth wanted a drawing made and a history of every cannon written out before each piece was sold for scrap.

Getting to work in earnest both Du Pont and Missroon believed the work would be finished quickly, "although the duty will be laborious, but is necessary—there is a great accumulation of *old horrors.*" Since his friend John Wily was hosting guests at his quarters, Frank roomed with Missroon at Mansion House.

Routinely, Frank and Missroon breakfasted before 8 A.M., started work before 9, and continued until 5 P.M. It took them three-quarters of an hour to reach Mansion House, traveling part of the distance by boat, so it was 6:30 P.M. before they could dine. Between supper and bedtime, Frank labored for two hours writing reports.

Missroon grew disgusted with the monotony of the work and considered applying to leave the Ordnance Bureau, but Frank persuaded him to stick it out. "I never shift duty when I am on it," he wrote Sophie, and "on this occasion I have taken great pains. . . . You would be astonished at the amount of writing, tedious ruling I have done."

One weekend Frank visited Rockwood, Mackenzie's home near Tarrytown, New York. The Mackenzies seemed cheerful, although the commander was "annoyed at being relieved from his brig. . . ." "I must say," Frank wrote Sophie, "I have never witnessed stronger external evidence of conscious rectitude of conduct than Mack^ie has exhibited. . . . I am convinced he has never yet had a doubt himself of the propriety of his course."

In early summer Frank returned to Delaware and vacationed with Sophie at Cape May. After this break he went back to the Brooklyn Navy Yard to finish the ordnance business. While there orders arrived to command the brig *Perry.* "What this has sprung from I cannot imagine," a disgruntled Du Pont wrote Sophie. "It's probably the start of a new system, in giving small vessels to commanders, but that they should have commenced by selecting me, who was on other duty I cannot comprehend. . . .

"This is part of my luck. I have had nothing but hard work & expense in this Ordnance duty, & just as some leisure & instruction were coming from the higher branches of it, I am shipped off. Though extremely disgusted & mortified, my path of duty is plain & with a new broom in the Dept., & the present condition & disrepute of the Navy, I cannot evade, or wish to change the matter. . . . I hope you will bear this disappointment & change in the happy future we had laid out for ourselves the other day."

The *Perry* lay anchored at Norfolk, a new brig "well spoken of." "The more I think of the order [to the *Perry*] under all the circumstances, the more indignant I feel—to compel me to go when others ought by every sense of justice to go, or place me in the very trying predicament of refusing sea service, has caused me deep annoyance."

After a stopover in Delaware, Frank headed for Washington. "It's out of the question to talk of getting off . . . the selection was entirely of the Secy. . . . You will be disappointed when I tell you . . . that the Brig goes to China."

Frank learned in Washington that the State Department had sent a commissioner, Caleb Cushing, with a considerable number of ships, to China to arrange a commercial treaty. He would sign a treaty on 3 July 1844, opening several Chinese ports to American merchants. When Du Pont reached China, he was to report to Cushing as an attaché. Frank's initial reaction to receiving command of the *Perry* was altered. Once the *Perry* had completed duty in China, Frank's long-cherished dream of circumnavigating the globe would be realized and he was happy at the prospect.

To a friend, he wrote, there "is a bright side to my orders to the Perry . . . the service is special & honorable, the selection intended to be as complimentary. . . . the vessel though undersized for such a voyage, is new & will probably be as comfortable as one of her class can be. . . . I could not look for a larger command for years."

By letter he asked Mackenzie to give "some general hints" about the management of brigs in gales, "the best mode of lying to, the best sailing trim." Mackenzie responded immediately, giving Frank detailed information obtained from East Indian traders and sending along a box with his commander's epaulettes. Do Pont was touched. "They will be the *first* pair to grace my shoulders and trust they will impart to me some of your zeal & efficiency as an officer. I value them greatly."

In September 1843, Frank, at the Gosport Navy Yard in Norfolk, took command of the *Perry*. "Though I have heard much of her . . . yet I must say . . . [she] more than realize[d] my expectations. She is in the first place most beautiful & larger than I thought—the Cabin is certainly very small—yet so superior to the accommodations of the other vessels. . . .

"I am very pleased with my officers. My crew though incomplete is very orderly, indeed I have never known so quiet a set of men, anxious to do their work. . . ." William R. Taylor was the *Perry's* first lieutenant, "a man of the highest competency, industry & force. . . ."

Frank returned to Delaware for a few days before sailing. From home, he wrote Mackenzie, "Our rival brig Lawrence . . . [came] down alongside us. She is 70 tons larger than the Perry with more accommodations, comforts for the crew and officers and more capacity for storage, yet I know not I would exchange, so much more a man of war look has the Perry and . . . will outsail her easily."

Returning to Norfolk in mid-November, Frank wrote Sophie, ". . . the men are getting a little tired of behaving well. I had to punish one yesterday. I took occasion to tell them of my future line of conduct—that every indulgence & comfort should be granted them, which the service & their conduct would permit me to extend to them. But I would rigidly enforce the regulations of the service. It seemed to have a good effect, yet I wish we were at sea, where everything would soon be regulated—here the work is hard, they are not yet comfortable & it is difficult to keep them in good humor."

On the eve of sailing, he wrote, "I feel in good spirits about the future. I have found myself heretofore come up to emergencies & responsibilities put upon me—my whole mind & attention will be given to my duties—my health is strong & promising, my brig has been fitted with an eye to what may be encountered, as far as a vessel of her class can admit, & she has a good & lucky name, not an indifferent circumstance to seamen. . . . I can only see success ahead. . . ."

Later, he added, "Last night it was gloomy & sad, as I sat alone in my little cabin, thinking of the future & what time had to elapse, & what distances had to be passed over, before we should meet again."

The *Perry* set sail from Hampton Roads for Rio de Janeiro on 2 December 1843. Officers and crew "bid adieu to our Pilot which seemed [like] severing the last link which united us still to our country & friends." Cape Henry faded in the distance.

On the following day, a gale struck the *Perry* and increased "to a tempest . . . the brig behaving beautifully, the waves rose to a fearful height & seemed every moment they would reach us, the fury of the winds kept us in advance of them—yet it was a dangerous operation. . . . It was an awful night. . . ." Although the winds, rain, and sea moderated occasionally, it took "ten days of hardship, by far the hardest & most trying that I ever passed at sea. Our little vessel has been sorely tried . . . she proved herself equal in every emergency. . . ."

The storm over, Sunday services were held. Du Pont wished that a chaplain were on board to instruct the men in religious matters, "but I would take it upon myself to say, that every man who gave

160

a thought to his Creator & who dwelt upon his own future state, & tried to prepare himself for it, would find the day come sooner or later, when he would consider moments so passed as the best spent of his life."

Frank read the service with "gravity & composure." Lieutenant Taylor and the surgeon read the responses. After the service, Frank read the *Articles of War*. "All seemed much pleased. . . . After all our gales & risks they were probably in a frame of mind to be a little more impressed than usual."

During his leisure moments, Frank perused the religious commentaries Sophie had sent, which "have done me much benefit. I am satisfied now, that I have made great progress in religious feeling & hope." He promised Sophie that he intended to be confirmed. "I left with regret, that I had put it off too long."

"I believe," Frank confided to Sophie later in this voyage, ". . . at last that my heart is changed, that the seed under God's mercy planted by yr. hand has germed at last—that I cannot believe any thing will deter me now from a continued, zealous, & heartfelt struggle to become a penitent & sincere follower of Christ. . . . a dreadful homesickness again coming over me I sought in every way to overcome it—& at last found relief in prayer."

He took advantage of the fine weather to exercise the crew at the cannon, to hand out fresh clothes, and to resecure the rigging and masts. He believed "everything [was] done to create efficiency & good order." and added, "The crew is of poor material, yet they are orderly. I have had to punish but very little, probably less than ever done before with a crew at the start."

After a passage of forty-two days, the *Perry* entered the harbor of Rio de Janeiro on 14 January 1844. The *Columbus* also arrived. Once anchored, the crew of the *Perry* began preparations for sea. While in port Frank became seriously ill with an "old digestive problem." To Sophie, he wrote, "I flattered myself that I was relieved from a chronic infirmity [diarrhea] under which I had been suffering for a number of years. A rule laid down by me never to decline any service which the Navy Department might require of me as long as I had health to execute it, together with a special desire to perform an Eastern cruise, led me to overlook too readily the probability of a return of the infirmity I speak of, on reaching tropical regions.

"The passage out to this port has proved to me my mistake, and

161

a relapse of the complaint with aggravated symptoms, convince me that I shall be prostrated by it in the climate of the East Indies and rendered unfit to discharge my duties with advantage to the Gov't."

Surgeons advised Frank that if he continued to the East Indies the complaint would turn into dysentery and would eventually be fatal. "I am better and have the disease under control, but the risk is too great . . . to go to the China sea. The physicians are most emphatic." He was forced to give up his command of the *Perry*.

The surgeons ordered Frank to a rest home in the countryside, where he could recover while he waited for the departure of the *Columbus* for the States. Depressed, he complained, "I should never have come in the miserable brig, that has given me every trouble, every annoyance, & to end with thankless results. Then again, I obeyed orders, fulfilled my duties, several under disheartening circumstances, as long as my health sustained me. When it failed I must yield to the will of God. . . ."

On 31 January, Frank, his health improved, returned from the rest home and handed over the command of the *Perry*. "I left the little brig with regret as far as the anticipated cruise around the world was concerned . . . but with none as to the vessel herself or those whom I left on her. It has been a command in which I have been disappointed or rather the extreme worry it gave me, & the bad faith of the department, added to the smallness of the command itself had a good deal disgusted me with it. Yet I was improving the vessel every day & probably would have been reconciled to everything disagreeable, could I have anticipated any degree of health whatever in the East Indies, or on the passage there even. . . ."

The *Boston* anchored in the harbor of Rio de Janeiro, but soon set sail for the La Plata River. The *Constellation* arrived from Callao, Peru, on her return from the East Indies. Commodore Thomas Ap Catesby Jones was on board.

Since the *Constellation* was scheduled to sail for the States before the *Columbus,* Frank switched to her. After boarding, he discovered that Commodore Jones's opinion of the *Somers* incident was the opposite of his own. "We had a good bout, after which the subject was tabooed between us."

Shortly after leaving Rio de Janeiro, Frank's "complaint returned" and he also suffered "an attack of inflammatory rheumatism." On the voyage home he felt "great bodily pain & loss of weight."

Physically exhausted, Frank arrived home in June. In a long letter to Mackenzie, he enumerated the disappointments of the cruise in the *Perry,* and concluded, "A long cherished cruise to circumnavigate, and the certainty of a larger command . . . all beckoned me on."

That fall Frank became immersed in the presidential campaign between the Whig, Henry Clay, and the Democrat, James K. Polk. He was passionately committed to Clay. The annexation of Texas was a key issue in the election. To Mackenzie, he wrote, "A better day I trust is dawning upon us in the certainty of Clay's election; indeed this certainty is more precious & desirable than ever since the nomination of the miserable political hack for the Presidency on the Democratic side. A man . . . who never took a national view of any measure in his life. . . . With the triumph of the Democratic party now, we are utterly gone"

Frank relished going to Delaware City to participate in a Whig demonstration, "the greatest meeting by far ever held in Delaware." Bands blared. Politicians harangued. The procession of wagons and carriages covered three and a half miles "in close order, all decorated most gloriously." Frank's brothers-in-law, Henry and Alexis, with their workers built a two-decker wagon, which carried 200 men drawn by thirty-three horses. "I never was so interested in a [presidential] contest before," he wrote Davis.

In November, New York City gave Polk a 2,100 majority and Pennsylvania went for him. Other states joined the bandwagon. "Mr. Clay is a used man!" Frank told Pendergrast. "I am too grieved to add another word."

"Mr. Polk," he admitted to Mackenzie, "was decidedly hostile to the Navy while in Congress—used to say that ships, officers & men could all be taken when wanted from the merchant service—but as its Commander in Chief, he may think differently."

During the winter of 1844–45, Frank made occasional forays to Philadelphia, "read . . . a good deal of solid matter," and gardened. Sophie was an invalid again, and "found it hard to maintain her usual cheerful resignation."

In the spring of 1845 President Polk appointed George Bancroft Secretary of the Navy. Frank went off immediately to Washington in response to the secretary's request. "I am greatly pleased at having been sent for. Bancroft struck me more favorably than I can well express. . . . [It was an] exceedingly agreeable & flattering

163

reception. . . . he has more polish of office than any Secret^y I have met."

Although pleased with the interview, Frank added, "The only thing unpleasant about him is the abuse of humanity—he is doubtless a man without sympathies & sensibilities. . . . Altogether he is a formidable fellow, & if he can be directed right & get fairly started may do us much good—or much harm."

After calling on Bancroft a second time at the Navy Department, Frank informed Sophie, ". . . You would be surprised at his pleasant manners, dropping occasionally a French word where it suited best—if I were as certain of the morals as I am of his cleverness I should have no fears. I hope he is honest. He expressed the utmost abhorrence of officers using . . . political influence. There is one thing certain. I believe the promotion of unworthy men . . . will be at an end and he is a foe to all loafers."

Frank quoted Bancroft to Pendergrast, " 'I think for some cause or other the Navy has lost some of the confidence of the country. I find the Navy Dept. tied up in matters where the War & Treas^y Depart. are left free, by a judicious course & the assistance of the Navy itself, all this can be won back. . . .'

"All this talk," Du Pont continued, "was over a bottle of Chateaux, which he enjoys like a gentleman, (one of the best traits I saw in him) & with as little reserve as if you & myself had been carrying it on. . . . I took the occasion to speak of you as I knew & felt."

While sojourning in Washington, Frank stayed at Coleman's, formerly Gadsby's—"clean apartments, excellent meals, white servants & chambermaids, instead of the indolent & dirty blackies, makes it a new abode." He contacted many old friends, but stayed on specifically to see more of Secretary Bancroft, ". . . the opp[ortunit]y is most favorable to give him some sound views on several subjects. . . ."

He called on Bancroft again, and was the secretary's guest one evening at a reunion. At this party "Old Mrs. Madison," wife of former President Madison, on hearing Du Pont's name, said, " 'I must see the son of Victor DuP.' " She was then living in Washington with her niece in a house on the northeast corner of Lafayette Square.

At the close of the evening, the secretary asked Du Pont to have dinner. "We had a téte a téte" for four hours, discussing dueling, merit promotion, the Mackenzie case, and the uniform. "I was greatly pleased on the whole." On another occasion he was Bancroft's guest at the White House to meet President Polk.

To Mackenzie, Frank reported, "Bancroft is not your friend—he seems fixed in his opinions. I pushed him hard about you . . . service, & that whatever difference of opinion there might exist surely neither himself, nor any of the old officers . . . could just see you kept from your command—he was silent. He seemed unacquainted with your professional acquirements & when I dwelt upon them with my whole soul, he seemed staggered."

While vacationing with Sophie at Cape May, Frank was recalled to Washington by the secretary to assist Commander Franklin Buchanan and Captain William McKean "in making a naval school to be located at [Fort Severn in] Annapolis." Buchanan had already been appointed superintendent.

During the 1820s and 1830s several secretaries of the Navy had pressed Congress to establish a naval academy similar to West Point, but political obstacles and naval traditions stymied any action. Western congressmen had no interest in the Navy, and Democrats favored fiscal restraint. Many naval officers and prominent civilians believed that the existing system of training midshipmen at sea provided all the education an officer required.

Two events during the early 1840s gave momentum to the movement for a naval academy. The introduction of steam propulsion in warships provided a new justification for educating midshipmen in engineering, and the near mutiny led by Midshipman Spencer on board the *Somers* focused public opinion on the need for improved methods of training midshipmen.

Officers, like Du Pont, supported Secretary Bancroft's effort to found a naval academy. The new secretary acted quickly to establish a school while Congress was recessed. In early June 1845, he initiated the transfer of Fort Severn at Annapolis from the Army to the Navy and, on 7 August, Bancroft ordered Buchanan to take possession of the fort and establish a naval academy.

In Washington, Buchanan, McKean, and Du Pont went to work planning a naval academy. "In a couple of days we made (on paper at least) as clever a naval school as need be." The three officers submitted "endless plans" and presented Bancroft with "grand programmes, throwing West Point into the shade." The curriculum presented included mathematics, steam, English, gunnery, chemistry, philosophy, navigation, French or Spanish, drawing, and swordsmanship. The course of study was to run for five years, of which the first and last were to be spent at the academy, the other three, at sea. Bancroft approved the plans and ordered the school to open in October 1845.

Across the United States rumors circulated that worsening relations with Mexico could culminate in war. Prior to leaving Washington, Frank met with Secretary Bancroft. Captain Robert F. Stockton, newly appointed commodore of the Pacific Squadron, had been sent to the frigate *Congress*, then moored at Norfolk. He was to relieve Commodore John D. Sloat. When Bancroft asked Stockton whom he wished to captain his flagship, "he . . . pressed my name hard." The secretary had replied that he would order Du Pont to the *Congress* if Frank did not object. Du Pont offered no objection, but pushed for an independent command. Bancroft replied that Frank would "not be a loser" if he accompanied Stockton on the *Congress* to the Pacific. Once in Pacific waters, he would relieve Captain William Mervine, who commanded the sloop of war *Cyane*. "I go to Norfolk in fine spirits," he told Pendergrast.

Returning to Delaware to prepare for sea, Frank wrote a description of the Washington trip to Pendergrast. "I was determined to look close into the affairs there, [to] move among the Polkites & judge for myself of the thousand rumors. . . ." Secretary Bancroft "took a violent fancy to me. We did not get to sleeping together but we did all else, téte a téte dinner &c &c. . . . He is a middle aged person of polished manners, dresses a good deal, & has great courtesy of office. He questions closely & is eminently a practical man. He has the Yankee characteristics, but . . . [this] is joined to high scholarship, & a higher range. Of his abilities I have no questions. I wish I could feel as sure of the *morale*."

Midshipman Samuel Francis Du Pont (Hagley Museum and Library)

USS Ontario, *one of the ships that "showed the flag" in the Mediterranean* (Naval Historical Center)

The United States Squadron departing from Port Mahon (Naval Historical Center)

Line-of-battle ship USS Ohio, *Commodore Isaac Hull's flagship* (Naval Historical Center)

USS Perry *with the American slave ship* Martha (Naval Historical Center)

Henry Winter Davis, United States Congressman from Maryland and a close friend of Du Pont's (Hagley Museum and Library)

Sophie M. Du Pont (Hagley Museum and Library)

USS Cyane, *Du Pont's ship during the Mexican War* (Naval Historical Center)

U.S. Steam Frigate Minnesota, *Du Pont's ship on the mission to China*
(Hagley Museum and Library)

The Du Pont home, Upper Louviers (Hagley Museum and Library)

USS Wabash, *Du Pont's flagship during the Civil War* (Hagley Museum and Library)

USS New Ironsides, *one of Du Pont's ships in the assault on Charleston* (Hagley Museum and Library)

XII

"My object was obtained"

On 4 September 1845, Frank arrived at the Gosport Navy Yard in Norfolk and found the *Congress* "very backward." Only 110 men were on board out of the 480 who were to compose the ship's complement. The officers, however, had all reported. Frank had liked Commodore Stockton ever since the days when he commanded the *Erie* in 1819. "He is everything that I could wish, and I hope it will so continue." It was not long, however, before he was complaining that Stockton was "*averse to work,* as his mind & plans are elsewhere." "Stockton does little or nothing," Frank wrote to Sophie, although "he is always the same courteous gentleman."

The commodore was a loner and his social isolation made him welcome his working partnership with Frank. The gregarious Du Pont regretted that Stockton did not have a warmer relationship with other officers or with the Norfolk community. The commodore's pleasure in meeting with him caused Frank to remark, "it has consumed a good deal of my time."

To Mackenzie, Frank expressed some uneasiness. ". . . how I shall get along with my *chief* has to be tried, socially & personally . . . yet I knew there are breakers ahead to be looked out for. He is a peculiar man—the service in its progress in a thousand ways has left him behind, and he does not assent readily to these changes. . . . I am curious to see how he will stand forty days at sea going to Rio. . . ."

While he supervised the crew as it overhauled the *Congress,* Frank took up rooms at Walter's Hotel near the navy yard. He often called on his many acquaintances in the vicinity, who were "amazed at my healthy & strong appearance, saying they never saw me looking so well or younger." He attended church regularly with Captain David Farragut.

As work on the *Congress* progressed, more crew members arrived. "I continue pleased with everything & discover as yet nothing to make me apprehend any thing unpleasant for the future."

While the frigate readied for sea, Stockton left for Washington on official business. During his absence, one evening while dining at Walter's Hotel, the waiter handed Frank a note from Secretary Bancroft. He had arrived unexpectedly in Norfolk and wanted to confer with Frank. At their meeting, the secretary was delighted to see him and spoke of the naval academy and his satisfaction with Du Pont and his colleagues' labors. After a pleasant chat, Frank left and slept on board the *Congress* for the first time. The following morning, after the secretary inspected the frigate, Bancroft "expressed himself highly gratified." Stockton soon joined them "in citizen dress," as he had lost his trunk in transit from Washington.

On 17 September the *Congress*—"as noble & majestic a frigate as the sun ever shone upon"—left the Gosport Navy Yard and soon anchored off the town. "My position here . . . is all I can wish for now & for the future. . . ."

"I never have been so happy," Du Pont wrote Mackenzie, "for I am emphatically a big ship man if I am anything."

In late September, Frank was able to return home to Delaware for a few days. He arrived back in Norfolk to discover, much to his distaste, that civilian passengers had boarded the *Congress*. At the request of the State Department, the *Congress* was to transport Anthony Ten Eyck and Joseph Turrill, respectively United States Commissioner and Consul-General, and their families to the Sandwich Islands (Hawaii). The contingent numbered thirteen passengers in all, men, women, children, nurses. Frank and the naval constructor had to arrange apartments for them. "I have to give up my room. . . . [The] women have one of the [water] *closets*, which can only be reached through my room, which of course I could not occupy. The forward cabin will be greatly circumscribed . . . [and] think of providing for such a mess for five months—it is awful in the extreme, but I bear it with perfect equanimity." These quarters proved unsatisfactory and soon the *Congress* returned to the navy yard to install a poop cabin for the passengers. When the laborers completed the cabin, the civilians moved out of Frank's cabin and into the new accommodation.

A packet of letters from Sophie was read and reread. To one of them, Frank replied, ". . . As you say 'true distinction will always follow the faithful performance of duty,' and I am determined as far as a weak creature can control such things to bend my whole mind to my work in hand & not suffer myself to be drawn off by speculations as to the future. . . . You have been all & all to me. . . .

"My situation here is all I could desire. . . . I see no difficulty ahead in controlling the crew & the commiss^d officers. . . . My desire is to govern as much as possible by moral influence, to avoid harsh measures as much as possible, yet I am perfectly aware that too much leniency is the nursery only of offences & increased severity afterwards. . . . my danger with Stockton is on this point— he is no disciplinarian. . . . We had a long conversation about punishment. . . . During our conversation I could see seeds of future difference. He goes for having privileged classes as it were. I am disposed to be more exacting of those who are most indulged. I do want to act in such a way as to satisfy *you* my precious Sophie, & have once or twice called upon our Father above for aid & right direction, just before making some decision which I thought important."

Early on the morning of 20 October 1845 the *Congress* got underway, and at 7 A.M., when just off Fort Monroe, all hands were mustered with the marines and band stationed on the poop deck. Stockton made a short speech. As soon as he finished, the "crew gave those hearty cheers." The chaplain gave a short prayer, "then boom away thirteen guns and the band struck up. . . . The weather is heavenly, indian summer. We are gliding along smoothly towards Cape Henry."

Two weeks out in the Atlantic, Frank wrote Sophie, "I can see nothing to mar the prospects of happy . . . successful cruise. . . . Of course there are many little annoyances to be met at the start in arranging properly so large a ship and controlling so many men.

"My desire to govern by moral persuasion and influence gives me additional labour. . . . The principal difficulty . . . is to be found in the conviction entertained by most of those under you, that the lash is the grand panacea for all evils in a man of war, and when this system is not followed to the extent they desire, they fail to aid you, in that watchful supervision and zeal, which alone is sufficient to prevent one half the offences, reducing of course by so much the necessity of punishment."

Commodore Stockton was described as "very unhappy," and

169

"terribly homesick for his family." In an attempt to cheer him up, Frank would engage him in social conversation in the evenings. "He is pleasant & often instructive, yet he cannot be called sound. . . . He is very extravagant in his opinions—these are set forth with quotes from Shakespeare . . . or a line from Milton."

When Frank discovered that Stockton was "an anxious man at sea, very much so," he was determined to ease his apprehension by being present whenever the commodore was on deck. Du Pont, who never climbed into bed until after midnight and often lay down in his clothes and boots, stated, "yet I sleep like a rock."

He found that Stockton's "whole course towards me is marked by the highest & kindest consideration." Yet, as the voyage continued, Frank gradually revised his estimate of the commodore. "He is an entirely changed man since I was with him years ago. He was then a dashing, bold, reckless young officer. . . . [Now] he is cautious, not to say timid about the ship. . . . He is a spoiled child of fortune, has always controlled others & been surrounded only by those who were the recipients of his favors."

Although the commodore had given outright command of the *Congress* to Du Pont, tact was required. The "most difficult thing which a man can attempt," Frank wrote Pendergrast, "is to introduce a new thing, system or measure on board a man of war. Now so many usages have crept in within the last twenty years, that are new to him [Stockton], it's difficult to get him reconciled to them. His mind is logical & argumentative. He can't understand the necessity of morning quarters, says there is more mustering now than he ever heard of, the men must be sick of it.

"However," he continued, "our friend is a noble fellow & my whole energies are devoted to [acquiring his] . . . confidence."

On the long voyage to Rio de Janeiro, Du Pont crowed, "I never knew what living could be had at sea before—the truth is I never lived so well on shore—every delicacy & nothing injurious [to eat]." Finding the water unsuitable, he had laid in an "immense stock of mineral water, the best I ever tasted, so great at sea I never dream't of." He had also brought along kegs of grapes, "a more grateful & healthful luxury can hardly be conceived." The commodore had filled his storeroom with the finest French wines. "Our cabin display could not be equalled," Frank told Pendergrast, "because Stockton has with him all the paraphernalia of table equipment & show," plates, saucers, cups, goblets, and candelabra.

170

Ship routine was shattered by an incident when the ship's company was at General Quarters. While Stockton and Du Pont were on the gun deck, the lookout cried, "Man overboard! Man overboard!" Instantly, Frank sprang into action "like a panther," shouting orders. The man in the water had scarcely passed the ship before the crew had lowered a boat manned by twelve men and an officer. Seamen cut life buoys, which fell near the struggling man. Frank realized the situation was hopeless when although the man's hands continued to thrash in the water, his head went under. He drowned in less than two minutes.

On 21 December, after logging 6,600 miles in 52 days, the *Congress* dropped anchor in Rio de Janeiro harbor. Several days later, Du Pont returned to the ship after dining ashore with Stockton. He was greeted by the news that some seamen had broken into the spirit room and handed out liquor in buckets to their friends. Several miscreants were staggering from the effects of alcohol. Two were so far gone that they had knocked down the sentries and abused their officers. Quickly, Frank had them clamped in irons.

The following day, Frank broke two petty officers and persuaded Stockton to order courts-martial for two ordinary seamen on charges of "violence and insubordination towards Sentrys." Frank then punished those who were not seriously implicated "to the full extent of my own authority." In the aftermath, when one man struck another, Frank severely punished him.

Frank admitted to Sophie, ". . . that some hundred lashes more in Norfolk & on the passage, might have saved us some here, possibly the trials, but to myself, the rock of my strength has been the comfortable feeling, that I put off the evil day to the last. . . . there is not a man who does not feel that he brought it on himself—& this is the reason why the exercise of my full powers were so instantly successful—another point gained, and a great one, & first remarked by the Chaplain, I know now *where* to strike. . . .

"I could never for a day have done at the start, what I am now doing, the Com^e would have stopped me . . . but my moderation, my forbearance, & my narrations to him of the conduct of all, have gradually brought him to see things just as I do, & the ordering of these courts I think will save us a thousand lashes during the cruise."

To Mackenzie, Frank wrote, "I have after taking the mild system as long as I could, to fall back upon the Cats with great energy." This, along with three courts-martial, "have given me the most perfect control over a crew with an admixture of the greatest scoundrels the sun ever shone upon. . . . The Commodore has come up to scratch seeing the necessity of punishing."

When the *Raritan, Plymouth,* and *Columbia* arrived in Rio de Janeiro, Frank went on board the latter to renew old acquaintances. When he returned to the *Congress,* he wrote Sophie that the arrival of the *Columbia* "has put me . . . in great conceit of the ship. We are far in advance of her. . . . I heard more swearing on the Columbia in ten minutes on deck than I have since we left. . . . I am determined . . . to stick by this ship. I see nothing but an honorable professional career & very respectable success before me. . . ."

On 15 January 1846, the *Congress* got underway from Rio de Janeiro, the helmsman steering southward toward Cape Horn. "Once more [I am] launched upon the ocean, and I am bound to new scenes, and at this moment I am further South then ever before."

Frank perused portions of Wilkes's *Exploring Expedition* and consumed every book available on Cape Horn, but found "there are but few points upon which two of them agree." "My whole mind is occupied in the ship. . . . My principle of action is to neglect no precaution, to be vigilant, to require it of others, and then to trust to a merciful Providence. . . . the life of a seaman is sudden with dangers, which no wise forethought can always avoid yet if any class of men are mercifully protected by a beneficent Creator, more than any other, it is that of the sailors. . . ."

Stockton was exhibiting a "new excentricity"—"you can hardly imagine his ignorance on general & miscellaneous matters—deficient in Geography, cannot remember proper names. . . ."

On 25 January Frank noted that six days had passed without the need to punish a man—"the men are much more efficient. I am satisfied my course in Rio has reaped its expected results. . . ."

The "southern ocean is more animated than the northern ocean," he observed. "We see more fish, more birds . . . [and] the brilliancy of the Stars & Planets is beyond measure grand."

On 2 February the *Congress* began a treacherous three-week passage around Cape Horn. On that day lookouts sighted the mountains of Staten Island off Tierra del Fuego. Du Pont held Sunday services as usual, but there was no sermon as the wind freshened and all hands reduced sail. The *Congress* plowed through larger swells. The clouds "rolled up in huge masses, black & threatening." The temperature plummeted. Cold rain fell. The ship rolled and pitched. "A more gloomy opening can scarcely be conceived." That day not a mile was gained.

Panicked by fears, a nervous Stockton confined himself to his cabin, dosing himself with "quack" remedies for an undiagnosed "disease," and "brought himself . . . to a very serious plight." Du Pont, clad in two pairs of flannel pants, a French paletot—"the greatest of coats"—and waterproof boots, was forced to shout every order to make himself heard. He enjoyed the comforter, which Sophie had given him—"I wore it altogether as a cravat . . . [and] pressed it to my lips every night when I laid down."

The next day the weather moderated. The ship had suffered no damage and Frank was "a very happy & thankful man." Progress westward continued to be slow going, "sometimes losing a little from the previous day, yet we carried every inch of sail that we dared to, reefing down when it came too hard, hoisting again the moment there was a lull."

The *Congress* inched westward, "though our track was literally a voyage in 'zigzag.' " By 13 February the frigate reached the meridian of Cape Horn, "quite a cheering item, & the worst half considered accomplished." But a gale on the 14th threw the *Congress* back. Finally on the next day the ship reached the meridian of Diego Ramirez, small rocky islands forty-five miles southwest of Cape Horn. On the 18th the *Congress* ran into "a six hour hurricane, for gale is too moderate a word to convey [its force] . . . but I was in time for it, as I have been on every occasion, my own observation & the Barometer never having deceived me." The sea was not as high as it had been on the 8th, but "nothing could excel however the fury of the beast." This wind proved to be the last heavy blow, although it continued to hail, snow, and squall while the frigate fought her way westward. The passage around Cape Horn was "the most trying, responsible, & fatiguing [work] that I ever went through for *that* length of time—one or two nights in the Perry were far more dangerous, but for a continued stretch of all the energies of body & mind, this has been my most laborious professional service."

On Sunday, 22 February, he was able to write Sophie, "We are 'round' at last." The passage took twenty-one days, "Three weeks from Sunday to Sunday since we rounded the east end of Staten Land.

"We have accomplished this without . . . breaking a spar, or hurting a man." The sick list failed to increase. Officers never called all the crew at night. The men had every meal punctually. "I have spent nearly the whole of this time on deck, never going to bed until between 1 & 2, & called every two hours & informed of the state of the weather, every reef has been taken in my presence. I am greatly thankful to a merciful Providence for so successful a result.

"This doubling of Cape Horn," he continued, "is an event in a seaman's life which I had long coveted; I found it a work of deep interest & of great professional gain. I cannot but feel some little pride but I trust an honest pride of having carried round a fifty gun ship under the circumstances in which I did this. I learn with pleasure . . . that all under me consider the service as having been ably performed. I was left wholly again as in the Brig [*Perry*] *to my own* resources. . . ."

Now for the first time in three weeks Stockton reappeared on deck. "His recuperative powers are great, & he seems to me about as well as usual so I am disposed to think part of his complaint is nervous & part imaginarie. I felt very much for him. . . . Although I felt for him, the fact that I was untrammelled during those three weeks of our passage round was a matter of congratulation to me & some on board have ventured to whisper that we should not have got round at all had he [Stockton] been out."

Once in the Pacific the *Congress* enjoyed fine weather as she headed for Valparaiso, Chile. The sea was smooth, and Frank was reminded of the Mediterranean.

By 6 March the *Congress* was at anchor in Valparaiso harbor, fifty-one days out from Rio de Janeiro. After a brief stay, she got underway again. On 27 March, the *Congress* dropped anchor in Callao Roads, Peru. Just before departing Callao, Stockton and Frank had "a long, confidential & friendly conversation, in which he expressed the warmest affection for me. The condition of the ship & her healthy discipline, acknowledged & conveyed to him from all quarters led to this." In a closing accolade the commodore told Frank that if a man could donate his place on the Navy List, he would resign his in favor of his commander.

The *Congress* shaped a course for the Sandwich Islands, "all glad to get away." On this voyage punishment almost disappeared. Frank discovered a "*pride of ship,* which for a long time I utterly despaired of. If this condition of things continue, I shall be greatly regarded, for I must confess . . . that nothing but the innate conviction that I was right, come what may, would have given me nerve enough to persevere to the end."

To Sophie, Frank disparaged his officers, "The order of their minds is *mediocre*," before softening his criticism by continuing, "I ought to remember that brighter minds bring with them darker characters. One of my failings I know is too great an admiration for intellect, irrespective of more important qualities."

All the officers looked forward to reaching the Sandwich Islands, where they would rid themselves of their passengers who had been on board since October 1845. Frank jested "that we are all alive & all speak to each other, it speaks well for every one."

By 15 June the *Congress* lay off Honolulu. "We are at last at the Sandwich Islands!" From the deck of the frigate, Honolulu was "half thatched, half modern in its structure, with one or two conspicuous buildings, the whole situated in a slight bend of the coast." A pilot was taken on board and directed the *Congress* to a berth just outside the harbor, a harbor where so large a ship as the *Congress* could not anchor.

As the days passed Frank grew enchanted with Honolulu, a town of 10,000. Merchants, consuls, and members of the government and their families composed the nucleus of society. "Hospitality is universal." The wealthy owned houses in town and also in the valley. Ladies rode horseback and "you see long habits & green veils streaming in the streets." Honolulu society entertained with dinners and balls every night. The *Congress* band attended many of the parties and played waltzes, gallops, and polkas. "The living is good," Frank informed Sophie. He was happily surprised when he "tasted of a 'loaau' of Pig and Tarro that is baked in the ground between hot stones." On one occasion he rode out through the valley east of Honolulu and "up to the summit, the Pali, the gap which overlooks the north end of the island."

On the day set aside for the presentation at the palace of Anthony Ten Eyck, the new American commissioner, Du Pont, Stockton, and many of the officers from the *Congress* attended in full dress uniforms. The frigate's band, dressed in red jackets, played. The audience also included the governor of Oahu, ministers, native chiefs, missionaries, and invited American and English citizens.

The king who passed through the hall and into the principal parlor, stood "erect & commanding, with a very handsome . . . uniform on, Scarlet & Gold." After Ten Eyck was presented and made a lengthy speech, the king responded in Hawaiian, which was translated. Stockton also spoke, "with the usual compliments to the missionaries, about whom he had never read one word in his life, &

did not know until after he doubled Cape Horn whether the Islands were in the North or South Pacific, or whether inhabited by Tartars, Africans, or whatnot." At the end of the ceremony, the commodore introduced all his officers to the king. "It was altogether . . . a very interesting scene—everything was conducted with great propriety & a quiet observance of the general rules of a mixed society."

While in Honolulu, Frank expanded his knowledge of the burgeoning whaling industry. "This whaling interest has become a matter of immense moment, & 700 ships [are] employed in it, & more than half come yearly to refit at the Sandwich Islands, carrying 10,000 seamen—they are the off scourings of our country; the ships are mostly in a state of anarchy, & mutinies occur frequently."

During the mid-1840s American interest in California had mounted, fueled by reports that the inhabitants were either passive or disloyal to the Mexican government. A merchant from New England, Thomas O. Larkin, had been appointed a confidential agent by the Secretary of State with orders to promote a pro-American feeling among the Californians. The secretary hoped that the United States could annex California without going to war with Mexico.

An expedition of United States Army Topographical Engineers, headed by Captain John C. Fremont, explored northern California in early 1846. The expedition's stated objective was to improve communication between Oregon and the United States, and the Mexican government tolerated this intrusion. Fremont used his soldiers to fan the flames of disaffection against Mexican control and helped the Californians form the Bear Flag Republic, which declared its independence from Mexico on 14 June 1846.

In May, Secretary Bancroft had dispatched official notice to commodores afloat of the beginning of the Mexican War, and dispatched orders to Commodore David Connor, commanding the Home Squadron in the Gulf of Mexico, to relay the news to Commodore Sloat in the Pacific. But the messengers were delayed; they failed to arrive in Mazatlán for several weeks.

On his flagship *Savannah*, Sloat received news on 31 May 1846 of the battles between American and Mexican troops at Palo Alto and Resaca de la Palma. Sloat, who had not received Bancroft's official notice, did not interpret these actions to mean that war had been declared, but on 8 June he set sail and joined the *Cyane* and *Levant* at Monterey, California. On 7 July Captain Mervine, commanding the *Cyane,* landed with his men and hoisted the Stars and Stripes over Monterey without incident. Officers from the warships acted as temporary civil officials and Sloat furnished arms and ammunition to equip a body of cavalry recruits commanded by naval officers. A member of this cavalry unit was Lieutenant Archibald H. Gillespie, United States Marine Corps, a secret envoy of President Polk and bearer of dispatches for Sloat and Fremont.

Commander John B. Montgomery on the *Portsmouth,* which lay anchored in San Francisco Bay, landed a force of sailors and marines, which took possession of Yerba Buena. As at Monterey, the Americans encountered no opposition.

When Captain Fremont arrived in Monterey with his troops, he protested Sloat's lack of action. The commodore, however, refused to cooperate until he learned the legal status of Fremont's forces. Lieutenant Gillespie joined Fremont's band.

The storeship *Erie* arrived in Honolulu from Mazatlán, with rumors of impending war. Frank could not believe the Mexicans would be "so foolish, for they must instantly lose California."

As talk of war escalated on board the *Congress,* "I can see every day reason for thinking more and more highly of the men who form the bulk of my profession," he wrote Sophie. "All seem ready to lay down their lives when the moment arrives . . . not to think whether their country be right or wrong (though I for one would give millions if I had them, that she should be right)."

In late June the *Congress* departed from Honolulu, setting a course for California. Since all the passengers had gone ashore in Honolulu, Frank was able to move into the poop cabin, which he described "as pretty, as neat, as beautifully clean & light, as it is comfortable in every respect, & to a degree I have never before experienced in the service. . . . It is without exception the most comfortable room I ever saw in a ship."

On the Fourth of July the commodore hosted a dinner party for Du Pont, two lieutenants, the purser, surgeon, chaplain, a passed midshipman, and the Lieutenant of Marines. Frank was not pleased. "I am more & more opposed on *ship board* of these reunions & festivities, where immunity for indulging, may be claimed for a day or event celebrated. . . . I despise patriotism which shows itself in drunkenness or breaks the rules of a ship."

On 15 July 1846 the *Congress* anchored in Monterey Bay. Through the fog her officers could make out the blue pendant of the *Savannah*. Soon an officer from the flagship arrived and boarded the *Congress* to direct Du Pont to the best anchorage.

The day after the *Congress*'s arrival, the British line-of-battle ship *Collingwood*, flagship of Rear Admiral George Seymour, stood in and dropped anchor. The *Savannah*'s band struck up "God Save the Queen," which was answered by the *Collingwood* with "Hail Columbia." Frank accompanied Sloat on a visit to Admiral Seymour, "a fine old gentleman, one side of his face very handsome, the other very much gashed by a scar from a wound received in battle."

When British officers boarded the *Congress*, "I was glad," Frank wrote, "to find that we were in every way equal to them in efficiency. . . . They cannot understand how with our democratic institutions we continue to keep up such strict discipline among our crews.

"I saw some of their men on shore in their boats *smoking*, & lieutenants getting in to them doing the same thing, such a thing with us would ruin the reputation of any ship. They are doing everything to increase the loyalty of their seamen with great success—but after seeing this ship, a very high specimen too—I doubt if . . . they are a match for us, you know I am no braggart and under their supposed great advancement I thought we might be behind hand, but our good ships I think [are] better than their good ones, and I suppose we have no more bad ones in proportion to theirs." A week later the *Collingwood* set sail for the Sandwich Islands.

Stockton ordered Fremont to "volunteer" to serve under his command, thereby denying the captain the glory of conquering California. Still lacking an official declaration of war with Mexico, Commodore Sloat, who still commanded the Pacific Squadron, resisted Commodore Stockton until convinced by Stockton's argument that it was imperative to take General José Castro, who commanded the enemy forces in California, or to drive him out of the territory. He saw no possibility of pacifying the area until either alternative was accomplished.*

---

* These details come from Robert E. Johnson, *Thence Round Cape Horn* (Annapolis, 1963), pp. 79–80. The Mexican War chapters concerning the Pacific Squadron rely heavily on Johnson's book.

Sloat finally permitted Stockton to relieve him as commodore of the Pacific Squadron on 23 July, and he sailed for Panama on the *Levant* six days later.

On board the *Congress,* Frank anticipated the arrival in Monterey of Captain Fremont, for whom he had an "almost . . . romantic admiration after reading all his Journeys." Soon after Du Pont went ashore, horsemen appeared "with rifles glittering, dressed in every costume imaginable, clouds of dust covering the column." Fremont commanded 150 "mounted western men, 50 who left Missouri with Fremont included—with 12 Delaware Indians, his hunters, guides, followed by droves of horses & mules—with the display of ships in the harbor, the surrounding scenery & great weather, made altogether a more thrilling sight and one which . . . produced more emotion & more pleasurable excitement & wonder, than I ever remember experiencing."

As horsemen approached, Frank spotted "a small well formed young man" wearing a white felt hat, clad in a light hunting frock, with a rifle slung across his saddle, and a Bowie knife in his belt. When Fremont reached Frank, he dismounted, and asked, " 'how are you Cap. D[u] P[ont]?' " The two Americans talked together for several minutes.

"No description can convey an idea of his men," Frank wrote, "covered with dust, dressed in buckskins, and every other possible garment, among them some blue sailor frocks, [as] they passed along—the most determined looking band, the brawniest men, and most sinewy looking people you can imagine. Yet all in order, & under the most perfect control by Fremont, who seems to be looked upon by these people, somewhat . . . [as] a kind of DemiGod."

Frank trailed Fremont and his troops up to their camps on the heights above the village where he observed them making fires, fetching water, and slaughtering a bullock. "I would not have missed this scene for anything." He asked Fremont for an introduction to the famed scout, Kit Carson. Lieutenant Gillespie led Frank to Carson, who was lying down, head resting against a tree. He rose and, as everyone gathered around, Frank shook hands and conversed with Carson. As the sun began to dip, Frank descended the gentle slope— "the ships showing most magnificently in the quiet waters of the bay, a sight which these wild men of the west could not turn from even to get their evening meal ready."

On another evening, Frank, at the request of Chaplain Colton, testified at a sailors' prayer meeting conducted in the *Congress*'s storeroom. When Frank entered the seamen were at prayers. As soon as they finished, Frank stepped forward and said, " 'Men, I have come to witness of what Mr. Colton has already told you I highly approve of. You have my entire countenance in this, & anything I can do to increase yr. interest or yr. comfort . . . I am ready to grant you. When I came down just now and saw forty seamen among our best men in all duties on their knees, the thought came to my mind, that a ship that could represent such a scene must prosper.' "

An appreciative Colton thanked Du Pont. " 'Capt. DP what you have done tonight will do more good, than fifty sermons presented by myself. . . . Heaven keep you.' "

After Commodore Sloat had boarded the *Levant* for the voyage to Panama, there was a reshuffling of commands. Stockton continued on the *Congress,* Du Pont relieved Captain Mervine on the *Cyane*—"a noble corvette"—and Mervine took command of the *Savannah.* Stockton ordered Gillespie to serve as Fremont's second in command. Fremont agreed to serve under Stockton, and his battalion decided to volunteer in the United States Army. Stockton appointed Fremont a brevet major, "but [by] what authority I know not."

Although transferring to the *Cyane* was a step up professionally as it was "a *separate* command," Frank left the *Congress* with "deep . . . regret." "The ship *[Cyane]* is all I could wish—a fine sea vessel and of large size, with beautiful cabin. Yet to break up & pack after being so comfortably fixed is no slight trial. . . . The Cyane is in fine order with a good crew. . . . a great gloom has been spread over here [on the *Congress*] at my going . . . but the future [here] was too doubtful for any hope of great usefulness. I have done all the good I could here & I consider it under a kind providence great good fortune to leave at what I think was my zenith here."

Just before leaving the *Congress,* Stockton and Frank were involved in an ugly scene. The commodore imagined that the officers and crew had treated him with disrespect during a Sunday worship service, and he made Frank the recipient of his displeasure. He said "what he had a right to say," but the time, circumstances, and "solemn silence in the presence of the crew," gave his words "all the appearance of a reprimand."

Frank restrained himself until he was behind the closed door of the commodore's cabin, "then I was into him—we had it hot &

heavy." They finally separated with "all cordiality." A half-hour after this confrontation, Stockton sent for Frank "to make some lame interpretation of opinion, we were soon at issue again." After each had expressed his indignation, the two overwrought men suddenly began to cry. Their tension relieved, they then shook hands.

The reassignment was welcome. It was "opportune" to leave after this incident, and Frank also feared that the commodore had grown "jealous of my authority, influence, & popularity with the officers & crew. . . . It was time for separation."

"I believe Stockton in his heart," he confided to Sophie, "would have been sorry had I preferred remaining in the Congress, yet I think he was inwardly wounded that I did not ask to do so. I felt that he had done me wrong. . . . No other man in the Navy could have managed as long as I did with the Com^e—had he been left to himself I think his command would have proven an entire failure. The ship was left in thorough discipline—no drunkenness, no profane swearing, no insolence. . . ."

The first lieutenant on board the *Cyane* was Stephen Rowan, "I doubt if I could have had better in the Navy . . . he is a tip top man."

Fremont's force, without their horses, 150 men in all—"American Arabs of the West"—boarded the *Cyane* and the sloop set sail for San Diego. Fremont shared Frank's cabin; Gillespie was quartered in the wardroom. The other officers and men "lay about . . . like pigs." Although the *Cyane* was overcrowded, Du Pont preferred "active & novel service" to lying in Monterey Bay.

When the *Cyane* reached San Diego, Fremont intended to commandeer horses and attempt to cut off General José Castro's Mexican army from Lower California. After an uneventful voyage, the *Cyane* reached San Diego harbor at noon on 29 July. Frank dispatched Lieutenant Rowan with the marines to town, where they raised the Stars and Stripes without opposition. This accomplished, Frank ordered Fremont and his men to land. Du Pont and Fremont took up separate quarters in San Diego.

Senor Juan Bandini, a Californian, formerly a member of the Mexican Congress, threw open his hacienda to the Americans, where every evening there was music and dancing, "the sole diversion of California." Frank appreciated the San Diegans and found the town a "much more agreeable place than Monterey, where I saw no society whatever."

181

His face shaded by a Panama hat, a blouse over his uniform coat, Frank relished daily rides into the countryside. He was armed with a rifle thrown across the saddle, his "revolving pistol," and his sword on these sorties.

In early August, a launch from the *Congress*, anchored at San Pedro, arrived with orders for the *Cyane* to head for that harbor. Fremont received notification to march northward toward Los Angeles. Stockton directed Du Pont not to leave any force in San Diego. Although the *Cyane* sailed on 9 August, calm winds and the capture of a Mexican vessel delayed the frigate's arrival until the 13th.

At San Pedro Stockton had previously landed with 360 sailors and marines and marched for Los Angeles. General Castro's troops, numbering only 100, were almost without arms and so dejected that they could not be counted on to obey orders. Faced with almost certain defeat, Castro and the Governor of California, Pio Pico, gave up all thought of thwarting Stockton's intrusion and fled into retirement.

Deprived of their leaders, the Californians made no resistance either to Stockton's advance or to Fremont's expedition moving northward from San Diego.

On 13 August the united forces of Stockton and Fremont triumphantly entered Los Angeles, ran up the flag, and received pledges of allegiance from its leading citizens. Four days later, Commodore Stockton proclaimed the province a territory of the United States, promoted Fremont to the rank of lieutenant colonel, and appointed him Governor of Upper California.

On his arrival, Du Pont had received orders to remain in the harbor and dispatch the frigate's marines to Los Angeles. As the contingent departed, Frank wryly commented, "Fear we will never see our Marines again, which have been sent for to make parades at Los Angeles."

The *Cyane* soon got underway and sailed with orders to blockade the port of San Blas on the coast of Mexico.

On 25 September she reached San Blas, the seaport for Tepic, twenty miles in the interior. On dropping anchor, Frank sent a proclamation of blockade to San Blas by boat before his crew seized a Mexican sloop loaded with valuable cargo. On the following day the seamen from the *Cyane* intercepted a Mexican brigantine, which was already in a sinking condition. After transferring the cargo, they hastened her descent to the bottom.

After eight days of blockade duty, sometimes at anchor, sometimes under sail, the *Cyane* left for Mazatlán, capturing another Mexican sloop along the way. At Mazatlán the *Cyane* rejoined the *Warren* and received orders to cruise and search for hostile gunboats. The frigate got underway and bore away for La Paz, the capital of Lower California. She anchored in a little harbor, six miles from La Paz, as the water near the town was too shallow. Frank sent Rowan with a unit of marines down the bay in boats to La Paz with orders to inform the governor that there would be no hostilities and no persons would be injured unless provocation was given.

After capturing nine Mexican vessels "big & small," Rowan landed at La Paz, where the governor acceded to Du Pont's wishes. Early the next morning the governor visited the *Cyane* and breakfasted with Frank. With a prize crew on board and the cargoes of other captured vessels, the *Julia* sailed for San Francisco. Frank would have burned the other craft, but he lacked orders to do so.

Despite the injury he had done by seizing their vessels, the citizens of La Paz treated him "with civility." "The Mexicans," Frank wrote in a broad observation to Sophie, "seem not to care to make money save for gambling, & the masses are the most degraded set you can imagine . . . nor are the foreigners settled among them much better, it is the custom with these people to live out of wedlock & rear large families."

However, this visit to La Paz was "altogether a pleasant change. . . . The greatest luxury was to get my clothes washed & done up well. . . ."

On 28 September the *Cyane* sailed from the little harbor near La Paz to establish a blockade up the Gulf of California, stopping at hamlets along the way to load supplies.

By 5 October she had reached Guaymas, which was nearly at the head of navigation for vessels of the *Cyane*'s size, and anchored in the inner harbor. Although Frank had been led to believe that Guaymas was one of the defenseless ports in Lower California, he noted soldiers on shore and also three vessels lying at anchor, one Ecuadorian, one Peruvian, one Mexican. Closer to town, he saw a Mexican gunboat, hard aground, dismantled without a mast or gun, a larger gunboat, also dismantled, and the Mexican Navy's brig *Condor*.

That evening members of the *Cyane*'s crew boarded the two neutral vessels and warned them of the blockade. The Ecuadorian captain came on board the frigate and reported that the skipper of a vessel captured at La Paz had journeyed to Guaymas and given the alarm, "by propagating terrible stories about us." At Guaymas the authorities' call for reinforcements had been answered by the arrival of a battalion.

Frank tried to gain his ends "by moderate measures." The next morning he wrote the commandant that the Americans did not want to provoke hostilities and preferred following the same conduct toward Guaymas as they had employed against La Paz. However, he said, the Mexican gunboats proved an exception and he requested that these be delivered to the *Cyane*. The commandant refused.

Immediately, Du Pont responded that the Americans would take the gunboats by force and, unless Guaymas was evacuated by 10 A.M. the next morning, the frigate would open fire on the town.

Early the following morning, a Mexican officer and several neutral merchants, under a flag of truce, boarded the *Cyane*. The commandant continued to refuse Du Pont's request. The merchants pleaded with Du Pont for a three-day delay to move their goods out of town.

Frank refused, since three days would give the Mexicans time to gather reinforcements, but he promised to wait until 11 A.M. before starting the bombardment. "I have done all I could to protect neutral property," he informed the merchants, "these are consequences of war, if you cannot influence the Commandant I am sorry for it, & regret extremely the necessity which compels my action."

The party left the *Cyane* "downcast & chagrined." As soon as they landed, soldiers set fire to the two dismantled gunboats and then warped the brig *Condor* into a cove near the barracks.

Frank hauled the *Cyane* closer to town so that she lay aground at low tide. At 11:30 the frigate opened fire on the barracks. Strong detachments under the command of lieutenants George Harrison and Edward Higgins boarded the *Cyane*'s launch and cutter and pulled toward the cove. A party clambered onto the deserted *Condor*. The launch and cutter towed her out.

Not wishing to cause unnecessary destruction, Frank ceased firing, whereupon the Mexican soldiers opened up on the launch and cutter. The *Cyane*'s cannon salvoed. When the broadsides stopped, the Mexicans promptly reopened on the boats, aided by a cross fire from a band of Indians on the other side of the cove. The *Cyane*'s cannon boomed again.

As soon as the crews rowed out of danger, Du Pont stopped the broadsides. The Americans set fire to the *Condor*. "My object was obtained."

The *Cyane* remained in the harbor, "the town was silent as a grave." "I could not but think it were well we had Mexicans to deal with. There we were, 300 miles up the Gulf with an enemy's coast on both sides, five miles within one of his closest harbors, surrounded by islands & high peaks—on any one of which a well served gun would have annoyed us terribly. A boat with fire combustibles with the land wind blowing right from the town every night could have set us on fire."

At high tide on 9 October, the *Cyane* departed from Guaymas and, with a fine breeze, soon arrived off Mazatlán, where the *Warren* lay anchored. To Sophie, Frank wrote, "Have you reflected upon my good fortune in being afloat during this war, instead of at home begging for service, with no prospect of getting it, & people believing you do not want to go?"

At Mazatlán, two Mexican sloops attempted to sneak into the harbor. Two of the *Cyane*'s boats pulled out and ran them aground. Ashore, Mexicans fired into the boats with artillery, but they were unscathed. The following day, two more sailed in. The *Cyane*'s boats cut them off from the harbor and ran them ashore. The Mexicans fired, and four enemy boats loaded with soldiers put out to cut off the Americans. The *Cyane*'s boats turned upon these hostile craft, which hightailed it to shore, soldiers jumping out and scampering off.

As her provisions were running short, the *Cyane* got underway and headed northward, stopping at San Jose, Lower California, to take on vegetables and water.

On 1 December 1846 the *Cyane* entered San Francisco Bay and anchored in "a cove called Sausalito," near the *Savannah*. Frank predicted, "San Francisco bay deserves its reputation—very safe, very extensive, with depth of water to admit the *Pennsylvania* & room for all navies of the world—a city like New York may rise in the next fifty years upon its shores. As yet it is all the grandeur of Nature. . . . a small miserable town which looks like a suburb of Honolulu called Yerba Buena lies opposite the island of that name."

XIII

"I stand high with the profession"

News reached San Francisco that a revolt had broken out in Los Angeles. Lieutenant Gillespie and his men, under siege by the Californians, had held out for a week, before taking refuge on a merchantman in San Pedro. Commodore Stockton sent a hurried note to Fremont, who was on recruiting duty in northern California, to return by forced marches. Prior to his arrival, Stockton made plans for another expedition against Los Angeles. By the second week in October, Fremont returned. Stockton was now ready to move. Fremont was to proceed by way of San Diego, while the commodore sailed to San Pedro. Lack of communication, however, played havoc with Stockton's plan, since Fremont violated orders and instead of going to San Diego landed at Monterey. The commodore, with only a token force at San Pedro, could not attack, and after waiting vainly for Fremont's appearance, he sailed southward to San Diego in November.

As the end of the year approached, the outlook for the United States' forces in California was dismal. Enemy troops held most of the towns in the interior and threatened coastal positions. Stockton was stalled at San Diego without sufficient troops to advance northward. Fremont was somewhere in the hinterland. General Stephen W. Kearny's cavalry force, riding overland from New Mexico, had only recently arrived at the California border. The commodore faced the necessity of concentrating at least some elements of his scattered forces as a prerequisite for attack. With Fremont's whereabouts unknown, Stockton sent a small party under Gillespie to inform General Kearny of the desperate situation at Los Angeles and to urge him to hasten to San Diego. Gillespie arrived at Kearny's camp on

5 December, and together they plotted an attack on an enemy unit in the San Pascual Valley. The assault failed. The enemy retreated with little loss after killing eighteen Americans and wounding many more. Both Gillespie and Kearny were listed as wounded. Their troops, short of both food and water, set up camp to await instruction from Stockton. A relief expedition of 250 men arrived at Kearny's camp on 11 December, and escorted the bedraggled troops into San Diego.

Kearny's arrival led to difficulties. He was now responsible for all military actions, while Stockton's authority was limited to naval operations. The general should have commanded all military units in California, but most of the men in the ranks came from the Pacific Squadron or from Fremont's regiments. Stockton refused to allow Fremont to be bumped from the position of military governor. After some argument, the commodore offered the general command of the expedition against Los Angeles, but Kearny refused and chose to serve as Stockton's chief of staff instead.

Commodore Stockton now turned his energy to the organization of a force composed of 600 seamen, marines, and cavalrymen, which he led overland toward Los Angeles. This contingent fought and won the battles of San Gabriel River and La Mesa on 8 and 9 January 1847. Fremont and his troops arrived at San Fernando from northern California. Facing certain defeat, the Californians capitulated at Cahuenga on 13 January. American forces now held all of Upper California.

The *Cyane* left San Francisco Bay for San Diego on Saturday, 19 December. On Christmas Day, Frank wrote Sophie, "My thoughts have been with you and our home-circle nearly all the time since I rose, picturing in my mind many little incidents likely to happen— not the gay, large assemblage of New Year's—but the quiet and more thoughtful temper—wending your way, possibly with sister Victorine, to church, amidst the uninterrupted occupations of the masses around you. Here we have enjoyed the day also, it is the first sunshine since we left San Francisco."

On 26 December the *Cyane* arrived in San Diego to take on provisions. After spending more than a month in the harbor, the *Cyane* sailed on 31 January 1847 for San Francisco with General Kearny and his staff on board. Entering Monterey for a brief stop, Du Pont discovered the frigate *Independence* with his old friend, Commodore William B. Shubrick on board.

Secretary Bancroft had ordered Shubrick to the Pacific on the *Independence*. He also directed Commodore James Biddle, commanding the East India Squadron in the line-of-battle ship *Columbus,* to proceed to California. Bancroft's orders to Shubrick were prompted by the information that Stockton had taken command of the Pacific Squadron. Bancroft felt that Stockton was too inexperienced to command a squadron and considered him only as an interim commander.

At Valparaiso Shubrick learned from Biddle that the latter had been directed to survey affairs in California, but to remain there only if the presence of his ship was necessary to ensure success. The *Independence* got underway for Monterey and Shubrick took command of the Pacific Squadron on 22 January 1847. Stockton later departed for Norfolk on the *Savannah*.

When the *Cyane* dropped anchor at Monterey, Du Pont immediately boarded the *Independence* and Shubrick received him cordially. On 11 February the *Cyane* sailed for San Francisco with General Kearny still on board. The general's staff was increased by the addition of Lieutenant Henry Halleck of the Army Engineers, who was in charge of defending the harbors. Du Pont was impressed with Halleck, who had delivered a series of lectures on military science at the Lowell Institute in 1846. These had been published and Frank had found them "interesting and instructive."

When the *Cyane* reached San Francisco, General Kearny and his staff, after transacting business on shore, left the ship.

"The quiet here has amounted to dullness," Frank assured Sophie, "but it has served to bring back things on board to order. The ship is neat and beautifully kept, and men have lost their careless, heedless, noisy way, created by the desultory life they have led.

"I think I may truly say I never knew a happier man-of-war, and I have never been with a set of men who seem so attached to me. Yet I have had to punish—not a great deal, but yet some. I have been very very firm, even stern, but I have succeeded, I believe, in convincing every man that I would at any time give him a jacket or a shirt, if he would spare me such a duty. . . ."

Southward in Monterey, Commodore Biddle in the *Columbus* arrived with orders to become commander-in-chief of the Pacific Squadron. Chagrined, Shubrick on the *Independence* demanded that he be sent home since the Secretary of the Navy had so little confidence in his ability. Biddle tactfully suggested that such a move would wreck Shubrick's naval career. Biddle promised to send Shubrick's letter of protest to Washington and to give him an opportunity to serve on independent missions in the meantime. Shubrick accepted Biddle's offer and soon departed for operations in Lower California.

From San Francisco an outraged Frank wrote Sophie, "I must tell you of Secretary Bancroft's . . . wicked, foul, malicious treachery to Shubrick who is superceded by Com^e Biddle . . . his orders leaving him no discretion, and he remains during the continuance of the war."

Frank continued, "I have a private letter from Commodore Shubrick, who is deeply mortified and indignant, as we all are. I cannot tell you how chagrined I am [with] this change, though of course I have no fault to find with Commodore Biddle, with whom I have long served. His capacity is equal to Commodore Shubrick's."

In April 1847 Frank received orders to get underway from San Francisco and sail southward to blockade Mazatlán. On 20 April the *Cyane* was off the western coast of Lower California. "Everything continues to prosper with me; I have no trials or troubles of a professional kind, and nothing but thankfulness should fill my heart. . . . The employment involved in an active command like that of this ship keeps my mind in exercise, and my earnest devotion to the conscientious discharge of my duties would appear to have met with a measure of success. The harmony, good order, and efficiency of my own ship, the contented spirit which seems to reign through her . . . still continues. My own intercourse with successive *new chiefs* [Sloat, Stockton, Shubrick, Biddle] . . . has been of the most agreeable and gratifying character. From Commodore Shubrick and . . . from Commodore Biddle, I have received every mark of regard and cordiality which I could possibly desire."

By late April, the *Cyane* was on station blockading the port of Mazatlán. The *Independence* with Commodore Shubrick on board came in and anchored near her.

The routine of blockade duty proved boring—"Time begins to pass wearily." Officers on board the *Cyane* itched for action and glory, and envied the ships in the Gulf of Mexico around Vera Cruz. "I have a good deal of amusement in keeping my officers *cool*, who, young yet, their whole minds are dwelling on lost chances of glory, etc. They seem indignant that the services of this ship last year have been filched from her, etc. I tell you it will all be right, and so it will; though it is curious how little had been said about her, while the operations of every petty revenue cutter, or small schooner or steamer, on the other side, fill paragraphs of the newspapers."

On 3 May Frank sat down and composed a lengthy letter about the war and the Mexicans. "My views about the war . . . moderate, and I believe that all is in the hand of Providence, and wholly inscrutable to us. I can see benefit to Mexico and to ourselves. They are a very arrogant and conceited people, the Mexicans, and the worst governed and the most selfish in existence. This latter trait is one secret of their strength. They are utterly indifferent to each other's sufferings; one province cares not for the disasters of another.

"Then *we* have learned what wars are; we, who were to swallow up at a mouthful the whole of Mexico, 'revel in six weeks in the halls of Montezuma,' with other grandiloquent and vainglorious nonsense, have seen a whole year roll round before twenty millions of people, with steam and all the arts and sciences of the age at their command, and money easily procured, could overcome seven millions of mixed Indian races, without an organized government even, the prey of every possible political evil, and physical and military want; and overcome they are not yet. . . .

"Should the war continue, we shall take quiet possession of whatever ports on this coast we may want, after the coming of the rains—say November. They are entirely without defence, and will be surrendered at any moment to the squadron. . . . Mexico seems without any power or force whatever on its west coast. There are but few soldiers, and these would not exist but for their internal dissensions. . . ."

News reached the ships off Mazatlán of the fall of Vera Cruz to the Americans with the Navy's participation. "Commodore Perry [commanding in the Gulf of Mexico] is a lucky man. We are, on this side, to use a sailor simile, 'lying on our oars.' . . . As I have told you, I am not satisfied professionally with our doings in this ocean. . . . We have not been fortunate out here (I mean the navy). Arduous and successful services, on the part of most or all the ships, have found no chroniclers, official or nonofficial. Then the successive changes of chiefs since have only tended to paralyze the action of all."

On 1 June 1847 the *Independence* departed and headed for Monterey. "So we are 'alone in our glory,' rolling, rolling, and rolling, looking out for the south-easters, and wishing the days to pass more rapidly."

As operations were running smoothly under Shubrick's command, Biddle decided that his presence was no longer needed in the Pacific. He sailed for the United States on the *Columbus* after turning over the squadron to Shubrick.

Du Pont recieved orders to sail in the *Cyane* for the Sandwich Islands to evade the southeaster season. On 27 June the *Cyane* left Mazatlán and headed westward. After a voyage of eighteen days the sloop of war anchored in the harbor of Hilo on the island of Hawaii. The ship was immediately surrounded by outrigger canoes. The friendly natives climbed on board and distributed fruit, "principally pineapples, the best I have ever eaten."

When the *Cyane* got underway from Hilo she steered for Honolulu, which she reached on 2 August. "This place looks improved," Frank wrote, "it has the air of a large city, when coming from the quiet hamlet like . . . Hilo. I am luxuriating in the comfort of being in a *close* har[b]or . . . where there is no swell & no anxiety."

Frank spent his weeks in Honolulu in social duties. "Dinners with the people of the world by day, teas with the missionaries at night, have been the order of our existence." In return the officers of the *Cyane* hosted parties on board. "This ship it is said . . . [has] produced more social intercourse among all classes than . . . [has] happened for years." Meanwhile the crew gave the ship a complete overhaul and painted her inside and out.

In late August Du Pont completed preparations for sea. "My visit here has been useful and honorable, if I can believe all I hear."

The *Cyane* sailed on 6 September 1847 for California. After a week at sea Frank wrote Sophie, "The ship never was in better discipline, in finer order, or more excellent harmony. The crew I am very proud of, and their conduct during our whole visit was most praiseworthy."

He continued, "From the 16th of July, when we entered Hilo . . . until the 6th of the present month, when we left Honolulu, has been an oasis in this long dreary desert, the North Pacific. I enjoyed it exceedingly, physically and morally, in every way. It has given us all a new lease in our powers of enduring this protracted cruise—or what promises to be so. . . . I have enjoyed much the opportunity of becoming acquainted with the actual condition of the Islands, their government, politics, parties, and men; their wants, their intercourse with foreign nations, etc., and the continued injustice they receive from these. I live in hopes that I may be able to do them some service at Washington."

On 18 September, while still at sea, Frank allowed himself to indulge his yearning for home. "This is your birthday, is it not?" he wrote Sophie. "What would I not give to know how and where you are! Perhaps at home, receiving visits and flowers, books, or other nice presents. The next one, if God in his mercy be willing, will be with you! though when I think of my return, which I rarely *dare* do, and still more fear to write to you about it, a strong feeling arises against the Navy Department, for its gross neglect of this station. . . . But enough of this. I will not get angry—not on your birthday anyhow."

The *Cyane* arrived in Monterey in late September, joining the *Independence, Warren,* and storeships *Erie* and *Southampton*. Frank received a box from Sophie, containing a comforter, religious verses, and cigars, "a great treat out here, where they are very bad & expensive. I do not smoke to excess, yet enjoy them greatly in the evening, for I am very fond of being alone in my cabin; after writing an hour or reading, I like to jump up, light a cigar & walk up & down & think of you."

Commodore Shubrick had decided to supplement the blockade of the Mexican coast by seizing as many ports as he could garrison. On 20 October, after an hour's bombardment, the *Congress* and *Portsmouth* had captured Guaymas.

Stopping to take on water at San Jose, Lower California, where the inhabitants were friendly, the *Cyane* and *Independence* were joined by the *Congress,* fresh from her attack at Guaymas. The three ships got underway and, on 10 November, approached Mazatlán under the signal to "prepare for battle" and anchored in the harbor at 8 A.M. "I am in the hands of my Maker," Frank assured Sophie. "I trust in him. He knows what is best. I have had no part or lot in bringing about the present condition of things; yet my duty is clear, and I have been given moral courage and physical nerve to meet any emergency, I think. If it should please God to take me away I dread the dreadful consequence to you."

At 8 A.M. the next morning the *Cyane* warped closer to shore. In the early morning light, the town looked deserted. The guns on a near point, close enough to have struck the *Cyane* with shot, had been removed. The barge from the *Congress* with Captain La Vallette and a body of officers, pulled toward the town flying a flag of truce in its bow. Soon the barge returned and La Vallette sent word that the town would capitulate at 12 noon that day. Frank received a message to take his crew alongside the *Independence* at 11. At the appointed time all boats from the *Independence, Congress,* and *Cyane* came together. Most of these boats were equipped with heavy pieces of artillery. "The sight was imposing."

Frank led the contingent of 500 sailors and 100 marines to the Mazatlán barracks where crew members ran up the Stars and Stripes. Lieutenant Halleck of the Army Engineers reconnoitered and designated the points to be occupied.

Shubrick appointed a four-man commission, headed by Du Pont, to meet with the Mexicans and agree on the terms of occupation. Frank grew noticeably annoyed at these meetings, and confessed, "I have never had my patience so sorely tried, yet it held out; but I can now understand why a peace with this country may be long delayed. There is an idiosyncrasy of temper among this people which is indescribable,—a shrewdness and obliquity combined,—attached the greatest importance to a single work, and for a word they would clasp their hands, smoke a cigar, and see destruction and ruin carried to thousands around them. They cannot appreciate consideration or liberality from the strong, for the reason they do not consider themselves weak, never mind what circumstances of ignominy they may be placed in."

The haggling continued for two days before the Mexicans signed the American articles. Frank remarked that people of property, who "daily expected to be sacked by their own soldiers," welcomed the Americans.

Although the sailors and marines had taken Mazatlán without opposition, Frank felt apprehensive about holding and administering a town of its size. "To govern a town of eleven thousand inhabitants is no small matter. The commodore is crowding me very much, but I will do all I can. He wishes me to collect the revenue. . . . Appraisers, weighers, gaugers, guards, and officers all to be taken from the navy and army, when we have not a man or officer to spare from the whole squadron, to say nothing of our ignorance of these duties. People will find, before we are done, what taking a town, without *suitable* force to keep it, will be. Not a ship can leave here for any other service."

A more normal situation was restored when, after further negotiation, the members of the municipal junta agreed to operate and govern the city at the pleasure of the occupying force. The inhabitants returned. "The *cuaretel* [barracks] is well fortified, the people friendly, and as the ships are going to remain we shall, I think, enjoy quiet possession."

News reached Mazatlán that General Winfield Scott and his army had marched triumphantly into Mexico City.

Ashore at Mazatlán marauding Mexicans, under the leadership of the former captain of the port, a German renegade, were roaming the outskirts of town, harassing townspeople, burning launches, and intercepting the mails. The Americans decided to land a force five miles up the beach from the town and, simultaneously, move out the force already in the barracks to "hem in" the Mexican renegades. "I thought rather well of the plan," Frank revealed, "looked upon it, however, as a wild goose chase to attempt to catch any of these people who know every bush, path, rock, and swamp,—but thought it would throw them back further into the country, and open more avenues for the rancheros with provisions to come in."

The *Cyane* furnished two boats, and the *Independence,* a third. On the night selected, the expedition, sixty strong, pulled toward the beach and landed. The sailors and marines found themselves near a party of forty Mexicans, the advance guard of the ex-captain of the port. The Americans lay low on the beach within seventy yards of the foe, and listened as Mexican reinforcements rode up.

On the *Cyane,* after seeing his boats depart, Frank felt anxious. He dared not trust messages from shore, so he landed and hiked up to the barracks. After talking with the officer in charge, Frank was reassured, and he returned to the *Cyane.*

The force from the barracks moved out at 10 P.M. with a detachment from the *Congress* in advance of the other companies. Lieutenants Halleck and Baldwin led. Abruptly, they confronted a knoll thick with bushes and were hailed by the Mexicans, once, twice. Baldwin ordered the men of the advance column to fire, and Halleck attempted to countermand the order, but he was too late. The rear column, hearing the gunshot, rushed forward "sailor-like." In the darkness, Baldwin's men mistook the onrushing column for the enemy, and fired. Twelve men slumped to the ground, dead. The Americans then charged the bushes but the enemy had vanished. The American forces moved on. Arriving at the ringleader's headquarters, they drove out a "nest of pirates," who scurried away, led by the ex-captain of the port. Soon the barracks force met the boat party. Neither side had gained or lost ground significantly in the skirmishing.

On 2 December the *Cyane* got underway for La Paz. The withdrawal of the *Dale* from that town had emboldened Mexican renegades to ride into La Paz at night and burn the houses of American sympathizers.

The *Cyane*'s arrival restored the confidence of these Mexican families, who promptly moved back to town. Frank, however, was convinced that unless the United States government sent out a regiment of regular troops, such insurrections would recur. American "tenure of the whole of the Californias, of Guaymas, of Mazatlan, to say the least of it, is not respectable, and unworthy of our country. A few sailors here, fewer marines there, ragged volunteers in a third place, give no evidence of the strength or power of a great nation. . . .

"This peninsula (L[ower] C[alifornia]) has suffered greatly from the war, first by breaking up of its commerce, which it was my lot to do in 1846 . . . then finally landing garrisons so weak and contemptible in numbers as would have invited the attack of a nation of Lilliputians; producing insurrections more disastrous by far to the country than its foreign foes. For it is one of the peculiar traits of Mexicans to be perfectly ruthless with respect to each other's property in such circumstances. Cattle have been destroyed . . . ranchos plundered without number.

"Had half the men-of-war which arrived in the Gulf after Vera Cruz had fallen, been dispatched to this station after that event, with the marines . . . we should now have been in *respectable* possession of Upper and Lower California, with every port on the west coast of Mexico from Guaymas to Acapulco; their environs clear of the enemy, commerce flourishing, and the advantages as apparent to the Mexicans as we could desire. All this, too, without the loss of a single life, and without knocking down towns which did not return a host. As it is, our tenures are almost disgraceful, and if Providence was not evidently with us in this war, and thus overruling evil for some great blessing yet hidden to our short sight, we should have been overwhelmed. We are now only overworked, everybody worn out; with no relief in view. I don't know sometimes whether my men are sailors or soldiers. How in their desultory life and duties I have kept the control of them, or my ship in decent order, I know not."

Christmas Day 1847. Frank yearned for home. "I cannot retire at the conclusion of this holy day, without saying a word to you, whose image has been flitting so before me—and with my mind so filled with speculations as to the welfare of all at home. I have been with you all in heart. . . . A Merry Christmas to you. I have a million things to say to you,—but it is so hard to dole them out through the nib of my faithful gold pen. 1848 is nearly here. I fairly long for it. I want so to be able to say, 'God willing, I shall see Sophie this year.' "

In La Paz Frank described himself as "locked up in the most stupid place" and reflected on the consequences of the war. "If we were to occupy all Mexico, it might be a great injury to *us*. I don't know how that would be; but oh, the countless blessings to Mexico herself no human being can doubt, who sees this country and knows its condition, moral and physical. It is not a *nation*,—the word should not be applied to it,—it wants the main element of cohesion, patriotism. They have been so badly governed it could not exist. . . . I look upon the demand of the Californias and north of the 32d parallel, that is, New Mexico, as moderate; territory which for years Mexico has utterly neglected, and had in consequence no control of, and from which she has derived not a single cent."

On Sunday, 13 February 1848, the *Cyane* upped anchor and headed for San Jose. "The long lay at La Paz was very irksome to most of the officers, and . . . in its present dejected state, is the least interesting place we have been in, even on this uninteresting coast. Yet I enjoyed the quiet very much, and somehow I did not find the days long."

As the *Cyane* arrived at San Jose her officers and crew were greeted by the sound of gunfire on shore. Leading a force of eighty-five men, Frank hastily landed to aid the garrison of sixty-two embattled sailors and marines and California volunteers under attack by insurrectionists. His men drove off the opposition and Frank was elated that not a man was lost. He believed that thirty-two of the marauders had been killed. "The service we rendered was opportune, was well done, attended with personal hazard, was crowned with complete success."

Back on board ship, Frank penned a long letter to Mackenzie. "You speak of better disposition of the force out here, blockading, &c. . . . we have never had a *decent* force . . . for the work in hand. . . . Blunders have been committed as elsewhere but the labor has been ceaseless in proportion to the means, far beyond the work anywhere else. . . ."

Describing his crew, Frank added, "They have been as true as steel to me—the pride of ship is at its tip top, the ship herself efficient in every part, & the happiest and proudest years of my professional life have been passed on board of her."

To Eleuthera, he mourned his lost youth, "I may literally say I have grown grey in this northwest coast of America; for in the life we have led, in the ceaseless excitement, the constant exposure harrassing responsibilities, time does not fall lightly upon one so situated." He added that he and the first lieutenant, "through a slow but gradual process have changed a pair of black whiskers, for a shade much resembling the coat of a beautiful Lower California Badger I have on board."

Intelligence from Mazatlán indicated that a peace treaty with Mexico had been signed, "and some hopes are entertained all round that it will result in something. Our joy at the fact has been greatly allayed here by finding Lower California is not included in the ceded territory."

By mid-April the *Cyane* lay anchored at Mazatlán along with the *Independence* and *Congress*. "We know not what awaits us—home, or the prolongation of an arduous cruise. Be this as it may, we have cause to be thankful to our merciful Father for His gracious protection during the last two or three months. The Lower California war is closed effectually, I believe, and the part this ship took in it I hope creditable and beneficial to all concerned."

By the Treaty of Guadalupe Hidalgo, ratified by the United States Senate, the United States obtained Upper California, New Mexico, and the Rio Grande boundary for $15 million and the assumption of the claims of United States citizens against Mexico. Frank was deeply disturbed. "Perhaps it will surprise you, if not *shock* you, when I tell you that nothing but the knowledge of the transcendent evils of war, brought home to me in our limited sphere out here, joined to my moral repugnance to it in the abstract, as every sane man must view war, that can reconcile me to such a treaty. I consider it disgraceful, and only less bad than war itself. . . . The Pusillanimity of its spirit will make the silly Mexicans reject it, persuaded we will beg still harder and take less if they hold out another year. . . . It is because I *want peace,* that I get so impatient at the ignorance displayed of the Mexican character."

On 6 May the *Ohio* with Commodore Thomas Ap Catesby Jones arrived from the Gulf of Mexico. "This has been a *great day,* fuss and excitement, salutes, guns, visits, swords and chapeaux, etc."

197

Jones relieved Shubrick as commander of the Pacific Squadron. This change of command marked the end of warlike activities in the Pacific.

Jones sent orders to Du Pont to ready the *Cyane* for home. "Joyful orders! We were congratulated on all sides, every one saying it is right, and lauding Jones for his decision. It has had a happy effect on the crews of the whole squadron."

Ashore at Mazatlán, skippers of coasters and traders congratulated Frank. One said, " 'Well, captain, we hear the Cyane is going home,—well you must be glad,—you have been out here a long time, but you have a good name on the coast.' "

On 1 June the *Cyane* sailed. As she crossed the stern of the *Ohio*, Frank's crew, dressed in white and lining the rigging, gave three lusty cheers. The *Ohio*'s sailors responded and her band struck up "Home, Sweet Home." When the *Cyane* cleared the *Ohio*, her seamen fired a thirteen-gun salute. Sailors of the *Congress* manned the rigging. Cheers were exchanged with the *Independence*.

The *Cyane* stopped at San Blas to take on water and food. Here Frank learned that the Mexican Senate had ratified the Treaty of Guadalupe Hidalgo, "and there is peace! Happy event! and a fortunate termination to a contest which, however wrong in its commencement, cannot yet be judged by man. The folly of not including Lower California is hard for us here to get over."

Arriving at Valparaiso, the crew immediately started refitting the ship. On 7 August the *Cyane* was underway again, this time for the States. On his voyage home, Frank pondered his years in the Pacific. "I made the cruise of this ship the thread upon which to weave the operations of the squadron in the Pacific, from the beginning to the end of the war."

The *Cyane* rounded Cape Horn easily. "We came down the west coast to the Cape with awful speed, before the north-west gales, scudding before seas that make a man's hair stand on end, under a close reef main topsail,—but this is the finest ship I ever saw for the most dangerous operation. We did not suffer from the cold."

On 11 September the *Cyane* was in the Atlantic and, a month later, she anchored off the Gosport Navy Yard in Norfolk. Frank met old friends, who complimented him on his appearance. "I find I stand high with the profession, just where I want to stand well."

By 26 October 1848 Frank was home in Louviers.

XIV

"It is important duty"

Du Pont returned proud of his service in the Mexican War. To Pendergrast, he wrote, ". . . in my profession I have had but one goal or ambition: to stand well with the worthy men of that profession. The cordial welcome I had at Norfolk from some choice spirits such as [Franklin] Buchanan . . . the joy your letter gave me . . . have made me feel proud indeed."

The Pacific Squadron's operations during the war, he continued, "were creditable to the Navy, as they have been important to the country—for the great result of the silly contest has been the acquisition of California, which is wholly & solely due to the Navy."

As was their custom, the du Pont family celebrated New Year's Day 1849 with a reunion. "Great has been my happiness to be at home at this annual period for the revival of social sympathies & domestic affections. Forty-seven of us met . . . at the old homestead over the creek, built just forty-six years ago by my uncle, within a few hundred yards of the recent remains of an Indian Wigwam," he wrote Pendergrast.

Frank often visited Washington "to catch up . . . in national affairs after three years in that wretched country of California." Early in January 1849 members of Congress debated the abolition of corporal punishment in the Navy. The arguments "were highly interesting, most animated I have ever listened to."

The "sickly sentimental" antiflogging reformers labored under three misapprehensions, Frank believed. The first was that there was a great deal of flogging in the Navy. He denied this. The second mistaken notion was that most seamen were whipped for offenses against their officers. Frank denied this, too. Nineteen out of twenty of the whippings were for the protection of the hardworking portion of a crew, a group always composing a large majority of every United States man-of-war.

The third erroneous assumption was that naval officers opposed the abolition of flogging. They did not, stressed Frank, but they wanted to be provided with an adequate substitute.

Attempting to halt the movement to abolish flogging by seeking senatorial support, Frank called Delaware Senator John M. Clayton's attention to the procedure followed by Great Britain in response to public and parliamentary concern over the amount of flogging in its armed service. A study by a royal commission had concluded that flogging could not be completely eliminated. Frank urged that a congressional committee make a rigid examination of punishments. Then, if changes were needed, Congress could enact them.

If Congress abolished flogging without granting naval officers some deterrent, Frank gravely predicted that law and order would vanish. In his opinion, if the abolition order was read on board any ship in the Pacific Squadron, its crew might seize the vessel and steer for the California gold mines.*

"The issue of punishment," Frank noted to Pendergrast, "is a vital one to our professional existence. . . . I will say . . . that I had about twenty of the greatest scoundrels that ever broke Jail, yet the certain conviction in their minds, that they were *sure* of punishment, prevented the necessity of resorting to it—but for the cats tied up in the bag, they would have kept the ship in a state of anarchy, if not taken her."

He was dismayed to read in a newspaper a letter from old Commodore Stewart favoring the abolition of corporal punishment, a letter "full of bad grammar—so evidently written by a man in his decline. It would be easy to overwhelm the old man, who spent a life punishing seamen, & never with a line in favor of any reform or amelioration of their condition—but he joins in a popular cry, & throws the weight of his name against the profession which has made him what he was."

Later Frank informed Pendergrast, "Although the abolition of it is certain, the candid people admit the necessity of providing substitutes."

---

* The flogging issues in this chapter rely on Harold D. Langley, *Social Reform in the United States Navy, 1798–1862* (Urbana, Ill., 1967), pp. 170–206.

While in Philadelphia, Du Pont purchased a copy of Herman Melville's novel, *White Jacket*. On reading the chapters relating to flogging, he became "indignant," and described the author as "an undyed villain." He "has given us through his talents & lies, the worst stab yet. . . . This fellow belongs to that class with whom crime is nothing—it is only the punishment which degrades.

"You can conceive," Frank continued to Davis, "an educated, gifted, unprincipaled man, brought by his vices to a whaler & man of war, ascribing his condition to anything or anybody but his own worthless self, with his intellect keen & his sense of degradation complete. . . . His lies are plausible, difficult to meet. . . ."

Frank urged Davis to review *White Jacket* for the newspapers. "You can add a laurel to your literary fame by holding that fellow up as he should be. . . . nobody but a naval officer can do it." Davis declined, but urged Frank to write a review.

On reading the entire book through, instead of in bits and pieces as he had done, Frank conceded that "parts are very interesting & some parts are admirably done." While on a visit to Annapolis, Frank was unable to persuade any of his friends that *White Jacket* "was likely to do harm—they say it is looked upon as a work of fiction."

Frank revised his opinion when he reread the book carefully. "I was somewhat disturbed at first on reading White Jacket, but on closer inspection I think it will do less harm than I thought," he concluded to a friend. "The general cleverness & spirit of the work seem disfigured, by the extreme of caricature & exaggerations of many scenes."

To Davis, Frank confessed that on a second reading his fears were "very much allayed. Yet it will do us *some* harm there is little doubt. . . .White Jacket is full of anachronisms. Melville seems to have availed himself of twelve months experience in a man of war, or rather to make these twelve months answer the purpose of showing up every enormity he has ever heard of on the ocean, & making the one frigate the stage on which they were exhibited. The flogging scene, with its attendant blasphemy on the part of the Captain, is given with such precision as to time and circumstances as to make the onus."

On 1 March 1849 Du Pont described President Polk's last levee in the White House—"It was the densest throng possible." All the officers, as requested by the secretaries of the Army and Navy, were resplendent in their dress uniforms—"it was very brilliant."

On the following day, Frank and some friends paid their respects to the President-elect, Zachary Taylor, "who shakes [everyone] . . . very cordially by the hand—his face is better than his pictures, & I think is feeble in his health, others say not." "I was pleased with the old general," Frank told Pendergrast, "he was more than I expected. He has the gift of sagacity." Taylor chose William Ballard Preston to be his Secretary of the Navy. Du Pont was not displeased by Preston's selection. "He is a man of talents, of integrity, considerable eloquence, a *western* Virginian. . . . [He] has some western attributes, can say *no*—is ambitious to make a name & to justify his sudden elevation."

On returning to Delaware, Frank and Sophie matured plans for the alterations of their "cottage." They were living in the first home of their own not far from Louviers. The cottage was "greatly out of repairs & I've concluded to make a new house of it. It will be sightly, commodious, and the grounds having been steadily improved, it will make a snug place. My brother has let me have as much land as I want, with deeds, etc. I will only take enough to add to the value of the house—a field & paddock with an enclosure for shrubbery," he wrote Pendergrast.

The couple planned to enlarge the house and make it "very comfortable, with handsome porticos." By increasing the acreage, Frank would have a fine field for pasture for his two horses and several cows. "My fences," he added to Pendergrast, "will enclose ten acres, & this is about my ideal of happiness; a rural residence, comprising gardens, fruits, pleasure grounds, & paddock, but *no farming*." The total cost of alterations and additions would be $3,500.

While carpenters repaired the cottage, Frank and Sophie were "billeted [with] different relations . . . our furniture was scattered in all directions."

In late July and early August Frank was in Annapolis, sitting on the Board of Examiners to test the midshipmen. "You would be surprised," he informed Sophie, by "the advantages . . . these young men have over what we had in our day [which] should make them very thankful."

When the Board of Examiners adjourned, its work completed, the Navy Department ordered Du Pont to Washington to serve on a board convened to reorganize the rules and regulations of the Naval Academy. This work was soon finished—"a capital programme."

The Secretary of the Navy was delighted with the board's effort, but Frank was chagrined to learn that "everything was still on the old footing . . . [the] middies going out & getting drunk!!" However, Secretary Preston cut through the red tape, and finally the new regulations went into effect.

In the interim, the secretary appointed Du Pont Superintendent of the naval academy. While he felt honored, Frank wrote to Preston, he had "reasons of a very imperative nature . . . to ask the favor of being relieved of this order." As Frank explained to Sophie, he "desired to get rid of Annapolis, not alone because it would be so complete a disruption of our domestic existence & ties, but I'm not clearly satisfied that the duties are sufficiently in my line to build any reputation upon—it would certainly be a place accompanied with a wear & tear of mind . . . that could bring but little compensation. However relatively easy it will be with a full code of Regulations, it is after all a thankless place."

In an interview with the secretary, Du Pont again declined the appointment, and Preston revoked the order. "It is a great relief. The Dept. are now fully aware that I want no shore duty, which takes me from my home."

Just before Christmas Frank and Sophie moved back into their cottage. "We are being now compensated for all our trouble and discomforts, by finding that all our anticipations are now more than realized, in having a cheerful & very comfortable abode with plenty of room for our friends when they come," he wrote Pendergrast.

During the first half of 1850 Frank sat on a court of inquiry at Annapolis, attended the funeral of President Taylor, and lobbied Congress to debar officers of the defunct Texas Navy from the ranks of the United States Navy. "The Texans are dead, without a doubt." Several years later Frank was to hear searing remarks made by Senator Sam Houston of Texas about his efforts to exclude these officers from the Navy. In August Frank journeyed to Cincinnati by way of Buffalo and Lake Erie to attend an Episcopal Church convention, where he was reunited with his best friend, Pendergrast.

On 28 September 1850 Congress passed a bill that abolished the flogging of naval personnel and, on the same day, President Millard Fillmore signed the appropriation bill containing the proviso.

When Frank returned to Delaware from Cincinnati, he discovered that he had been appointed a member of the temporary Lighthouse Board, a committee "to be concerned in relation to lighthouses, boats,

& buoys." The members of the board included Commodore William B. Shubrick; Brevet Brigadier General Joseph G. Totten, Corps of Engineers; Lieutenant Colonel James Kearney, Topographical Engineers; Professor Alexander D. Bache, Superintendent Coast Survey; and Naval Lieutenant Thornton A. Jenkins. Since lighthouses were under the jurisdiction of the Treasury Department, the Secretary of the Treasury, Thomas Corwin, charged the board "to inquire into the condition of the light-house establishment of the United States, and make a general detailed report and programme to guide legislation in extending and improving our present system of construction, illumination, inspection, and superintendence."

Board members set up offices in the Winder Building in Washington. At the first meeting in early May 1851 the board placed Frank on two committees, one with Kearney to check the relative expenses of the system of lighthouses in the United States and Europe, and one with Shubrick to prepare directives for the guidance of lightkeepers. To Sophie, he admitted, "This duty is going to interfere much with our domestic happiness, & yet, though I would have given a good deal, that I had not been selected, I cannot see that I could have declined it—it will be improving, it is honorable, & will be of professional service to me in every way." Three days later, he conceded, ". . . It is important duty & as you say connected with benefit to one's fellow creatures. I did not seek it, & it gives me position, & means of improvement."

To Davis, he explained, ". . . it was one of those honors which I could not decline, & yet would have preferred that it had been given [to] some one else. I felt also very doubtful as to being able to fill it with advantage to anyone. But when there is a will there is a way—and the reading up [is] not difficult, for cargoes have been written on the subject."

The board received orders from Secretary Corwin on 29 May 1851 to inspect Flynn's Knoll in New York Harbor and report on the proper lighthouse structure for it. Members of the board traveled to New York, and registered at the Astor House. For two days they inspected lighthouses, a light vessel, and Flynn's Knoll. On his return to the hotel after the first day, Frank wrote Sophie, "We had good meals & were as merry as crickets." The work completed, Frank made a quick trip to Delaware.

He received orders from the Navy Department to comment on the proposed modifications of the harbor defense fortifications, pursuant to a matter laid before Congress by Secretary of War C. M. Conrad.

Frank rejoined the other Lighthouse Board members in Washington, and journeyed with them to Norfolk, before returning with the group to New York with orders to proceed to Newport, Rhode Island; Boston; and Portland, Maine.

By mid-July 1851 Frank was able to return to Delaware, where he turned his attention to coastal defense as requested by the Navy Department. With the help of Davis through correspondence, Frank finished his report. He addressed himself to the questions, "To what extent, if any ought the present system of fortifications, for the protection of our seaboard, be modified, in consequence of the application of steam to vessels of war? Could seacoast forts be abolished and leave the defense of harbors to the Navy alone?"

Du Pont pointed out the main function of the Navy was not defensive. "Indeed, this arm can only fill its special mission in war, that of *aggression,* by being enabled to *leave* the great seaports and exposed points of our maritime frontier to a more certain and more economical system of protection, in order to carry the 'sword of the state' upon the broad ocean, sweep from it the enemy's commerce, capture or scatter the vessels of war protecting it, cover and convoy our own to its destined havens, and be ready to meet hostile fleets; in other words, to contend for the mastery of the seas, where alone it can be obtained, on the sea itself."

As to the value of forts, Frank contended that "forts . . . are the only permanent defences and the most economical; for, with the present science in construction and choice of materials, the outlay is there once for all, for the repairs are next to nothing. Forts offer means by which a small force is enabled to resist a large one; a smaller number of men a large army. . . . Forts can be made impregnable against any naval force that could be brought against them, and are needed for the protection of our own fleets while preparing for hostilities on the ocean. They are secure depots for munitions of war, and render defence certain and easy. . . .

"How would a naval force, for home defence, be partitioned out to the different cities and stations, without endless vexation, dissatisfaction, and dispute? To employ our active navy, in whole or in part, to the entire or partial abandonment of our system of fortifications, would be to supplant impregnable bulwarks by pregnable ones, a fixed security by a changeable one. . . ."

Du Pont underscored, "A navy becomes efficient just in proportion as it is relieved from harbor defence; and in a war, even defensive in its origin and object, the navy, in almost every case, must assume an offensive attitude. We lose the vantage ground if we wait the assault of an enemy. . . ."

In the past naval successes against forts, he stressed, were due to the forts being poorly equipped and manned. Then he listed the effectiveness of forts against fleets, and pointed out that both France and England, while building war steamers, were also adding to the fixed defenses of their seaboards.

"After mature examination, I am of the opinion that, in a system of national defence, forts cannot be dispensed with without entailing enormous expenditures for uncertain results."

With California now a part of the United States, Du Pont, with keen insight, emphasized the importance of the Sandwich Islands to America's defense in the Pacific. "It is impossible to estimate too highly the value and importance of the Sandwich Islands, whether in a commercial or military point of view. Should circumstances ever place them in our hands, they would prove the most important acquisition we could make in the whole Pacific ocean, an acquisition intimately connected with our commercial and naval supremacy in those seas; be this as it may, these islands should never be permitted to pass into the possession of any European power."

In his report, Du Pont did not lose the opportunity to push for a much bigger navy. "The naval power of England is greater than ever before in her history, and the disparity between us is yearly increasing, particularly in her steam navy.

"In conclusion, whatever may be decided in relation to the national defence by fortifications . . . I beg leave to express an emphatic dissent from all theories having for their object the substitution of active ships of war for permanent works. This would be placing the navy in a false position before the country; giving its duties to perform to which its organization is inapplicable. . . .

"To retain the navy for harbor defence was seriously entertained at the commencement of the last war with England [1812]; the proposition to do so sprung from the apprehension that it could not compete with the vastly superior England force upon the ocean. But at that time some brave and sagacious officers in the high ranks saved the navy from the fate that threatened it, and to these gentlemen it owes all its subsequent honors, usefulness, and prosperity. If any such ideas prevail at this day, in or out of the profession, those holding them would do well to pause and consider what the navy would have lost, and what the country would have lost, if our ships of war had at that eventful period been deprived of the opportunity of filling so bright a page in the nation's history of their achievements upon the open sea."

The Secretary of War was pleased by Du Pont's report on coastal defenses. He told a naval friend of Frank's, "I know Cap. D[u Pont] through a very able report he has made to my Dept. I wish he would call & see me. All the Navy reports were able, but I like his best."

Frank returned to Washington to meet with other members of the Lighthouse Board to write their final report—"it will be a creditable work." The board pointed out many deficiencies. The lighthouses, light vessels, beacons, buoys, and their accessories "were not as efficient as the interest of commerce, navigation, and humanity demanded." The lighthouse establishment of the United States did not compare favorably with those of Great Britain or France. The towers and building had not been constructed of the best materials, nor were they under the supervision of competent engineers. The lanterns were of improper dimensions, and constructed of "ill-adapted, and . . . not economical materials." The illuminating apparatus "was of the description now nearly obsolete throughout all maritime countries." There was no system of inspection "to render the light-house establishment moderately useful or efficient."

To correct these and other deficiencies, the board made lengthy recommendations. In conclusion the members wrote, "The board have not sought so much to discover defects and point them out, as to show the necessity of a better system. Commerce and navigation, in which every citizen of this nation is interested, either directly or indirectly, claim it; the weather-beaten sailor asks it, and humanity demands it."

The night the members signed the report, 30 January 1852, the Secretary of the Navy hosted a dinner, "a grand affair." Frank made new acquaintances and renewed old ones with senators and representatives. He especially enjoyed chatting with Senator Daniel Webster.

The following morning, Frank waited on President Fillmore and remained an hour and a half. Frank took the opportunity to tell the President that he had filed an application at the Navy Department for a pursership for a nephew, who was "a member of a large family, in various branches of manufacturing," who were zealous Whigs. "No one could be more gracious or behave more as a President should on these occasions." Despite Frank's lobbying efforts, the young man did not receive the appointment.

Throughout the early months of 1852 Frank often traveled to Washington, still caught up in Lighthouse Board affairs, or visited Annapolis to sit on the Board of Examination. After inspecting the naval academy, Frank wrote Charles Davis, "This is a noble institution. I came here with some prejudice against the revised system, although I was responsible in part for what led to it. But it all works well. I was fearful that the course was too scientific & less practical than it should be, although I am convinced true science can never be carried too far in a general sense, but the objects & ends in view must also have their weight—but the practice ship reverses all objections. These boys knew more than midship[men] after a first cruise, simply because the whole duty of the officers on board is turned to their instructions."

To Sophie, he wrote in a similar vein. "I am exceedingly pleased with this institution & I know no place in the whole country where I would rather see a boy go than here. Manly exercises at the cannon, muskets, broad sword, come in as recreations & producing fine physical development, while the proficiency of the youngsters & their regular advancement in their studies is very striking—then there is no violation of discipline & the habits of self denial & self restraint are so firmly, yet so kindly insisted upon, that it must leave its influence through life. . . ."

In early September Frank returned to Washington to lobby the passage of the lighthouse bill, and listen to the debates in Congress. He was overjoyed when the bill passed—"a rare triumph." To his friend Henry Winter Davis, congressman from Maryland, who helped push the bill through the House, Frank wrote, ". . . our Lighthouse work of the last eighteen months has been crowned with high & unexpected success. Both Houses have adopted our plan for reorganization, by a decided vote but yet after the most violent & hostile opposition in the House & Senate. . . ."

XV

"I was speechless for a while"

In February 1853 Du Pont gained permission from the Navy Department to become general superintendent of the Exhibition of the Industry of All Nations, better known as the Crystal Palace Exhibition, in New York, the first American World's Fair. The huge success of the London Exhibition in Hyde Park in 1851 inspired the American venture. The Crystal Palace Exhibition was the brainchild of a prominent Boston carriage dealer, Edward Riddle, an imaginative promoter. Riddle had served as American Commissioner at the London Exhibition and, at its closing, British exhibitors, anxious to develop an overseas market, approached him. Impressed by the profits generated at the London fair, he hatched the idea of an American exhibition and hurried to New York to gain support for the project. New York merchants and bankers agreed to back such a venture. The New York Common Council granted Riddle a lease on Reservoir Square (now Bryant Park) at the northernmost limits of the city. Then, unsure of the exhibition's success, Riddle impetuously withdrew and sold his lease to his supporters for $10,000.

On Riddle's departure, the new association of businessmen received a charter from the New York Legislature, incorporating "The Association for the Exhibition of the Industry of All Nations" for a five-year period with a capital of $200,000, and issued a call for stock subscriptions.

National pride motivated the Crystal Palace Exhibition. A display for the manufacturers and raw materials of America would introduce Europe and the entire world to the nation's technological progress. A parade of European manufactures would stimulate American industry to even greater progress.* The fair would serve as a university for the masses, an "encyclopedia of the science of life, for their education and edification."

The highest hurdle confronting the directors was the erection of an exhibition building. Meeting in August 1852, the committee selected a design submitted by George Carstensen and Charles Gildmeister, two unknown Danish architects residing in New York. It was "most on the Venetian style," shaped like a Greek cross surmounted at the intersection by a huge dome. When completed, this glass and iron building with its ground floor and galleries would provide nearly four acres of space. Essentially, it was the London Crystal Palace surmounted by a dome.

Workmen raised the first column of the Crystal Palace on 30 October 1852. Almost immediately, difficulties surfaced caused by administrative bungling. Construction lagged. To rescue the exhibition, its directors, possibly because of family connections, sought to engage Commander Samuel Francis Du Pont as superintendent and Lieutenant Charles Davis as his assistant, hoping that they might add prestige to the venture.

Twice Frank refused. Finally, Theodore Sedgwick, the President of the Crystal Palace Association, visited Delaware in an effort to convince Du Pont to accept the challenge. Sophie was against the move, but Frank weighed the possibilities. He wrote Henry Winter Davis, "The whole thing is in the hands of gentlemen of the first stamp, & its success seems assured. I feel I confess some timidity, in consequence of the sphere being so new. . . . Yet I feel I have some elements for this thing."

Undecided whether to accept the assignment, Frank went to Washington to seek advice. Commodore Shubrick considered "it an *honor*," although he foresaw difficulties to overcome. Other officers agreed with this assessment. Frank set forth the pros and cons in a letter to Charles Davis: "It is admitted I believe to be complimentary to the Navy—it will offer an opportunity for improvement, & be still more the occasion of making valuable acquaintances, which to men of our roving profession may be agreeable & advantageous

---

* Material for the Crystal Palace Exhibition was gained from Charles Hirschfeld, "America on Exhibition: The New York Crystal Palace," *American Quarterly* 9 (1957): 101–16; and Monte A. Calvert, "American Technology at World Fairs, 1851–1876," unpublished M.A. thesis, University of Delaware, 1962.

at some future day. . . . I do not see much distinction or fame to be gained, it seems rather the result of our present position & reputation, which I feel to be much overrated, in my case & which may be [more] damaged than added to." Frank urged his friend to consider becoming the assistant superintendent.

In early February 1853, despite Sophie's misgivings, he went to New York and met with Davis and, together, they accepted the positions with the Crystal Palace. Settled at the St. Nicholas Hotel, Frank reassured Sophie, "I feel much easier than I expected . . . because the whole thing is akin to regulating a large man of war."

In another letter Frank continued, "The more I think of this the more I like it, for among other things I was thinking . . . that you would like it. It would give your mind new channels of thought. . . . The advance of art, knowledge, science &c. are . . . great . . . information & new ideas meet you. . . . I feel already my mental vigor stimulated."

Du Pont and Davis opened an office for the Crystal Palace at 53 Broadway. When they visited the construction site, they were shocked by the "chaos & confusion," the want of space, the absence of "all organization, the jawing between architects & builders, the rows . . . the local committees having no clear conception of what they were entering into." He concluded his description of this disorganization to Henry Winter Davis with the comment, "I say if I could convey to you a little of this & all its ramifications, even you would consider me a very bold man to have gone into such a kettle of fish. In fact I can hardly realize yet that I have done so."

The "neighborhood [is] a miserable one, & the mud was awful," he wrote Sophie. After meeting with the contractors, he stated, "My coming has stirred up everything & given a new life to the whole concern. . . . Our service consisting more in the confidence inspired among all concerned than as yet in any actual service. . . . it is . . . like taking a huge line of battle ship on the stocks & getting her equipped, manned, & in safe condition on the ocean."

In early March Frank left New York to go home to see Sophie, before traveling to Washington on Lighthouse Board business and to attend the inauguration of President Franklin Pierce. "The inauguration went off well. If he sustains the effect he has produced on every one, his success will be prodigious," he optimistically predicted. Several days later—"a day of ceremony"—a large body of naval officers, "superbly dressed," were introduced to the new Secretary of the Navy, James C. Dobbin, and with him, called on the new President. Afterward they visited with former President Fillmore and the new Secretary of War, Jefferson Davis.

A dispatch from Charles Davis urged Du Pont to return to New York. On his arrival on 10 March, he discovered everything "in a terrible snarl." The biggest problem proved to be the weatherproofing on the roof of the Crystal Palace. Many crates had arrived, but exhibitors, domestic and foreign, refused to open their boxes while rain continued to pour into the structure. A solution was finally worked out by altering the roof level.

After his return to New York, Sophie admitted to him, "I am so thankful you are well—& tis a relief to me you are out of Wash^n (I hope tis not 'out of the frying pan into the fire, tho'). . . . I cannot but be very anxious about the Crystal Palace. What you say gives fresh impulse to the fear I already so strongly entertained, that the building being behind hand, could be hurried, & every other consideration yielding to the necessity of its completion, it would be imperfectly done . . . & therefore be unsafe. . . . do give special attention to this—it is not only solicitude for *you* that prompts my anxiety; but you can readily conceive how many lives might be endangered. . . . Now that you *are* in New York, it is better for you to stay till you have got through with all that needs your personal attention. . . . These perpetual journeyings are *wearing* out to the body. . . . But I am resigned to this trial now. . . ."

By mid-March Frank still hoped to open the exhibition in May, if the workmen made "some great exertion." He met with the directors and apprised them of the situation. They promptly voted more money "to give new impetus to the work." Frank and Davis made the rounds, despite a raging storm, visiting the men at work, the foundries and machine shops, placating the architects.

Frank was encouraged by the news from abroad. Statuary, paintings, and "articles of rare value" were promised. National support for the event was developing. State legislatures voted money to assist their exhibitors. Rumors persisted that President Pierce and governors from various states would attend the opening.

Frank decided to bring Sophie to New York. He rented an apartment at 7 Waverly Place. Its rooms were large, "handsomely furnished, with bureaux, [and] large commode." He was impressed with "the quiet, genteel privacy of the establishment." In early May he left for Philadelphia where he met Sophie to escort her to New York.

As soon as she had settled in the apartment, Sophie wrote her sisters, "I must write you a few lines ere Frank goes to the office. . . . We arrived here very safely. . . . I was a great deal tired . . . tho' otherwise very well. . . . Our quarters here are most comfortable in every respect—quiet to an astonishing degree. I can scarcely believe we are in this modern Babylon—this busy bustling city. . . ."

To one of her sisters, Sophie painted a word picture of the apartment and their routine. "Our parlor is most comfortably furnished; there is a large centre table where we have our meals and a variety of nice little tables of all sorts—two of the nicest most comfortable sofas, & chairs of the most delightful easy kind—there is one sofa near one of the windows which I have adopted, it has near it the nicest of little tables for my work & with a drawer where I can put the inkstand & any other matters—this is *my corner,* that I have adopted specially. Our meals are of the nicest kind, no pretentions, but all neat & excellent, & sufficient. Frank seems happy to have me here that it makes me doubly glad to be able to come."

Inspections of the Crystal Palace convinced Frank that the exhibition's hoped-for opening in May was unfeasible. It was set back to 14 July, "a mortifying delay, not to say a disgraceful one," he wrote Henry Winter Davis. "My comfort in having embarked in a sinking ship . . . is that I may have saved her from foundering out right, for the ultimate sweep I have no doubt, & I believe the whole thing will meet the high expectations of the country."

In early July, carpenters and mechanics completed work. At 2 P.M. on the afternoon of 14 July, undaunted by the delays, the directors opened the exhibition with pageantry and enthusiasm. President Pierce journeyed up from Washington to take part. Ten thousand visitors crowded the Crystal Palace for the occasion. The speeches, sandwiched between the invocation and choral music, proved few and short. Theodore Sedgwick introduced the President, who spoke briefly, and the Crystal Palace Exhibition was declared open. It marked, in the words of a *New York Times* correspondent, "a day hallowed in American History," which saw "the sun of American industrial splendor" rise, never to sink again. The Crystal Palace was an achievement of American engineering. The spirit of the New York exhibition declared that the United States could exceed what England had achieved and that Americans were proud of it.

Ordinary citizens strolled about awed. They admired the huge bronzed dome and shiny interior galleries, decorated in rich cream relieved by red, blue, and yellow combinations, and enclosed by only glass and iron. The Crystal Palace symbolized American progress, "the first decided stand of America among the industrial & artistic nations of the earth," wrote a reporter. The exhibit hall was, emphasized Walt Whitman in an editorial, "certainly unsurpassed anywhere for beauty . . . an original, aesthetic, perfectly proportioned American edifice—one of the few of modern times not beneath old times. . . ."

Visitors enthused over the variety of exhibits from Europe, the jewelry, silverware, porcelain, metalwork, furniture, and fabrics. American displays demonstrated human ingenuity: reapers, mowers, threshers, plows, sewing machines, printing presses, grain separators, power rock drills, and portable hydraulic presses. Mixed in were carnival displays, statues modeled in spermaceti, stuffed birds, stag horns, and artificial fish. Sightseers could inquire about the "West-Indian Tincture and Abification Tooth Powder," "The Great National Instantaneous Liquid Hair Dye," and the "Anti-Scourbutic Soap."

Art critics condemned the works shown in the picture gallery as trash and humbugs. The majority of these were European paintings, largely from the romantic Düsseldorf School.

The midway atmosphere was heightened by establishments that were not an official part of the exhibition. Abutting the Crystal Palace, these grog shops, gambling dens, sideshows, and cockfight arenas irked more respectable citizens.

Opening day fervor dissipated when people learned that only one-third of the displays were in place. Such incompleteness inhibited sightseers. The New York *Tribune* dissuaded people from attending until September.

In late August Frank and Sophie left New York so he could travel to Washington on Lighthouse Board business. "I leave quite happy at the near completion of the Exhibition, at its unsurpassed beauty, & at the smooth & almost perfect working of our organization," Frank optimistically wrote his friend William Whetten, secretary of the Association. "We all *deserve* success in *every way*, that's certain."

Before Frank went on to Washington, he and Sophie settled into their cottage. They found the "place more attractive than ever. . . . the perfect quiet & the luxury of having not only nothing to torment me, but absolutely nothing to do, after the life I had led for the last four months, baffles all description . . . ," he wrote Henry Winter Davis. "I left New York perfectly happy, having accomplished more than I ever had dared to hope."

In early September, he arrived in Washington and realized there was much to be done—"but I will go at it like a Beaver," he wrote Sophie. "I do like so much this Light House work & association—our board are so clever & so amiable."

Frank returned to New York in late September. "Many beautiful things have been added," he reported to Sophie. "The picture gallery is most surpassing & the machinery arcade contains wonderful things never before collected together." After an evening trip to see the Crystal Palace fully lighted, he declared, "I was speechless for a while with the transcendent beauty of the scene—as the London one was never lighted. This is a distinctive feature for the Crystal Palace, it being the largest building in the world that was ever lighted up & shown at night. A band of music adds to the effect. There are *a few more* gas lights than in the whole city of New York in the streets!"

Although the exhibition drew praise, its directors faced a "terrible financial deficit." "The Directors," Frank confessed to Sophie, "have lost their heart & I cannot blame them, for their never was so much beauty, magnificence, and instruction wasted upon a nation." Attendance flagged.

Du Pont was eager to quit the superintendency. "I would . . . give a pretty round sum to be able to walk out of the Palace & never see it again," he wrote Charles Davis, who had returned to Cambridge. "But the connection is a delicate one to sever."

Finally in October Du Pont and Davis tendered their resignations to take effect on 1 November. They explained their action to Theodore Sedgwick: "It has been our desire to unite with you in promoting what we believe will prove a noted epoch in the industrial progress of our country, and in our own sphere to do something, however little for the maintenance of national pride & patriotism, for the removal of national prejudice, & for the extension of knowledge. However inconvenient it might be to remain, we should still hesitate to offer our resignations, if we were not satisfied that our retirement will prove compatible with the interests of the Association. The various branches of the Executive Department have been for a length of time in uninterrupted action, & we feel confident

215

that a prudent watchfulness only is necessary to secure its regular & efficient operation."

That fall the directors of the Crystal Palace installed stoves, hoping to attract visitors throughout the winter, but attendance continued to plummet. In the spring, the famed showman P. T. Barnum seized the presidency of the association and converted the building into a place of amusement. But, like his predecessors, Barnum floundered in red ink and resigned. The association collapsed into bankruptcy. A receiver took over for the creditors and managed the Crystal Palace for nearly four years, renting the site for various public functions until fire destroyed the building.

XVI

"The excitement . . .
is astonishing"

Throughout the spring and fall of 1854 Frank continued to commute to Washington on Lighthouse Board affairs, which also took him to the Delaware Capes, New York, Boston, Cape Cod, and Portland. During his time in Washington, Frank often took the opportunity to call on Secretary of the Navy Dobbin. On one occasion, after spending an entire evening in his company, he commented, "I was greatly pleased with him, because no one man ever impressed me more that had truly the interest of the Navy at Heart & he has become very familiar with the subject. . . . his [annual] report is one of the best, if not the best we ever have had."

Since 1850 a major effort had been spent on an attempt to draft a congressional bill that would improve the efficiency of the Navy. In his annual report for 1853, Secretary Dobbin had underlined the inefficiency of the naval establishment so far as its commissioned personnel was concerned, and had called for action on the part of Congress, although no legislation was forthcoming. In his annual report for 1854 he again requested Congress to take action, and this time it responded.

In January 1855, Du Pont was in Washington when congressmen were considering "An Act to Promote the Efficiency of the Navy." The object of the bill was to increase the efficiency of the Navy by eliminating incompetent officers, making the promotions of good men easier. The bill aimed to break the logjam created by elderly officers who were over age in grade. Many thirty-year-old passed midshipmen and forty-five-year-old lieutenants clogged the pipeline,

217

slowing the promotion of young and talented officers. A large majority of senior officers were well past middle age, and in some cases physically unfit for sea duty. Other officers, although healthy, were incapable of commanding a man-of-war.*

Asked by Secretary Dobbin to write a paper supporting the efficiency bill, Frank accomplished the task quickly, calling it "a good resume of the stagnant condition of the Navy." Perhaps more than any other officer, he lobbied for the bill's passage. He emphasized to both Delaware senators, Clayton and Bayard, that "this measure is right," and urged them "to give it a good life."

On 13 February the bill passed the House. Immediately after the vote, Frank hurried to the be first to tell Secretary Dobbin, "who was greatly elated and said some kind things."

While the bill was debated in the Senate, Frank continued to press for passage as he anxiously watched "the halt, the blind, the unfortunate, & the vicious . . . pouring in by every train to throw their weight against . . . the bill."

On 28 February the bill made it through the Senate. To implement the new law, a board of officers was to be appointed to examine the qualifications of all naval officers from the rank of passed midshipman upward. This board was to report its evaluations to Secretary Dobbin, who would review the findings, add his recommendations, and send them on to the President for executive action.

Throughout his career, Frank had been extremely critical of his superior officers, finding most of them incompetent. Now he saw a chance to rid the service of the deadwood. He was concerned that Secretary Dobbin appoint able officers to serve on the board, who were of "sufficient firmness to carry it out." On more than one occasion, he conversed with Dobbin, advising him as to the membership. Frank felt it vital that his friends, men who shared his views, be selected. Navy men were cognizant that Du Pont had the secretary's confidence "to a considerable extent." To Commander Andrew H. Foote, Frank confided, "My own fear is, that he [Dobbin] is not *quite* impressed with what a *fight* this is to be—before the country. . . . he thinks every thing is going as smooth as oil."

Acceptance of an appointment to the board would "require more *moral* courage than any task an officer could be called upon to

*Details for this chapter are taken from Frances L. Williams, *Matthew Fontaine Maury, Scientist of the Sea* (New Brunswick, N.J., 1963), pp. 269–93.

perform," Frank believed. "It would be a fortunate thing for *me* if I could be excused," he wrote Charles Davis, and "Pendergrast says I ought to be—he says the Dept. & the Navy ought to wish to spare me the *ire* which will be concentrated on me & almost on me alone. But I shrink from nothing connected with the work."

The board's composition should include, he continued, "men who are ready to defend the law & the action of the Board under it, in . . . public . . . , before Congress, in short who feel the full importance of the crisis & are willing to devote their energies until victory is won."

In early June, Secretary Dobbin named the officers who would constitute the Efficiency Board: captains William B. Shubrick, presiding officer, Matthew C. Perry, Charles S. McCauley, Cornelius K. Stribling, Abraham Bigelow; commanders Du Pont, Garrett J. Pendergrast, Franklin Buchanan, Samuel Barron, Andrew H. Foote; lieutenants John S. Missroon, Richard L. Page, Sylvanus W. Godon, William L. Maury, James S. Biddle.

"The board on the whole," Frank wrote Charles Davis, "is good." Later, he added, "all looks well, more than well, & with the exception of a certain member from Delaware we have a very large representation of the strongest men in the Navy." To Henry Winter Davis, he exulted, "it is the strongest board we could have had."

Just before the board met, Du Pont and Pendergrast, along with several other members, checked into Mrs. Smith's boarding house at 233 F Street, on the corner of 14th, close to Willard's Hotel. The Efficiency Board commenced deliberations on 20 June in an unoccupied house near the Navy Department. Members sat on weekdays from 10 A.M. until 3 P.M..

"I am following the Secretary of the Navy's appeal to me personally to be conciliatory, and I have been occupied in inculcating this spirit on others," Frank wrote Sophie. After the first few sessions, he favored her with short sketches of key members of the committee. "Perry is always wrong in the first impulse, his second thought is an improvement & the third distillation produces quite palatable results. . . . I do not think he likes this work & winces under some fancied responsibility which may make him unpopular."

McCauley, Stribling, and Bigelow "are too honest to falter." Shubrick "is nearly always right in what he does, & wrong in what he says—he is opposed to the . . . law, but he is too honorable to have accepted his orders if he did not intend to fulfill their requirements." Of the commanders, Pendergrast "looms up as the emergency calls for."

Throughout July the board continued its deliberations. "Our work [has] revealed the necessity for this great reform—how the Navy existed with the amount of dead weight fastened to it, seems inexplicable."

During the evenings and on Saturdays and Sundays, he sought out other members of the board, especially Shubrick. Frank exerted himself to convert them to his way of thinking about the officers in question. As the work of the Efficiency Board neared its end, he found time to write his friend Charles Davis, "I am free to say that the duty has been ably & fearlessly performed. The *whole amount* is perfectly awful to think of, yet most necessary & wise. All motives of expediency were thrown aside—no connexions social or political, no friendships however strong, were permitted to weigh a feather, if the individual came under the law."

All the members feared the resentment of those officers who were dropped or placed on the reserved list, and were deeply concerned about the reaction of the general public and the press.

On 26 July the Efficiency Board concluded its deliberations. Its findings concerning 712 officers whose careers had been reviewed were dispatched to Secretary Dobbin. Out of those 712 only 49 were dropped as incompetent or unworthy. The board placed seventy-one officers on the "reserved" (retired) list with leave-of-absence pay, and eighty-one on the "reserved" list with furlough pay, which was one-half of the former. Once Dobbin received the report, he sent for Du Pont. They spent two hours at the secretary's home reviewing the committee's work. After a careful study, Dobbin forwarded the findings to President Pierce.

Two days later the Secretary of the Navy, Commodore Shubrick, and Du Pont were summoned to the White House to explain each case. "We got through this satisfactorily," Frank told Sophie. "I left with the conviction that the result of the report, *not the names,* would be published immediately," he wrote Henry Winter Davis. "The Secretary of the Navy struck me as a man whose judgment, reason, & pride were all in the reform measure. He told me if he had done nothing else in this department, that one measure would satisfy his ambition. But while in this courageous mood, I could see him discover a bugaboo sitting in the corner in the shape of the public press."

President Pierce approved the Efficiency Board's report. "I hereby express my approval of the 'finding' of the Board as set forth in their report," he wrote Secretary Dobbin. "Proper orders will accordingly be issued in pursuance of the provisions of the law."

The committee's actions were communicated to the officers concerned. Then the storm broke. With rare exceptions, the officers placed on the reserved list, together with those dropped from the service, joined with relatives, friends, and politicians to protest vehemently. The recommendations of the board incurred reaction in public and private circles, and became a principal topic of discussion in the press.

The acrimony did not come as a surprise. In mid-September Frank wrote Lieutenant James S. Biddle, "The storm seems a little black, but less so than I expected." "Since the labors of the Board have been published, I have received several letters from retired officers or their relatives," he explained to Henry Winter Davis. "These, mostly written in good spirit, I have managed to answer though the task was not easy & moreover painful."

As public attacks against the board mounted, Frank informed Henry Winter Davis, "the efforts of the wounded are prodigious." The law setting up the Efficiency Board was attacked, and pressure increased to repeal it and to restore those retired or dropped to active duty. Singled out as incompetent, those on the lists felt humiliated. Ego and purse were both injured. "The extent of the clamor is not greater than I expected, but there is more bitterness than I fancied."

The most vehement in his denunciation of the board's action was Du Pont's friend, Lieutenant Matthew C. Maury, Superintendent of the United States Naval Observatory, the man who had charted the winds and currents of the oceans, the man who had authored *Physical Geography of the Sea,* the man who had fought for naval reform. This world-renowned hydrographer had been crippled by a leg injury, which had forced him to shore duty. Cognizant of his contributions, he was indignant to find himself placed on the reserved list on leave-of-absence pay. Frank explained Maury's reduced status to Charles Davis as due to his inability to "perform promptly & efficiently all his duties ashore and afloat."

Although he was not detached from the Naval Observatory, Maury was stunned by his reclassification. He immediately wrote Secretary Dobbin. In part he said, ". . . in the judgment of the Board I . . .

have been placed under official disgrace. This is a severe blow, and I feel it as a grievous wrong." He wished to know the accusations and who his accusers were on the board.

The secretary replied that the Efficiency Board had reported no reasons and therefore he could not grant Maury's request to know what accusations were made or who made them.

"I hear Maury is going *to fight*—is furious—& talking of civil suits," a concerned Frank informed Biddle.

To Charles Davis, he wrote, "The Reserved List is an honorable list. . . . Why should Maury if he cannot go to sea object to be[ing] placed [there?] . . . Remember he would carry there all his emoluments, equal to those of an officer two grades in advance of him, and his position before the world [would] be in no manner changed. One thing he would not get—his promotion. Do you think he cares in the slightest degree for it? *Lieutenant* Maury are household words now in both hemispheres that he would not care to change."

Frank seemed impervious to his friend's chagrin and pain. When he received an angry letter from Maury, Frank, who had cast his vote to put him on the reserved list, brusquely replied, "I with the other members of the Board were instruments of the law, and did what in our judgment the law made it our duty to do: the action of the Board was submitted to the revision of the Executive & approved, & the law neither makes us responsible for the results to your interrogations. Excuse me also for saying that my individual vote is not a fit matter for enquiry."

After a short visit home in November, Frank returned to Washington "to strengthen up Dobbin." "He is . . . firm. Yet the position of the Department in reference to the Board & the outside pressure is not what it should be," he complained to Biddle. Du Pont called on Dobbin and reiterated that members of the committee did not want him or the President to stand in front, but "to be supporting columns behind." Frank tried to undercut Maury by suggesting that he be removed from the superintendency of the Naval Observatory because from "this aegis," he could attack board members. With superior political judgment and aware of Maury's popularity, Dobbin refused.

Newspapers continued to denounce the Efficiency Board for placing Maury on the reserved list. And in January 1856 Senator John Bell of Tennessee presented a petition to Congress for the restoration of Lieutenant Maury's previous status in the naval service. The

House, busy with other matters, neglected to take immediate action. But in the Senate a long and vicious debate on the actions of the efficiency Board was underway.

The chairman of the Senate Naval Affairs Committee, Senator Stephen R. Mallory of Florida, led the defense of the board. Supporting him were Senator John Clayton of Delaware, Senator Judah P. Benjamin of Louisiana, and Senator Albert G. Brown of Mississippi. Leaders of the attack against the Efficiency Board were Senator Bell, Senator Robert Toombs of Georgia, Senator John J. Crittenden of Kentucky, Senator Robert Hale of New Hampshire, and Senator Sam Houston of Texas. During these debates, Du Pont was a frequent visitor at Senator Clayton's home, helping him write his speeches defending the board and explaining in detail the measures taken. Clayton admitted to Frank that the pressure to reverse the board's conclusions was "very great," and recommended that Du Pont advise all "who were interested . . . [to] move on their friends in the Senate."

Distressed by the ferocity of the debates, Frank listened with intensity as he continued to campaign for the board's findings. On learning that Senator Houston was about to denounce him on the Senate floor, he cautioned Charles Davis, "You will see a determined effort to drag me down & to break me down if they can. What I can learn is that . . . Houston of Texas . . . [is] the special instrument to carry on this cowardly attack from the shelter of Senatorial parliamentary privileges. I am calm & self poised, but in so unequal a contest, with the hate & perversion, & detraction & lies of the cropped & slanderous pens in the press; it behooves me to think of my friends."

With the exception of hasty visits home and a trip to Philadelphia to act as a witness at a court-martial, Frank stayed on in Washington. "I think it is more comfortable to be *near* the fire than to be at distance," he confided to Sophie. Later, he admitted, "The excitement of the Senate on this subject is astonishing & all the hostility seems directed against the Board. We stand up firmly & fearless, but I do fear the reform is in danger."

In March Sam Houston, who had appointed Maury a midshipman thirty-one years earlier, took the Senate floor. He harangued the Senate for three hours, finally unable to continue his attack because of hoarseness. His defense of Maury castigated Du Pont for his influence over the Secretary of the Navy and for his "criminal part" in the board's action. He dredged up the quarrel between Du Pont and Commodore Hull over the orlop deck. Houston denounced Du Pont as "responsible . . . for the outrage that has been done to the nation . . . [and] for throngs of individuals."

Frank was rankled by Houston's "infamous speech," declaring that "malice, sneering, lying are its sole ingredients. . . . Our senate has been humbled . . . by permitting such a man to vent his spleen." To Pendergrast, he fumed, "His hate to me, by whom instigated I know not, knows no bounds."

Both Delaware senators and Senator Mallory replied to Houston with "remarkable vehemence." Senator Clayton, abetted by Frank, who worked with him on his remarks, answered Houston's "low speech, which delighted everyone but the Texan himself."

During a lull in the debates, Frank journeyed to Annapolis to see Pendergrast, who had command of the new steam frigate *Merrimack*. Frank went out to the frigate, which lay anchored five miles off the harbor. With his friend he inspected "the Engines, was initiated into the mysteries of propellers, by models & drawings; talked [of the] ship, shells, big guns, steam; all the risks & hazards . . . of the new . . . ships, and never alluded or thought of the Naval [Efficiency] Board once. Altogether it was very refreshing & my visit will be of much service to me, invaluable if I should get one of these ships."

Still smarting from Houston's accusations, Frank made the decision to write a lengthy letter to Senator Bayard to be read on the Senate floor. "I had an impulse to get something on record *over my own name*," he explained. He returned to Washington, showed the letter to Clayton, who "took out the sharp & severest things," and presented the edited version to Bayard, who "read *it* with excellent effect."

In part the letter stated, "For some reason unknown to me, although I was but one of the commanders assigned by the Secretary of the Navy as a member of the Naval Board, I have been subjected to an unusual share of censure. It would not be that the object of the attacks on me was merely to destroy so humble an individual as myself; and if it was intended by them to impair public confidence in the decisions of the Naval Board, surely nothing could be more unjust than to condemn the judgment of fifteen men, for the delinquencies of one. . . .

"When about to be assigned on the Naval Board, I desired the

Hon. Secretary to excuse me from that service, for considerations peculiar to myself. He refused, and ordered me to that duty. That order was my law. I obeyed, and discharged my duty without fear, favor or prejudice . . . that obedience constitutes the ground, on which I have been arraigned before the Senate. Of this injustice it is that I complain, and I desire that complaint to be laid before the country."

In August 1856, a letter from Secretary Dobbin arrived enclosing a captain's commission from the President with the consent of the Senate, dating from 14 September 1855. Quickly, Frank replied, "I respectfully request Sea Service under this Commission."

During the summer of 1856 Frank sensed that the measures taken by the Efficiency Board were still in danger "from the immense pressure brought to bear on the Executive & Congress to return the reserved & dropped to the active list of the Navy." Officers affected by the board's actions and their friends continued their efforts to have the findings of the committee set aside. Under extreme pressure, the Senate passed the long debated "Act to Amend 'An Act to Promote the Efficiency of the Navy.' " The major provisions of the bill granted all officers affected the right to request a naval court of inquiry, where they could show cause why their status should be restored. Conclusions of each court would be sent to the President for final action. In case of a favorable verdict, the action of the Efficiency Board would be reversed and the officer reinstated to his former rank on the active list. Later the House passed the measure.

The new law forced the Navy to review 108 of the dismissals and to reverse a majority of them, including that of Lieutenant Maury.

During the early months of 1857, Frank was frequently in Washington on Lighthouse Board affairs. On 6 March, two days after the inauguration of President James Buchanan, Du Pont, uniformed in "bright full dress," was part of a contingent of Navy and Marine officers, "the handsomest turn out that I have ever seen," who paid an official call on the new President. The "show in the East Room was striking." Commodore Shubrick "spoke very handsomely & [we] were all introduced." President Buchanan's reply "was very sensible & [with] feeling."

In the pre–Civil War era, fervent optimism in America's destiny was hampered by a sectional power struggle. Sectional fears deepened as traditional checks retreated before individual enterprise and market forces. Increasingly, the struggle centered on the slavery question, polarizing values, interests, and hopes into different versions of the nation's mission. The battlefield for these differing conceptions of the American dream focused on the West.

The acquisition of huge territories in the Southwest and Far West at the end of the Mexican War forced the country to confront decisions that produced volatile conflicts. Northern determination to raise barriers against the spread of slavery was rooted in moral conviction and in an unwillingness to compete with slave labor in the newly won territories. The South, which felt threatened, clamored for slavery's expansion westward. The North geared to prevent it.

Attempting to resolve the issues, Congress passed the Compromise of 1850, which strengthened the Fugitive Slave Law, left the future of slavery in New Mexico and Utah in the hands of its citizens, abolished the slave trade in the District of Columbia, admitted California as a free state, and practically eliminated slavery north of the old Missouri Compromise border, latitude 36°-30'. Unfortunately, the settlement failed to resolve the central conflict, although it offered the illusion of sectional reconciliation.

In 1854 Senator Stephen Douglas of Illinois, a Democrat, revived the slavery issue when he secured the passage of a bill for local determination of the slavery question in the Kansas and Nebraska territory (both north of the Missouri Compromise line). When the federal government tried to force on Kansas settlers a proslavery constitution that conflicted with the feelings of many Kansas, civil war erupted in the territory.

Kansas divided the Democratic party and split the last national institution to have survived the sectional struggle over slavery. The Democratic party became increasingly southern and proslavery.

Originated in 1854, the Republican party began as a one-issue group—opposed to slavery in the territories. The Republicans made a good showing in the presidential election of 1856, and were subsequently aided by the leadership of men such as Abraham Lincoln of Illinois and Senator William Seward of New York.

During the Lincoln-Douglas Senate race of 1858, Lincoln argued that Douglas's indifference to slavery stamped him as unwilling to confront the slave power and thus disqualified him from leadership. Lincoln's "House Divided" speech was a turning point in American political history because in it Lincoln argued that expedience and moral indifference had upset the Founding Fathers' assumption that slavery was on the path to extinction. Lincoln was no abolitionist, but he did believe that the prohibition of slavery in the territories would ultimately squash the institution. Although Lincoln lost the election, he became nationally prominent in the defense of a position that was morally firm and constitutionally moderate.

With heightened sectional resentment, it is interesting that Du Pont, resident of a slave state, whose family did not own slaves, scarcely mentioned these events in his extensive correspondence. Although in one letter to a friend, he expressed his opinion on the slavery issue when he wrote, ". . . our General government . . . which represents the nation at large, has no power to deal with slavery—the authority which alone can do this is altogether local & belongs to the States within which it exists. . . . If our Congress were to attempt to do this, it would immediately dissolve our Union of States, without in any way benefitting the person of the slave himself. . . . Neither myself nor any of my blood connexion own a slave. . . ."

XVII

*"Everything has prospered
with me"*

During the first half of the nineteenth century, relations between the United States and China were, on the whole, good. The United States maintained the East India Squadron to protect American lives and property in that far-flung region. American trade flourished as merchant ships exchanged sea otter pelts from the northwest coast of America for tea and silks obtained in Canton, the only port open to foreigners. There seemed little need for a formal trading agreement between the two nations.

By the mid-nineteenth century the Opium War of 1839–42 between Great Britain and China altered the situation. This first armed conflict between the West and the Celestial Empire established a pattern. Under the Treaty of Nanking that followed, the British kept the island of Hong Kong, already occupied, and China opened five more ports for trade. Western powers exercised vastly superior military might to secure the trading agreements they desired. In 1844 Caleb Cushing secured the Treaty of Wanghia, the first formal treaty between the United States and China, which gave Americans all the rights and privileges the British had gained by waging war against the Chinese.

Continuous piracy along the Chinese coast created friction between the Chinese and British. When the *Arrow*, flying the British flag, was seized by Chinese officials a sharp British ultimatum, only partially met, brought on a full-scale war. Enraged at the murder of a missionary, France cooperated with Great Britain.

To negotiate a new treaty, the United States government planned to send William Reed as the first diplomat since Caleb Cushing to be accredited to the Chinese government with the rank of envoy extraordinary and minister plenipotentiary. A close friend of President Buchanan, Reed was a Philadelphia lawyer and Professor of History at the University of Pennsylvania. He was to sail in the new steam frigate *Minnesota,* the pride of the Navy, and to have some control over the entire East India Squadron. The new Secretary of the Navy, Isaac Toucey, instructed Commodore James Armstrong,* commanding in the Far East, to accede to Reed's wishes even to the extent of concentrating all of the squadron's ships at any point that Reed might choose.

Still marking time commuting between the Brandywine and the Potomac, still eager for sea duty, Du Pont badly wanted the command of the *Minnesota* on her cruise to the Far East. "I am making a desperate effort for the Minnesota," he confided to his Navy friend, Captain George Smith Blake, while urging him to use his friendship with the Secretary of the Navy in his behalf. He also wrote Secretary Toucey, "I beg leave to renew my application for sea service on file in the Department and would respectfully request to be considered an applicant for duty on the Expedition as announced as fitting out for China." Frank also contacted Reed, with whom he had a "long friendly acquaintance," seeking his backing.

He purposely checked into Willard's Hotel, where Reed was staying, as "a sure & easy way" of seeing him. In conversation Reed assured Du Pont that he wanted him to command the *Minnesota.*

In mid-April Secretary Toucey gave Reed a list of fifteen captains awaiting orders who had applied for the China mission. Although Du Pont's name was at the bottom of the list, Reed expressed his preference for him when he made his choice.

"I have the *Minnesota!*" Frank jubilantly wrote Sophie.

When Frank informed Captain Blake that Toucey had selected him to command the *Minnesota,* he acknowledged, "My Navy friends

---

* Armstrong was informed that Congress had established a naval rank senior to that of captain, "commodore" being merely a courtesy title. Unwilling to accept any of the various grades of admiral with their supposedly aristocratic connotations, Congress settled on the title "flag officer."

Portions of this chapter depend on Robert E. Johnson, *Far China Station: The U.S. Navy in Asian Waters, 1800–1898* (Annapolis, Md., 1979), pp. 95–113; and Robert A. Thompson, "Samuel Francis Du Pont and the William B. Reed Mission to China, 1857–1859," unpublished M. A. thesis, University of Delaware, 1965.

behaved nobly & my first impulse is to write to those whom I know were deeply sympathising with me . . . . My friends are wild with joy, civil & naval—I am thankful, but subdued to my tone in view of the long separation from home, and of the great responsibilities involved in such a command—but I find myself with unusual energy of mind & with a very hopeful, but not proud spirit God willing therefore I shall not disappoint the confidence of my friends."

The screw-propelled steam frigate *Minnesota,* designed by Chief Constructor of the Navy, John Lenthall, was built at the Washington Navy Yard, and launched on 1 December 1855. In these early days of steam warships, steam was only an auxiliary to sail. Workmen fitted the *Minnesota* for sea at the yard until the end of July, when she moved down the Potomac River to Alexandria, where mechanics completed the work.

To Du Pont, the *Minnesota* represented "the grandest and most successful combination of sail and steam yet reached." But he took command with misgivings since he feared the possibility of conflict between the Reed contingent and naval personnel on board. He confided to William Whetten that he realized that he would be "required to get along with a minister & his large suite, who may have to reside on board, bringing up the old vexed question of civil & military authority—relations which heretofore with but one or two exceptions have resulted in disagreeable quarrels, the cause & disgrace being almost always on the side of the Navy."

A large vessel like the *Minnesota* would also pose problems—"sailing of such a ship alone . . . in such shallow seas is no trifle," he continued to his friend of his Crystal Palace days. The last drawback, he felt, would be his "painful" separation from Sophie for the length of time required by an Asian cruise.

From Alexandria, the *Minnesota* steamed north to the Philadelphia Navy Yard, where Du Pont took formal command. On 2 May 1857, he wrote Blake that "I was in every hole & corner of her & know her like a book already." To Alexander Bache of the Lighthouse Board, Frank admitted, "The ship is all that professional ambition could desire." He speculated that Senator Sam Houston found this prized command "a bitter pill."

On 29 May the formal inspection of the ship was celebrated as stewards poured wine and notables spoke. After this gala event, the frigate got underway for Norfolk to receive her armament. Frank was elated by his first command of a steam warship. "The engines worked splendidly," he extolled. "I was down in the midst of them & it was certainly a grand sight."

Shortly after the *Minnesota* reached Norfolk in early June, Sophie joined her husband for a stay at the Ocean House in Portsmouth, Virginia.

By the end of June, the frigate was ready for sea, and entertained at a huge reception on board for Reed, attended by "all the soldiers, officers, and their families, the Norfolk navy and their families, with many guests from the Hotel."

Early on 1 July, Frank, "sore at heart but holding up bravely," kissed Sophie good-bye before he boarded the ship, which weighed anchor. "My crew," he described to Whetten, as "young, very green, but I hope of good material."

Four days out of Norfolk, Frank, unaccustomed to a steam frigate, wrote Sophie, "these ships have an ugly noise & jar under steam, very disagreeable, and the sea sick people . . . declared they began to get well the moment the propeller stopped." By 1 August the *Minnesota* had crossed the Equator, and six days later she was off the coast of Brazil.

Already Frank expressed annoyance with his passenger, William Reed—"a man of *ability, intellect,* of mental & literary culture, of affable manner—and yet we have not the slightest congeniality—an hour with Winter Davis leaves more solid & pleasurable impression, than a day or week with this gentleman."

At the end of a "long and tedious voyage" across the Atlantic, the *Minnesota* anchored in Table Bay, Capetown, at the southern tip of Africa on 7 September 1857, where she was visited by the British governor and other notables. A week later, Du Pont reported to Secretary Toucey that "the general health on board is good: that harmony prevails, that the discipline of the crew, their exercise and drills are progressing as satisfactorily as I could hope with the material at hand to work upon, which I regret to say is below mediocrity."

After coaling, the *Minnesota* departed Table Bay for Hong Kong. On 16 October the frigate arrived at Java Head, completing the voyage in twenty-six days, "the shortest passage by steam or sail . . . ever made between the two points."

After taking on coal and water, the *Minnesota* got underway again for Hong Kong. "I never steam when I can help it & this is the true intent of these ships," Frank explained to Sophie. "Steam is the auxiliary, but I am free to confess it has served me a grand purpose in these China seas."

Du Pont put the engines to the test when, on 31 October, the *Minnesota* ran into a monsoon, to which was "superadded a typhone of great violence." He called on the engineers "to do their work, and nobly did they respond." The frigate continued to plow ahead, "never getting below 4 knots."

Finally on 5 November, the *Minnesota* anchored at Hong Kong. On that same day, Frank expressed his relief to Sophie, "this long voyage ended today at 2 ock when we dropped anchor—the rattling of that [anchor] cable as it went out was a grateful sound in my ears, & I did not fail to give thanks to our heavenly Father for his merciful preservation of us & safe arrival in our destined haven from the beginning to the end, it seemed that we should be called upon to struggle more or less in making this passage, yet it all went right. . . ."

The scars from the harsh treatment he had received on the Senate floor were still painful, and he admitted to anxiety during the voyage. "I have much to be thankful for—one thing I confess to *you*. I desired *earnestly,* though I should have borne up manfully I hope had it been otherwise, viz. I did not want nothing to happen on the *passage out* to the ship or myself that could be distorted by malice against me—any vicissitudes occurring *during* the *cruise,* will be all secondary to any thing taking place in such a voyage, calling for comment—looked upon as the test of a man's fittness to command."

Later, he added, "do not think steam . . . as dangerous—had we been a sailing ship I should have not been in yet."

When the *Minnesota,* which Frank nicknamed "The Leviathan," arrived in Hong Kong, honors commenced for Minister Reed. First, the *Portsmouth* and *Levant* fired nineteen-gun salutes. Then a message from Sir Michael Seymour, the British admiral, announced that he would salute Reed with nineteen guns and call on him. Du Pont fired twenty-one guns "to the nationality ashore," then replied to all the nineteen-gun salutes fired for Reed. Officers hastened on board to pay their respects to Reed. For the days to come, there were more calls. The *Minnesota*'s officers returned these courtesies.

The harbor was crowded with British frigates and gunboats. Within six days of the *Minnesota*'s arrival, Du Pont became acquainted with Admiral Seymour, various other British officers, and was introduced to the Governor of Hong Kong. "The unexpected grandeur of this ship & her gigantic proportions," a delighted Frank wrote Sophie, "have had its effect . . . I feel an unusual show of courtesy & respect from every body here.

"I am free to confess," he continued, that "her presence here has done us good nationally—people think that a country that can turn out such a ship, must be a first rate naval power. Yet we are children compared to these Englishmen in naval resources & readiness."

As an American he was gratified, "the ship . . . is superior to any thing in England or France by the acknowledgment of their officers. . . ."

Although he considered the *Minnesota* to be "the grandest & most successful combination of sail & steam yet reached," he was not uncritical. "She is three hundred feet long & her draught of water is 13 ft. 6 in. so that she is . . . [not] well suited for the navigation of these seas."

"But the Department should never regret sending her," Frank concluded to a friend, "as she has done more to impress upon French, English, & all foreigners of our capability & knowledge of naval architecture, ordnance, & equipment generally, than anything that could have occurred—she has helped to raise us with the Chinese."

In Hong Kong the British and French, still at war with the Chinese, were preparing for an assault up the Canton River to capture Canton. Some sixty vessels carrying 5,000 sailors and marines started to move up river on 28 November.

The Americans, of course, were neutral. "Our part is nothing in all these affairs. To be neutrals is not a pleasant position, when we have equal interest with the belligerents, but still may be all right— but to follow as spectators if not spies, ready to take a share of the benefits without a share in the risks . . . is a different thing."

In describing the United States' coattail policy to Biddle, Frank wrote, "Our position of frigid neutrality in this Anglo, Franco, Chinese question, is awkward at best—watching & standing by, to reap the first advantages, of results, gained by means which we pretend to condemn. . . . We navy men find it . . . trying . . . to see . . . preparations for active conflict & lay listlessly on our oars to the evident disappointment of the French & English, and without any gain whatever in the good opinion of these . . . [Chinese], who have much more respect for those who drub them, than for those who stand by & see it done."

British naval strength in the Far East profoundly impressed Frank.

In Hong Kong the British had concentrated the "flower of the Baltic, Black Sea & Arctic fleets." Many of these vessels were light draft gunboats that could easily navigate and maneuver in the tricky, shallow Chinese rivers.

Canton fell to British and French forces in January 1858. The capture of the city, the first phase of the British plan to gain a desired treaty revision, made little impression on the Emperor in Peking, who regarded the Cantonese with indifference. This attitude led the allied ministers* to agree to meet at Shanghai before the end of March to confront the Chinese with a united front. If, after this session, negotiations with the Chinese failed to produce results, the allies would move northward to Peking and apply direct pressure.

Meanwhile, Flag Officer Josiah Tattnall reached Hong Kong and relieved Commodore Armstrong, who hauled down his flag on 29 January. Tattnall chartered the 450-ton *Antelope* from Russell and Company for Reed's personal use and assigned her to the *Minnesota* as a tender.

Although Frank had doubted his ability to maintain a cordial situation with the Reed contingent, his relationship with Reed was good at first. "My intercourse with the Minister," he wrote Biddle, "is agreeable & harmonious & he remaining on board in preference to living on shore . . . indicates that he himself is satisfied." Reed did, however, rent a furnished house at nearby Macao for the winter months.

In time, however, Reed's belief that the *Minnesota* was at his personal disposal, coupled with Du Pont's conviction that the diplomatic demands interfered with the good order of the ship, placed stress on this happy state of affairs. Du Pont and many of his officers thought that Reed made rather burdensome demands which, occasionally, were resented. Although the *Minnesota* afforded Reed the best accommodations she could offer, Reed found them lacking because Lord Elgin and Baron Gros had some special designation or honor that he did not possess. Attempting to be agreeable, Du Pont sought to supply the minister with whatever was necessary: a lieutenant to escort him, a flag for his tender, the *Antelope,* proper gun salutes, and facilities on board for entertaining.

---

*William Reed, United States; Lord Elgin, England; Baron Gros, France; and Admiral Putiatin, Russia. Like the United States, Russia was neutral.

Later, Frank was to admit, "I have often been tried by my intercourse with the minister; have frequently been impelled by my feelings to *do* something or to *say* something—but have always fortunately taken time to reflect, & have endeavored to shape my course in accordance with two sentiments which I have labored to keep uppermost in my mind; my duty as a Christian man in the exercise of patience & forbearance, and my self respect as a gentlemen and an officer.

"I am bound to say for the minister that his personal bearing towards me has ever been most respectful & differential—his errors have been, claiming *as rights* what was given him as courtesies, not to me, but reaching me through *gossip*—his utter selfishness in reference to movements of the *ship, talking* as if all the ordinary operations of a vessel of war were to be suspended if they contrascend[ed] his plans—and that . . . her officers & crew were here for no purpose whatsoever but to cater to his *personal* convenience as well as to forward his official duties. . . ."

The United States government had sent Reed to China to revise the Treaty of Wanghia of 1844. Specifically, three concessions were considered vital. The United States wanted to place a resident minister at Peking to deal directly with the Imperial commissioners, it hoped to open up additional trading ports, and it wished to clarify the terms of extraterritoriality once and for all. Basically, extraterritoriality provided that foreigners were subject only to the laws of their home nation and would not be tried or detained under Chinese law. As applied to the treaty ports, extraterritoriality became a powerful tool for the opening of China commercially as it made foreign merchants and missionaries immune to Chinese authority.

In mid-February 1858, Du Pont and Reed traveled up the Canton River as guests in a British gunboat to see the results of the allied bombardment. Although he does not refer to it, Frank's bilingualism stood him in good stead as they called on the French admiral. Before leaving they visited with the British general, and explored the city. "Chinese cities are all alike," Frank commented, "& are literally very poor, there being no public spirit, of course there are no public buildings . . . the Buddhist Temple alone excepted. . . ."

Back on board the *Minnesota*, Frank confided his feelings to Sophie. In part, he said, "I am as happy as I have ever been, separated from you. I am seeing service while yet in the vigor of health. . . .

if his [God's] blessings continue, I have no hesitation in saying that I should like to have service which would take me home in July '59 & not before—so much do I like my command, but still more do I feel the importance to me professionally to see a couple of years service in my present grade."

To celebrate George Washington's birthday in Hong Kong, "I thought I would honor the day by dispensing a little hospitality which would at the same time enable me to pay off all my debts in that way." He invited the entire American community of Hong Kong on board, all the American merchant captains in the harbor, the officers on board British men-of-war, and several Dutch and French officers. He ordered the Stars and Stripes hoisted on all the *Minnesota*'s mastheads. At noon the frigate fired a twenty-one-gun salute, while at the same time the English, French, and Dutch vessels responded. "All went off beautifully—great moderation in the drinking way."

On orders from Flag Officer Tattnall, the *Minnesota* with Reed on board visited Manila in early March, where the squadron commander maintained a residence on shore. From the Philippines the *Minnesota* headed for Wu-sung, twelve miles from Shanghai, situated on the narrow Huang-p'u River, which flows into the Yangtze Kiang estuary. Access to Shanghai was difficult because of the dangerous entrance to the estuary.

After the *Minnesota* dropped anchor, Reed traveled to Shanghai by boat to attend the meeting of allied ministers. Within a week it became apparent that nothing of consequence was to be accomplished. A note from the Chinese Governor General was received, which bluntly stated, "no Imperial Commissioner ever conducts business at Shanghai." No option remained but to head north in force for the Pei Ho River to coerce Peking into acceding to Western demands.

Reed left for the Pei Ho River on the *Mississippi* because the *Minnesota*'s rudder was broken. Once her mechanical problems were solved, the *Minnesota* rejoined the Western flotilla off the Pei Ho River on 26 April. "Here we are," Frank wrote Sophie, ". . . 60 miles from where the great wall of China touches the shore of this Gulf." Of the seventeen warships at anchor, only the *Mississippi* and *Minnesota* were American. This show of sea power caused the allies to be optimistic about the outcome of their negotiations, as they were confident their naval display would force Chinese cooperation. Du Pont's hubris led him to make the claim, "the Chinese were obstinate until overawed by the presence of the Minnesota."

When the Chinese commissioners arrived at Ta-ku, a village just above the fortifications guarding the Pei Ho River mouth, the allied ministers landed to start negotiations. On 3 May, Du Pont and Reed, accompanied by three marines, the secretary of the American legation, and an interpreter, landed from the *Antelope* at Ta-ku to meet with Chinese commissioner Tau. With his entourage, Tau welcomed them in a huge tent appointed with a rich red lining. Servants set tables with dried fruits, sweetmeats, and nuts. Chinese hospitality, manners, and elaborate costumes impressed the Americans.

Tau appeared cooperative, which encouraged them to assume a satisfactory outcome. He declared that his high rank would enable him to submit the entire treaty, when it was concluded, to the emperor himself. After arranging for the next meeting, Du Pont and Reed left the tent with their entourage, believing that the "meeting had been satisfactory."

The *Antelope*'s return to the *Minnesota* gave Frank the opportunity to view the fortifications guarding the river. "My observation of the poor Chinese on shore was that I could take all their forts with my crew alone."

During the second interview with Tau, Reed discovered that despite the cordiality of their first meeting, the Chinese refused to discuss receiving an American envoy at Peking or to listen to arguments about the opening of river forts to foreign navigation. The commissioner promised that President Buchanan's letter to the emperor would be received and opened by him "alone & with due honor."

While negotiations with other ministers continued, British and French warships concentrated off the Pei Ho River to impress the Chinese with the ability of the allies to gain their ends by force. The commissioners, however, emphasized that the forts on both sides of the river would repel any invaders. "Events have occurred of much importance; how far they will induce results most desirous, peaceful relations with China and an extended commerce with her no man can tell," Frank informed Sophie, "because I have often said to you to judge of Chinese by our standards is altogether fallacious, & to get at their process of reasoning requires a long intercourse with them & knowledge of their language."

Reed, who was ill, asked Du Pont to deliver the President's letter. On 18 May, Frank, resplendent in full dress uniform, accompanied by a detachment of marines, called on Commissioner Tau at the tent in Ta-ku. The letter was presented with great ceremony. Altogether everything went well, "the poor creatures knew an evil hour was fast approaching them and they had the mark of panic in their faces, though making every effort to betray no apprehension."

When the negotiations with the Chinese reached an impasse, Lord Elgin and Baron Gros decided to resort to force. Du Pont, Reed, and several officers boarded the *Antelope* to witness the bombardment and storming of the forts by the Europeans on 20 May.

At 2 P.M. cannon flashed from eight British and four French gunboats, loaded with marines. British gunboat *Cormorant* moved into position under one of the forts on the right bank of the river. Chinese cannon opened up, but without damage to the ship. Other gunboats maneuvered to positions under the covering fire of the *Cormorant.* Those on the *Antelope,* which kept well back, saw the shells careen into the forts' walls with effect.

The bombardment lasted an hour and a half before the troops moved in. French marines captured forts on the right bank; those on the left fell to British forces. Allied casualties were few. With the seizure of the forts, Chinese resistance ended.

Frank described the battle to Sophie as "very animated & exciting scene throughout. The Chinese did much better than at Canton. For the batteries were not sufficiently silenced until bombarded one hour & a quarter to authorise the landing of men & the storming of the different forts. . . .

"I feel proud . . . that though the whole affair was handsomely done, the thought *was strong within me* that there was nothing in the operations, that under like circumstances, with the same material, we could not have *quite equalled* & you know, I am not given to self exultation or conceit." This operation convinced Du Pont that steamers could successfully attack forts.

With hostilities halted, Du Pont and other officers from the *Minnesota* inspected the captured forts to examine the effect of the bombardment. Rummaging about, they discovered amid the dead bodies many "duds," waiting to be detonated. They also found iron cannon of poor quality alongside beautiful brass pieces, which were marked for London and Paris, ready for shipment. They saw untouched meals still on the tables, and playing cards on the ground.

Frank wrote Sophie later, ". . . all we saw was very curious—part of it very horrible for many dead bodies had not been removed—the utter helplessness of these people in the art of war against western nations."

When the barriers had been cleared from the Pei Ho, the gunboats steamed upriver to unfortified Tientsin. British Admiral Seymour moored his vessel opposite the entrance to the Imperial Canal, the waterway to Peking, to symbolize his ability to deny Peking access to its river outlet. In the wake of their successful action against the Chinese, Elgin and Gros expressed their wish to reopen negotiations with them. The two neutral envoys, Putiatin and Reed, moved upstream in the Russian tender *America* so that they could take advantage of the Anglo-French operation.

In Tientsin British and French negotiators were lodged in a renovated temple, while Putiatin and Reed shared the house of a wealthy merchant—"The rooms of all kinds are around a large open space, which is a Chinese garden filled with trees, shrubbery . . . [and] ponds."

Flag Officer Tattnall in the *Powhatan* arrived off the Pei Ho and ordered the *Mississippi* southward to Hong Kong to reprovision.

To communicate with Reed, Tattnall sent Du Pont upriver in a British gunboat, which made semiweekly runs to the city. At Tientsin, Frank went directly to Reed's residence. Serious negotiations were underway between the Chinese commissioners and the individual ministers.

Admiral Putiatin was the first to sign a satisfactory treaty, while other ministers reported progress despite hostility, which was expressed by spontaneous attacks on foreigners in the city streets. Relations between the Westerner and the average Chinese citizen were not as disciplined as the cool, polite atmosphere maintained between the commissioners and the allied envoys. When Admiral Seymour arrived in Tientsin, he was almost mobbed, and two British captains while touring the city were pelted and forced to run.

When Reed's valet rushed into the house with the news that Du Pont's Chinese servant, Ahling, had been abducted while walking in the city, Frank immediately responded. Summoning twelve marines of Reed's ceremonial guard and a midshipman, using the valet as a guide, he set out to secure Ahling's release. The American force attracted the attention of a growing and unruly mob as it proceeded through Tientsin. Anticipating trouble, Chinese merchants closed their stores as the crowd filled the streets. A marine pointed out to Du Pont three mandarins, "dreadfully alarmed," on the steps of their yamen. Frank halted, and sent the midshipman back to fetch an interpreter, "feeling how complicated things might become if we could not make ourselves understood."

When the interpreter arrived, Frank explained the situation to the mandarins. They responded that the boy would be freed and requested that the Americans return to their quarters. When Frank refused, the mandarins invited the contingent inside to wait. This he acquiesced in as the crowd in the streets had multiplied "beyond conception . . . [and] they were getting very excited." The mandarins quickly conducted the Americans into the courtyard of the yamen. They could hear the pandemonium outside as servants served tea. Soon Du Pont came to the realization that the yamen was the official residence of the high Imperial Commissioner and understood that "the crowd was excited for it thought we had come to seize their great men." After an interval Frank informed his hosts that he would take possession of the yamen at 10 P.M. if the boy were not returned, and he left with his marines. They retraced their steps toward Reed's house, "the crowd not pushing us, & a police officer walking ahead to keep away the populace. . . ." On reaching the residence, they discovered Ahling.

The next day, after church services at British headquarters, Lord Elgin expressed his belief that the Americans' prompt show of firmness would hasten the negotiation of the treaties to conclusion. " 'I am very glad Capt D[u] P[ont] you acted with so much promptitude, it will have [an] excellent effect.' " On Monday Frank took passage on a British gunboat to return to the *Minnesota*.

The Sino-American treaty of Tientsin, signed on 18 June 1858, opened eleven Chinese ports to American trade. It also provided for a United States minister in Peking so long as any other foreign diplomat resided there. Christians, whether foreign or Chinese, would be protected. By 22 June, the British and French had signed treaties. The Western diplomats had forced the Chinese to grant all of their demands. Frank put it simply, "I believe all has been got that was asked for. . . ."

On 5 July 1858 Flag Officer Tattnall in the paddle frigate *Powhatan* left for Nagasaki, Japan, and the *Minnesota* with Reed on board departed on 6 July for Wu-sung. At Nagasaki Tattnall found the crew of the *Mississippi* to be sickly so he ordered her to the cooler climate of Hakodate before going on to Shimoda in the *Powhatan*. There he learned that Consul General Townsend Harris had successfully negotiated a desired commercial treaty with Japan, but its formal signing was not to occur until 1 September.

Aware that Lord Elgin and Admiral Putiatin would soon reach Japan to conclude similar pacts, Tattnall convinced Harris that his treaty should be signed first, whereupon the consul general informed the authorities at Shimoda of his intention to travel to the capital, Edo, later Tokyo, in the *Powhatan*. As the frigate entered Edo Bay, the guard boats got underway from shore. Tattnall ordered full speed ahead and the boats were left far behind.

Harris sent a messenger to Edo as soon as the *Powhatan* had dropped anchor off Yokohama. The Japanese commissioners arrived, and the Treaty of Edo was signed on board Tattnall's flagship on 29 July. The pact opened the ports of Nagasaki, Yokohama, and Hakodate to American trade, and provided that other ports would soon be permitted to conduct commerce with American ships. "A Capital New Treaty!" rejoiced Frank when he received news of the details.

On his return to Wu-sung from the Pei Ho River, Frank reflected on his cruise to the Far East. "Everything has prospered with me," he wrote Sophie, "it has pleased a merciful God to endow me with health & energy to meet trials and circumstances. . . . The station has been altogether agreeable. . . . I have had too, great professional experience & interest, with a large & most intimate acquaintance with the first men of the Br[itish] Navy, cemented by genial hospitality on both sides. . . .

"Our minister is . . . well pleased with his position out here. . . . He has got through his work well I think—our position *nationally* was all right I presume—practically it was awkward—to tell John Bull with . . . virtuous indignation that we would join in no hostilities, & yet always be on hand for a share of what hostilities *alone* could produce, seemed a little like the difference between the receiver & the thief, not that I think there was any stealing on any part."

The dreaded disease cholera, a common ailment for those on China station, struck the *Minnesota*. When Du Pont returned to the ship from Wu-sung, Seaman Clough was sick although he had failed to report himself on the binnacle list for three days. After Clough died, another sailor, who also had been ashore, succumbed. The third fatal case appeared three days later. The ship's surgeon discovered that this man, and several others who were also sick, had purchased "samshu," a Chinese alcoholic drink, from men in a coaling barge. Later at muster petty officers discovered several seamen drunk. Officers and crew feared the quick spread of disease. Three panicky sailors jumped overboard in an attempt to escape the epidemic.

Deeply concerned, Frank believed that the only solution was to go to sea, "where all the seeds of disease will be soon blown away." The *Minnesota* got underway for Nagasaki on 5 August. When she departed, Du Pont counted eight men claimed by cholera. The frigate left without Reed, who remained in Shanghai to complete the final details of his negotiations.

On 15 August the *Minnesota* arrived in Nagasaki. The surgeon reported no new cases and the general good health of the crew slowly returned. Sea breezes and a storm had "cleared the air," and arrival at Nagasaki, which enjoyed "the most pure and perfect atmosphere ever experienced," added to their well-being.

The stay at Nagasaki was, for Frank, "the green spot of our China cruise." He enthusiastically described it to Sophie: "The harbour is not so grand as New York, Naples . . . or Constantinople, but it is more beautiful, more picturesque, more unique than any sheet of water I have seen. . . ."

The return voyage to Wu-sung was uneventful. When Reed again saw Frank in Shanghai, he remarked that the captain looked trimmer and more vigorous than on his arrival in China. "How very thankful I ought to be," Frank wrote Sophie, "I live systematically, never eat suppers, never eat at night . . . at sea, which I formally did, never touch alcoholic liquors, & rarely drink *water*, which I consider the most injurious thing in China—between one & two [o'clock] every day I feel a little craving for food in anticipating for dinner—I then take a piece of cake, a tumbler of Porter, or Claret, or any light wine, & on this I am satisfied for 24 hours so far as drinking is concerned. . . ."

In mid-September, the *Minnesota* left Wu-sung for a second run to Nagasaki with Reed on board. In his letter to her of the 18th, Frank was appreciative of his wife's support, "This is your birthday precious Sophie. . . . All these anniversaries special to *us* seem to bring home to me more and more dearest how much I owe you in my worldly career. I can more distinctly trace as I grow older to your influence—great and many as my short comings may be, I am thinking of you more than ever just now. . . ."

After the *Minnesota* returned to Wu-sung, Reed reported that work with the Chinese commissioners was completed and he was anxious to start for home. He planned to go in the *Minnesota* as far as Bombay, where he would disembark and return to the United States via Paris.

On 10 November 1858, the *Minnesota* got underway from Wu-sung for Hong Kong. "The mission is considered as closed and successful," Frank wrote Sophie with satisfaction. By the 16th the frigate had arrived in Hong Kong, where she recoaled and took on provisions. "It is quite a relief to get back here in the midst of a flourishing Eng[lish] colony, with its varied evidences of business & life—a *close,* quiet & safe harbor, with plenty of water under one's keel, after the turbid & shallow waters . . . [near the Pei Ho River] . . . the still muddier . . . Yang-tse, with [its] deceptive & shifting flats & bars—these all served one good purpose, however, of giving a zest to the picturesque beauties of Japan, which no words can convey.

"I have been duly thankful, for the closing up without accident of our northern cruise [to the Pei Ho] . . . I [am] much *satisfied* with this Eastern cruise, it has been altogether profitable. . . ."

At 11 A.M. on 8 December the *Minnesota* "got underway prettily" from Hong Kong. Flag Officer Tattnall saluted with thirteen guns, which the *Minnesota* returned. The housetops and wharves of Hong Kong were lined with people, and the riggings on numerous ships were filled with cheering sailors. "We are actually *off* and *homeward bound,*" Frank observed, "what a thrilling thought and what a cause for thankfulness."

After a short stay at Singapore, the *Minnesota* sailed through the Strait of Malacca—"this is the largest ship that ever passed through"—and anchored to Penang to take on supplies. The ship's company spent Christmas Day there. "Christmas," Frank wrote Sophie, "how much I thought of you—after breakfast I went to my room, read . . . some prayers in my little book, a couple of chapters in my bible, & then got on my knees and prayed long & earnestly, thanking our heavenly Father for his numberless mercies to me, for his long protection & enjoyments of life—prayer for *you* as I hardly ever had done before. . . ."

The *Minnesota* departed Penang and was off the Nicobar Islands, Bay of Bengal on the last day of December. She was under sail, which "relieves the Engine, still more the Firemen, who are getting sick pretty fast. I do not wonder at it—while steaming they have to stand the great heats of making the fires, & when stopped have to repair the Engine—so they really have a hard time of it & no leisure time."

By mid-January 1859 the *Minnesota* lay off Colombo, Ceylon, where Du Pont, Reed, and several officers spent an evening with the acting governor and his wife. "This will be our last *stage* with the Minister—in a few days now we land him in Bombay."

The *Minnesota* arrived at Bombay on the 17th, and eight days later Reed disembarked. After shaking the minister's hand and wishing him well, Frank, with a sense of relief, fired off a nineteen-gun salute and ordered the crew to man the yards. "Oho, what a nightmare removed from the ship. I had been a sort of official butler long enough," he reflected.

As Reed left the *Minnesota* to board a mail steamer for Europe, he had reason to be proud. His mission had been crowned by triumph, and the *Minnesota* had created a favorable impression on observers throughout the Far East. Whether from preoccupation with his negotiations or from a lack of appreciation, he made no effort to indicate to Du Pont and his officers that they shared responsibility for a portion of his success. "We are all glad to get rid of him," Frank wrote, "none more than myself."

Ashore in Bombay, the officers were entertained in royal fashion. "The only drawback was the excess of hospitality."

On leaving India on 14 February, Frank remarked to Sophie that this interval, free of pressure, had restored him. "To myself, it was not only a period of agreeable . . . relaxation mentally & morally, but of positive benefit to my physical—for it was only after I felt the renewed vigor, & improved appetite, and indifference to fatigue, that I was made aware that *I had let down some. . . .* I left Bombay a rejuvinated man. . . ."

Six days out of Bombay, the *Minnesota* anchored in Muscat harbor. Here Frank called on the Imam. "I had no business in coming to Muscat, save to pay my respects to him to present him the compliment of the President of the U.S., who expressed the hope that friendly relations which had existed between the two countries, during the life time of his Father . . . would continue under the domain of his Son.

"He replied that he was all the same as his father, and was glad to see an American frigate come to Muscat. I told him she was the largest ship ever sent to the East." As to the town, Frank characterized it, "Oh! what a destitute, wretched place—a perfect mudhole."

"I am glad however that I went," he added to Sophie, ". . . because evidently the State Dept, considered it of some moment to have a man of war go, and because others had avoided the duty, it being 18 yrs. since our last ship was there. . . ."

The *Minnesota* left at sundown on 20 February and finally reached Table Bay, Capetown. "A day of thankfulness, dearest Sophie—another safe arrival, after sailing over many thousand miles, & passing through unsurveyed Seas without accident of any kind."

On 29 May 1859 the *Minnesota* put in at Boston amid the hoopla of gun salutes from other ships. Despite the "disarray & confusion incident to anchoring," Du Pont held Sunday services, "for I had in my own heart to return thanks. . . . I am looked upon as a man of *luck* (which I despise as I grow older) as always coming out with what I want, & this has been attributed *by many* to having service on board, & being what is called a *religious man*—my! how far I am from it, though it is something to know & feel this delinquency."

Before going home, Frank set down an appraisal of his tour. "The size of the Minnesota, [and the] great beauty of her lines . . . not to mention her order and discipline so credible to her officers and crew, made her an object of universal attraction and admiration in the Eastern seas. . . .

"All feeling of national prejudice or rivalry seemed discarded, and from the distinguished Admirals commanding the very large fleets of Britain and French to all grades under them, commendation was uttered without stint. . . . To our countrymen domiciled in the East and to the intelligent commanders of our noble mercantile clippers, usually numerous just then, she was an object of especial national pride.

"In the moral effect thus produced the Minnesota paid for herself many times over, as an evidence of the progress of the country in nautical sciences; of what we could do in naval architecture, and in those specific & practical combinations, which constitute her class the most effective ships of their day. . . ."

To Bache of the Lighthouse Board, he summed up, "The last two years from beginning to end, have been the most instructive and gratifying of my professional life."

XVIII

"My land cruise with the Japanese"

On leave in Delaware, Frank applied himself to the garden and continued his interest in Asia by further reading on China and Japan. He traveled frequently to Washington and made occasional visits to Philadelphia.

On learning that Midshipman Alexander Slidell Mackenzie, Jr., son of his close friend, was assigned to the steam frigate *Wabash*, headed for the Far East, Frank immediately wrote him. His advice to the youngster, ready to board his first ship, mirrors the principles that guided Frank throughout his career. "You are going to a very interesting part of the world—to a station well calculated to develop professional knowledge, and in a class of ship the best of all to acquire that knowledge—where steam does not supplant sails, nor do the latter interfere with learning the management of a steam engine in conducting a ship.

"The proficiency and cleverness you have shown at the Academy will doubtless be followed up in the more practical part of your profession—and I write not so much to encourage you in this line, as to urge upon you something without which all this capacity as an officer will be as naught.

"I allude to that high tone and bearing, that correctness and morality of conduct, which should distinguish an officer from the great mass of sailors under him. To be free from their vices is, the first step towards obtaining that moral influence now more than ever necessary to secure a proper control over them.

"Never swear, or use epithets—a scrupulous avoidance of this will give you immediately the consideration of the men—not to mention that by doing so would violate the divine law and the regulations of the Navy. Do not smoke or chew tobacco, nor ever taste alcoholic drinks. Other temptations will you meet with—I beseech you to avoid them with all the earnestness you are master of—and if you succeed during your first cruise in escaping these rocks & shoals of a ship life, in all after time the task will be comparatively light. Remembering of course that conquest over self & the avoidance of evil must come from a source & strength greater than our own—never therefore be ashamed to acknowledge this, and stand up like a man in the faith & principles you have been nurtured in with so much care and solicitude.

"Next to moral culture in importance, comes intellectual; and you will find it not only a present enjoyment, but a source of after usefulness & expansion of mind, to make it a practice of reading the best books you can get on countries you visit; thus adding the collected experience of others to your own observations."

News of John Brown's attack on Harpers Ferry in Virginia impinged on the placid domesticity of the Du Ponts. On 16 October 1859, abolitionist John Brown, intent on freeing the slaves, with a party of eighteen men marched into Harpers Ferry, seized hostages, and occupied the firehouse of the federal arsenal. With a force of United States troops, Colonel Robert E. Lee crushed the raid. Brown was captured and later tried and hanged. The South saw Brown as an instrument of the North's malicious intentions toward it; northern reformers regarded Brown as the embodiment of courage united to principle.

In a memorandum to a friend, Frank wrote, "You allude to the execution of John Brown—after a most impartial trial he was executed, for treason & murder; he was a fanatic & crazy . . . and was seeking to make innocent blood including that of women & children to flow like water. . . ."

To Reverend Edward Syle, brother-in-law of Henry Winter Davis, Frank described John Brown's action at Harpers Ferry as a "fanatical, wicked, & bloody raid . . . an event which circumstances have rendered very momentous, & it has threatened & shaken our union more than ever before."

In 1860 Japan was on a threshold. The necessary stimulus for her transformation had been set in motion by the Western powers, in particular by the United States, when Townsend Harris signed the commercial treaty of 1858 with her. The first official Japanese embassy arrived in the United States in 1860.*

This delegation was the first in Japan's history to be accredited to a Western nation. A formerly closed society had taken a small step onto the international stage.

When the *Powhatan* carrying the Japanese arrived in San Francisco on 22 March 1860, enthusiastic crowds were at the dock. After a sojourn of eight days, the Japanese proceeded directly down the coast to the Isthmus of Panama, which they crossed by rail. On reaching the other coast, they boarded the screw frigate *Roanoke* for Norfolk.

Qualified by his Asian tour, Du Pont was selected by the Secretary of State as senior member of the naval commission delegated to accompany the Japanese embassy. Concurring orders were issued by the Secretary of the Navy. On 10 May, Du Pont called on President Buchanan, who was "sensible & gracious," for last-minute instructions.

Of his appointment, Frank wrote Pendergrast, "I had been laboring under a happy delusion that my Japan cruise was all over when suddenly I find myself launched amid shoals & quick sands, more dangerous than any I had to contend with, off the shores of that mysterious land. Suddenly & most unexpectedly I was ordered to report to the State Dept.—& there was astounded by hearing the object of my summons. I beg off like a *hound* on the grounds of great personal inconvenience, that I had done my share to establish friendly relations with the Japanese & bring about the preference they had shown our country; by two visits, & spending money freely among them—that other officers were on the spot who had likewise been to Japan & were more capable than myself, etc. etc. But it seemed to avail nothing. . . . I yielded . . . [and] the President & *every* member of the Cabinet . . . giving me their thanks after I had accepted.

"Before doing this . . . I stated my views—looking out especially for my own *status,* as an officer & a gentleman, telling the old general [Secretary of State Lewis Cass] that while it could & doubtless would be a place of high honor under all the novelty & peculiar

* Details in this chapter come from Chitoshi Yanga, "The First Japanese Embassy to the United States," *Pacific Historical Review* 9 (1940), pp. 113–39.

circumstances of the case, yet if this were not attended to, my position might run down into that of a travelling agent with a party of Sioux or Dakotahs. I also presented a programme of organization simple & abundantly cheap, as three fourths of it, are navy officers, whom are to get nothing but mileage & reasonable expenses! All was accorded frankly & fully . . . . [Secretary of the Navy] Toucey . . . let me have [Commander Sidney S.] Lee & [Lieutenant David Dixon] Porter who have embarked with me full of zeal—the latter worth his weight in gold in just such an undertaking, relieving me of a thousand details. . . . my Crystal Palace experience has already come to my help."

Du Pont, Lee, and Porter left Washington on the chartered steamer *Philadelphia* and arrived at Norfolk on 12 May. The following day Du Pont and his party, amid the pomp created by martial music, boarded the *Roanoke*. The crew manned the yards as Du Pont presented himself to the Japanese delegation. "Everything so far has gone off beyond any thing I could hope for. . . . The Japanese are not good looking, but full of intelligence, refined, & delighted people. . . . The rice they eat would astonish a Chinaman."

The importance attached to this historic visit is reflected in the speech of a congressman from Philadelphia: "We ought to remember that we are a preferred nation; that this embassy is sent to us in preference over all other nations of the world who have solicited the Japanese to send embassies to them. We cannot do it too much honor; and I hope that, waiving all other consideration, we will agree to unite with the executive branch of the Government to do full honor to this Embassy."

The House of Representatives passed a resolution to adjourn until 3:00 P.M., Monday, 14 May, to enable the members to witness the Japanese debarcation at the Washington Navy Yard.

A jubilant crowd turned out in holiday attire to welcome the visitors. A military contingent escorted the carriages along the route to Willard's Hotel as crowds inched forward to glimpse the Japanese. "The [presidential] inaugurations have been literally nothing [compared to this]. So with the interest in the whole thing, it amounts to an excitement I have never seen. Some of it vulgar curiosity & ignorant curiosity too, but a large share seem to think of the historic event & the consequences it may result in."

From the moment the delegations reached their quarters at the hotel, the streets were packed with the curious from every stratum of society. Flagstaffs flew the flag of the rising sun. So great was the interest that clothing stores stocked Japanese costumes, minstrels entertained by inventing Japanese jokes, and enterprising merchants touted Japanese fans.

From Willard's Hotel to the White House the diplomats in open carriages, dressed in ceremonial costumes, rode in a procession, accompanied by Du Pont, Lee, and Porter, behind tall standards carried by Japanese soldiers. Frank's account to Sophie described the embassy as resplendent in "their full costumes of very rich things, but more peculiar than anything I saw in Japan."

The delegation entered the anteroom of the White House, described as "rich & beautiful," the decor highlighted by a lovely show of flowers. The Japanese guests were presented with "magnificent presents from Townsend Harris." The East Room was "more brilliant than I ever saw." President Buchanan occupied its center opposite the main door. The embassy proceeded to a large area left clear for it, up a lane created by Navy officers on one side in full dress, who faced Army officers headed by General Winfield Scott on the other. "I never saw anything handsomer in my life of the kind."

"The Japanese went through their part with ease, & with aplomb." After presenting the letter from the "Tycoon," the Japanese retired to the anteroom before returning to make their address, which the chief ambassador delivered. He conveyed the Shogun's wish to establish peace and commerce between the two nations on a firm and lasting basis. President Buchanan replied by expressing gratification that the first Japanese embassy ever accredited to a Western power had been sent to the United States, and stating his sincere belief that the treaty of commerce of 1858 "cannot fail to be productive of benefits and blessings to the people of both Japan and the United States."

When Buchanan concluded, he shook hands with his guests, which the Japanese considered a big compliment.

The exchange of ratifications of the treaty took place at the State Department. After this formality, the envoys devoted their energies to touring Washington, including a visit to the Capitol. Conducting the visitors about and satisfying their curiosity kept Frank occupied as he noted in a letter to Sophie: "Since my foot touched this hotel [Willard's] at 6 ock [in the evening], I have not had a single moment to myself, the pressure having increased, yet I am less fatigued than the first week."

Before the Japanese departed Washington, they took leave of the President, "saying they had not yet expressed thanks for the most important kindness the government had done them, that of placing them under the care & protection of D[u Pont], L[ee], and P[orter] from whom they had received such important assistance . . . & kindness from the first day of their acquaintance—& to this the President replied . . . complimentary to us that we were the flower of the Navy. . . ."

After twenty-four days in Washington, the diplomats boarded a special train for Baltimore. After a night in that city, they continued north to Philadelphia. Conducted by members of the city council, they toured the waterworks, a city park, a foundry, a locomotive factory, the fire department, and a machine shop, where mechanics demonstrated the processes of forging, molding, triphammering, and boring.

On 16 June the party, including Du Pont, Lee, and Porter, entered New York Harbor on the ship *Alida*. After working their way up Broadway, and through Grand Street, the Bowery, and Fourth Avenue, the procession arrived at Union Square, where they witnessed a military review of 7,000 troops. Then the visitors proceeded down Broadway to the Metropolitan Hotel, where they were quartered.

The diplomats' stay in New York was climaxed by a huge ball at Niblo's given in their honor. Ten thousand persons crowded the hall. For a single night's entertainment, the city spent $40,000.

American technology fascinated the Japanese. They inspected sewing machines and washing machines, studied the art of galvanizing and electroplating, saw a soap factory, toured a glass factory, stopped at a sugar refinery, visited a newspaper office, and were entertained at P. T. Barnum's Museum.

Finally, on 30 June, the diplomats departed for home on the *Niagara*, which had been specially refitted and furnished in a "style of Oriental splendor, leaving nothing to be desired which comfort or luxury of the distinguished guests could desire," reported *The New York Times*.

Du Pont, his "land cruise with the Japanese" over, wrote Henry Winter Davis that he had seen a letter from the State Department to the Secretary of the Navy that "could not have been more warmly appreciated of our services. . . . We are very nicely on the official records, and as officers this is all we should desire.

"The further we went with the objects of our charge," he continued, "the more was I satisfied how important our duties were & how disastrous any ordinary mode in reference to such an embassy, would have been—this buoyed me along, otherwise the intensity of the fatigue & bodily & mental, would have broken me down. The Crystal Palace & a Typhone in the China Sea were childs play in comparison."

The visit of the Japanese inspired numerous expressions of hope and anticipation for warm, mutually beneficial American-Japanese relations. *Harper's Weekly* reported that "the establishment of friendly relations with the Japanese can not fail to be of marked advantage to our Pacific states," and stressed Japan's economic value to the United States.

XIX

"I cast my lot"

With the election of Abraham Lincoln as President in November 1860 the South feared the worst. In Charleston, South Carolina, the excitement and indignation of the crowds thronging the streets reflected a genuine determination to be done with the Union. The South Carolina legislature passed a law on 13 November calling a convention to consider "the dangers incident to the position of the State in the Federal Union."

Writing from Washington, Frank described the mood of the capital to Sophie. "This is the gloomiest place politically that I have yet been in—everyone believes that the Union will be dissolved." On 29 November, he added, "Alas . . . things look worse & worse. S Car is certainly going out [of the Union] & I believe four other states will join her—the Union men [in the South] who could prevent this see no support from any where. The [Buchanan] Administration seems paralyzed. . . ."

To Biddle, a distressed Frank wrote, ". . . things look squally in S C. I have always sympathized with the southern people though often condemning their leaders."

"If S.C. is allowed to withdraw," he confided to Henry Winter Davis, "then our nationality has been a fiction, a compact without solid foundation. On the other hand coercion created a Southern Confederacy & sooner or later a civil war. One thing [is] certain, there never was so little call for secession."

After visiting Washington again in early December, Frank told a friend, ". . . my time [was] greatly taken up by visits from my Navy friends, who are so much affected by the pending crisis—the questions of state allegiance or national obligation will soon be disturbing many of them and in the Army as well as the Navy.

"As I never believed that I was serving *two* masters unscriptual at best, I gave my opinions freely. . . . the Election of Mr. Lincoln is the pretext not the cause [of South Carolina's threats of secession]. In the Gulf States there is some latent loyalty & love of the Union, but in S.C. there is nothing but alienation . . . & hate. . . . How there can be peaceful secession I cannot imagine. . . . In my warmth for the Union & determination to stand by it let my state go where it will. . . ."

Frank learned that Commodore Stewart, with whom he had made his first cruise on the *Franklin* in 1817–18, had applied to be relieved from the command of the Philadelphia Navy Yard. Immediately he wrote the Secretary of the Navy asking for orders to that station. Later, he wrote William Whetten, "When . . . [this] matter was submitted to the President, he said, 'If Captain DP's claims are at all on an equality with others I wish him to have it, for *we* have been looking round to show him some mark of the appreciation of his management of the Japanese embassy.' I suppose the 'we' meant himself and the Cabinet."

On 20 December the Navy Department ordered Du Pont to relieve Stewart. "The orders are gratifying & especially agreeable to Mrs. Du Pont," he informed Biddle.

On that same day, by a unanimous vote of its 169 members, the South Carolina convention solemnly passed an ordinance declaring that "the union now subsisting between South Carolina and other States, under the name of the United States of America, is here dissolved." South Carolina was now avowedly a separate nation. Secession spread. Alabama, Florida, Mississippi, Louisiana, and Texas soon followed.

Prior to the outbreak of the Civil War Frank had pleaded with southern associates not to jettison their Navy commissions. They, while lamenting secession, considered devotion and loyalty to their states primary. They responded to the appeals of their families and the harangues of the southern politicians.

In December, before taking command of the Philadelphia Navy Yard, Frank described his southern colleagues' attitude and his own position to old Commodore Shubrick, a South Carolinian, then living in Washington. He was senior officer in the Navy and still chairman of the Lighthouse Board. "On arriving in Washington," Frank informed him, "I was surprised to find that my Navy friends from the South, while deprecating the sad condition of the country, seemed very generally to consider allegiance to their states as paramount to any obligations to their whole country and to the national government—or to be more accurate, they considered that the laying down of their commissions absolved them from these obligations.

"My own views are so different and would impel so different a course of action that I felt it my duty to express my dissent from theirs. . . .

"Commodore, I may be all wrong, but I never believed I was serving *two* masters. I have been nurtured, clothed, and fed by the general government of my whole country, have had the honor of carrying her flag abroad and representing her sovereignty on the ocean. I have been paid whether employed or not—and I have asked myself whether this could have been, had Congress for a moment thought that I held my national obligations and my oath 'to bear true allegiance to the United States of America' in subjection to state duties, state ties and affinities.

"To Delaware I owe the duty of a good citizen," Frank continued. "I pay my taxes to support the state government—my means add to her industrial wealth; I promote her welfare in every way that I am able. Among these duties as a citizen I have held myself ever ready day or night to assist the United States marshal when called upon by him to execute the fugitive slave law. But nothing in my relations to my state can cancel my obligations to the general government, and I believe every intelligent citizen of my state so understands my position."

He added, "If the general government ever came to *oppress* my state, then the question of cleaving to the one and leaving the other might arise; but this has never yet happened either in its unity or by any of its coordinate branches, legislative, executive, or judicial; nor has the general government been so charged by any of the states North or South—so that neither you nor I have ever served a ('vulgar oppressor'). . . .

"Be this as it may, however, if the ship of state is to founder she will sink gradually; she may get down to the original number, though not the same '*thirteen*' but she will hold on to the stars and stripes, and with these I cast my lot."

His loyalty unshaken, Frank conceded to his friend, Captain Louis Goldsborough, that "The South has just cause of complaint and it has in the last ten years become much alienated—South Carolina has been entirely so, and sincerely thinks herself oppressed and humiliated—but there is not the shadow of an excuse to go to the extreme. . . ."

Du Pont assumed command of the Philadelphia Navy Yard on 31 December. In early January 1861 he traveled to Annapolis to preside over a board to examine midshipmen. Arriving back in Philadelphia, he wrote his impression of Lincoln to William Whetten: "I have said nothing of the President-elect—the reporters garbled his speeches and made poor sayings for him, but he made a very favorable impression here. Younger and much finer looking than his portraits, [he] created always at first pleasurable surprise—tall and gaunt like Clay and without the latter's grace, he is still very pleasing and evidently self-reliant and far above the crowd who composed his suite. . . ."

In March 1861, Sophie joined him in Philadelphia, where she and Frank took up housekeeping in "very pleasant lodgings (room and parlor)" at 1333 Spruce Street near Broad. Here Frank learned that President Lincoln had selected a Connecticut Yankee, Gideon Welles, to be Secretary of the Navy. Welles had previously served as chief of the Navy's Bureau of Provisions and Clothing, but claimed no technical or intimate knowledge of the Navy. He was, however, better equipped than many naval secretaries had been, and was to prove a quiet and unswerving executive.

Welles's limitations were adequately compensated for by the Assistant Secretary of the Navy, Gustavus Vasa Fox, who had served eighteen years in the Navy. Resigning his commission in 1856, he had accepted a job with a woolen mill in Lawrence, Massachusetts, where he had acquired administrative skills.

At 5 P.M., 12 April 1861, telegraph wires crackled with news from Charleston. Cannon of the Palmetto Guard had bombarded Fort Sumter, garrisoned by Union troops. Washington was "thrown into intense excitement." Editors posted news of Charleston in the streets and hotel lobbies. Information from the Associated Press agent in South Carolina was immediately dispatched to the White House, where President Lincoln, "anxious but calm," had summoned the Cabinet.

The American nation was plunged into civil war when Fort Sumter surrendered on 13 April. Immediately, Lincoln issued a call for volunteers to suppress the rebellion, and on 19 April he proclaimed a blockade of the southern states. On the following day, Virginia militia seized the Gosport Navy Yard in Norfolk with its enormous stores of ordnance, munitions, and the hull of the frigate *Merrimack,* promptly rebuilt and rechristened the *Virginia.*

In Washington secretaries Welles and Fox concluded that the Navy was in poor shape to meet its obligations. Only forty-two of its ninety ships were in commission, and most of them were stationed in distant waters. Only three were ready for immediate service along the American coast. Trained for deep-water operations, the Navy had little experience with the coastal work that would be needed during the war. To bolster federal forces in home waters, Welles and Fox quickly chartered or purchased merchantmen for conversion into warships contracting for the construction of new vessels.

Sophie returned to Louviers and Frank took up quarters at La Pierre House. His duties caused him to put in long days at the navy yard, from "ten to any hour at night, but generally until three o'clock, fitting out all the ships here, chartering and arming steamers, etc."

He was dismayed at the number of southern officers who resigned to join their states. To Whetten, he mourned, "The defection of the Army and Navy has continued . . . most of my most intimate friends have gone. Moral insanity came over them and it has made my heart bleed—but it should only nerve those who have remained to greater exertion. I am anxious for the *blockade* to get established; that will squeeze the South more than anything. [Matthew Fontaine] Maury, honored so by the North, is among the traitors and has been in treaty with the South for some time past; by the way, Charles Davis takes his place at the Observatory."

Frank did not conceal his disapproval from his close Navy friend, Franklin Buchanan, who had defected to the South, "My dear 'Buck,' . . . My standpoint in viewing this grave question is so different from yours that it is due to you and to me to know what these views are and have ever been. They are that the resigning of a commission cannot cancel the obligation and sanctity of the oath we took to bear allegiance to the United States and to support the Constitution—the commission may be laid down, for good and sufficient reason, but the oath is recorded *above.*

"When I saw you last November in Washington, I discovered you and nearly all my Southern friends were breathing an impure moral atmosphere and were troubling yourselves with the political issues, with which you and I had nothing to do. Among the observations made in reply to remarks of mine that our allegiance to our states was altogether subordinate to our obligations to the United States, I was always met: 'But we are no longer United States—these are disunited.' To my view a man might as well tell me the Mississippi no longer empties into the Gulf of Mexico, because acres and miles of its banks are torn away." *

In Washington, Frank's friend Alexander Bache of the United States Coastal Survey suggested to Secretary Fox that he appoint a strategy board to study the problem of the blockade and offensive operations against the South and make recommendations for proper action. He urged Fox to appoint Du Pont as senior member. Du Pont's Mexican War experience in blockading the California coast and his study of the coastal defenses of the United States stood him in good stead. Fox immediately wrote Du Pont, ". . . I only seek the good of the country and the Navy. Will you give up the Yard and come with us to the bitter end?" Frank agreed, and went to Washington on 25 June 1861. He and Bache chose the other two members of the board: Major John G. Barnard of the United States Corps of Engineers, "deaf as a post" but an expert in harbor defenses, and Frank's old friend, Commander Charles Davis.

In Washington, Frank rented rooms at Wormley's boarding house. "I have much less comfort where I am than at Willard's," he wrote Sophie, "but it is much less expensive."

The Blockade Board convened secretly at the Smithsonian Institution where it studied charts and culled intelligence reports as it reached the conclusion that the Navy faced a "Herculean" task. The outer coastline of the Confederacy from the northern boundary of Virginia to Mexico extended more than 3,000 miles and the exterior shoreline along the south Atlantic seabord was merely the outer edge of a series of islands, behind which lay sounds, rivers, and connecting channels and canals. These created a protected and almost continuous inland waterway from Virginia to Florida, navigable for small vessels. Along the outer shoreline countless inlets or openings connected the Atlantic Ocean with this interior waterway. Although a major port could be effectively policed by Union warships, blockade runners and Confederate privateers could sneak

---

* Helpful for the Civil War chapters were John D. Hayes, *Samuel Francis Du Pont, A Selection from His Civil War Letters* (Ithaca, N.Y., 1969) 3 vols.; and James M. Merrill, "Naval Operations along the South Atlantic Coast, 1861–1865," doctoral dissertation, UCLA, 1954.

through an inlet many miles above or below a principal port, and steam unmolested to their destinations within the Confederacy. The Blockade Board informed Welles that to be effective the blockade must strangle the flow of traffic along this inland waterway. The Union Navy, however, was incapable of efficiently policing this coastline at the onset of hostilities.

The problem of supplying the blockaders disturbed the board. Vessels stationed off North and South Carolina were forced to steam north to Hampton Roads for coal and water, while those off Florida had to go into Key West.

A responsibility of the Blockade Board, Frank wrote Sophie, was ". . . the selection of two ports, one in South Carolina, another in the confines of Georgia and Florida for coal depots, these will have to be taken and five or ten thousand men landed, to fortify and entrench. It seems impossible to supply the blockading fleet with coal without these depots." In its reports submitted to Welles, the board recommended points along the Confederate coast to be seized for bases and coaling depots.

To increase efficiency, the board suggested that the Atlantic Blockading Squadron be split. The advantage of this was that different portions of the south Atlantic seaboard possessed different topographical features and required different treatment. With minor variations the Navy Department carried out this recommendation. It detailed four units to operate along the Rebel shores: the North Atlantic, South Atlantic, East Gulf, and West Gulf squadrons.

Welles and Fox, acting on the board's suggestions, undertook to strengthen the blockade by planning land-sea operations to close the inland waterways to southern commerce, and to plant naval supply bases along the Confederate coast.

Meanwhile, General Irvin McDowell marched his ill-trained troops over the red clay roads of Virginia and into the jaws of Confederate guns at Bull Run. By late afternoon of 21 July 1861, the general saw his formations disintegrating, men stumbling over interested spectators, in a pell-mell retreat to Washington and safety. Gloom enveloped the North. McDowell relinquished command of the Army of the Potomac to George B. McClellan, the little Napoleon, fresh from campaigning in western Virginia.

To Sophie, Frank confided soon after the Battle of Bull Run, ". . . the demoralization of the Army here is *complete* and the officers are worse than the men inasmuch as they are crowding the hotels, instead of reorganizing their companies and regiments. It is the most fortunate thing that the enemy, strange as it may seem, are still in utter ignorance of the extent of their victory, or this place could have been taken without any difficulty. . . ."

On 25 July the members of the Blockade Board convened with Welles and Fox at the Navy Department. The "subject of the expeditions was entered into," Frank wrote Sophie. "The Cabinet have had our papers again and the President [has] been told up and down by Mr. Fox . . . that the blockading squadron[s] cannot keep at sea in the winter without depots for coal, etc. . . . It is thought two expeditions will go at once and pounce upon two ports little suspected and watched. There is nothing that could be done now so important and so sure to strike terror and do away with the recent reverse [Bull Run] as this. . . .

"It seems quite settled in Fox's mind that I shall go to New York and fit them out, for he told the President the Department had an officer ready. . . . I shall obey all orders in such matters or even requests, for I see so little zeal in the country's cause where most should be, that those whose hearts are right about it should exert themselves. . . ."

Several days later, he wrote in a similar vein, "I had been content to remain where the war found me and where I was doing quite as much good as I could blockading—probably a good deal more— but since the affair at Bull Run I have not been comfortable, and have felt that every man who could be doing anything in addition to his previous work, this hour of need required him to do so."

On 5 August Du Pont received confidential orders from Gideon Welles to prepare the naval part of a land-sea expedition to attack the south Atlantic coast as suggested by the Blockade Board. "The invasion and occupation of the seacoasts of the states in rebellion, as proposed by the Navy Department, having been accepted by the government, and an officer of great merit [General Thomas W. Sherman]* designated by the War Department to organize the expedition in conjunction with the Navy, you are hereby selected to cooperate with this officer.

"The importance of this expedition upon the flank of the enemy cannot be overestimated; and in confiding its preparation and or-

* Not to be confused with General William T. Sherman.

ganization to your hands, the Department hereby gives you the full authority necessary to ensure success.

"You will proceed to New York, as early as practicable, and communicate this order to the officer selected by the War Department; and you will lose no time in getting afloat."

To Sophie, Frank pointed out, "These orders are the natural sequence of events. . . . dearest, the country is in peril, I tell you it is—and if those who have health and life to serve her, and a measure of ability, do not step forth, she will not overcome the danger."

Frank left Washington and journeyed to New York, where he registered at the Astor House. He received orders detaching him from the Philadelphia Navy Yard and from the Blockade Board to take command of the newly formed South Atlantic Blockading Squadron.

On 27 August the first joint Army-Navy expedition under Flag Officer Silas Stringham and General Benjamin Butler arrived off Cape Hatteras, North Carolina, with seven ships and 900 soldiers. The squadron shelled into submission the two forts guarding Hatteras Inlet. Butler's troops occupied the forts, and the Union assumed control of the channel through which at least 100 blockade runners had steamed in the previous six weeks.

At his desk in Washington, Welles, surveying the result of his first amphibious expedition, remarked, "the whole country . . . desire[s] more of the same sort! This they ought to have, and that speedily."

"The first fruits of the labors of my associates and myself came out on the North Carolina coast—the first gleam of light from the ocean again as in 1812, when our Army was whipped along the whole Canada line . . . ," Frank rejoiced in a letter to Henry Winter Davis. "If I had not fairly *insisted* upon the expedition going, and . . . [told] the Secretary his Department might as well be shut if he did not compel the flag officer to execute his orders, he never would have sailed. . . . the great moral effect and encouragement to the country are of incalculable service just now."

Promoted from captain to flag officer, Du Pont started to assemble his squadron. The Navy's acquisition program for vessels was well under way, but the ships, purchased or chartered, had to be repaired and refitted with guns, magazines, and shell rooms. "But, alas!" Du Pont reported, trying to convert a merchantman into a man-of-war is like "altering a vest in[to] a shirt." Transports, ferryboats, and canal steamers clogged the Brooklyn Navy Yard, while in other yards on the East Coast, workers pounded to completion four new "90-day" gunboats.

Besides contracting and purchasing and converting vessels into warships, Du Pont conscientiously coralled navigational aids, directed repairs, supervised the installation of cannon, and hired pilots. In Washington, the Navy Department assigned some of its most competent officers to the squadron.

Ordered to round up volunteers for the southern expedition, General Sherman beat the recruiting drums in New England, and appealed to state governors for regiments. Gathering "good, sound, and safe" troopships, coal, ordnance, water, and food supplies proved difficult. Thirteen thousand men and their equipment were hastily loaded, unloaded, and reloaded as they were transported from Long Island to Washington and, finally, Annapolis.

Du Pont's initial encounter with General Sherman in early September was favorable. To Sophie, he wrote, "I had a long visit this afternoon from G[eneral] S[herman]—he grows upon you, inasmuch as everything he says indicates a man of principle and, I believe, a religious man. . . . He is also and evidently a *thorough officer* and understands what he is about and what is before him."

Aware of the pitfalls ahead, Frank continued, "I began to feel today for the first time the *extent* of the responsibilities put upon me in the projected enterprise. . . . I am more and more persuaded that it was my duty to accept this business, indeed I could not have declined it with honor, and I never should have been satisfied to remain on shore, when the service on the ocean was changing its character from blockade to maritime war—and no service on shore, however useful, could be considered anything after the war. But I must pray for guidance and direction."

In mid-September Frank returned to Washington to dine with Fox, "the object soi-disant was to discuss the expedition—but he only spoke to me about it, in a little aparte, which was satisfactory as far as it went, accompanied with much kindness and interest."

By now Frank was exercising considerable influence with the Navy Department. Fox had confidence in his judgment, and the two men commenced a friendship, based on an appreciation of each other's qualities. During that summer, many officers, like Du Pont, believed that Fox, not Welles, was actually functioning as Secretary of the Navy, making the important decisions. "Mr. Fox . . . *is the Secre-*

tary and well it is." Fox's personality and naval background over-shadowed Welles, who was learning the ropes of the Navy Department during this period. Thrown into close contact with Fox in planning the amphibious assaults against the South, Frank unfortunately underestimated Welles's abilities.

Frank returned to Louviers to see Sophie for a few days. While at Louviers, Frank expressed concern for the success of his expedition to his friend, Captain Blake, now superintendent of the Naval Academy. "I shall meet the great responsibility placed upon me with all the vigor and zeal I can bring to bear. It is awkward to be thrown into an invidious position, but with God's support I shall not, I trust, disappoint my friends."

Frank and Sophie left Louviers for the Astor House in New York. No sooner had they arrived than Frank was recalled to Washington for a meeting with President Lincoln at Secretary of State William H. Seward's home. Members of the Cabinet, Assistant Secretary Fox, and generals McClellan and Thomas Sherman attended. As the meeting progressed, Lincoln appeared in "a great hurry" to end it. Although he expressed little hope for the expedition, he was vexed by the delays, and badgered Welles to get the amphibious force underway in four days.

The nation was eager for action. Although the Hatteras expedition temporarily relieved northern despondency, the shadow of Bull Run lingered.

A little more than a week after Lincoln's four-day ultimatum, the naval contingent of the expedition, led by Du Pont's flagship, *Wabash*, hoisted anchor off the Battery in New York Harbor on 16 October, and slipped down the channel and out to sea.

XX

"The victory was complete"

At Hampton Roads, Du Pont's squadron rendezvoused with General Sherman's troopships. The Roads, exclaimed Fox on an inspection tour, "are filled with vessels as far as the eye can reach all filled with troops or bristling with guns. . . . There is a great deal of enthusiasm."

On board the *Wabash* Du Pont and Sherman conferred to determine the expedition's target. They discarded both Charleston and Savannah as being too strongly fortified. Fox urged Du Pont to seize Port Royal, South Carolina, first, one of the finest harbors on the southern coast, instead of Bull's Bay, South Carolina, or Fernandina, Florida, areas recommended by the Blockade Board. The assistant secretary sensed that the occupation of such a harbor would be of far greater consequence to the war effort than the capture of a more obscure base.

The commanders selected Port Royal, but Frank expressed some concern. Late one night on board the *Wabash,* he wrote Fox, "Sherman and I [decided] *to try* [Port Royal]—But I tell you it is a much greater job than you and I contemplated. . . ." The arrival of Charles O. Boutelle of the Coast Survey, an expert on the Port Royal area, eased Du Pont's apprehension.

Into Port Royal Sound flowed two navigable rivers important to the defense of South Carolina. Thirty miles up the Broad River lay Coosawhatchie, a main junction of the Charleston and Savannah Railroad. Ten miles up the Beaufort River was Beaufort, the nearest town to the Port Royal forts, and forty miles in the same direction, via a maze of small rivers and inlets, was an inland passage to Charleston. In the opposite direction, twenty miles from Port Royal, lay Savannah. With a population of 40,000, mostly slaves, the Port

Royal area had an estimated productive value of $3,000,000 per year, and was the producer of the bulk of sea island cotton, reportedly the best cotton in the world.

Winds, squalls, and swells made an early departure for Port Royal futile. Weeks slipped by while the expedition remained at anchor. Food supplies dwindled; water shortages threatened. Amid the preparations for sea, Frank and Sophie corresponded frequently. He wrote with affection, "I read over your letters with delight. I know how your dear heart yearns about me and it is a blessed thought and it keeps mine tender, if it wanted any such ailment, dearest Sophie. I love you so deeply—I pray for you and myself daily and keep my mind directed to a high sense of duty, seeking above for judgment and direction."

A temporary break finally occurred in the weather and, on 28 October 1861, the convoy of twenty-five supply vessels moved out of Hampton Roads and steered southward. The attack force, consisting of seventeen armed ships and thirty-three transports with 13,000 soldiers and marines, the largest fleet ever commanded by an officer of the United States Navy—"an armada"—took departure the following day. "I feel drawn towards you," Frank told Sophie, "and a sigh comes up now and then and my heart overflows with love and my eyes are wet, but I am hopeful and thankful—prepared to do my duty to my country to the utmost of my ability and with the bravery which belongs to our descent and family, and be resigned to the will of God who has been merciful to us both for many long years. I promise you not to do anything for mere eclat under danger, but to do all that duty and a fitting example in a chief demand. As I see things now, it is probably I may not have to land."

On 1 November a storm of hurricane proportions struck Du Pont's force off the Carolina shore. Distress rockets illuminated the wind-tossed ships, which were awash. On board the *Wabash*, Frank reported, "we closed ports and bailed bucket after [bucket] from off the carpets. . . . During the night it was the old story—fetching away of furniture, rolling of glasses and bottles about the sideboard, rolling of sofas. So hot and close below, blowing great guns above with torrents of rain. In spite of the engines the ship drifting fast ashore, great many lights still in sight from the ships—collision occupying our minds some, but mine more on the small fry, thinking if this great leviathan could be made to twist, roll, and writhe as she did, what must those tiny vessels in comparison be doing."

The side-wheeler *Governor,* with 300 marines, her rudder gone, smokestack overboard, decks crowded with men, rolled heavily and began to sink. Rescue operations saved most of the crew and marines.

Fortunately, the storm abated and the ships, strewn in all directions, rejoined the steaming formation. The casualty list included three cargo ships, one transport, and several men.

Du Pont's squadron dropped anchor off the bar approaching Port Royal Roads on 4 November. On the following day, after successfully traversing the shallow water, they steamed to an anchorage at a safe distance from two Confederate forts, Walker and Beauregard, described by a Confederate as "watch towers of our holy temple. . . ." To enter Port Royal, Du Pont's ships would have to slide through the channel amid a crossfire from these forts.

On board the *Wabash,* naval and military commanders pored over a chart spread out on a table, as they worked out battle plans. They agreed that the forts should first be reduced by naval gunfire. After entering Port Royal Sound the main force was to turn in a snakelike movement and head southeast closing in toward Fort Walker. These maneuvers were to continue until Fort Walker's batteries were knocked out. Du Pont's plan kept the vessels in constant motion and utilized the maneuverability of steamships. The Rebels were never allowed to direct their fire at stationary targets. The vessels "might as well be sailing ships if we threw away the advantages of steam," observed Du Pont.

On 7 November the ships bustled with activity. In high spirits the "jolly tars" sanded down the decks, extinguished the fires, rigged the pumps, while barefooted powder boys hauled up ammunition. Soldiers crowded the decks of the transports.

At 8:00, the signal to get underway was run up on the *Wabash*'s halyards. Commanding officers ordered, "All hands up anchor" and, forward on the forecastles, men at the capstans and bars worked methodically to the tune of the fifers' flutes. Underway, the warships steered for positions in the order of battle. The main attack force, led by the *Wabash,* was followed closely by the frigate *Susquehanna.* Suddenly guns flashed. On board the *Wabash,* gunners rammed in ammunition, ran out the guns, and fired again. *Susquehanna*'s guns belched a "terrible rain of hail." Salvos plowed up the embankments of the forts, burying their guns in showers of sand.

The first run past the forts completed, *Wabash* and *Susquehanna* turned slowly in the Sound and swept back down the channel, while the other vessels of the attack force, in constant motion, steered various courses near the forts and fired. Closing the range to Fort Walker, *Wabash*'s starboard guns boomed. The barrage was heavy. On board the transport *Atlantic*, General Sherman watched fascinated by this display of naval might.

The ships started on their third run, this time closing to a range of 600 yards from Fort Walker. The racket of gunfire was deafening and the air was thick with smoke and dust. The *Wabash* had been "struck in all directions" and was "much cut up in her rigging." Ten hits on the *Susquehanna* had slashed away iron stays, ropes and rigging, and heavy shrouds. Struck four times, the *Pawnee* lost frame timbers, launches, guns, wardroom bulkheads, and an iron safe. Wisely, Du Pont had closed the gap to Fort Walker on successive runs. The Confederate guns could not bear at so close a range, while those of Fort Beauregard were too distant to inflict damage.

The prevailing opinion in 1861 was that one gun on land was the equal of five or ten on shipboard. At Port Royal, this theory evaporated. With its defenses ripped up and only three cannon in working order, Fort Walker weakened.

From the bridge of the *Wabash,* officers saw Confederates stream out of forts Walker and Beauregard and at 2:30 in the early afternoon the American flag floated over both. Out in the Roads, where the troopships lay anchored, soldiers "acting like mad" danced wildly on decks, shouting "Glory!" Bands struck up "The Star Spangled Banner."

The casualty lists included thirty-five Union dead and wounded, and sixty-six Confederates, although Yankees counted an additional "twenty or thirty" Rebel bodies in and around the fort.

The transports got underway and steamed up the channel, where they anchored a few hundred yards off shore. A brigade slowly and tediously disembarked into surf boats and, to the tune of "Yankee Doodle," headed toward the beach to occupy the captured ground.

Once ashore, soldiers began construction of a camp, which a New Hampshire volunteer described as located among "cotton, sweet potatoes, corn, beans, oranges, palmetto trees, mules, Southern pines, palms, and peanuts." General Sherman set up headquarters in a plantation mansion.

With victory in hand, Du Pont stood at the pinnacle of his profession—the first naval hero of the Civil War. From a mere midshipman in 1815, he had risen through careful career moves, exerting family and political influence when needed. His Mediterranean cruises, his Mexican War experience, and his Far Eastern tour had been his training ground. After forty-six years of service, Frank had finally achieved his goal.

That night Frank described the action to Sophie. "A half hour after I closed and sealed my letter we were under the batteries on both sides. . . . We returned both; I did not anchor, but kept the ships moving slowly around so as to prevent giving the enemy fixed objects to aim at. *Entre nous,* this ship did *nearly all* the work, the *Susquehanna* doing nobly behind us, though the gunboats did well, too, but did not follow around with us in the order prescribed. . . . In our first turn and attack I was not satisfied with the execution of this ship, though the effect turned out to be much greater than I thought—but on our second attack I can remember nothing in naval history that came up to this ship in the repetitions of her broadsides. . . . The victory was complete and attended with circumstances which gave it a glare of brilliancy which I never looked forward to—I mention this because it is a fact, not because I value such things. . . .

"You will have seen by the tone of my letters, precious, that I did not permit troubles and reverses and trials of the expedition to worry me—so I am not going to permit myself any elation of my success, but be thankful to Him who gave it. I have kneeled and poured out the feelings of a grateful heart at my preservation, and the success of my arms, and the cause of my country."

Later, Frank added, "This is a wonderful sheet of water—the navies of the world could ride here. I shall write for light vessels, pilot boats, etc. and we shall have a teeming life which probably another century would not have brought about but for this wicked rebellion. It is not my temper to rejoice over fallen foes, but this is a gloomy night in Charleston. . . ."

In Charleston dismay was fanned by rumors that Du Pont's true objective was to burn the city. A slave revolt threatened. Municipal control was vested in a five-man committee that had full authority to act in the emergency. The Charleston *Courier* urged readers to offer up prayers on their knees.

Carolinians rushed to arms. Volunteer units, the South Carolina Rangers, Sumter Guard, Charleston Light Dragoons, and Hibernian

Guards ordered their members to report for training.

A tremor of excitement ran through the North. New York was "in ecstasies" to see the war "at last carried into Africa." "On to Charleston! On to Charleston!" echoed throughout the city. In Wall Street the stock market jumped "Up! Up! Up!"

In Washington Secretary of the Treasury Salmon P. Chase informed reporters, "Uncle Sam is about out of the woods"; a naval officer prophesied, "We'll drive the insurgents to the moon." At the Navy Department, Welles, calculating that the seizure of Port Royal had "taken the vitals out of the rebellion," wrote his son, "trust our arms will go on 'conquering and to conquer,' until it is utterly exterminated. . . . our friends have only to follow up the good work and this I think they will do."

From Port Royal, Du Pont wrote to Fox, "the magnitude of our operation is growing upon me and the blow is ringing all over this Southern country." Ashore, Army privates gathered up the sea island cotton, which had not been burned by departing planters, and loaded it on ships headed north to be sold at auction. From the north lumber, machinery, and equipment arrived with which to construct storehouses, hospitals, and wharves.

A short distance away, at Confederate military headquarters in Coosawhatchie, South Carolina, General Robert E. Lee, who commanded the district, finished a report, "We have no guns that can resist their batteries, and I fear there are but few State troops ready for the field." Scattered along the coasts of Georgia and South Carolina, Lee had only 7,000 infantrymen, some of whom were armed with only "sporting rifles." To bolster his feeble force, the general received permission to employ temporarily units then passing through South Carolina to other fronts. Richmond dispatched five regiments and one battalion to join Lee's forces. Without heavy guns to halt the warships, Lee elected to erect crude obstructions in the rivers and inlets and to prepare the defenses of Charleston and Savannah for a heavier bombardment than they had been built to sustain. In the interim, he remained fearful. "The strength of the enemy exceeds the whole force we have in the State. It can be thrown with great celerity against any point, and far outnumbers any force we can bring against it in the field."

Unaware of South Carolina's vulnerability, Du Pont and Sherman's follow-up offensive stalled. Unfortunately, they waited for reinforcements instead of taking active steps to subdue the entire region. "If the government would send immediately 20,000 men down," Frank informed Sophie, "both Charleston and Savannah with our assistance could fall before New Year's Day."

General Sherman pleaded for more cavalry, infantry, artillery, engineers, steamers, ferryboats, and even a quartermaster officer. He "damned and God damned officers and men to their faces," insisting that a secure base at Port Royal be established before launching any offensive operation. Later, after assessing the enemy's strength, Frank told Sophie, "There is no question now, both Savannah and Charleston could have been taken *without loss* after our blow here, as easy as Washington after Bull Run by the rebels—but then delays seem inherent on both sides. I do not blame the generals. . . ."

"I felt at times fairly *oppressed* by the inordinate expectations in the public mind from the expedition," Frank wrote Whetten. "Our people had witnessed the closing of the Potomac by the rebels, in the immediate presence of an army numbering 150,000 men and a flotilla of twenty-seven sail, yet some miracle was to be achieved by General Sherman with 13,000 and a few frigates and gunboats. . . . Surely I ought to be grateful to our merciful Father for enabling me to meet in any degree such a craving on the part of the country. . . ."

The quick capitulation of the Port Royal forts, except for a scheme to capture Fernandina, left Du Pont and Sherman without plans to take advantage of the momentum their victory had generated. "I never thought I could carry it out so fast," Frank confided to Fox. As a result Savannah, Charleston, and the Charleston and Savannah Railroad went unscathed. "The golden opportunity," lamented an officer, "is passed."

Slowly, the immediate environs were put under control. Gunboats steamed up the river to seize Beaufort, only to find it abandoned except for one intoxicated resident. Naval units quietly occupied the entrances to the Savannah River: Tybee Island, just out of range from Confederate-held Fort Pulaski, which guarded the approaches to Savannah, and Wassaw Inlet, southwest of Tybee— "our flag flies over Georgia too." Such operations around Savannah secured points of refuge for blockaders, and aided materially in sealing off Georgia's leading seaport for the duration of the war.

To Senator James W. Grimes, a member of the Naval Affairs Committee, Frank wrote, "The effectual closing up of Savannah by a division of my squadron occupying Tybee Roads, which we took possession of . . . has given us a foothold in the state of *Georgia* almost as satisfactory to me as to see the one waving here [Port Royal]. . . .

"My greatest care now is about the blockade—the character of our coast, unlike any other on the globe, makes an effectual covering of the ports most difficult. Charleston is more thoroughly watched than ever owing to the fearless character of the commander of the *Susquehanna,* who lays in so close that he has even cut off their fish; but besides, I have covered three other ports in that state besides Georgetown, viz., Edisto, Bull's Bay, and Stono Inlet. . . ."

Northward from Port Royal a naval force seized abandoned St. Helena Sound—"the key to everything in this part of the country"—which commanded the inland route to Charleston, and whose rivers supplied the interior communication with the state of South Carolina. Another flotilla steamed up the South and North Edisto rivers, located just beyond St. Helena Sound toward Charleston, and occupied an abandoned fort and the harbor of South Edisto.

During the pacification of the Port Royal area, Frank described an inspection of the naval force. "I devoted the forenoon [18 November] to visiting the ships of the squadron present . . . I examined the shot holes, some of which are wonderful, said a kind word to the wounded, and assembled informally the crews and, in a pleasant manner, said I desired to express to them in person what I had already conveyed in my general order—my thanks for their good behavior, etc.—and took occasion to lay great stress on the proper treatment of the people on shore and to express my abhorrence of plunder and depredations of all kinds, how they sullied all victories. . . . It was well taken, and all went off well and I think was much appreciated by officers and men . . . . All the vessels are in excellent order."

From Washington Gideon Welles wrote Du Pont, "Your reconnaissances and demonstrations have given great satisfaction. We are all proud of our arm of the service, which has certainly struck effective blows when it has made the attempt. This is important in the war we are waging. There should be no defeats. Let us have success whenever we do move, and the country will forget its impatience. . . . your whole management of the work in which you have engaged has exhibited so much judgment, skill, ability, and right comprehension that you have commanded general confidence. . . ."

On 6 December 1861 Sherman's army moved. A brigade formally occupied the town of Beaufort. "Glad to hear of any movement," Frank remarked sarcastically to Fox, "but Beaufort is not Savannah, nor the way to get to it." With promptings from Du Pont, Sherman sent six companies to occupy St. Helena Sound permanently and a regiment to Tybee Island for the same purpose. With the occupation of Port Royal, Tybee, Wassaw, St. Helena, and North Edisto, Du Pont's squadron was depleted to a degree that threatened to embarrass the blockade. Frank pleaded for more gunboats, and promised Welles that if he were provided with them, the whole coast of Georgia and the greater part of South Carolina would be under United States control in no distant period.

Although in January 1862 Fernandina, Charleston, and Savannah remained in Confederate hands, Du Pont's second in command, Captain C. R. P. Rodgers, pointed out that the five "important harbors of refuge now in our keeping; [were] far more than the government ever expected from *this* expedition."

The Port Royal assault accomplished its basic objective, the acquisition of a well-protected harbor on the south Atlantic coast. Strategically, Du Pont's feat, coupled with the recovery of Hatteras Inlet earlier in August, gave the Federal Navy command of nearly the whole coast of North and South Carolina and Georgia and of the water route between Charleston and Savannah. Several of Du Pont's contemporaries proclaimed, with much justification, that the Port Royal victory secured the most important naval station in the Civil War.

The joint expedition could have accomplished much more against the inadequately armed south Atlantic coast. Du Pont, Sherman, their naval and military superiors in Washington completely misjudged the strength of Lee's forces and the ability of coastal fortifications to withstand an attack by steam vessels. Had the order of Du Pont and Sherman been more explicit about follow-up operations, had the commanders been more daring, or had Du Pont exerted greater pressure on the general, the South might have lost Savannah or Charleston, or at least experienced considerable damage to these two ports.

Du Pont's victory brought the war to the shores of South Carolina and Georgia and, in the North, an observer reflected, "it came when the gloom of many failures depressed the national spirit to its lowest point, and instantly raised it to a conscious confidence in the power and fortune of the republic."

On 25 December Frank wrote home, "Christmas Day. Merry Christmas, dearest Sophie, if anything can be merry in these times of war and troubles. I think of all at home and the children of the Brandywine and of your going to church. Compliments of the season to all. . . .

"Our ships look . . . nice today, and I have given the squadron Christmas. A sprig of fir is on all the guns; I never saw this before in all my service and it looks beautifully. I never told you of our prayer meetings; they hold them near the cabin door in the evenings and open with a hymn, sweet beyond description, for I never heard such voices in a man-of-war before."

Early in the war the Navy Department toyed with the idea of sinking ships loaded with stone at the entrance of Rebel harbors, to choke the channels and prevent blockade runners from entering. In the summer of 1861 the Blockade Board devoted hours to mulling over such a plan. Secretary Welles concluded that this operation would prove "the most economical and satisfactory method" of halting "the flow of commerce" at Savannah and Charleston.

Welles ordered his purchasing agent to secure twenty-four old vessels of not less than 250 tons each, sell all unnecessary articles on board, and load each with blocks of granite to the "utmost extent." The agent "absorbed nearly all the cheap ones," and anchored them to New Bedford, Massachusetts, and other New England coastal towns. Valves consisting of a large screw fixed in the bottom of each vessel were rigged to scuttle this "Rat Hole Squadron." When unscrewed, the valves would allow a steam of water "as big as a man's leg" to gush in. An inquiring reporter from the New York *Evening Post,* inspecting some of the ships, mostly whalers, described them as "a hard looking set," and estimated that for the "best of the lot" the government paid out $6,000.

In November 1861 the stone ships sailed southward from New England. At Port Royal Frank delayed other operations long enough to try this new experiment. The stone ships arrived in early December off Federal-held Tybee Island, near the mouth of the Savannah River. There, while approaching their anchorage, two sank immediately, and another, in a sinking condition, was towed to Tybee Island to be employed as a breakwater.

With the Union occupation of Tybee Island and the other entrances around Savannah, Frank decided to concentrate the stone fleet at Charleston. "I think we can make it effectual, for three or four months anyhow," he wrote Sophie, "and this will give us the winter. It can be done without going under the fire of the forts."

For four days the blockaders of Charleston engaged in scuttling operations. After soundings were taken around the entrances to the harbor, sixteen whalers towed by steamers were planted in designated spots and submerged in the main channel, creating "eddies, whirlpools, and countercurrents," and rendering navigation hazardous and uncertain. Other stone ships were sunk in another Charleston channel.

Complaints about "this atrocious experiment" reverberated from the Confederacy and Great Britain. "What . . . could be more savage . . . or more unlike a civilized or a Christian nation?" inquired a Confederate naval officer. General Lee termed it "an abortive expression of . . . malice and revenge." *The Times* in London claimed that such actions were "something unheard of" in naval warfare, while in the British Parliament, an admiral called them an "indelible blot . . . a national shame."

These recriminations were premature. "The Rat Hole Squadron" proved a failure. By 12 February 1862 a Confederate major at Fort Sumter reported that "little was to be seen of . . . [the] hulls" of the stone fleet. Tides and currents in the Charleston entrances had washed equally good channels around the side of the sunken hulls, and blockade runners continued to slip safely by the cordon of Union ships on station off Charleston. The "novel mode of blockade" ended ingloriously.

Meanwhile Frank arranged for his blockading squadron to perform ship repairs at Port Royal and thus reduce dependency on Northern shipyards. On two hulks of the stone fleet workmen constructed carpenter, blacksmith, boiler, foundry, and machine shops. They also converted a sailing ship of the line, *Vermont*, into a receiving ship, complete with barracks and a hospital.

XXI

"Do not go it half cocked"

On board the *Wabash* preparations were being made to attack Fernandina, Florida, and the inland waterway from Fernandina to Savannah traversed by light draft Confederate vessels evading the blockade. Only 430 miles from Nassau, a major base for ships arriving from England with cargoes, Fernandina carried on a brisk traffic. This town of 2,000 was the eastern terminus of the Cedar Keys Railroad, which stretched westward across Florida to the Gulf of Mexico. Secretary Welles declared it "probably the most important port to close up on the eastern coast of Florida."

Fernandina was almost defenseless. The regiment stationed there was demoralized because of a drunken colonel and, at nearby Fort Clinch, soldiers possessed only four guns, all lacking ammunition. Florida's governor and the state's representatives in the Confederate capital of Richmond all pleaded for military aid, but little was forthcoming. To placate the state, a few cannon and supplies as well as a pitifully small number of troops were dispatched southward.

On 28 February 1862 Du Pont's naval force and Army transports with 4,000 troops on board cleared Port Royal and headed for the Florida coast. From the *Wabash*, Frank optimistically wrote his brother, "if God is with us, I shall sweep the whole lower coast, which will close up pretty much all *my* work . . . save the few places to blockade which are not held by my vessels. . . . I do not apprehend much difficulty or danger. . . ."

A day later the flotilla churned into St. Andrew Inlet and anchored in Cumberland Sound, twenty miles from Fernandina. Here the transports and the heavy drafted naval vessels remained all day, while the smaller gunboats maneuvered in the sound for reconnaissance.

Southward at Fernandina, Confederate officers ordered their soldiers to break camp, transport equipment to the railroad station, and head into the interior. When dispatches flooded into military headquarters reporting enemy gunboats in Cumberland Sound, there was a "pell mell stampede" of civilians to the railroad station.

Out in the sound on 2 March, Frank received information from a black that the Confederate batteries had been abandoned. To prevent Rebels from burning their property, he dispatched gunboats directly to Fernandina together with a portion of the troops on board the *Boston*. Confederate abandonment of the shore batteries made it unnecessary for the heavier ships to navigate the difficult inland passage, so Du Pont's main fleet retraced its course out of the sound toward the main ship entrance.

The light draft gunboats and three armed launches from the transports *Boston* and *McClellan* slid down Cumberland Sound toward Fernandina but, due to treacherous waters, only the *Ottawa* successfully maneuvered the channel. From on board the *Ottawa* seamen saw white flags on shore. As the long gunboat neared the town, a few rifle shots rang out from the bushes and from the railroad train, which was just leaving for the Florida interior. After a two-mile running skirmish between the Union gunboat and the Confederate train along the banks of the sound, the locomotive and its cars successfully escaped.

On the arrival of the Union gunboats *Pawnee* and *Huron*, marines and sailors occupied Fernandina. Seamen guarded the railroad and, in the course of a day, commandeered two locomotives and three railroad cars.

Cursing the "heat and mosquitoes," the sailors discovered that the town presented "a peculiarly desolate and deserted appearance." The few white inhabitants touched their hats or bowed as the Federals passed, but all had "a half-frightened, half hang-dog look."

On 4 March Du Pont's main force anchored off the town. The soldiers on board the transports disembarked and garrisoned Fernandina. Inspecting Fort Clinch, Frank felt surprised that the defenses had been voluntarily abandoned. "A great day this, dearest Sophie. I am almost too much excited to write and not a little fatigued. . . ."

To Secretary Welles, Frank proudly declared, "The victory at Fernandina was bloodless, but most complete in results."

The occupation of surrounding towns, hamlets, sounds, and inlets was begun until the whole east coast of Florida from St. Augustine northward and parts of Georgia were held by Federal forces.

Once St. Simons Sound and the neighboring sounds in Georgia were secured, Frank reported to Welles, "I take great pleasure in reminding the Department that one of the principal and ultimate objects of the naval expedition which I have the honor to command was, in its first conception, to take and keep under control the whole line of seacoast of Georgia, knowing . . . 'that the naval power that controls the seacoast of Georgia controls the state of Georgia.' . . . the entire sea coast of Georgia is now either actually in my possession or under my control, and thus the views of the Government have been accomplished."

Frank's assessment of his contribution to the Union was bolstered by "a vote of thanks of Congress for his services and gallantry displayed in the capture of Forts Walker and Beauregard, commanding the entrance of Port Royal Harbor, on the 7th of November, 1861."

The squadron's work was far from over along the southern coast. Du Pont's forces had to continue the blockade, flush out Confederates from minor batteries, and secure the sounds and creeks.

On board the *Wabash*, Frank reviewed the work. After the capture of Port Royal, the Union forces had gained control of the entrance to the Savannah River and the neighboring sounds in Georgia, Florida, and South Carolina. This allowed Du Pont to station vessels in the sounds and establish an effective inner blockade.

In Washington Secretary of State Seward declared, "One half of the coast of South Carolina, the whole coast of Georgia, and the harbors, cities and coasts of East Florida, are occupied. . . . There is scarce a harbor on the whole coast. . . which is not hermetically sealed. . . ."

While the Navy searched out pockets of Rebels, in April 1862 the Army captured Fort Pulaski, guarding the approaches to Savannah. "Hurrah Pulaski's down," noted a naval officer, of this purely military operation. The Navy gained considerably. The occupation of nearby Tybee Island in the winter of 1861 had tightened the Savannah blockade and now, with the fall of Fort Pulaski, Savannah was practically lost as a port to the Confederacy.

At Port Royal, General David Hunter relieved General Sherman as commander of the newly constituted Department of the South, comprising the states of South Carolina, Georgia, and Florida. "General Hunter," Frank wrote Sophie, "is a man of the finest bearing, tone, and address; silent, but not like most silent men, he is uncommonly gracious and benign in his intercourse. He is easy in his private means, and very independent of thought and action, has no fear of responsibility, yet very devoid of pretention. . . ."

After a call on General Hunter, Frank wrote Sophie, "I have just been to tea, we had blackberries, which reminded me you had asked me in one of your letters if I had fruit—this is the first we have seen. Just now we are 'hard up,' to use a nautical phrase—no fresh beef or mutton, no macaroni; these three things seem absolutely necessary to me—so we have salt beef which is very good of its kind, then some excellent pea soup in which I cut up immense pieces of the *fattest* but very sweet pork, put up in Philadelphia and which Doctor [Benjamin F.] Bache said was good for me. On this I make out—and am holding my own very well, on the whole. I have gained a good deal in health, I think on looking back, and ought to be very thankful. I attribute it, under Providence, to having entirely over-come a desire for drinking water, taking but a cup of tea or coffee and no sugar, except what is in the milk. Then I have eaten *no* vegetables and, strange to say, macaroni supplies their place per-fectly—the steward cooks it very well, with a liaison of tomatoes generally; the beef and mutton I eat when we have it is fabulous. Some sherry wine and *bitters* before dinner stimulate this appetite—and before going to bed at night I take a great tumbler of brown stout. . . . Champagnes and sauternes, and all those light wines I used to like so well, I not only do not take any more but I have lost the taste for them—even when we have ice to put in them. . . ."

Blockade runners continued to slip into Charleston evading the vigilance of Yankee commanders. Frank dispatched general orders to his squadron that the blockade must be "strict and absolute," the Union commerce must be protected from depredations of Con-federate privateers, and that a lawful blockade demanded the actual presence of an adequate force stationed at the entrance of each port. Every captain was ordered to keep his vessel "at all times" in the "most perfect condition for service." In May 1862 the South Atlan-tic Blockading Squadron maintained ten ships off Charleston and twenty-two elsewhere along the South Carolina, Georgia, and Flor-ida coasts. Du Pont's blockade organization became the model for other squadrons.

Cases involving captured vessels were adjudicated in federal prize courts. The gross proceeds from condemnation of British vessels seized by the South Atlantic Blockading Squadron exceeded $2,000,000;

those of Rebel vessels equaled $400,000. Of this sum, the prize money given to the capturing crews totaled $1,500,000, of which Frank's share was almost $75,000.

After the historic battle between the *Monitor* and *Virginia* (ex-*Merrimack*) in March 1862, Assistant Secretary Fox and others caught "iron fever." The naval engagement at Hampton Roads gave the Union Navy Department the hope that its iron, turreted vessels might do what its wooden ships could not. Faith in this class of gunboats was so great that some hypothesized that a "couple of ironclads" could destory Gibraltar "in a couple of hours." Fox stated to a congressional committee that naval commanders would have no "hesitation in taking *Monitor* into Charleston." To John Ericsson, the designer of the *Monitor,* Fox confided, "From the beginning I have advocated the product of your brain and staked the reputation of the Navy on the results." The iron contagion infected the entire North. "Unless we are greatly mistaken, the naval battle . . . in Hampton Roads has changed the whole aspect of naval warfare and harbor defenses" praised the editor of *Frank Leslie's Illustrated Newspaper.* "It is evident that the monitor can sail unharmed into any harbor of the world, however well defended, and laugh at the fire of the forts."

Without further testing, Welles and Fox launched an extensive building program. Ericsson received contracts for six more monitors; other builders started construction on twenty-one single- and double-turreted monitors. Designs were drafted for seagoing ironclads. The *Roanoke,* sister ship of the *Merrimack,* was armored and provided with turrets.

Fox channeled his enthusiasm into a plan for the capture of Charleston Harbor with the monitors. He sounded out Du Pont less than a month after the *Virginia-Monitor* mêlée. "Our summer's work must be Charleston by the Navy," he informed Du Pont. "We can give you the Monitor . . . [which] can go up to Charleston and return in perfect safety. . . . What do you say to it?" With several monitors, Fox asked, "Don't you think we can . . . make it *purely navy?* Any other plan we play second."

Dubious of the monitors' ability to subdue Charleston, Frank replied that the Confederate effort in and around the harbor had been "ceaseless day and night," as they reinforced Fort Sumter. "Do not," he stressed, "under-rate the work."

Fox, undeterred, replied, ". . . the 'Monitor' can go all over . . . ."

She is absolutely impregnable. . . . I pray you give us Charleston. . . . The Fall of Charleston is the fall of Satan's Kingdom."

Du Pont felt that Fox's confidence in the ironclads was misplaced. "Fox writes about *Charleston,*" Frank remarked to Charles Henry Davis, ". . . My information is the harbor is entirely obstructed. . . ."

To his friend and attorney in Philadelphia, Benjamin Gerhard, Frank wrote, "I [brought] . . . a powerful glass to bear on Charleston. One long year of unremitted work has been applied to its defenses and they are formidable in the extreme. . . ."

In Washington, the rank of rear admiral was established, and on 30 July, Samuel Francis Du Pont and eight others were promoted.

The North craved a naval victory at Charleston. The Union army under General McClellan was stalemated in Virginia. General Lee stopped the Federal advance up the Yorktown Peninsula in the Seven Days' Battle. Washington recalled McClellan and replaced him with General John Pope. Consternation followed as Lee crushed Pope at the Second Battle of Bull Run, while another Confederate Army advanced under General Braxton Bragg into Kentucky to threaten Louisville.

Restored to command, McClellan checked Lee at Antietam in September, and the Confederate Army in the west, under Bragg, retreated into southeastern Tennessee. The feeling of relief could not compensate for the disappointment of earlier hopes. Among men of all political parties the conviction grew that the efforts of the people in generously supplying the government with the means to conduct the war had been ill repaid.

"Our army," wrote Welles to his wife in September 1862, "is back where it was last winter. . . . I trust no time will be lost in reviews and showy parades, but that early and rapid blows will be struck, so as to send the rebels far South."

Welles worried about the prestige of the Navy. The "navy will be attacked before long," he predicted, "some misfortune or indiscretion will bring down furious denunciations from little whelps."

To quiet criticism on the conduct of the war, Fox told one senator that he hoped the Navy would give him Charleston before Christmas and, to Flag Officer David Farragut in the Gulf of Mexico, he disclosed that the first strike by the new monitors "must be Charleston."

The possibility of an expedition to Charleston was frequently discussed in Cabinet meetings. On 13 September secretaries Chase and Seward went to the Navy Department. With Welles and Fox, they examined charts and talked of the monitors, which would soon be ready for sea. Welles suggested to Chase that the monitors "might take Richmond as preliminary to Charleston."

At Port Royal, on board the *Wabash*, Frank doubted that either city could be subdued by monitors. "This is too serious a matter," he warned Fox. "Do not go it half cocked . . . it is a bigger job than Port Royal, putting the coast of these . . . rebel states in irons. . . . let us consult together again—Loss of life is nothing, but *failure* now at Charleston is ten times the failure elsewhere."

The Navy Department recalled Frank to Washington for discussions. He left Port Royal on 27 September, and three days later he arrived at New Castle. He went directly home. Together with Sophie, he journeyed to the capital. He had already concluded that the attack on Charleston should be a combined naval and military assault with at least 25,000 troops. However, at the conference table Fox monopolized the discussion. Du Pont said very little. The assistant secretary insisted that the monitors were invulnerable, argued that success depended on the Navy alone, and discarded the idea of a joint operation. Fox's confidence in the monitors "was so profound as to lead him to say that one monitor alone would cause the immediate evacuation of Charleston." Despite Fox's faith, one monitor, two ironclads, and several wooden gunboats had failed to capture Fort Darling in Virginia. Frank's stubborn silence convinced both Welles and Fox that the admiral's views coincided with their own and the secretaries spoke of the upcoming operation as "the crowning glory of a successful career." As the meetings ended, they shook hands with Frank and predicted that when he next returned he would be "loaded with honors justly due" to one "who avenges Sumter."

Frank and Sophie returned to Louviers. After a brief stay, he went to Washington to meet with President Lincoln. "He alluded to my successes," Frank wrote Sophie, ". . . I explained the general nature of our occupation off the seacoasts of the three rebel states and the moral effect of this, particularly as one of them was South Carolina." That evening Frank dined with Seward, who said that "the occupation of the whole coast and every port is much more important abroad than the capture of Richmond."

On 18 October Frank set down his conclusions for Sophie. "I leave under *no more plans* than the first day: a vague impression that Charleston must be taken—a marked appetite on the part of the government officials that it should be, and that very speedily, captured. Six weeks is considered a long time, especially by Mr. Seward. Officers talk of the 'grand attack' and all underrate the difficulties. But it pleases God to give me equanimity under these circumstances, and it is a great mercy that He shows me. . . ."

At Washington, Frank and Fox, after an inspection of the monitors at the navy yard, boarded the gunboat *Ellen* for the trip to Hampton Roads. "We had long and earnest conversations on the capture of Charleston," Frank informed Sophie, "Fox modulating his sanguine hopes and impulsive certainty into a calm investigation of all the difficulties. It was a matter of mutual benefit to us and I feel better than I did because matters have been a good deal digested, which they were not at all at my first visit to Washington."

At Hampton Roads, after inspecting the *New Ironsides,* "one of the wonders of the world, for she is a *seagoing* plated ship," Frank and Fox boarded the *Keystone State* after dark, "letting Mr. Fox depart, who was anxious to be . . . in Washington. I was much pleased with him and I spoke earnestly to him not to allow the Cabinet ministers or unhealthy public opinion to push him prematurely into an operation. . . ."

During the autumn of 1862, Welles and Fox spurred the shipyards to greater activity. Welles demanded that the monitors be ready by early winter because he did not want "to depend upon the army even for cooperation" at Charleston. Under the influence of Fox, Welles, whose caution had vanished with his junior's extreme optimism, decided on a naval attack against the South Carolina stronghold.

Welles and Fox ignored the fact that few harbors of the Confederacy possessed greater natural defensive advantages than did Charleston. The city lay seven miles from the harbor entrance, which was formed by Sullivan's Island to the north and Morris Island to the south. The main ship channel into Charleston was circuitous, lined on each side by shoals. Before the Civil War the seaward entrance was defended only by Fort Moultrie on Sullivan's Island, Fort Sumter, which was erected in the harbor on artificial foundations, and Castle Pinckney, an "old fashioned brick work," located a mile east of Charleston on Folly Island.

After the war broke out the Confederates strengthened the defenses of the city. In addition to the three forts, which were intended to resist naval attacks, workmen erected strong earthworks on the upper and lower ends of both Morris and Sullivan's islands. Laborers rebuilt and armed old Fort Johnson on James Island, and established batteries on the beach, running in a southeasternly direction. Southerners devised torpedo mines, created a Torpedo Bureau, and rigged submersibles in the harbors.

General Pierre Gustave T. Beauregard assumed responsibility for the city's defenses. He reinforced forts Sumter and Moultrie, and other defensive works of the harbor. Beauregard increased the number of mines in the channel, and stretched a rope obstruction across the water close to the city. The general hoped that Federal gunboats would be slowed by the mines, ropes, and piles, permitting the forts to take careful aim and concentrate their fire. "The great object of the enemy," Beauregard's chief aide declared, "will . . . be to run by and every effort must be made to crush him."

Frank, less sanguine than Welles and Fox, wrote Charles Henry Davis, "The work on the defenses of Charleston has never ceased. . . . I believe he [Beauregard] has exhausted his science and applied every conceivable means. He is fully confident that he can successfully defend the harbor. . . . I have always been of [the] opinion that it [the attack] should be a joint [Army-Navy] operation, carefully devised—and I trust I am not insensible to the honor of a *naval* capture, though I am infinitely more alive to the absolute *necessity* of *success* than of any special glory to our arm of the service, or of personal distinction to myself. We cannot afford a failure in this crisis, political as well as military, through which we are now passing. . . ."

In the North, the monitors were acclaimed as they neared completion. One correspondent announced "Charleston, Savannah, and Mobile will probably hear of them before Christmas," while a senator prematurely asserted, "And what a glorious triumph it will be! It will thrill every loyal heart with delight."

One of Ericsson's new monitors, *Passaic*, was launched in November. The commanding officer detested the vessel. He cursed the breakdowns, and denounced the public clamor, bluntly stating that if his monitor engaged forts, she would be "hors de combat in a very little while." He privately noted, "I begin to rue the day when I got into the iron clad business, the discomforts I can stand, but

283

not the want of efficiency which becomes more and more apparent every day."

In Washington, Fox disregarded the complaints and ignored the monitors' deficiencies as he scrounged for scraps of information on the harbor. He suggested that Confederate obstructions in the Charleston channel could be overcome. If the enemy relied chiefly on pile obstructions, the Navy was to plow through them with an iron raft pushed by one of the monitors. He urged Ericsson to construct an instrument for "continuous butting," and hired two "torpedo men" to construct rams.

At Port Royal, Frank was deeply concerned by the widespread feeling that the arrival of the monitors spelled the capitulation of Charleston. He wrote to a friend, "I feel that very heavy work is before me, for there seems a morbid appetite in the land to have Charleston. . . . The difficulties to be overcome . . . have increased a thousand-fold. . . . English people who have been into Charleston . . . smile at the idea of it being taken. The Department thinks it can be done with a few monitors. . . . You are aware there is no running by; the harbor is a bog . . . to say nothing of the obstructions, which ironclads are much less serviceable in removing . . . than wooden vessels with their boats and appliances. I hope and believe we can do the job as well as most people. I shall certainly try."

By early winter the monitors were still in northern shipyards undergoing trials. Defeatism, especially in the West, was growing. In December 1862 General Ambrose Burnside and his Union army met disastrous defeat at Fredericksburg. "This defeat," a depressed Frank explained to Sophie, "I take for granted, will turn all eyes on Charleston and all hopes. It is a *sentiment* in the national heart that it should be captured, but it will not put down the rebellion. . . . The attempt to be made soon, I presume, though we have not an iron vessel yet, is as complete an *experiment* as can be imagined. I am satisfied that the power of aggression and even endurance of the ironclads are as much overrated by Mr. Fox and others as the extent and nature of the defenses of Charleston are underrated."

Later, he clarified his viewpoint to Sophie. "I have but one rule of [thumb] in reference to such things: it is my duty to carry out the views of the government, to stand by those who, constitutionally elected, are carrying on this war, however badly, to the best of their ability. I want to do *my* duty to the cause and to the country. . . ."

Disaster temporarily set back the proposed Charleston attack. On her passage from Hampton Roads southward the *Monitor,* towed by the *Rhode Island,* encountered heavy gales. She sank, with the loss of two officers and twenty-four men.

By February 1863, the *New Ironsides, Passaic,* and *Montauk* had reached Port Royal, while other monitors towed by steamers arrived in March. Ten thousand Yankee troops were sent to Port Royal to act as Du Pont and General Hunter saw fit. But Secretary Welles impressed on Du Pont that "the capture of this most important port, however, rests solely upon the success of the naval force. . . ."

Fox increased the pressure on Frank by reminding him that "The eyes of the whole country are upon you, and knowing your skill, and resource, and reliance upon Him who gives victory, I commend you to His keeping, no misgivings as to the result. . . ." Anticipating victory, the Department ordered Du Pont, after the fall of Charleston, to capture Savannah, then dispatch the monitors around to the Gulf for use against Mobile.

Throughout the early months of 1863 Union officers at Port Royal interrogated runaway slaves, explored rumors, and conducted night surveys of Charleston Harbor. They ascertained that nets and mines, some of them "extraordinary in size," had been laid down in the channels, and estimated that 140 guns could be brought to bear against approaching vessels. To a friend, Frank described the Rebel defenses as "simply fabulous." He warned Fox that "The *Experiment,* for it is nothing else, is too momentous to be trifled with." He told Sophie, "I am quite sure that the Department is not all alive to the magnitude of the undertaking, nor does it contemplate as it should the disaster to our cause by failure."

Frank's squadron was fast deteriorating. Many of its ships had been at Port Royal since November 1861 and needed repairs. Their crews required rest. Frank complained that he disliked "running willing horses to death," and pointed to his sailors who, after continuous service, had never landed anywhere on the coast "but to fight." Morale was at rock bottom. Officers and men on the *Huron* were ill with fevers. A near mutiny broke out on one gunboat when the crew purloined liquor from the spirit room, and rioted on the berth deck. On board the *Western World,* "perforated by worms," the sailors reluctantly returned to their work only after the captain threatened to shoot them all dead. A boat crew of the *Georgia* deserted.

The *Ottawa* "broke down completely and was utterly worthless," and the *Mohawk, Madgie, Potomska, Quaker City, Water Witch,* and *Norwich* suffered mechanical failures. Operating out of Charleston Harbor, two Rebel rams knocked the *Mercedita* and *Keystone State* out of commission. The monitors arrived at Port Royal needing repairs. "I mention these details," Frank complained to Fox, "in order that the Department may be informed of the true condition of things."

Frank decided to test the monitors under fire. The *Montauk,* towed by the *James Adger,* and four wooden gunboats pushed up the Great Ogeechee River in Georgia toward Fort McAllister. The Union vessels anchored below the earthwork and salvoed. The light gun fort retaliated. Four hours later, after expending all the ammunition, the *Montauk* and other vessels ceased firing and stood downriver. Neither fort nor ship received injury. Du Pont correctly pointed out to Welles, "whatever degree of impenetrability they [the monitors] might have, there was no corresponding quality of aggression or destructiveness as against forts, the slowness of fire giving full time for the gunners in the fort to take shelter in the bombproofs. . . . This experiment also convinces me . . . that in all such operations to secure success troops are necessary."

"Altogether this experience," Frank confided to Sophie, "was desirable, and I am glad I made the experiment. I suppose the rebels will make the most of having resisted a monitor. . . . The truth is . . . the panic produced by gunboats has passed away—the terror caused by the capture of Port Royal gave us all the coast but Savannah and Charleston, and more foresight and vigor with the Army would have given us them . . . . their defenses are better everywhere. . . ."

To a friend, Frank evaluated the possibility of success against Charleston. "The monitor was struck thirteen or fourteen times, which would have sunk a gunboat easily but did no injury whatever to the *Montauk*—speaking well for *impenetrability* of these vessels—though the distance was greater than what would constitute a fair test. But the slow firing, the inaccuracy of aim—for you can't see to aim properly from the turret, and only six shell[s] went in out of sixty—give no corresponding powers of aggression or destructiveness. . . . He [Fox] thought the appearance of *one* on the coast would make people run away for hundreds of miles. Well, I asked *myself* this morning, while dressing, if one ironclad cannot take eight guns, how are five to take 147 guns in Charleston harbor? . . . I wish they had invented some cast-iron men and officers for them. . . ."

Fort McAllister became "a thorn" in "Du Pont's flesh." Two more attacks, once with three monitors, to knock out the Georgia fort were carried out. Both times the monitors failed. One Federal officer believed that the fort could not be reduced no matter how many monitors were in the river. A naval engineer realized, "we must have more to be successful against Charleston." On these expeditions river obstructions proved troublesome, and the monitors' fifteen-inch guns were not as efficient as expected.

After the "practice" runs, Frank noted that two out of seven monitors had gone aground, two had their concussion boxes injured, one had her fifteen-inch gun carriage shattered, some had their decks torn up slightly, and one had hit a mine. Asked how his monitor took enemy shells, an officer described it as "like an electric shock."

One captain pointed out that the fight did "not promise much" because the effect of the monitors' guns was "very slight." "There is little doubt in my mind," he confided to a friend, "that with very considerable powers of endurance, the Monitors have only a very limited one of inflicting injury on . . . forts, and this arises from their few guns and the slowness with which the fire from these is delivered. . . . I for one began to have serious doubts on the subject of the few iron clads at our disposal, being able to do much toward reduction of . . . [the] city."

"I think the attempt on Charleston will fail!" announced another captain, "the officers of the Navy . . . are losing faith in the Monitors." On board the monitor *Weehawken*, Commander John Rodgers wrote home, "I hope we shall succeed but I do not feel as sure as I could wish." The skippers of the monitors *Nahant* and *Montauk* did not consider this type of vessel "yet perfected," and the captain of the *New Ironsides* reported to Fox, "I confess that I am by no means confident."

Northern correspondents, watching the progress of the South Atlantic Blockading Squadron, felt the pessimism and began to doubt the monitors' ability to succeed against Charleston. "I learned by degrees," reported one newsman, "that from the chief commander down to the lieutenants, the officers of the fleet had not much faith in either the offensive or the speed of the new forms of ironclads."

In Washington, Fox prodded Du Pont to attack. "Finances, politics, foreign relations, all seem to ask for Charleston," he declared. "The people will have nothing but success and they are right."

President Lincoln visited the Navy Department to tell Welles that he had "but slight expectation that we shall have any great success from Du Pont. He as well as McClellan hesitates—he has the slows. . . . Du Pont is everlastingly asking for more . . . iron-clads. He will do nothing with any. He has intelligence and system, and will maintain a good blockade. You did well in selecting him for that command, but he will never take Sumter or get to Charleston. . . ."

Welles's assessment of Frank was unflattering. He noted that ". . . Du Pont shrinks from responsibility, dreads the conflict he has sought, yet is unwilling that any other should undertake it, is afraid the reputation of Du Pont will suffer. This jeopardizes the whole—makes a botched thing of it. I am disappointed, but not wholly surprised. . . ."

Du Pont and his monitor captains were not alone in pinpointing the monitors' limitations. John Ericsson firmly held that his monitors could not capture Charleston. "Your confidence in the great naval attack," he informed Fox, "astounds me—You have not turrets enough . . . you have not guns enough. For a naval contest you would be all powerful. . . . How different is the case in your present undertaking—I hope I may be wrong but at the same time pray that you will not commence the attack until you have all your turrets present."

Fox remained optimistic. He confided to Ericsson that, "Though everybody is despondent about Charleston, and even the President thinks we shall be defeated, I must say that I have never had a shadow of a doubt as to our success, and the confidence arises from a careful study of . . . [the] marvelous vessels."

Fox was so unrealistic that he wrote Frank, "I hope you will hold to the idea of carrying in your flag supreme and superb, defiant and disdainful, silent amid the 200 guns, until you arrive at the center of this wicked rebellion and there demand the surrender of the forts, or swift destruction. *The President and Mr. Welles are very much struck with this programme. . . .*"

Aware that he must use the monitors against the Charleston forts, Frank confided to Sophie, "I consider the pending event so momentous to the country first, to the Navy next, and to myself and to *you* and all my family as connected with my reputation and *honor* as an officer, that I will send you all the *official* papers, touching immediately upon these matters."

Several days later, he added, "Now comes a great *experiment,* with the public mind intensified and the national heart sore from its want of success elsewhere—believing in a victory, impatient of delay. No more knowledge of the instruments with which the problem is to be solved, and of the work to be accomplished, than of Egyptian hieroglyphics. Yet with all this, while the sanguine are going *down,* I feel composed, hopeful, reliant that all that can be done we will do, but nothing more. No visions of success, nothing sanguine—just as I felt in the gale, when my fleet was scattered. Success is not in my hands, to do my duty is—and with God's help I will do that."

A week before the attack, Frank wrote again, "I wanted to begin this letter to you last night, but it was crowded out even on a Sunday evening by things which could not be deferred and which [at] this moment of great pressure demand my attention. It pleases God, however, in His infinite mercies to sustain me in these hours of immense responsibility, the greatest by far of my life, because I think the result at Charleston may decide the fate of the nation—a matter overlooked by our rulers entirely who only think of a blow being struck to help them politically.

"They no more know what the bravest hearts here think and feel about the matter than, when alongside a comfortable fire, they remember a man outside in a snowdrift. The ignorance about Charleston is appalling on their part, for it is the only way to account for the impatience which seem to manifest itself. . . . What precious lives I am taking in with me to solve what is only an experiment! . . . I put my trust in a merciful God, who has so mercifully preserved me thus far and allowed me prosperity. . . .

"I have your dear picture in the pocket nearest my heart and in a little *Sailor's Prayer Book* as a portfolio for it. It gives me comfort to have it there."

Just before the attack in Charleston, Frank switched his flag to the broadside type of ironclad, the *New Ironsides,* and sent his "Order of Battle, and Plan of Attack upon Charleston, South Carolina," to the monitor captains.

XXII

"We have met a sad repulse"

On the evening before the Federal assault against Charleston, 6 April 1863, a New York *Tribune* correspondent wandered around the deck of Du Pont's flagship, the *New Ironsides,* anchored off the entrance of the main ship channel of the harbor. Groups of sailors sat on the gundeck singing, joking, and playing cards, and aft, a bluejacket remarked that if the ship were to hit a mine the next day, she "would sink like a stone, and they would be drowned like rats." To the newsman, the *New Ironsides* looked like "a machine of destruction."

Off in the haze as crews readied the monitors for the next day, commanding officers dropped into small boats and headed for the flagship to receive their final instructions. Clanking up the Jacob's ladder of the *New Ironsides,* they entered Du Pont's cabin. Together with the admiral, they reviewed the plans for the forthcoming attack. The seven monitors and *New Ironsides* with their thirty-two guns were to pass up the channel and open fire on Fort Sumter. After that stronghold was reduced, the flotilla was to proceed to the city, training their guns on other harbor installations. Du Pont designated the monitor *Weehawken* to head the battle line.

The next day at mid-morning, Frank jotted a short note to Sophie, "We shall move at twelve and the contest will soon after commence. The *verse* today is equally encouraging. I feel better physically today than yesterday having slept more last night. . . ."

At 12 noon Du Pont's flagship signaled the monitors to get underway. Drums beat for general muster on the *New Ironsides* and, from "the Admiral down to the powder boys," all knelt and listened to "a short, touching prayer."

Preliminary maneuvering completed, the monitors steamed into Charleston channel toward Fort Sumter. A reserve squadron of wooden ships was held in readiness. Suddenly on the *New Ironsides,* "a dull sound, like that of a sledge-hammer upon an anvil, was heard on the bow port side," reported a correspondent. ". . . A second and a third, more violently than the first, shook the sides of the ship. Soon came the humming and whizzing of rifled and round shot and shell overhead. . . . Bang, bang, their shot went against the side of the ship."

The Union attempt to take Charleston "by machinery" had commenced. On the *New Ironsides,* only three persons could squeeze into the pilot house. When the pilot panicked, the *New Ironsides* collided with a monitor, went aground, and anchored. "This ship," the surgeon recalled, "was of no more use than if she had been at the Philadelphia navy yard."

Inside Fort Sumter, there was a "terrific din." Guns boomed. Shells exploded.

By 3:30 P.M. Charleston Harbor was "a seething caldron." With the *New Ironsides* out of action, the monitors maneuvered to assigned stations, hammered at the fort at a range of 800 yards, and attempted to pass and head up to the city. The lead monitors discovered the channel obstructed by "rows of casks" and piles. Unable to blast a way through, the *Weehawken, Passaic, Nahant,* and others turned sharply, and the battle line became entangled. The monitors were caught in a crossfire. Turrets and guns jammed.

A shell exploded on board the *Nahant.* Bolts torn loose in the pilot house killed the quartermaster and knocked the pilot senseless. The steering gear became defective, forcing the captain to order the ship to retire from action. Below in the wardroom, the surgeon, cursing the " 'Balls, shells, and bolts that rattled like hail, ' " shouted, " 'G-d, we are catching it now!' "

Rebel guns severely pummeled the other monitors. The *Weehawken*'s deck was ripped up. The *Passaic*'s pilot house was "mashed in." Hit ninety times and "completely shattered," the *Keokuk* withdrew only to sink in the channel, fortunately without loss of life.

At forts Sumter and Moultrie sixty-five cannon blazed away at the "eight black specks." The eastern wall of Sumter "was pretty badly struck in two or three places" by the "not very accurate fire of the Yankees," but there was no serious injury. The monitors' guns failed to reach the other harbor installations.

On board the *New Ironsides,* struggling to maneuver into firing range, Frank recognized that the monitors had "made no impression upon the fort." With darkness coming on, he ran up the signal to withdraw from action. He intended to renew the attack the following day. "I think I may say with safety," a monitor commander declared, "that an hour more would pretty much have finished the fleet."

That evening the monitor captains climbed to the quarterdeck of the *New Ironsides* and went aft to a large cabin, where Frank was seated at a table. Once comfortable, each commander gave his report. The conversation was "as solemn as a scene of death." "I am convinced," stated one commander, "that although this class of vessel can stand a very heavy fire, yet the want of more guns will render them comparatively harmless before formidable . . . forts."

"With our present means, I could not if I were asked," seconded another captain, "recommend a renewal of the attack."

Tired "enough of war," Commander John Rodgers of the *Weehawken* concluded that "the obstructions kept us from getting the Charleston—not the batteries." The consensus was that the two-gun monitors were deficient in firepower, although they were praised for their "endurance of pounding."

Frank sat quietly. After the commanders had reported he adjourned the meeting.

In the early morning hours of 8 April Frank dressed, went out on deck, and walked around the *New Ironsides.* He found his friend and chief of staff, C. R. P. Rodgers. They conversed in low tones. " 'I have given careful thought during the night,' " Frank informed him, " 'to all the bearings of this matter, and have come to the positive determination from which I shall not swerve. . . . I have decided not to renew the attack.' "

Rodgers remained silent while Frank continued. " 'During the few minutes we were under the heaviest fire of the batteries we engaged, half our turret-ships were in part or wholly disabled. We have only encountered the outer line of defense, and if we force our way into the harbor we have not men to occupy the forts we may take, and we can have no communication with our force outside except by running the gauntlet. In the end we shall retire, leaving some of our ironclads in the hands of the enemy, to be refitted and turned against our blockade with deplorable effect. We have met a sad repulse; I shall not turn it into a great disaster.' "

Later, Rodgers was to declare, " 'The matter has now been fairly tried. With favoring circumstances, with good officers, with good management, the experiment has completely failed. . . . We fought only about 40 minutes, and the unanimous conclusions of the officers is that an hour of that fire would have destroyed us . . . the Admiral took the responsibility of avoiding greater evil, by saving the fleet and abandoning an enterprise which we think has been fairly impossible.' "

Months earlier Frank had anticipated that the monitors would be unable to reduce the forts and take Charleston. The assault of 7 April bolstered his belief in the inability of the monitors to subdue shore installations. "These monitors," he wrote General Hunter on the 8th, "are miserable failures where forts are concerned." They had been able to fire only 139 times, while "an incessant storm of . . . shot and shell, rifled projectiles of all descriptions, and red-hot shot" by the Confederates rained on them, and partially disabled five. "I attempted to take the bull by the horns, but he was too much for us," Frank confessed.

On the evening of 8 April, a distraught Frank justified his defeat to Sophie. "We have failed as I felt sure we would, but have been mercifully spared from any serious disaster, and have left none of my fleet behind me—though the *Keokuk,* so gallantly fought, went down this morning. We saved all on board, including some wounded men."

After describing the action, he added, "Finding it was too late to accomplish anything, I made signal to cease action and to fall out of range. When I did this I had no doubt but that I would renew the attempt this morning—but when I found the extent of our damages and the very slight *if any* impression [that] had been made upon the fort, which being of brick we did think we could knock down—showing how hopeless to do anything to the earthworks—I made up my mind instantly . . . that it would be sheer folly to renew the attempt. . . . I found after I had made this decision that there was but one opinion among all my captains who came on board last night—that it was impossible to take Charleston and futile to renew the attempt. . . .

"Do not be worried about this. I am quite calm and unruffled myself, knowing I have done all that was right and been mercifully

293

protected by God, for had we got where we were going I believe we should have lost the whole fleet. . . .

"Of course I must look for the effects of want of success, as compared with success. The monitor people will be my worst enemies. . . ."

That same evening, Frank wrote Welles, ". . . Charleston cannot be taken by a purely naval attack. . . ."

To Charles Davis, Frank explained, "I am quite prepared for any *howl.* Success is very different from a reverse in the public mind, but I want to say that the same Providence which has never deserted me has never been more true in its support than now. I never felt more certain that I was right than in my present position. . . . I could never take from our friend Mr. Fox that extraordinary faith he has in these monitors—they have admirable qualities, but they are dead failures with forts, either brick or earthworks. . . ."

When the smoke of battle cleared, Charlestonians were overjoyed. Their guns had fired more than 2,000 times and the vaunted monitors, "though formidable engines of war," were not "invulnerable or invincible." Southerners had watched their guns explode the monitor myth. No longer was there to be "the superstitious fear" of the vessels with "steel corsets."

Analyzing the Confederate victory, General Beauregard pronounced, "Upon the whole, I think the Abolitionists will come to the conclusion, if they have not already done so, that their monitors are great humbugs; more terrible in imagination than in reality. Forts McAllister and Sumter have been terrible blows to them, and they will become the laughing-stock of Europe."

Conflicting reports arrived North. On 6 April the New York *Herald* ran a story, credited to "prominent officers of the government," that the monitors had bombarded Charleston and that Federal land forces were in control of the city. More news trickled in. Editors of the Cincinnati *Gazette* learned from Nashville, Tennessee, that in " 'a terrible battle . . . at Charleston' " the ironclads had been repulsed.

In Washington, Fox sifted through the reports. He wrote to Ericsson, "I believe we are now in possession of the city. . . ." He found it difficult to accept news of failure. As the situation looked darker, Fox declared that the "attack was for the purpose of obtaining full information. He stated that Du Pont was just preparing for "more desirous work" and could see "no reason whatever to be in the least discouraged."

Secretary Welles agreed that the reports merely indicated a Federal "reconnaissance . . . to feel and pioneer the way for a grand attack."

On 12 April, the situation was clarified. At the Washington Navy Yard, the steamer *Flambeau*, carrying Lieutenant Commander L. C. Rhind, docked. This officer, "disgusted, demoralized, and wholly upset," hustled off the ship and arrived at Welles's house in mid-afternoon. The secretary had just written Du Pont, "God grant . . . the destruction of that fortress," when Rhind, the commander of the ill-fated *Keokuk*, stepped into the room, and handed him the admiral's dispatches. Accompanied by Rhind, Welles carried the dispatches up Pennsylvania Avenue to the White House to report to the President.

Welles attributed the debacle to Du Pont, who "gave up too soon." He had been supplied with the "best officers and vessels in the service, and his force was in every respect picked and chosen." But when the test came, the Admiral had fought for only thirty-five minutes. Welles attributed the defeat to Du Pont's lack of confidence and suggested that he was unequal to the responsibility, which had "depressed and oppressed" him. "A magnetic power" at the head of the Federal expedition was wanting.

The North, which had accepted the claim that the monitors were invincible, reacted with shock. Newspapers reported that "The day for the people to be fooled and bamboozled is over," and ridiculed those who were surprised that "the monitors were not walking about on land in the rear of Charleston."

The Chicago *Times* reported that administration officials charged that Du Pont was "incompetent and almost a coward," and found monitor commanders inferior to seafarers of the "Paul Jones stamp," who would have renewed the action and "would have taken Charleston or perished in the attempt." Despite such disparaging coverage, Du Pont felt that the press, on the whole, was favorable toward him—"We are struck with the fairness generally of the public press and of the tone and true sympathy of the private letters."

At the Navy Department Lincoln informed reporters that he was "not pleased with the results," before departing "with a downcast, haggard, bewildered look, unshaven, with neckcloth all awry—the very picture of a man whose wits had left him." The Senate and House passed resolutions demanding that the Secretary of the Navy send them all dispatches relating to the actions of the ironclads.

Fox equivocated. He informed reporters not to regard the result of "this preliminary bombardment as decisive or essentially discouraging," adding that on reading the official reports, he was in a "much more cheerful and hopeful state of mind." His refusal to accept the truth was reinforced by a letter from a monitor engineer: "When . . . victory was ours . . . [we were] ordered away. . . . It looks like treason."

The Navy Department delayed publishing the adverse battle reports on the ground that all the monitor captains had been "tutored" by Du Pont. Despite the repulse, Welles and Fox continued to believe the monitors were capable of capturing Charleston.

At Port Royal Frank regarded it "madness" and "sheer folly" to attack again with the "miserable monitors," despite President Lincoln's telegraphed order urging another assault: "a real one (though not a desperate one)."

Protests from Port Royal reached the administration. Monitor commanders wrote letters to Secretary Welles demanding the vindication of Du Pont. If "persons can be found who believe Charleston is to be taken by sea attack," wrote one captain, "just send them down here to attempt it, instead of vaporing about in bar rooms and political meetings." Commander Rodgers criticized Ericsson for "lack of common sense," and declared that the "ingenious follies" should have been tested in New York instead of Charleston Harbor. . . . if our tools had been what they were supposed to be, we should have taken Sumter and . . . Charleston, but they failed—and we failed."

Defeat dampened Frank's spirit, doubt eroded his confidence. Nothing could stir him to attempt an amphibious assault, although General Hunter was "absolutely delighted" with the idea. With the help of a covering fire from the monitors, Hunter was certain that Morris Island could be taken and used to reduce Fort Sumter. Naval officers countered that they could not cover a landing without danger of being driven ashore and wrecked by the first breeze from the northwest.

Hoping to ward off administrative wrath by having friends intercede on his behalf, Frank wrote Henry Winter Davis an account of his action at Charleston. He concluded by admitting, "I do not feel amiable towards men who have robbed me of the prestige pertaining up to this hour of my first reverse after a long life of successful service, but I can be just to them and true to them. If they attempt any injustice towards me I will certainly not lamely submit,

I hope for Fox's own sake that he will behave like a man—but I have no idea how the Department will behave. I know, however, how *I* will—they must not venture to censure or rebuke. . . .

"I wish you would quietly ascertain what the feeling in the Cabinet is. I would not go to the Navy men you know. . . . The administration, if they were wise, would thank me for saving their fleet and standing between them and the morbid appetite of the people for Charleston. . . ."

In the absence of correspondence from Welles or Fox, Frank wrote Davis again, "It is evident that the silence of the Navy Department . . . is *ominous*. With this, John Rodgers of the *Weehawken* has letters from his family in Washington . . . which state that the Department is evidently casting round for my relief—which if it be true means war in favor of the ironclad plunderers, to sustain them I must be sacrificed. . . ."

Finally in mid-May Frank received a dispatch from Welles. "If the results at Charleston were not all that we wished, there was much in them that was gratifying. Brief as was the conflict, the fire brought to bear on the monitor vessels was such as could have been sustained by no ordinary boats and demonstrates their power of resistance and their adaption for harbor purposes. . . .

"I would be wrong to say we have not been in some degree disappointed. . . . I did suppose the attack on Charleston had your hearty approval. . . . Had you at any time expressed an opinion against the expediency of an attack, or a belief that it would be disastrous, such was my confidence in you and my respect for your intelligence and capability that I should certainly have reviewed the subject, and not unlikely an entirely different arrangement of our forces would have been projected. . . .

"I have been disappointed in receiving from you no suggestion in regard to future movements since the conclusion you arrived at that a purely naval attack on Charleston cannot be successful. . . ."

Welles privately noted in his diary, "Du Pont is prejudiced against the monitor class . . . and would attribute the failure to them, but it is evident he has no taste for rough, close fighting." He continued, "I fear he can no longer be useful in his present command, and am mortified and vexed that I did not earlier detect his vanity and weakness."

On 3 June Secretary Welles notified Du Pont, ". . . The government is unwilling to relinquish all further efforts upon a place that has been so conspicuous in this rebellion, and which continues to stimulate treason and resistance to the Union and the government, and whose reduction is so essential. I regret that you do not concur in these views. . . .

"From the tenor of your letters it appears that your judgment is in opposition to a renewed attack on Charleston; and in view of this fact, with your prolonged continuance on the blockade, the Department has concluded to relieve you of the command of the South Atlantic Blockading Squadron, and to order Rear Admiral Foote in your place."

Frank received this dispatch stoically. He confided to Sophie, "I received a letter from the Department informing me I would be relieved by Admiral Foote. . . . I would rather be in my place than in theirs—their subtlety, or rather Fox's, is very great. I think the word *mean* is the only one to apply to the transaction; as it was expected by me, of course, it caused me not the slightest excitement. I have been as calm as I ever was in my life—it is hard after forty-seven years of service, and serving actively through the Mexican War and this from its inception, at great personal sacrifice and against some ill health, to be disposed of in this way by upstarts temporarily in office. But I am going to keep my mouth shut and take all things patiently and, I trust, wisely—I am right on the record. So you see Providence has opened a way for me to be with you this summer where I long to be beyond description. . . ."

Secretary Welles had wished to replace Du Pont with Foote, "a dogged fighter . . . the Oliver Cromwell of our Navy," but Foote became ill, and Welles was forced to appoint Admiral John Dahlgren, who had spent the war at the Naval Ordnance Bureau. General John Gillmore took command of the Department of the South from Hunter. Jubilant, Fox declared that Dahlgren and Gillmore would "certainly take Charleston," and planned to shift operations to Wilmington, North Carolina, as soon as Fort Sumter fell. But Charleston did not fall that year and remained immune from capture until the waning stages of the war.

The major share of the responsibility for the failure at Charleston on 7 April 1863 lies with Welles and Fox, who believed that they were presenting the keys of Charleston to Du Pont when they sent him the monitors. These turreted vessels went southward without having undergone adequate shakedown cruises. Although Du Pont did not specifically or officially tell Welles or Fox that he feared a

repulse at Charleston, they ignored reiterated warnings of the difficulties he faced attacking that fortified port. One monitor commander suggested, "Experiments should be tried when their failures
shall involve no loss—before our own canon. . . ."

The Navy Department erred by pushing aside the suggestion of
Army cooperation. Amphibious landings had worked extremely well
during the early phases of the coastal war. A noted British military
observer believed that had the Army and Navy combined their efforts, the Charleston failure might have been turned into victory.
"This cooperating action of the naval and military services mutually
supporting each other," he wrote, "and the fact that neither can be
neglected without direct detriment to the other, seem to be among
the most important lessons taught in the whole history of the American Civil War."

Another error committed by the Navy Department was its failure
to evaluate carefully Du Pont's reports from October 1862 to April
1863. Welles and Fox should have been cognizant of the admiral's
distaste for the Charleston scheme, the monitors' shortcomings before Fort McAllister, and the squadron's gradual deterioration. Although Welles came to question Du Pont's assertiveness, he failed
to take positive action.

Before leaving Port Royal, Frank consoled himself with thoughts
of his reunion with Sophie. He wrote to her at the end of June, "I
have never alluded to our wedding day. How many years have
passed!—how many of these have we been separated from each other.
Yet we have had many blessings. I feel I owe much to our merciful
Father in Heaven—and I have no repinings at the past, speaking in
a wordly sense. You have been of unspeakable comfort, happiness,
and benefit to me, and we have been spared when so many younger
have passed off in whom we had near and deep interest. If God will
unite us again and allow us to be together and serve Him as we
ought, how His blessings will have been continued." By mid-July
Frank was at Louviers.

Throughout the summer, Frank, embittered and disconsolate, reviewed the operations at Charleston and mulled over his grievances
against Welles and Fox. He mailed copies of his official dispatches
to friends with political clout, to Senator Grimes, and to Henry
Winter Davis who had recently won back his seat in Congress. He
forwarded copies to his Navy friends James S. Biddle and captains

C. R. P. Rodgers and Percival Drayton. Davis advised that the correspondence could not be allowed to stand on record unanswered.

Frank, with Davis's help, composed a letter to Welles. This responded to the secretary's letter of 26 June in which he had said, in part, ". . . it is to be regretted that you did not make known your distrust [of the monitors]. . . ." Frank also pointed out that Admiral Dahlgren had failed before Charleston on 8 September, suggesting that Dahlgren's repulse "sufficiently vindicate[s] my judgment." Incensed, Welles wrote Frank a rambling and insulting letter.

Under pressure from Sophie and certain Navy friends, Frank decided to discontinue the correspondence. Davis, however, was not through. He badgered Congress to demand the official dispatches on Charleston, which Welles declined to deliver because the letters might prejudice the public mind. This call from Congress resulted in Welles's publishing later a 600-page government document, *Report . . . in Relation to Armored Vessels,* which, he emphasized, contained all the important correspondence on the monitors. The secretary gained a victory over Davis, and Frank's reputation sustained a further blow.

Du Pont never again agreed to a permanent duty station. In his retirement at Louviers he was surrounded by a circle of relatives and close friends.

In March 1865, while in Washington serving on a Navy board, he caught cold, which resulted in bronchial attacks. Such an attack resulted in his death in a Philadelphia hotel room on 23 June 1865.* His beloved Sophie was at his side. Sophie survived him for many years. Historians are indebted to her for preserving her husband's letters and collecting other correspondence. She died on 9 January 1888.

In 1817, as a young, highly motivated midshipman, Frank Du Pont told his mother that he hoped some day "to do honor to my country." This hope was realized.

Du Pont was a proud officer, and one of the true intellectuals in the Navy. The privilege of rank was important to him. He weighed every career move cautiously, making sure that it would, in his judgment, promote himself. Self-disciplined, he was eager to excel. If he concluded that an assignment might impede his progress, he

* Hayes, *Du Pont,* I, xc-xciii.

tried, by direct appeal or by exerting political pressure, to avoid it.

During his early service, Du Pont termed himself "a rebel," and criticized his superiors, both naval and civil, for incompetence and censured them for failing to meet the high standards he expected.

He possessed a high degree of physical courage and confidence in his shiphandling capacity. He enjoyed the challenge of maneuvering a ship to a difficult anchorage and despised overly cautious captains. Unawed by rank, he became aroused when he believed his rights were being usurped by higher authority.

As Du Pont matured, and especially after he assumed the responsibilities of a captain in 1855, he no longer publicly disagreed with decisions taken by the Navy Department.

At the outbreak of the Civil War he was the darling of the Navy Department, highly respected by his fellow officers and, perhaps, the best known naval officer in the nation. His contemporaries regarded him as a skilled and dedicated officer with a flair for diplomacy, an officer who relished the politics of the naval profession. His failure to stand up and speak out on the monitors proved costly to his career. In his meetings with Welles and Fox concerning the assault on Charleston, Du Pont, fearful that his objections would be misinterpreted, chose to remain silent and not raise the issue of a joint expedition. He earnestly believed that as an admiral he was to carry out his duties, and not question the Department's directives. Du Pont compromised his reputation as an aggressive admiral when he made the correct decision not to attack the Charleston forts a second time. That action would have resulted in the loss of most of the squadron and Du Pont exercised courage when he took his commanders' advice and withdrew, refusing, as he stressed, to turn a defeat into a disaster. Welles and Fox decided to mask their blunders and make Du Pont the scapegoat for the reverse at Charleston.

Current opinion, however, does not condemn him for not ordering a second assault. If he had succeeded at Charleston, Du Pont would have stood with Admirals David G. Farragut and David D. Porter as one of the foremost naval heroes of the Civil War. Although his force captured Port Royal, the Union's first major victory, Du Pont's repulse at Charleston prevented him from reaching the same plateau as the other two. In the decades following the war, Du Pont's name gradually slipped into obscurity. Present-day historians characterize him as a minor player in the grand sweep of the Civil War. They fail to recognize his contribution to the naval effort, his chairing the Blockade Board, his organizing the blockade of the southern coast, and his pioneering of joint Army-Navy expeditions against Confederate ports.

Du Pont's contribution to naval history does not rest on his Civil War laurels or his defeat with the monitors. His lasting gift is the record he left through his letters of serving on distant stations, helping to organize the Naval Academy, chasing pirates, fighting in the Mexican War, experiencing the change over from sail to steam, assisting several naval boards, and acting as a diplomat. It is a record that accurately mirrors the history of the United States Navy from 1815 to 1865.

Bibliography

Manuscripts

Hagley Museum and Library: Samuel Francis Du Pont and Mrs. Samuel Francis Du Pont papers. Library of Congress: Alexander H. Bache, John Ericsson, John Rodgers, Gideon Welles papers. New York Public Library: Percival Drayton, Gideon Welles papers. New York Historical Society: John Ericsson, Gustavus Vasa Fox papers. Henry E. Huntington Library: Gideon Welles papers. National Archives: Naval Records Collection, Record Group 45, Letters from Officers Commanding Squadrons, South Atlantic Blockading Squadron; General Orders Issued by R. A. Samuel F. Du Pont, Commanding South Atlantic Blockading Squadron; Letters by C. R. Perry Rodgers, Commanding *Wabash;* Letters from Officers of Rank below that of Commander; Letters from Rear Admirals, Commodores, and Captains; Secret Survey of Charleston Harbor by Charles O. Boutelle of the Coast Survey, Subject File, Box 394.

United States Government Documents

Annual Report of the Secretary of the Navy, 1828–1865; *Congressional Globe; Laws of the United States of America,* 1830; *Official Records of the Union and Confederate Navies in the War of the Rebellion,* 26 vols., Washington 1894–1922; *The War of the Rebellion: A Compilation of the Official Records of the Union and Confederate Armies,* 128 vols. Washington, 1880–1901; "Message from the President of the United States, Transmitting Copies of the correspondence relating to the negotiation of the Treaty with the Sublime Porte, &c. &c. &c.," *House Doc. No. 250,* 22 Cong., 1 sess. Washington, 1832; "Letter of the Secretary of the Navy to the Chairman of the Committee on Naval Affairs of the Senate of the United States, In relation to the construction of iron-clad steamers, &c.," *Senate Misc. Doc. No. 70,* 37 Cong., 22 sess. Washington, 1862; "Letter from the Secretary of the Navy, In answer to A resolution of the House of the 11th instant [June, 1862], transmitting reports of the wreck of the transport steamer Governor and search for United States ship Vermont by the Frigate Sabine," *House Exec. Doc. No. 139,* 37 Cong., 2 sess. Washington, 1862; "Letter from the Secretary of the Navy, addressed to the Committee on Naval Affairs, in relation to iron-clad ships, ordnance, &c.," *House Misc. Doc. No. 82*, 37 Cong., 2 sess. Washington, 1862; "Letter from the Secretary of the Navy, In answer to resolutions of the House and Senate in relation to the operations of armored vessels employed in the service of the United States," *House Exec. Doc. No. 69*, 38 Cong., 1 sess. Washington, 1864; "Message from the President of the United States, recommending A vote of thanks by Congress, to Captain Samuel F. Du Pont for his services," *House Exec. Doc. No. 82*, 37 Cong., 2 sess. Washington, 1862; "Report of the Joint Committee on the Conduct of the War," *Senate Report No. 108*, 37 Cong., 3 sess. 3 parts, Washington, 1863; "Report of the Joint Committee on the Conduct of the War," *Senate Report No. 142*, 38 Cong., 2 sess. 3 parts, Washington, 1865; "Report of the Board of the Officers convened under Instructions from the Hon. Thomas Corwin, Secretary of the Treasury, to Inquire into the Condition of the Light-House Establishment of the United States." Washington, 1852.

Periodicals

Frank Leslie's Illustrated Newspaper; Harper's Weekly.

Newspapers

Charleston *Courier;* Charleston *Mercury;* Chicago *Times; The New York Times;* Philadelphia *Public Ledger.*

Other Sources

Abbot, Willis J., *Blue Jackets of '61* (New York, 1886); Albion, Robert G., "Distant Stations," *United States Naval Institute Proceedings*, LXXX (1954), 265–73; Allen Gardner, W., ed., *Papers of Isaac Hull*, (Boston, 1929); Ammen, Daniel, *The Atlantic Coast* (New York, 1883); *Id.* "Du Pont and the Port Royal Expedition," *Battles and Leaders of the Civil War*, I (1884–87), 671–91; Anderson, Roger, "Samuel Francis Du Pont and the Voyage of the *North Carolina*, 1825–1827," unpublished Bachelor of Arts Honors' Thesis (University of Delaware, 1970); Anonymous, "The First Cruise of the 'Monitor' Passaic," *Harper's New Monthly Magazine*, XXVII (1863), 577–95; Baxter, James P., *The Introduction of the Ironclad Warship* (Cambridge, MA, 1933); Beauregard, G. T., "The Defense of Charleston," *Battles and Leaders of the Civil War*, IV (1884–1887), 1–23; Belknap, George E., "Reminiscent of the 'New Ironsides' off Charleston," *The United States Service*, I (1879), 63–82; Blum, John M., *et al., The National Experience*, (New York, 1973), vol. I; Bauer, K. Jack, *Surfboats and Horse Marines, U.S. Naval Operations in the Mexican War, 1846–48* (Annapolis, 1969); Burr, Henry L., *Education in the Early Navy* (Philadelphia, 1939); Burton, Amos, *A Journal of the Cruise of the U.S. Ship Susquehanna* (New York, 1863); Burton, E. Milby, *The Siege of Charleston, 1861–1865* (Columbia, SC, 1971); Calvert, Monte A., "American Technology at World Fairs, 1851–1876," unpublished Master of Arts Thesis (University of Delaware, 1962); Carstensen, George & Charles Gildemeister, *New York Crystal Palace* (New York, 1854); Chapelle, Howard I., *The History of the American Sailing Navy* (New York, 1949); Church, William C., *The*

Life of John Ericsson (New York, 1906), 2 vols.; *Id.* "The Naval Victory at Port Royal, S.C., November 7, 1861," "Military Order of the Loyal Legion of the United States, New York Commandery," *Personal Recollections of the War of the Rebellion*, II (1897), 255–66; Cleland, Robert G., *A History of California: The American Period* (New York, 1939); Dahlgren, Madeleine V., *Memoir of John A. Dahlgren* (Boston, 1882); Davis, Charles H., Jr., *Life of Charles Henry Davis* (Boston, 1899); Dennett, Tyler, ed., *Lincoln and the Civil War in the Diaries and Letters of John Hay* (New York, 1939); Du Pont, H. A., *Rear-Admiral Samuel Francis Du Pont* (New York, 1926); Du Pont, Samuel Francis, *Extracts from Private Journal-Letters of Captain S. F. Du Pont while in Command of the Cyane during the War with Mexico* (Wilmington, 1885); *Id., Official Dispatches and Letters of Rear Admiral Du Pont* (Wilmington, 1883); *Id., Report on the National Defences* (Washington, 1852); East, Omega G., "St. Augustine during the Civil War," *The Florida Historical Quarterly*, XXXI (1952), 75–91; Enos, Jonathan C., "Captain Samuel Francis Du Pont and the William B. Reed Mission to China, 1857–1859," unpublished undergraduate research paper (University of Delaware, 1978); Ericsson, John, "The Early Monitors," *Battles and Leaders of the Civil War*, IV (1884–87), 30–31; Fernald, Jean W. "The Role of Sophie Madeleine du Pont: An Invalid in the Brandywine Sisterhood," *Working Papers from the Regional Economic Research Center*, V (1982), 138–48; Fishwick, Marshall W., *Launching an Admiral: The Boyhood of Samuel Francis Du Pont* (Wilmington, 19—); Freeman, Douglas Southall, *R. E. Lee* (New York, 1934–35), 4 vols.; Hayes, John D., ed., *Samuel Francis Du Pont. A Selection from his Civil War Papers* (Ithaca, NY, 1969), 3 vols.; Hening, Gerald S., "Admiral Samuel F. Du Pont, The Navy Department, and the Attack on Charleston, April 1863," *Naval War College Review*, XXXII (1979), 68–77; Hirschfeld, Charles, "America on Exhibition: The New York Crystal Palace," *American Quarterly*, IX (1957), 101–16; Johnson, Mary, "Victorine du Pont: Heiress to the Educational Dream of Pierre Samuel du Pont de Nemours," XIX (1980), *Delaware History*, 88–105; *Id.*, "Madame E. I du Pont and Madame Victorine Bauduy, The First Mistresses of Eleutherian Mills: Models of Domesticity in the Brandywine Valley During the Antebellum Era," *Working Papers from the Regional Economic History Research Center*, V (1982), 13–45; Johnson, Robert E., *Far China Station, The U.S. Navy in Asian Waters, 1800–1898* (Annapolis, 1979); *Id., Rear Admiral John Rodgers, 1812–1882* (Annapolis, 1967); *Id., Thence Round Cape Horn, The Story of United States Naval Forces on Pacific Station, 1818–1923* (Annapolis, 1963); Langley, Harold D., *Social Reform in the United States Navy, 1798–1862* (Urbana, IL, 1967); Lewis, Charles L., *Admiral Franklin Buchanan* (Baltimore, 1929); Mackenzie, Alexander Slidell, *A Year in Spain* (New York, 1847); Low, Betty-Bright & Jacqueline Hinsley, "A Family Party: Daily Life on the Brandywine, 1823–1833, Caricatured by Sophie Madeleine Du Pont," unpublished manuscript (Wilmington, 19–); McPherson, James M., *Ordeal by Fire, The Civil War and Reconstruction* (New York, 1982); Merrill, James M., *The Rebel Shore, Union Sea Power in the Civil War* (Boston, 1957); *Id.*, "Strategy Makers in the Union Navy Department, 1861–1865," *Mid-America*, XLIV (1962), 19–32; *Id.*, "The First Cruise of a Delaware Midshipman: Samuel Francis Du Pont and the *Franklin*," *Delaware History*, XX (1983), 256–68; *Id.*, "Midshipman Du Pont and the Cruise of *North Carolina*, 1825–1827," *The American Neptune*, XL

(1980), 211–25; *Id.*, "The Asiatic Squadron, 1835–1907," *The American Neptune*, XXIX (1969), 106–17; *Id.*, "Naval Operations along the South Atlantic Coast, 1861–1865," doctoral dissertation (UCLA, 1954); Millis, Walter, "The Iron Sea Elephants," *The American Neptune*, X (January, 1950), 15–32; Moore, Frank, ed., *The Rebellion Record* (New York, 1862–1868), 12 vols.; Morison, Samuel Eliot, *"Old Bruin," Commodore Matthew C. Perry, 1794–1858* (Boston, 1967); Munroe, John A., *History of Delaware (Newark, DE, 1984); "Naval Letters from Captain Percival Drayton, 1861–1865,"* New York Public Library, *Bulletin*, X (1906), 583–625, 639–81; Niven, John, *Gideon Welles, Lincoln's Secretary of the Navy* (New York, 1973); Nordhoff, Charles, "Two Weeks at Port Royal, *Harper's New Monthly Magazine*, XXVII (1863), 110–18; Odgers, Merle M., *Alexander Dallas Bache, Scientist and Educator, 1806–1867* (Philadelphia, 1947); Paullin, Charles O., *Commodore John Rodgers: Captain, Commodore, and Senior Officer of the American Navy, 1773–1838* (Cleveland, 1910); *Id.*, "President Lincoln and the Navy," *The American Historical Review*, XIV (1909), 284–303; Potter, E. B., ed., *Sea Power* (Englewood Cliffs, NJ, 1960); Price, Marcus, "Ships that Tested the Blockade of the Carolina Ports," *The American Neptune*, VIII (1948), 196–241; *Id.*, "Blockade Running as a Business in South Carolina during the War between the States, 1861–1865," IX (1949), 31–62; Randall, J. G., & David Donald, *The Civil War and Reconstruction* (Lexington, MA, 1969); Riggs, John Beverley, *A Guide to the Manuscripts in the Eleutherian Mills Historical Library. Accessions through the Year 1965* (Greenville, DE, 1970); Rodgers, C. R. Perry, "Du Pont's Attack at Charleston," *Battles and Leaders of the Civil War*, IV (1884–1887), 32–47; Singletary, Otis A., *The Mexican War* (Chicago, 1960); Thompson, Robert A., "Samuel Francis Du Pont and the William B. Reed Mission to China, 1857–1859," unpublished Master of Arts Thesis, (University of Delaware, 1965); Thompson, Robert M., & Richard Wainwright, eds., *Confidential Correspondence of Gustavus Vasa Fox* (New York, 1918), 2 vols.; Tyler, David B., *The Wilkes Expedition, The First United States Exploring Expedition (1838–1841)* (Philadelphia, 1968); Valle, James E., *Rocks and Shoals, Order and Discipline in the Old Navy, 1800–1861* (Annapolis, 1980); Wainwright, Nicholas B., "Voyage of the Frigate *Congress*, 1823," *Pennsylvania Magazine of History and Biography*, LXXV (1951), 170–88; Weeks, Grenville M., "The Last Cruise of the Monitor," *Atlantic Monthly*, XI (1863), 366–72; Williams, Frances L., *Matthew Fontaine Maury, Scientist of the Sea* (New Brunswick, N.J., 1963); Wolseley, Viscount, "An English View of the Civil War," *North American Review*, CXLIV (1889), 594–606; Yanga, Chitoshi, "The First Japanese Embassy to the United States," *The Pacific Historical Review*, IX (1940), 113–39.

Index

307

Index